P9-CFG-785

NEVER DONE

A HISTORY OF AMERICAN HOUSEWORK

Susan Strasser

PANTHEON BOOKS

NEW YORK

Copyright © 1982 by Susan Strasser

All rights reserved under International and Pan-American
Copyright Conventions. Published in the United States by
Pantheon Books, a division of Random House, Inc., New York,
and simultaneously in Canada by Random House of Canada
Limited, Toronto.

Library of Congress Cataloging in Publication Data

Strasser, Susan, 1948–
Never done.

Bibliography: p.
Includes index.
1. Home economics—United States—History.
2. Housewives—United States—History.
I. Title.
TX23.S77   640'.973   81–48234
ISBN 0–394–51024–0   AACR2
ISBN 0–394–70841–5 (pbk.)

Typographic design by Susan Mitchell

Manufactured in the United States of America
First Edition

To the memory of my mother,
Maxine Harriet Hochberg Strasser,
and of the millions of other women
whose work motivated my own.

Contents

Acknowledgments

Most male authors save for last their thanks to their wives, who bring them coffee, cook their meals, do their laundry, check their sources, challenge their assumptions, type their drafts, put up with and rescue them from their self-pity, comfort and console them, and above all, believe in them. I did my own laundry and typed all but the final draft, but a number of people cooked for me and offered love, critical support, and important ideas. The length of the list and the geographical dispersion of the people I must thank suggest both my peripatetic habits and the nature of my personal struggle for love and community as a single woman in the United States of the 1980s. My love and thanks to Joel Bradbury, Phil Brenner, Carie Cable, Gary Chase, Susie Huston, Lisa Marshall, Eve Miller, Diane Morrison, Alan Nasser, Paul Repetowski, Karen Smith, Matthew Smith, Susan Smith, Judy Strasser, Margaret Stratton, Bethany Weidner, Carl Witchel, and Larry Wolken. Two women performed some of the wifely duties when I could no longer see my own mistakes—Peggy Lenzi, who typed the final manuscript, and Peggy Cahill, who helped keep track of final details.

Many persons contributed by lending me materials, asking and answering questions, and commenting on previous stages of the work. I received financial support for an earlier stage of the project from the Smithsonian Institution and The Evergreen State College. I worked at many libraries and spoke with many librarians, but am especially indebted to the members of the staff of the telephone reference service at the Seattle Public Library, and nearly all of the staff of the Evergreen library, whose help went beyond the bounds of normal service to faculty at an undergraduate institution more dedicated to teaching than to research. Nearly all my students and colleagues at Evergreen have sharpened my historical understanding and taught me how to communicate it; in the final stages, the students in Foundations of American Enterprise helped me clarify my sense of the large historical picture, and Nancy Allen, Hazel Jo Reed, and the women enrolled in Reintroduction to Education helped with the specifics.

I have received much direct help and encouragement from Chris Bose, Peter Hall, Karen Hanson, Heidi Hartmann, Dorie Klein, Karyl Lee Kibler, Mathilda Larson, Rodris Roth, Barbara Spector, and the participants in the 1978 Conference on Women and Domestic Life, held at MIT, especially Ruth Cowan, Dolores Hayden, and Ann Lane. At that conference, I was encouraged to write a book, and started on the path that led to Jeannette Hopkins, who understood from the start my intention to turn my scholarly work into a book for a more general audience, and who taught me what I know about being a "real author" by editing my writing and asking hard questions; despite the frustrations that she warned me about the day we met, the book is incalculably better for her help. George Talbot of the iconography department of the State Historical Society of Wisconsin gave me an intensive lesson in illustration and provided welcome encouragement; Shari Segel, of Research Reports, filled in some final holes in the illustrations. People at Pantheon—especially Don Guttenplan, Philip Pochoda, Susan Mitchell, and Jeanne Morton—have provided welcome encouragement and contributed their superb professional skills.

Others who made few specific contributions to this book have left me with longstanding intellectual debts; along with many of those above, these persons made me into the historian I am, and I hope they will recognize themselves here. By introducing me to social history and encouraging my notion that housewives might make reasonable subjects for historical research at a time when few historians studied even influential women, David Allmendinger ended my career as an indifferent student. He sent me to Stony Brook to study with William R. Taylor, whose influence shows in these pages even though he often encouraged me most by leaving me alone. There a number supported and challenged me at the intersection of our scholarly work, our political practice, our commitment as teachers, and our personal lives, among them Marty Gold, Walter Harp, Gene Lebovics, Victoria Lebovics, Tim Patterson, Laura Schwartz, and Michael Schwartz.

Preface

My research on housework began in 1968 for an undergraduate thesis on the literature of advice to American women during the mid-nineteenth century. Studying cookbooks, etiquette books, women's magazines, and household manuals, I concluded that this literature offered a kind of "domestic feminism" that suggested that women could and must establish a place for themselves within their own "sphere," the home. Writing the thesis was frustrating. Investigating the ideas in the advice literature failed to answer my major questions: I wanted to know what women in nineteenth-century homes *did*, not merely what they were *told* to do. I decided to study the development of household technology in the context of ideas about the household; most of the research on which this book is based is incorporated in my doctoral dissertation, "Never Done: The Ideology and Technology of Household Work, 1850–1930" (State University of New York, Stony Brook, 1977). I have continued to work on this research for more than a decade in part because it has offered a channel for my personal questions about my own place as a woman during the second half of the twentieth century. I received so much encouragement that I came to feel responsible for sharing my work outside the academic professions. It became apparent to me, moreover, that I could not clarify my own point of view without making some explicit nonacademic statements about the implications of my historical work for the society I live in. As a result this book is not a revision of the dissertation but a new work, intended for a general as well as a scholarly audience.

I was not alone in my intention to counter the sexism and class bias that had made housewives of the past seem unfit subjects for "professional" historical work. The women's liberation movement has generated new interest in women's history, at first outside a resistant historical profession, finally within it as well. Concentrating at first on leaders of social and political movements and women pioneers in the professions, many women's historians attempted to offer modern women heroines and role models, characters in a "herstory" long ignored; many of these leaders left papers, which new women's research libraries began to collect. Women leaders have become almost as accessible to the historian as presidents and kings. Housewives remained "hidden from history," however; women's history could be as distant from the activities of most women of the past as traditional political and economic history had been from the activities of the soldiers and workers who fought the wars and enriched the industrial entrepreneurs.

Eventually women's historians combined their efforts and their critique of the historical profession with those of the advocates of a "new social history," who insisted on researching the story of the many rather than the privileged few. This "history from the bottom up" produced articles in professional journals and local oral history projects that used a variety of unconventional techniques to tell the tale of everyday life in the past. Combined with the traditional "top down" methods and emphases, and with sophisticated quantitative methodology and theoretical models, social history has begun to give a more complete picture. Social historians of women studied the women who worked in the early textile mills, who sewed in the sweatshops of the late nineteenth century, and who entered the labor force in this century as clerical and sales workers. Combining the new emphases with the old methods of intellectual history, historians examined popular literature, the ideology that defined women's roles and established the notion that women's place was in the home. Still, few studied housework itself, the major activity of half the population.

The topic of housework is complex, and lends itself poorly to the specialized monographic work that delights historical scholars. Some of the best new social histories derive their power from a combination of analysis that has wide-ranging implications and research that concentrates on detailed examination of a local situation or an individual industry. A history of housework—the individual job done by more people than any other—presents many more complications. Just as the individual housewife cannot define her work outside the context of her family's well-being or categorize her tasks discretely, so the story of American housework cannot be separated from the broader social and economic history of the United States. The women who did it served the rest of the population as they built the factories and the cities. Manufactured products and urbanization, in turn, transformed women's work in their homes. Good monographic work on the history of everyday products is, in most cases, in its early stages.

With sparse information from specialized research, I had to resist the temptation to make generalizations that served theory. The history of housework bears on at least two large theoretical questions, both commonly asked by sociological theorists and neither a useful way of posing the historical issues. What did industrialization do to the family? The historical viewpoint suggests that the family must be considered as part and parcel of society, not as a separate institution destroyed by changes in some larger arena—the latter idea is a legacy of the nineteenth-century doctrine of "separate spheres" for men and women. The functions of the household have changed in conjunction with changes in the methods, structures, and products of business and government, not simply as a result of economic and political change. Did technology free women from the home? Theoretical constructs about technology and social change suggest neat statements of cause and effect; in fact, technology transformed housework in the context of many other changes in economic and social life—new ideas about women's roles, new opportunities for women in new sectors of the economy, and a general economic transformation—and no neat statement may be made, even for those who believe that women are now "freed from the home." Theorists base such questions not in social change but in analytic logic, which, as historian E. P. Thompson points out, must "handle unambiguous terms and hold them steadily in a single place." History, ambiguous by nature, changes the terms, especially when the historical investigation covers a period as long as two centuries.

I came to understand my task as the exercise of historical imagination, trying at the same time to remain conscious that my research examined real people's lives. It is easy to romanticize the past and impose modern conceptions on it, as did the two women I heard commenting on the Smithsonian's model of an eighteenth-century kitchen. "There's something so attractive about the simplicity of it all," they agreed. They failed to comprehend the immense labor involved in hauling water and building fires in a kitchen with neither sink nor stove. I also tried to learn to extrapolate limited amounts of evidence to large numbers of people, in order to make statements about the past like those we make about the present from our experience. Most readers will agree, for example, that with the exception of the very poor in rural areas, contemporary Americans have electricity and indoor plumbing—and published statistics show this to be the case. I used a variety of sources to draw similar social pictures about various implements and devices in the past. My generalizations do not necessarily hold true for any individual woman's experience.

I could not find many answers in the patent records, a traditional source for the history of technology, because I wanted to know when things became commonplace, not when they were invented; other sources provided better information. Starting at the beginning of this century, several kinds of agencies surveyed American consumption habits: reformers working for charitable organizations gathered evidence for their contentions about intolerable living conditions; government bureaus collected information in order to describe standards of living; sociologists established their profession by describing daily life; and eventually market researchers surveyed what people had in the interests of manufacturers who intended to sell them more. The manufacturers' advertisements for their products offer another kind of perspective on those goods; with due attention to what advertisers call the "target audience," the historian can uncover attitudes both about the products and about the older methods and equipment those products were intended to replace.

Neither consumption statistics nor national advertising existed before the end of the nineteenth century, however; for the earlier period, I had to rely on secondary works by others who had researched particular aspects of social and economic development, and on several major categories of primary sources. Catalogues tell what consumers could buy; those from Sears and Montgomery Ward tell more than most because, as the first nationwide mass distributors, they tried to sell nearly everything and to attract customers from all classes except the very wealthy. Travel accounts written by visiting Europeans, a popular form of literature on both sides of the Atlantic when the United States represented a social experiment in democracy, describe places, objects, and customs that Americans took for granted; Frances Trollope's *Domestic Manners of the Americans* describes household life in more detail than most because the author set up housekeeping in Cincinnati for about two years. Novels describe domestic scenes less explicitly—a phrase here or there hints at attitudes about chores or illuminates the corner of a room; the ones written by women, especially Harriet Beecher Stowe and Louisa May Alcott, naturally provide the most evidence. Direct testimony from housewives' diaries and letters, in obvious ways the best kinds of sources and illustrations, raise two difficulties: women's archives have barely begun to gather them from private family collections, and even the richest of them shed less light on the generalizations of social history than do documents intended for large numbers of people. I used them more frequently for illustration, therefore, than for evidence on which to base generalizations.

I continually returned to the literature of advice, those cookbooks, women's magazines, and manuals for running households that so plagued me at the start. They addressed a limited audience during the nineteenth century, since books and even magazines cost a great deal of money, but women exchanged magazines, saved reference books for years, and passed on their information and advice about housework to friends and daughters. Advice literature suggests ways of doing housework, gives information about equipment, and counsels women on how they should think about their work. Its shortcomings for the researcher stem not only from class but from the fact that these books and magazines tell what the writers prescribed, not what most women actually did. The manuals that offered the most information sold best, had the most influence, and can most easily be found in rare-book stores, libraries, reprint editions, and microfilm collections. Harriet Beecher Stowe's sister Catharine Beecher wrote the most comprehensive manuals, coloring her advice with a coherent theory about women's place and the function of women's work; the changes in her successive revisions of A Treatise on Domestic Economy (1841), published over four decades, demonstrate essential changes in household technology and in middle-class expectations during that time.

Beecher's books and the other advice literature constitute an ideology about housework, a set of doctrines about women's work that must be studied in conjunction with information about household technology and economic development. Again, the exercise of historical imagination puts them in their contemporary context: they tell neither more nor less about reality than the current issue of McCall's or the latest edition of The Joy of Cooking. This literature shapes people's reality; it is also shaped by it. Women do not necessarily believe everything they read, and the advice literature often contradicted their own experience, presented inconsistent ideas, or offered doctrines that were at variance with their own cultural backgrounds.

Investigating the changing work of the household, I came to understand everyday objects and common ideas about daily life as historical phenomena: literally, they come and they go. Dating coffeepots, detergent powder, school lunches, and the idea that women belong at home presented a more complicated problem than dating a treaty or an election, but these became in my mind no more eternal than the War of 1812 or Millard Fillmore's term as president. This encouraged in me—and I hope it encourages in others—a critical viewpoint about modern society: McDonald's became a phenomenon as transitory as the wash boiler. It motivated me to remain conscious of the connection between my daily life and the activities of distant corporations and politicians.

At times, I have seen myself as an embodiment of my real subject: I am an economically independent woman living alone in a city three thousand miles from my birthplace, depending on the telephone for much emotional support, sharing home-cooked meals with others only irregularly. I am hooked on my own individuality and privacy, yet yearn for intimacy; I use electricity to grind the coffee I drink while I write about the social effects of energy and product dependence. My life is both filled with work that has meaning to me and impoverished by its lack of the daily responsibilities and emotional ties that have long given women's lives another dimension. I can and do take advantage of privileged options unavailable to most women, but understand my personal choices merely as one version of individual adaptation to a set of dilemmas posed by the historical developments I describe here. I teach and write history because I believe that only people who understand that societies can and must change will have enough faith to work for a better future: imagining the differences of the past challenges a hopelessly static conception of the present. I hope this book will serve to assist in the genuine solutions to the problems of our daily lives, which will come neither from books nor from individual adaptation but from collective action.

S. S.

Seattle, Washington
April 1981

Prologue: Never Done

Mathilda Larson, an eighty-eight-year-old woman who was raised on a North Dakota farm, lists the household tasks and remembers the tools—doing laundry with tubs, washboards, and flatirons, cooking on a wood stove with iron pots, growing and preserving food, sewing and mending, cleaning filthy kerosene lamps—and speaks with little nostalgia: "I'd hate to go through it again. Took us all day to do a big washing." Near the end

of a lifetime of making cakes from scratch, at home and in the bakery she ran with her husband, she now serves a cake made from a packaged mix: "Not as good, but easy."

Mrs. Larson dates her first electric lights by her daughter's age—"My daughter is sixty-two now, and I think she was about three years old, so it must have been fifty-nine years ago." She brings out her own wedding pictures to display her wedding dress, made of silk poplin, sixty cents a yard. She speaks as readily of the work she did for money, first as a seamstress before her marriage, later at the bakery, but the two kinds of work hold very different meanings for her. Housework for her family is tied in with other components of her life, and she cannot discuss its "working conditions" without telling tales of the people she loved and worked for; sewing and baking for money were "jobs," and she speaks of them as such. Mrs. Larson could not believe that her unpaid work had any importance to a historian. Why did I want to record "this junk," she asked, referring to anecdotes about her mother's roasting and grinding "coffee" from barley and refilling the mattresses yearly with new straw. After a lifetime of hard work, she discounted her experience.

Oral historians often interview subjects who consider their lives of little importance, believing history to be a matter of presidents and generals and kings. For Mrs. Larson, as for other housewives, humility finds daily reinforcement in a society that measures value in money and holds the work of those who earn no money to be without value. In a society where most people distinguish between "life" and "work," women who supervise their own work at home do not seem to be "working." This devaluation appears on all levels, from Mathilda Larson's incredulity at being interviewed to conventional social intercourse ("Is she working?") to the economist's numerical expression of national well-being, the gross national product. Defined as the sum of the values of all the goods and services produced during a year, the GNP ignores unpaid housework; the man who marries his paid housekeeper and stops paying her thereby literally lowers the GNP. Conventional economic analysis affords little insight into the historical process that changed American women's lives during Mrs. Larson's lifetime; understanding that process requires reflection on the relationship between household work and the broader social and economic world.

No static conception of the function of housework in the economy will provide the theoretical basis for a clear historical picture. The colonial household *was* colonial society, as one historian, calling it "the little commonwealth," points out; it served the functions of home, factory, school, and welfare institution. One by one, private industry and government have assumed those functions, moving the work of the household from the private realm to the public. Before industrialization, most housework produced goods and services used within the household: women spun and wove cloth and sewed it into clothes, grew food and prepared it for eating or storage, made soap and candles, and washed clothes for other family members, who shared those tasks and—according to the sexual division of labor—worked in the fields and as small craftsmen. As increasing numbers of men and single women went to work in factories during the nineteenth century, housewives served their society by reproducing the labor force, both in the literal sense of conceiving, bearing, and caring for children and in the broader one of preparing workers to go to work daily. At the end of the century, as households began to consume the products of American industry, as the economy expanded and factories produced a wide variety of consumer goods on a mass scale, housewives began to serve the economy by organizing consumption for individual households.

Mathilda Larson's story suggests that even this more dynamic description oversimplifies: at the turn of the twentieth century her farm family still produced most of what they used, and consumed few industrial products. Even in the colonial period, few households produced everything they used, and today, despite frozen foods and day-care centers, households continue to produce some goods and do some of the work of reproducing the labor force. An account of the housewife's services to the economy and to the rest of the population over the past two centuries provides a key to understanding some of the fundamental changes in the nature of the work itself, and gives insight into the distinctions between housework and wage labor that have often been regarded as if they resulted from biological differences between women and men.

The industrial revolution removed textile manufacture from the home and brought crafts like shoemaking, formerly done by independent craftspersons, into factories. Entrepreneurs gathered workers together to produce goods for profit, assigning them different tasks for greater efficiency, supplying them with machines and raw materials, and supervising their labor to ensure peak production. Most people still farmed, and by modern standards those factories look small and inefficient, but as the new industrial order developed, people came to consider the home as separate from the rest of society. There married women labored alone, supervising themselves, isolated from the dominant trends of the new society in what popular writers, around 1825, began to call their own "sphere." Although not totally accurate, this ideology of separate spheres for men and women reflected the new and growing reality of industrial society.

By the middle of the century, however, the distinctions between the spheres of the household and the world of industry had blurred. Households had to adapt to industrial workers' new schedules; natural cycles of light and dark could not dictate routine when some family members lived by the clock. Factories had begun to produce goods that helped people adapt to urban industrial life—soap for urban dwellers who had no re-

serves of fat left from slaughtering, lamps and lamp oils to brighten the time left after work, textiles that lightened the burdens of preindustrial housework. Domestic writers recognized and confronted these trends, along with the degradation of unpaid domestic labor that went along with the steady expansion of the money economy, but they held to the ideology that set the working world of women apart from that of men.

That ideology still rang true, in large part. Because only the very wealthy could afford gas or plumbing, industrialization hardly changed the major daily tasks of housework. For the vast majority of married women before the twentieth century, housework was, by definition, a full-time chore, largely taken up with building fires and hauling water. Women who needed money earned it by increasing their housework, by taking in laundry, sewing, or boarders. Men had bosses; married women bossed themselves, deciding what needed to be done according to the task and not the clock, controlling their own work process. Men left home to work; women's work remained intertwined with the rest of their lives, their time restructured by new products and by the demands of their husbands' jobs, but still fundamentally their own. Although they adapted their work to the schedules of the industrial order and used money to buy some of its products, most married women continued to work under conditions sufficiently different from those of their husbands to obscure the connection between the spheres.

Between about 1890 and 1920, mass production and mass distribution brought new products and services—gas, electricity, running water, pre-pared foods, ready-made clothes, and factory-made furniture and utensils —to large numbers of American families. With these products, house-holds became the direct beneficiaries of an economic transformation as profound as the industrial revolution, during which business corporations assumed their modern structure and united Americans into a national consumer market. Standardized, uniform goods that cost money replaced the various makeshifts that had constituted most people's subsistence, dealing blows to the satisfactions of home production but bringing about a general end to the arduous labor of the household and a general rise in the standard of living. Those goods began to substitute for much of the massive productive and maintenance work that housewives had provided throughout the nineteenth century.

Their burdens lightened by the new technology, married women con-tinued to work alone in homes increasingly dominated by industrial pro-duction, preparing daily meals, caring for children, and organizing the social and affectional lives of their families. A network of reformers, re-sponding to the new trends, had redefined the relationship of the home to the larger society. Like the ideas of their predecessors during the indus-trial revolution, the ideas of these reformers may best be understood as expressions of reality, formed during an important period of economic transition, that helped to shape the social and economic changes that followed. Working with other reformers during what has come to be known as the Progressive Era, those interested in household life established the home economics profession and campaigned against the traditional ways in which women had made money without becoming wage laborers for the entrepreneurs. They defined new tasks in mothering and in consumption, tasks to be overseen by experts who claimed to combine the rationality of science with the efficiency of business, replacing love, common sense, and old-fashioned ways as guides for housework. These ideas set the stage for changes in housework during the rest of the twentieth century. Even the functions that remained in the home at its start—cooking, child care, and emotional life—became public matters, increasingly fulfilled by commodities and services designed by corporations for their own profit.

The history of housework provides a description of fundamental changes in American daily life as the economy developed; just as it demonstrates the effects on individuals of the periods of economic transformation, so it also demonstrates the effects of long-run trends. Because the American economy was capitalist, it had to grow: capitalists by definition went into business to make profits, which they invested in new ventures, and they sought new areas of investment that would expand the economy as a whole. Food, shelter, and clothing became matters of social production, not private, created by profitable industrial manufacture; new kinds of transportation, communication, and business methods created new distribution systems, facilitating that growth. As the factories and the railroads multiplied, so did the social relations that went with them: American economic expansion substituted the new roles of boss and worker, manufacturer and consumer, for the old ones of male and female subsistence farmer, who worked for themselves and consumed what they produced. As it expanded, the economic system became increasingly centralized. During most of the nineteenth century, bankers and financiers dominated the economy, investing their money in building the transportation and communication structure that would assure continued growth; centralization was not yet a feature of production in the industries making goods for households—soap, lamp oil, and cast-iron stoves came from small, local companies. By the end of the century, large corporations were coming to dominate the distribution and production of household goods, making their decisions on the basis of their own profit.

The increased availability of consumer goods only partially obscured the fact that the profit motive outweighed the well-being of workers and consumers. Bloody battles characterized worker-employer relations for decades after the first nationwide strike, which paralyzed the railroads in July 1877; rank-and-file resistance and militant union organization eventually brought industrial workers decent wages, hours, and working con-

ditions, concessions to industrial peace from employers who earlier had bestowed libraries on starving steelworkers or displayed the profits from their workers' labor in ostentatious houses for themselves. No such resistance from consumers greeted their similar disregard for the needs of the housewife. Industrialists ignored most of the patents for household labor-saving devices because they could not produce them profitably; they produced others, like canned foods and washing machines, for military and commercial applications decades before they offered them to households. The commercial laundry industry, which removed a chore from the home, suffered in competition with the more profitable washing-machine industry; Edison developed the basic elements of electric service under constraints that ensured its competition with gas. American manufacturers offered little to ease the work of most households before 1900, and they introduced the new products of mass production with newly developed advertising techniques that eventually assured their domination of the so-called private sphere.

With their advertising, the manufacturers joined the home economists —who welcomed them from the start—in their roles as household experts, perverting the role in the interest of selling goods. Advertisements used guilt and fear to promote dependence on products, creating artificial burdens to substitute for the disappearing real ones. (Women, it seemed, were meant to be burdened.) Manufacturers advanced the notion that convenience constituted an end in itself, holding out the promise that the burdens might be lightened with enough of the latest products. They attempted to end the conviction that money (the currency of the public sphere) cannot buy love (the central feature of the private), using sex to sell things, suggesting that buying things for loved ones would bring love to the purchaser, and promoting products and the act of consumption itself as substitutes for intimate relationships. Plugging individual consumption of standardized goods, they created an illusion of individualism, leaving consumers stranded in the marketplace, isolated in a mass. Mass production replaced the monotonous nineteenth-century winter diet with burgers and fries; it transformed the dimly lit family circle, an arena of intimacy and productive work, into a scene of corporate-sponsored leisure, no better illuminated by the flickering TV. Women lost the compensations of nineteenth-century housework: satisfaction in their craft, intimate connections with their families and with other women formed through work, and the sense of value derived from work done for love, not money.

They suffered the loss of their old compensations, however, in the context of new ones. Craft satisfaction, intimacy, and community went along with grueling amounts of heavy labor, a lack of privacy that most modern Americans would find intolerable, and the oppression of women on both individual and social levels. Women took for granted a staggering burden of household work—"We expected to do those things, we didn't know any different," says Mathilda Larson—and made little of the compensations, which they took equally for granted. Mass communications brought information about the rest of the world, and new ideas about doing household work, along with the advertisements; gas and electricity rescued Americans from severe discomfort and from virtual slavery to the seasons as it took them farther from the cycles of nature. Tainted water supplies, rancid food, soot and skin burns from open fires, and full chamber pots offer a more accurate picture of daily life for most people before the twentieth century than the less frequent pleasures of the quilting bee.

Women had plumbing installed to make their lives easier; they preferred electric lights to kerosene lamps because electricity gave more light with none of the dirty work; they bought ready-made clothing because they wanted to spend their time on other things besides sewing. Like that of Mathilda Larson, who did not buy an electric iron until about ten years after she had electric lights, most women's lives changed incrementally; many events in their own lives and in the rest of the world—new technology, their children's growth, new kinds of job opportunities, and new attitudes that came from their neighbors as well as from the popular media—combined to make those changes. Over the long run, bit by bit, seemingly unconnected and unprofound events in millions of lives formed patterns that the participants, who considered the events either trivial or wholly personal, could not necessarily see.

Many of the changes in housework matched changes in other kinds of work during the long process of industrialization. Shorter hours and better working conditions—less hard, constant physical labor, in safer and more comfortable circumstances—distinguish twentieth-century housework as they distinguish other twentieth-century labor. Like other workers, the housewife lost control of her work process; manufacturers exerted their control on her through product design and advertising rather than through direct supervision. The clock and the calendar replaced the sun as arbiter of everyone's time. Yet the isolation of the full-time housewife increased. While other workers went to work in groups, however thoroughly supervised, full-time housewives lost the growing daughters and full-time servants who worked with them at home, the iceman and the street vendors who came to their houses, the sewing circle and the group of women around the well. That isolation, combined with the illusory individualism of consumerism, intensified the notion that individuals could control their private lives at home, protected behind the portals of their houses from the domination of others: the central legacy of the doctrine of separate spheres.

Those spheres were never separate in fact, and the apparent distinctions between the household and the outside world continue to erode.

Ecological concerns suggest that private decisions have social consequences; distinctions between men's work and women's work have lost their former clarity, both in household work and in work for pay. For all the private distress of the rising divorce rate, and despite the continued refusal of many employers to pay women wages equal to those of men, women need no longer accept either housework or marriage as their inevitable lot in life, terminable only by death, nor can they assume that marriage will provide them with a permanent deliverance from the world of bosses, as their grandmothers could. Modern women, who can wash their laundry in automatic machines and pick up both their dinners and their children on the way home from their jobs, must consider the implications of the lost satisfactions of old-fashioned housework and find ways to re-create some of those satisfactions in their daily lives both as workers and as consumers. At the same time, they must avoid romanticizing the past. The lost satisfactions must be balanced against the thorough subjugation of women, their work, and the values they were charged to protect at home as industrial society developed, the economic dependence that allowed that subjugation to persist and stultified individual women's life choices, and the staggering burden of running households where women's work was truly never done.

ONE

Daily Bread

During the nineteenth century, many Americans began for the first time to buy their food. Poor people still struggled to produce as much as they could even in urban areas, and rural Americans outnumbered urban until 1920; however, nineteenth-century changes in the production and distribution of food set the stage for a profound transformation. In 1790, the year of the first United States census, one American lived in a town of 2,500

or more for every eighteen who lived in the country; a century later, nearly 40 percent of the population lived in urban territory. "Urbanization," as the historians describe this process, like its frequent partner "industrialization," changed the American landscape—rural as well as urban—and the most intimate rituals of everyday existence.

City living and industrial development created food consumers out of producers; consumers were progressively removed from the sources of their food—in miles and in numbers of intermediary people and processes. Even the food itself changed. Modern transportation and food-preservation techniques lengthened the seasons and introduced variety even in the diets of the poor. In 1900, the distinctions between rich and poor, urban and rural, continued to dominate food habits—poor people and rural dwellers produced more of what they ate—but mass distribution, large-scale commercial agriculture, mass production, and the new corporate structure paved the way for universal change.

Although never entirely self-sufficient, American farming families before the twentieth century depended on their own labor and their own land for most of their food. Even as early as the colonial period, when almost everybody farmed, rural people sold extra produce to the few townsfolk; they bartered their surplus or used the money from sales to pay the millers who ground their meal and sawed their logs, the blacksmiths who forged their tools, the merchants who imported their coffee, tea, sugar, molasses, salt, and luxury goods, and the professionals who tended their legal and spiritual needs. They needed cash also to pay the governments, landlords, and moneylenders whose demands for taxes, mortgages, and debt payments established a conflict between farmers and commercial interests well before the Revolution, a conflict expressed in local rebellions and national political movements through the nineteenth century, and echoed in the contemporary complaints of the farmers who blocked the Mall in Washington, D.C., with their John Deere tractors in 1979.

For these modern militants their kitchen gardens and freezers are a supplement to their cash crops and their paying jobs in town, but for colonial farmers and frontier settlers subsistence farming was primary, supplemented with sales. Rebecca Burlend and her husband, arriving in Illinois with their five children in 1831, bought some venison from a man who had just killed a deer and one bushel of ground corn at a third the price of wheat flour. After these initial purchases, the Burlends ate almost exclusively what they could produce for the first few years, except for coffee, "which we used sparingly, for want of money"; they spent the cash from their first wheat crop on shoes, a plow, two tin milk bowls, "a few pounds of coffee, and a little meal." Established farmers, by contrast, bought and bartered for food, tools, clothing, medicine, and liquor; Illinois storekeepers (who often ran sawmills and grain mills as well) sold

Home production of food. "Woman hoeing tomatoes," photo probably posed for advertising purposes, 1904.

bartered food to newcomers and travelers, or sent it "to New Orleans, or some other place where it can be readily sold." The further development of Western cash-crop farming had to wait for future agricultural methods and devices, the coming of the railroads, and the emergence of a national market for farm products. In the meantime, the Burlends' neighbors and other frontier settlers, like their predecessors in the original colonies, sold what they could to buy some of what they needed.

All these close-to-subsistence farmers ate monotonous diets, heavily dependent on a few staples abundant in their region—New Englanders fished for cod, Southerners grew sweet potatoes. The scarcity of cash, seasonal limitations, and ineffectual storage and preservation made meals repetitious, heavy with salt pork and corn. Indigenous to America, less susceptible to blight and more versatile than wheat, corn appeared on farmers' tables in many forms: fresh, mixed with rye or wheat in breads, soaked and converted into hominy, and as pork, which historian Richard Cummings calls "a form of condensed corn." Because hogs required little attention and preserved pork kept well and tasted good, farmers favored it over other meats; eaten fresh only at slaughtering time, pork, salted and smoked, provided the mainstay of the American diet. In fact, many people disliked fresh meat, believing that it was "unwholesome," lacking in "strength," or simply something to be left to "those who have a mind to swallow or be swallowed by flies." Salted meat and cornmeal, which could be kept all year, dominated winter diets; summer brought milk and fresh produce, but milk spoiled in the Southern hot weather. There, as everywhere, butter and cheese prevailed among dairy products because they kept better. Leafy vegetables also spoiled, and many farmers did not plant them because of the need for constant care, limiting their diets to wild greens or vegetables that could be stored or preserved, such as turnips, pumpkins, and beans. They raised orchard fruits more for cider and brandy than for eating, and picked and ate wild berries (rarely preserved because of the high cost of sugar). Rebecca Burlend's description of the Illinois settler's diet, a steady fare of bread, butter, coffee, and bacon, appears accurate for farmers everywhere before the middle of the nineteenth century who depended almost entirely on their own efforts for their living.

Almost from the beginning of colonial settlement, farming families made money by selling goods at the town market; outdoor public marketing began in Boston in 1634, four years after John Winthrop established the town. Other colonial cities followed suit, setting up outdoor marketplaces and hours of operation, and later constructing enclosed market buildings; by 1742, when Boston built its first enclosed market, Faneuil Hall, most other cities already had at least an outdoor one. Town authorities maintained these markets as arenas for direct sales to consumers by producers (farmers and fishermen) and processors (butchers and bakers):

they forbade food sales at the markets by retailers other than importers, and enacted regulations to keep hucksters from "forestalling"—arriving early at the market and buying all the farmers' wares before the general public got there.

At best the regulations hampered the hucksters by preventing them from buying before an appointed time or by forbidding them to meet farmers "at the end of the Streets" to buy up their goods; no rules ended street vending of vegetables, fish, meat, and dairy products, common in colonial cities and continuing well into the twentieth century. In addition to the professional hucksters, farmers and their spouses sometimes preferred to sell their surplus in the street instead of the market; they would keep to a regular schedule with regular customers or opt for random sales through neighborhoods until their wares were gone. For the urban house-

Souvenir photo of Military Plaza market, San Antonio, Texas, 1887. "At dark," reads the back, "the south side from East to West is filled with tables loaded with bread, chicken, *tamales, chilli con carne, enchilades,* and other Mexican dishes. . . . North of these tables are the plaza merchants selling jewelry, fruit and notions. At day light the merchants have vanished, their places are filled with vegetable stands."

wife without refrigeration and with little or no transportation, street vendors provided a constant supply of fresh food.

Many urban people raised food in their own backyard gardens; some kept livestock. Scavenger pigs who roamed the cities early in the nineteenth century were caught and eaten by laborers' families; when New York outlawed homeless pigs in 1830 and sent carts to collect them, hungry housewives battled the drivers. Twelve years later, Charles Dickens wrote in *American Notes* of pigs "roaming towards bed by scores" in the early evening, "eating their way to the last" along Broadway, losing their ears and tails to vagrant dogs with whom they shared the streets. He advised pedestrians to "take care of the pigs"; the pig, he wrote, goes where he pleases, "mingling with the best society, on an equal, if not superior footing, for every one makes way when he appears, and the haughtiest give him the wall, if he prefer it." Frances Trollope, whose *Domestic Manners of the Americans* outsold even Dickens's book among Europeans' accounts of their American travels, discovered "more ways than one of keeping a cow" in Cincinnati in the late 1820s. Many families fed and milked a cow at the door every morning and evening, "leaving the republican cow to walk away, to take her pleasure on the hills, or in the gutters, as may suit her fancy best." More than once, Mrs. Trollope could not get milk for breakfast because "the cow was not come home."

Until the 1840s, city as well as country diets lacked milk, fresh fruits, and vegetables; produce was scarce in winter and perishable in summer, and what little showed up fresh in the market might wilt in the sun before the day ended. The growing urban wage-earning class subsisted instead on bread, potatoes, crackers, salt pork, and blood pudding, a sausage made of chopped pork with hog or beef blood stuffed in a casing. More prosperous urbanites enjoyed wider variety—jellies and fruits preserved in expensive imported sugar, white bread, trifles, ice cream, coffee, and tea. But even the most elegant and affluent homes were limited to available supplies: a trifle served at a dinner at President Washington's New York residence tasted of rancid cream, and at another dinner there in August 1789, described by a senator as the finest he had ever eaten, the lengthy menu included no vegetables. Still, greater abundance and variety probably protected the wealthy from the vitamin deficiencies of the urban poor—who, unlike the rural poor, could not forage for wild greens.

A nutritional class distinction widened with the technological progress of the nineteenth century. Faster transportation—with, toward the end of the century, more efficient cold storage in refrigerated railroad cars and steamships—lengthened the seasons for fresh fruits and vegetables, especially for the rich, and made shipment of all kinds of perishable goods possible over long distances, adding variety to the markets and to some extent reducing prices on meat, dairy products, and fresh produce. Milk consumption in New York, for example, tripled or quadrupled during the

1840s, following the construction of the Erie Railroad. Railroads also stimulated the growth of truck farming in districts outlying the cities; hundreds of acres in upstate New York, Long Island, New Jersey, Delaware, Maryland, and eastern Virginia produced tomatoes, strawberries, and other fresh produce for the cities. As early as the 1850s, orchards and vineyards as far away as California, Florida, and the Caribbean supplied some fruit to the Northeast in unrefrigerated railroad cars and steamships. Prices were high because of transportation costs and spoilage. Perishables were occasionally shipped in ice before the Civil War, but the prototype for the refrigerated railroad car was not patented until 1867, and refrigerator car lines not established until the 1870s.

The rail networks were responsible for the heyday of the public markets in the middle of the century. In addition to milk and produce, the railroads brought fish and meat; for example, wild game became a staple

Refrigeration, railroads, and the eventual combination of the two in the refrigerated railroad car revolutionized food and farming. Farm Security Administration photo by Jack Delano, 1940.

market offering by 1867. Before the railroads, venison, moose, bison, raccoon, and opossum, already scarce in the areas surrounding the cities, had been advertised in the newspapers as special items when available.

Foreign visitors commented on the size of American markets and the "almost endless variety of the choicest articles of food—meat, poultry, fish, vegetables, and fruits from all parts," conveyed by steamboat and railroad. In large cities people could no longer depend on a single public market; by 1860, Boston and St. Louis each had ten large markets, San Francisco had five, and other cities had made appropriations for additional market spaces. Public markets, today a tourist attraction in a few large cities, served as central arenas of daily life all over America in the mid-nineteenth century. Even small towns in the Midwest, essentially service centers for farmers, supported central markets until after the 1870s, when they had begun to disappear in all but a few older towns.

Although middlemen between farmer and consumer and the owners of shops dominated mid-century markets, transient farmers could still rent stalls. Women and their daughters put up apple butter, applesauce, and sauerkraut to sell in the fall after the summer produce was exhausted; they also offered household products—feathers for pillows, cattails for stuffing mattresses, bulrushes for scrubbing or for chair bottoms, broom straw and finished brooms, soap, baskets, potted plants, dried bouquets, and Christmas greens. Producing and selling afforded rural women a means of making money compatible with routine household tasks. Farm families did their business among, and sometimes in competition with, the permanent vendors who held the power at the markets. In poultry stalls feathers flew and chanting salesmen tried to outsquawk live chickens, turkeys, and geese. Butchers sold beef, mutton, veal, pork, and wild game; fish and dairy and the new greengrocery stalls handled produce arriving by rail.

Street vendors continued to compete with the markets. Professional hucksters had begun to ride into the country to buy supplies, or they bought produce from commercial outfits at the markets, too impatient to wait to buy out supplies from farmers' stalls. Two nineteenth-century shopping manuals, one written by a New York market butcher and the other by the editor of the *New York Market Journal*, warned against patronizing these vendors, who, with lower overhead, could sell at lower prices. Their "inferior" produce, the manuals claimed, came from the markets' oversupplies and refuse.

Inferior produce could certainly be found at the markets as well. Jo March, the heroine of Louisa May Alcott's *Little Women*, charged by her mother with the housekeeping for a day, went off to market to buy "a very young lobster, some very old asparagus, and two boxes of acid strawberries," thinking she had made good bargains. Early public health investigators castigated the markets for selling deteriorated and adulterated food; the New York city inspector called the famous Washington and Fulton markets—so often celebrated in travelers' accounts for marvelous variety—"a singular agglomeration of rotten wood, worn-out masonry, and collected filth, without system in their construction, or any visible appearance which would enable the stranger to discover why they are permitted to exist." The markets did provide some consumer protection against obviously fraudulent practices like short-weighting, which could be brought to the attention of the municipal officials who supervised market operations; still, officials took action more often against occasional renters and operators of small stalls than against the powerful permanent market operators.

Whatever the quality of their produce, unregulated street vendors were convenient, even necessary, for consumers without refrigeration who were compelled to shop frequently, especially in the summertime. Although the first icebox patent was issued in 1803, the high cost of ice made iceboxes exceptional until after 1827, when two inventions—the ice cutter and a new icehouse that drastically reduced the rate of melting—dropped the price by more than 60 percent. Harvesting, storing, and shipping natural ice developed into a substantial industry. Henry David Thoreau described the process at Walden Pond in the winter of 1846–1847: "A hundred Irishmen, with Yankee overseers, came from Cambridge every day" for sixteen days, hired by a man who "wanted to double his money, which, as I understood, amounted to half a million already; but in order to cover each one of his dollars with another, he took off the only coat, ay, the skin itself, of Walden Pond in the midst of a hard winter." They scored the frozen pond into a checkerboard using horse-drawn ice cutters, then pried the scored blocks apart, "and these, being sledded to the shore, were rapidly hauled off on to an ice platform, and raised by grappling irons and block and tackle, worked by horses, on to a stack, as surely as so many barrels of flour, and there placed evenly side by side, and row upon row, as if they formed the solid base of an obelisk designed to pierce the clouds." The Walden workmen told Thoreau "they had some in the ice-houses at Fresh Pond five years old which was as good as ever."

All over the Northern states, ice harvesters duplicated the scene at Walden Pond, storing the blocks in icehouses. The ice waited there for shipping, either local delivery (available in cities from ice carts making regular rounds by the 1850s) or long-distance transport. Natural ice remained a luxury, mostly used for commercial food storage, for cooling drinks, or for that extravagant treat, ice cream. "Is it fairies?" asked *Little Women*'s Amy March, beholding Mr. Laurence's gift of sweets and fruit and ice cream ("actually two dishes of it, pink and white"). "It's Santa Claus," said her sister Beth. More sophisticated diners, especially European travelers, considered the confection no less delicious.

Ice cut from Northern lakes and ponds provided the supply of commercial ice before artificial refrigeration. From an 1846 lithograph.

Domestic refrigerators were widely advertised and ice deliveries in urban areas were regular and reliable by mid-century, but per capita ice consumption remained low. Home iceboxes were rare; cookbooks and domestic manuals, which sometimes recommended use of refrigerators, suggested cold-storage methods for families who had none. Sarah Josepha Hale (later the editor of *Godey's Lady's Book*, for many years the most influential American women's magazine) told the readers of *The Good Housekeeper* in 1844 to pack meat in snow to keep it frozen for "many days, even weeks." Catharine Beecher, who wrote the most comprehensive nineteenth-century housekeeping manuals, in 1846 published directions for converting a barrel into an inexpensive substitute for the "superior" manufactured refrigerator. Twenty-three years later, in 1869, refrigerators were still so rare that Beecher provided a detailed description in *The American Woman's Home*. In addition to a wire or tin closet for cold meats and cream, kept in the cellar ("if ants are troublesome, set the legs in tin cups of water"), she advocated "a refrigerator, or a large wooden-box, on feet, with a lining of tin or zinc, and a space between the tin and wood filled with powdered charcoal, having at the bottom a place for ice, a drain to carry off the water, and also movable shelves and partitions. In this, articles are kept cool." As late as 1869, Catharine Beecher's middle-class readers might not even have known what a refrigerator was.

Technical innovation continued both in harvesting and storing natural ice and in artificial ice production, which became an important manufacturing business in the South during the 1870s and 1880s, and in the North after two mild winters in 1888–1890. After that time, the numbers of homes with refrigerators and the amount of ice used increased rapidly, as reflected both in the statistics of the ice industry (Philadelphia, Baltimore, and Chicago used over five times as much in 1914 as in 1880) and in those of the refrigerator manufacturers (who made products with almost fifteen

Ice delivery was available in cities beginning in the mid-1850s. This photo was taken for the Washington Souvenir Company in 1919, when many ice men traveled in gasoline-powered vehicles.

times the value in 1919 as in 1879). About four-fifths of the families studied in a 1908 survey of New York working people reported owning refrigerators. The iceman came to fewer homes in the country and in smaller towns and cities, where houses had cellars and back porches that could be used for cold storage. As late as the 1920s, according to an ice industry estimate, half the urban homes in the United States bought no ice even in the summer; a model budget for Portland, Oregon workers' families in 1925 declared ice dispensable, merely "a convenience to be desired during a short season."

The nostalgic picture of mammoth gardens and gargantuan rows of home-canned goods, formed after the turn of the century, obscures the truth that home preserving of vegetables by methods other than drying or keeping them in root cellars was uncommon during the nineteenth century. Most cookbooks included directions for salting meat and making preserves, but so do modern cookbooks, and probably many of these directions, then as now, served only as reference for occasional use. By 1871, one "Housekeeper's Guide" reserved directions for making cheese and curing bacon and ham to the "Farmer's Department," amid the advice for planting strawberries and washing sheep. The "Culinary Department" of the guide contained recipes for jams and jellies; there urban readers also found advice for choosing meat at the butcher's and preserving it with pepper and charcoal. Sugar preserving, which requires sterilized containers but not hermetical sealing, used the process familiar to modern preservers: sterilizing jars, filling them with hot fruit, preserves, or jelly, and covering them with wax or tight lids. But, wrote Helen Campbell in an 1881 manual for country housekeeping, "most people consider it difficult" because "the directions generally given are so troublesome that one can not wonder it is not attempted oftener." The high cost of sugar throughout the century further limited home preserving.

Nicolas Appert, a Frenchman, had invented hermetical sealing in 1809, in response to a competition for a method of preserving food to supply the troops for the Napoleonic Wars. By the 1850s, self-sealing jars were sold in American country stores, but acid fruits and brined vegetables stored in them often spoiled because of poor seals. Vegetables and non-acid fruits could not be canned without the pressure cooker, "the only method recommended" in modern home canning, available for household use only after World War I. Campbell's country manual did not even suggest the boiling-water bath recommended by modern cookbooks; she provided no recipes for canned vegetables other than tomatoes and an okra-tomato combination for soups. Another 1880s cookbook offered recipes for canned peaches, grapes, strawberries, quinces, pineapple, fruit juices, tomatoes, corn, peas, plums, mincemeat, boiled cider, and pumpkin. The real impetus for home canning came only after 1900, with the invention of machines that could make the glass jars that formerly had to be hand-blown, and with government campaigns to promote home-canned foods, especially the produce of World War I victory gardens—"We Can Can Vegetables and the Kaiser Too."

Until the end of the century, expeditions and military campaigns used most of the food that was canned commercially; the California gold rush and the Civil War, for example, produced demand for American canned foods, although few unsuccessful forty-niners or enlisted soldiers ate so luxuriously. Appert's method processed food in glass jars, which were supplanted commercially by cheaper and sturdier tin cans after 1839. For the rest of the century inventors tinkered with the canning process, designing machines to cut the cans and solder their seams, adding chemicals, or devising new kettles that would raise the heat, shorten the processing time, and lower the cost of canning food. By the 1880s, cookbooks recommended can openers as necessary kitchen equipment, though canned food was too expensive for most until after the turn of the century. Writing in the advertising journal *Printer's Ink* in 1893, the treasurer of Franco-American detailed the history of their campaign to lure consumers to canned food. The first ad appeared in the *American Yachtsman* (suggesting both the class status of canned foods and their continuing use for special expeditions). After five years of advertising, Franco-American had found that the best returns came from the middle-class magazines—*The Century, Harper's, Cosmopolitan,* and *Scribner's.* Franco-American had tried daily newspapers in Chicago and Boston, but dropped that advertising because "dailies go to a large percentage of people who do not use our class of goods."

Bread was the one prepared food product in common use among urban working people; bakers plied their trade almost from the start of colonial cities. In 1664, ten bakers operated in New York, and the Boston selectmen turned down a request for a permit to "set up the Trade of a Baker," probably because so many others were already operating. Few city people owned ovens, which, before cast-iron stoves, had to be custom-built into fireplaces or as separate structures outside. As stoves became more common during the nineteenth century, baker's bread remained economical during the summer, when to fire up the stove used fuel and overheated the kitchen. Cookbooks, however, advised against the use of baker's bread: Sarah Josepha Hale decried it as tasteless, unhealthy (those who made their own bread could be certain of the quality of the flour), and wasteful when the stove was already used for heating. Country women, she pointed out, baked their own bread, but "in our cities, ladies marry and commence housekeeping, without knowing anything of breadmaking" and entrusted the task to servants without even supervising it "the way they do their cakes." Urban people without servants ate baker's bread. One Midwestern baker maintained that "the people who lived in the better homes and kept help in 1890 never thought of buying bread

Baker's bread was available in towns from the beginning of the colonies. Prang's Aids, lithographed in color, showed various trades and occupàtions, 1875.

unless to fill in when the home-baked bread ran short. They regarded baker's bread as poor-folksy; it was the working class who bought baker's bread." Crackers—longer-lasting and easier to store—provided an additional market for bakers; long used on ships and as military provisions, they filled barrels in country stores before the Civil War, producing enough demand to stimulate establishment of large commercial cracker bakeries as early as the 1850s.

Those country stores underwent a radical transformation in the second half of the century when enormous changes in transportation, communications, agricultural methods, production techniques, merchandising policies, company structures—in short, everything that goes together to make an economy—combined in a nationwide distribution system. Dominated by the manufacturers, that system eventually replaced the cracker barrel with Uneeda Biscuits, offering a wide variety of brand-name prepared food products to consumers around the turn of the century. Before 1850, traditional mercantile firms dominated distribution; "business was carried on in much the same manner as it had been in fourteenth-century Venice or Florence." Usually they operated on commission, not owning the goods but facilitating their transport.

During the 1850s and 1860s, two new groups, agricultural commodity dealers and wholesalers of manufactured goods, took over distribution, shipping by rail and steamship and communicating by telegraph and an improved postal system. In agriculture, still the central business in an economy only beginning to industrialize, new marketing methods were combined with liberal land policies (embodied in the Homestead Act of 1862) and new agricultural implements (the steel plow, the mechanical reaper, the threshing machine, and the combine). The new system transformed Midwestern farms like the Burlends'—largely self-sufficient operations supplemented with barter and small sales—into cash-producing cogs in the big wheel of agricultural business. In manufacturing, the new wholesalers replaced the traditional independent country peddlers; they worked for large firms under the supervision of a general manager, traveling by rail, handing out samples and catalogues, and helping small storekeepers learn the accounting methods they needed for dealing with the wholesale firms. Both the agricultural commodity dealers and the wholesalers depended on new financial procedures: futures trading in the agricultural market, and credit reporting in the wholesaling of manufactured goods. These new procedures, the new transportation and communication, and new company structures made it possible for the firms to move more goods; the real savings came, not from company size, but from rapid stock turnover.

In the next decades, mass distribution was followed by new methods for making more goods: mass production. The first factories, arenas for

John Hecker's machine-made bread, an advertisement from around 1858.

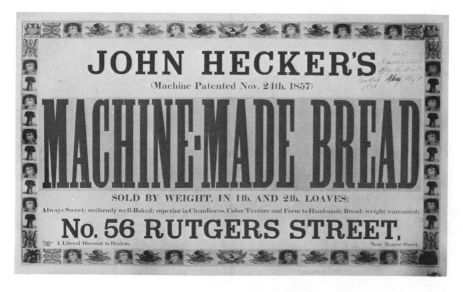

production where manufacturers brought workers and machines together, had, by the Civil War, replaced homes and shops as the basis of manufacturing. Now the new transportation and communications systems assured a steady flow of raw materials into factories and of finished goods out, while the new wholesalers, purchasing directly, left factory owners free to invest profits in plants and machinery instead of tying them up in the hands of the commission merchants. The new factories of the 1880s relied on "continuous process" machines and methods that turned out goods automatically or moved them continuously through a factory from one stage to the next, the basis of mass production. Henry Ford's 1913 Model T assembly line, the fullest application of the principles, used methods applied decades before to simpler products like processed foods. "New process" mills transformed wheat, rye, barley, and oats into flour and breakfast cereals after 1879; the first "automatic line" can factory, cutting and soldering tin cans at unprecedented speeds in a coordinated, almost completely automated process, opened in 1883.

Hauling loads of corn to the canning factory, Eau Claire, Wisconsin, around 1920.

Cans being sterilized in steam before filling and sealing, at the Phillips tomato-packing company, Cambridge, Maryland, 1941. Farm Security Administration photo by John Collier.

During the 1880s and 1890s, large corporations combined the new techniques of mass distribution and mass production, and marketed the products they made, creating the modern corporate structure with different departments to handle purchasing, production, and marketing. From the start, these enterprises served the entire country; by the turn of the century they advertised and distributed brand-name products to a national market. Campbell's Soups, Quaker Oats, Gold Medal and Pillsbury Flour, Heinz's 57 Varieties of pickles, relishes, and sauces, Libby's canned

meats, Borden's Milk—these and others became household words thanks
to national advertising by firms that bypassed the wholesalers in marketing
and advertising operations, while often continuing to use them to distribute goods to retailers. After 1900, as firms like these, which could
effectively exploit the economies of mass production, came to dominate
industrial activity, prices of manufactured goods began to drop. Prepared
foods began their move away from the luxury category, and by the 1920s
the giant corporations' products could be found on many ordinary tables.

Up until the turn of the century, however, working people used few of
the new factory-prepared foods; many continued to produce as much as
they could, avoiding the money economy as much as possible. Pigs and
goats still lived in Manhattan as far south as 42nd Street; many urban
families kept chickens well into the twentieth century. Margaret Byington, a social worker studying family life in the steel town of Homestead,
Pennsylvania, in 1908, heard "a curious noise beneath my chair" and
looked down to find "a friendly chicken which had come for a feast of
crumbs." One steelworker's widow sold eggs "to add a little to a slender
income." In the cotton-mill town of Manchester, New Hampshire, around
the same time, it was very common to see a man walking down the street
with a cow, one resident remembered. "Most everybody" had chickens.

Most everybody had gardens, too. A seed-store proprietor who had
lived in Muncie, Indiana, since the Civil War estimated that 75 to 80
percent of the town's families gardened in 1890; by the early 1920s his
estimate was "certainly not over 40 or 60 percent." The 1890 gardens were
"considerably larger." Poorer people continued to garden in greater numbers. One Homestead family refused to give Byington an account of their
food expenditures because "it would not fairly represent their table expenses," thanks to their garden; another put the expenditure for seeds on
the food account.

Byington commented that gardens developed "neighborliness of spirit,"
since the women talked about them over the fence; the Manchester
resident laughed about putting chicken coops "on the far side of the lot
. . . near your neighbor's house," and the neighbors putting up with it.
Neighborliness could go too far, but both comments indicate how food
production contributed to a sense of community now gone, along with
meeting at the well or pump or hydrant to get water, comparing laundry
hanging in adjoining yards or on adjoining lines in the same alley, and
frequent trips outside to get wood or go to the outhouse. People shared
the food they produced; just as frontier people gave freshly slaughtered
meat to their neighbors "with the view of receiving as much again when
they kill theirs," so backyard gardeners everywhere traded the extra produce that they could not preserve. This surplus disappeared as food
became a purchased commodity: everybody bought just what they
needed.

Seasons limited diets when people ate only what they could grow, and continued to do so to the end of the century even for those who purchased food. An 1887 cookbook, listing "the varieties of seasonable food to be obtained in our markets" month by month, reveals that shoppers as well as gardeners ate only tubers and root vegetables (beets, carrots, turnips, potatoes, parsnips), winter squashes, celery, and cabbages from November through April. One Muncie housewife described the 1890 "winter diet": "Steak, roasts, macaroni, Irish potatoes, sweet potatoes, turnips, cole slaw, fried apples, and stewed tomatoes, with Indian pudding, rice, cake, or pie for dessert." To make it less boring, they "swapped around from one combination to another, using pickles and chow-chow to make the familiar starchy food relishing. We never thought of having fresh fruit or green vegetables and could not have got them if we had." Spring brought welcome relief—variety, and an end to serious seasonal vitamin deficiencies.

Few manufactured products relieved the housewives' tasks once they had brought the food home. All year round, food arrived in the kitchen unprepared. Shoppers returned from the market with live chickens that had to be killed, or dead ones that had to be plucked; their work at home matched that of the farmer or the poor urban chicken keeper. Even purchased fish had scales; even purchased hams had to be soaked or blanched. Roasting and grinding green coffee, grinding and sifting whole spices, cutting and pounding lump or loaf sugar, sifting heavy flour that might be full of impurities, soaking oatmeal overnight, shelling nuts, grinding cocoa shells, seeding raisins, making and nurturing yeast, drying herbs: tasks like these accompanied nearly every ingredient of every recipe, whether it came from the garden or the market.

Those tasks began to disappear around the beginning of the twentieth century, as manufacturers took over the work of precooking preparation, packing food to advertise and distribute to a national market and selling it at affordable prices. American industrialization and urbanization had transformed food, once the primary product of home industry and the primary resource for barter, into a commodity, produced by large companies and sold for profit. Throughout the nineteenth century, new methods and implements in business and commercial agriculture, and the general economic expansion that was both cause and effect of those innovations, brought food into the marketplace, usually raw and unprepared, and introduced middlemen between consumers and the farmers who produced it. Prepared food in cans and boxes, the result of mass production and mass distribution, entered consumers' kitchens during the first decades of the twentieth century, eventually to be followed by fully prepared meals from the supermarket freezer and the fast-food restaurant. Throughout the uneven process of this transformation, wealthy families bought more food than poor ones, rural dwellers produced more

The new packaged foods transformed small-town stores like the Richmond Grocery, Lodi, Wisconsin. Grace Richmond is shown here behind the counter, sometime between 1903 and 1913.

than city folks, and some home production coexisted with the railroads and factories; in 1900, three-fifths of the American population still lived in rural territory, and many poor urban people still produced as much food as they could.

Even so, nearly everybody felt the effects of the new developments: farmers produced cash crops for a national agricultural market, and shopped at markets when they went to town. Progress in transportation, food preservation, factory production, distribution, and marketing— components of the general expansion and centralization of the money economy—had begun to alter Americans' diets, their most intimate daily habits, their attitudes toward food, and their relationships with their families and communities. With refrigeration, they ate less spoiled food; with mass-produced glass jars, they preserved more; with better transportation, they enjoyed greater variety with longer seasons. This variety brought better nutrition, a major element in the higher standard of living that industrialization offered the average person. It is true that as they relinquished the hard work of home production, they also lost its satisfactions, becoming dependent on industrial products as consumers and surrendering the pleasures of planting, harvesting, and trading the surplus with others. Modern backyard gardeners who celebrate those pleasures, however, do so in the context of their otherwise industrialized lives. At the end of the nineteenth century, overburdened housewives might well opt for any savings in time and labor that they could afford.

Out of the Frying Pan

Bef efore gas and electricity, cooking was hard, hot, heavy, and even hazardous. Food came into the kitchen unprepared, to be transformed into meals that would sustain a nation laboring more with its bodies than with its brains. During a century of industrial revolution, with technological change the central trait of American factory production, inventors patented many devices that could have eased women's labor in the kitchen, but none changed the fundamental character of cooking. It remained a source of enormous fatigue from heat and hard work, an arduous thrice-daily household ritual. Only two technological innovations were bought in sufficient numbers to make a substantial impact on American cooking. One was the cheap geared metal Dover eggbeater and the other the cast-iron stove, which conserved fuel and reduced the hazards of cooking with wood and coal. By the end of the century, the iron stove was within most families' means, a large purchase that could last many years.

The hearth was the heart of every room until the mid-nineteenth century, and the kitchen fireplace with its open hearth was the center of the house. Many houses, especially in rural areas and small villages, had only one heated room; the "hall" of colonial New England served as kitchen, dining room, living room, den or recreation room, workshop, and sometimes bedroom as well. The kitchen fireplace of large and small houses was built wider and deeper than fireplaces intended for heating alone, to accommodate pots and reflector ovens and joints of meat. The central architectural feature of indoor space, the kitchen fireplace dominated women's lives. Throughout the day, they poked the fire, added fuel, and moved pots to adjust the heat on slow-cooking dishes. At mealtimes, they gathered the members of their households—menfolk, children, and sometimes other relatives or even hired help—to share the products of their labors at the hearth.

By the beginning of the nineteenth century, large houses in the developing cities had separate rooms to serve as kitchens, often staffed by servants, and rooms for dining as well. Southern plantation houses had kitchen outbuildings, effectively shielding the planters' families and guests from slaves' activities and from the oppressive heat of cooking during Southern summers. In homes with large numbers of slaves or servants, mistresses superintended the cooking, assisting in preparing meals and overseeing an eating ritual generally more elaborate than in a household run on a single woman's labor. Few households, Northern or Southern, had enough extra hands to permit the lady of the house to be an administrator and hostess alone. Most with any help had a single woman slave, or one neighboring farm girl come to "live in."

In large houses, kitchen fireplaces were crowded with equipment, including pots, skillets, and other utensils on legs or legged trivets, designed to lift the pots above the burning coals. Pots were hung from bars and hooks if their legs were too short, or if the dish required long cooking—a less stable arrangement, especially when the suspension device depended on wood or rope rather than iron, and undoubtedly the cause of many a lost dinner. A number of kitchen fireplaces were equipped with back-bars of green wood or iron, iron hooks, chains, and cranes and jacks, designed to hang pots and joints of meat and to move utensils away from or toward the burning logs. Complicated built-in arrangements and mechanical de-

The kitchen was the heart—and often the only heated room—of the colonial home.

vices that responded automatically to heat or smoke were common only in the homes of the wealthy. Ordinary folk made do with a simple bar or crane, and with a few pots. Kitchen utensils were valuable, often listed in colonial household inventories as part of probate records.

Hearth utensils were usually made of iron, although a few families of means owned copper ones as well. Gridirons to broil meat, skillets, and waffle irons, with long handles to spare the cook from the flames, were made of wrought iron by local blacksmiths. Toasting "forks" were usually not forks at all, but rather wire frames to hold slices of bread. Long-handled skimmers and ladles, wooden or iron, removed scum from boiling kettles and served as basters. The common wooden "peel" or "slice," a large spatula used for moving bread and meat in and out of ovens and fireplaces, sat by the hearth along with other equipment.

Although in Europe even small towns had professional bakers or public bakehouses, where women brought their own dough to be baked under the bakers' supervision, public bakehouses were unusual in America, and professional bakers sold bread only in the city. Rural people usually ate pancakes instead of bread; European travelers often commented on the hoecakes, johnnycakes, and other breads baked in American homes above the heat source. Some women baked on their hearths either with a reflector oven or "roasting kitchen," a boxlike utensil on legs usually used for roasting birds, or with a Dutch oven for rolls and biscuits, a strong covered iron kettle on legs, around which coals were placed. A few homes provided brick bake ovens, built into the side of the kitchen fireplace with a flue to conduct smoke up the chimney, or as a separate structure outside the house. The fire was made directly in these ovens; after the ashes and coals were swept out, the baked goods went in. The oven, heated "so hot as to allow it to be closed fifteen minutes after clearing, before the heat is reduced enough to use it," was hard to regulate; determining the right heat required considerable experience. As many as four bakings (of items requiring successively less heat) could be done after one fire. The cooling

Fireplace cooking utensils. Clockwise: 1. Gridiron, for broiling meat, with revolving circular top. 2. Common gridiron. 3. Chop roaster, of tin, which stood before the open fire, the bright metal reflecting the heat; chops hung on the hooks and drippings fell into the pan. 4. Toaster, or "toasting fork," with top that revolves on a pivot. 5. Roasting kitchen, or Dutch oven, of tin, for meat or fowl, which was fastened to the central rod with iron skewers and turned with the handle. A door at the back of the oven was opened for basting; drippings were poured out through a spout at the side of the oven.

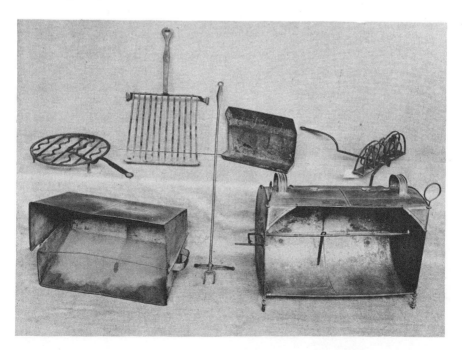

oven functioned properly for yeast breads, a characteristic imitated in most modern bread recipes by preheating the oven to a high temperature and then lowering it after the bread has baked for ten or fifteen minutes.

Only constant fire tending—poking, shifting logs, and adding wood—could keep a hot fire going in brick ovens and fireplaces. Wood had to be felled, chopped, and carried into the house; usually men and boys cut the trees down, but much chopping and wood hauling was women's work as well. The job of cooking on those fires was hot and dangerous. Despite long-handled utensils, cooks had to bend and kneel and reach into the flames. Burning cinders flew from unscreened kitchen fires, skin and clothing scorched at the grate, and small children were seldom safe in their own homes. In the summer, heat from the fireplace could be nearly intolerable.

Cast-iron cooking stoves reduced, but did not eliminate, most of the hazards and difficulties of fireplace cooking. Foundries began to specialize in stove casting in the 1830s, and by the middle of the century, small works manufactured stoves all over the country. Thanks to improved transportation and distribution, stove casting soon became one of the most significant branches of iron founding, with some foundries making and assembling stove plates, others making plates to be assembled locally by individual craftsmen. During the decades before the Civil War, cookbooks gave directions for both fireplace and stove cookery; they recommended interchangeable equipment—pots and pans without legs, and trivets to convert the pots to fireplace cooking. They offered advice on brick ovens and recommended adjustments in method for baking in iron stoves. The language of most recipes could apply to either stoves or fireplaces: "put it on the fire," "set it in a well-heated oven," "fry them a light brown," "simmer the water they were boiled in to half a pint," "stew it gently about an hour." But women still roasted and broiled at the fire, and recipes referred directly and matter-of-factly to fireplaces, telling the cook to "set the pot in the chimney corner with the lid off." The transition from fireplaces to stoves was in progress by the middle of the century, but not yet complete.

Controversy accompanied this transition. Meat broiled over coals, as every backyard barbecuer knows, tastes different from meat broiled under a flame. Cast-iron stoves had no broilers—gridirons, used on stoves or fireplaces, kept their place as the only broilers available—but they did have ovens. Cooks could try to duplicate hearth-roasted meat in ovens instead of hanging it or turning it on a spit at the fire, but some cookbook writers argued that meat roasted at the fire possessed a flavor and texture meat baked in an iron oven could never match. As late as 1885, a cookbook emphasized the distinction between roast beef made at a fire and "Baked Beef (or beef roasted in the oven)." The iron oven had its drawbacks for other baking, also. Catharine Beecher, who celebrated convection in cooking stoves as "the most convenient, economical, and labor-saving mode of employing heat," maintained in 1869 that "we cannot but regret, for the sake of bread, that our old steady brick ovens have been almost universally superseded by those of ranges and cooking stoves, which are infinite in their caprices, and forbid all general rules." She sidestepped the roasting controversy by recommending a cooking stove that incorporated "a common tin oven, in which roasting can be done in front of the stove, the oven doors being removed for the purpose. The roast will be done as perfectly as by an open fire."

This built-in reflector oven, only one of a wide variety of stove options available by the 1840s, epitomizes historian Siegfried Giedion's characterization of the cast-iron stove as "a vigorously plastic type, having a base and a superstructure." The basic stove design, typified by Philo P. Stewart's Oberlin Stove, patented in 1834, concentrated the heat in a perforated fire chamber surrounded by air. The "superstructure" included movable grates (at first for wood, later for coal or for both wood and coal); ash sifters, and other devices to grade chunks of fuel; hot-water systems, from built-in boilers on top of the stove to elaborate systems of

Catharine Beecher's recommended stove, with raised tin baking cover. From *The American Woman's Home,* 1869.

pipes that carried hot smoke from the fire, heating water along the way; and storage cupboards, including warming closets useful for heating plates, keeping food warm, and drying fruit. Accessories further broadened the range of cooking options: a huge raised tin lid, for example, could enclose the heat radiating above the stove to furnish more baking space. Many technical devices and improvements better understood by the thermodynamics engineer than the cook—corrugated woodboxes, tapering fireboxes that concentrated heat in a conical chamber, insulators, flues, and dampers—provided hotter, longer-lasting, less smoky, and more fuel-efficient fires.

Sears's offerings at the end of the century included many of these options. In 1897, they sold twelve diverse "Sunshine" stoves and ranges, most available in different sizes and fitted for either coal or wood or (for extra money) both. The cheapest Southern Sunshine Cook, a plain square stove with four 7-inch pot holes and an oven 16 by 17 by 12 inches fitted for wood, cost $5.97: "Though low in price it is a strong and durable stove." For a higher price there were more and larger pot holes, ventilated ovens twice as big as the oven on the Southern Sunshine Cook, stoves with high decorated backs with or without shelves and towel racks, built-in ash sifters, and extensive systems of dampers and flues. Arrangements for heating water ranged from the plain reservoir available (at extra cost) with every model to the most expensive circulating boiler on the $48.00 Family Sunshine Range; only a plumber could install the $48.00 range, connected to the town water system or to an elevated tank, "placed at sufficient height to force the water to any part of the house where hot water is desired."

Coal and wood stoves continued to change even after the turn of the century, by which time they had long since supplanted fireplaces, and gas provided the competition. The era of the all-cast-iron stove had ended: new machines for rolling steel, and new processes that changed the composition of steel and perfected control over heat treatment, produced new kinds of steel, lighter and less brittle than cast iron. Easier to transport, rolled steel conformed better to turn-of-the-century systems of centralized production and national distribution, making for a general switchover from locally produced cast iron to centrally produced rolled steel in American industry. Stoves were no exception: in 1908, Sears offered only asbestos-lined sheet-steel ranges, with cast-iron fittings—doors, water reservoirs, firebacks, legs, grates, and cooking tops. Innovation continued: the 1908 ranges offered warming ovens, oven-door thermostats, poker doors, and a top that could be raised by a ratchet, "which has entirely done away with having to lay the fire by removing the lids and sliding them around over the top of the range."

Home economist Nellie Kedzie Jones, who wrote a women's column in the Curtis farm journal *The Country Gentleman* from 1912 to 1916, applauded many of these improvements. "The best" kitchen range, she said,

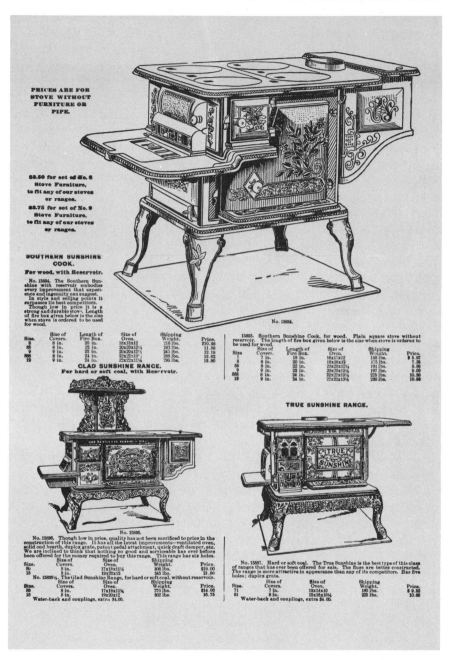

Three of the twelve "Sunshine" stoves and ranges offered by Sears in their 1897 catalogue. The Southern Sunshine Cook, shown here with hot-water reservoir, was fitted for wood; the Glad Sunshine and True Sunshine ranges were designed for hard or soft coal.

"is none too good. You had better economize anywhere else than on that. Good cookery is impossible on a poor stove." A farm kitchen needed a large six-hole stove, with a firebox large enough to hold "quite big wood," a damper in the stovepipe ("a wonderful fuel saver"), and a large water reservoir ("you can't have too much hot water"). She celebrated the "indispensable" warming oven, baking ovens with glass doors, "and of course a thermometer. Without it your baking is guesswork." "Aunt Nellie" was less enthusiastic about the less practical stove embellishments. "Get a range as plain as possible," she advised. "Much nickeling, curlicues, scrolls and gingerbread work generally are a pest to keep clean and are often, from an artistic standpoint, atrocities. A plain surface is easier to black and to clean."

Even the most modest cast-iron or steel stove—the plain box with cookholes, an oven, and a firebox—offered thermal efficiency far beyond that of the best fireplaces. With a stove, less fuel could produce more heat with less tending. And stoves were safer, less fascinating to small children than open fires, and less likely to send flying sparks and hot cinders into the room. Stove tops at near waist-level eliminated much of the bending and lifting of fireplace cookery. New houses could be built without fireplaces, at considerable savings. With advantages like these, less flavorful oven-baked beef handily won the competition with the hearth-roasted variety. Stoves became standard household equipment during the decades after 1869, when Catharine Beecher called them "the most common modes of cooking, where open fires are relinquished." By the end of the century, open fires had been relinquished everywhere, in rural areas and the rapidly developing urban ones, in the hovels and tenements of the poor and the mansions of the rich.

Coal and wood stoves, for all their advantages, were by no means perfect. They cut down on house fires, but not on skin burns; with large expanses of hot metal in every household, burns were mentioned frequently in accounts of nineteenth-century life. Stove heat, although more even than fireplace heat for boiling and frying, could change with the wind outside; it was certainly uneven by modern standards. Dampers required a great deal of fiddling; the more sophisticated the stove, the more sophisticated the damper arrangement. Flues might be blocked, dampers might be loose. Sometimes it was hard to tell even whether a damper was open or closed, except by the results: a dead fire, or an oven cold because the damper for the water-reservoir heat was open.

Although stoves reduced fire tending, untended fires could and did go out. When Jo March's mother in *Little Women* went off one day, leaving her daughters to do the housekeeping, a dead fire was the first of many disasters. " 'Here's a sweet prospect,' muttered Jo, slamming the stove-door open, and poking vigorously among the cinders." She rekindled the fire, but could not wash dishes until the water was hot. Housekeepers more experienced than Jo kept an eye on their stoves, but had to rekindle them every morning. Helen Campbell gave complete directions in a manual published for country housekeepers in 1881. First, dispose of the remains of the last fire: remove the stove lids; gather the ashes and cinders into the grate; replace the lids; close the doors and drafts; dump the cinders and ashes into a pan below the grate and sift either in a sifter built into the stove or in a regular ash sifter (placed over a barrel); set a fire with shavings or paper, small sticks of wood, and a few larger pieces; reopen the drafts, light the fire, and add large pieces of wood or coal; now close the dampers. A good fire in a good stove, Campbell wrote, would last four hours; rekindling meant raking ashes, adding more fuel, and readjusting dampers.

The experienced coal-stove or wood-stove user managed to pare down the time required for all these operations. Still, in an experiment conducted in 1899 by Boston's School of Housekeeping, it took almost an hour a day to care for an up-to-date coal stove. In a six-day period, twenty minutes were spent in sifting ashes, twenty-four minutes in laying fires, one hour and forty-eight minutes in tending fires, thirty minutes in emptying ashes, fifteen minutes in carrying coal, and two hours and nine minutes on blacking the stove to keep it from rusting. It was heavy work: 292 pounds of new coal were put in the stove in those six days, 27 pounds sifted out of the ashes, and more than 14 pounds of kindling. The authors of the Boston study complained that they had trouble calculating the cost of cooking fuel because the fire had so many uses: "a given fire will cook not one but many articles at the same time," and it heated the kitchen and the hot-water reservoir as well as the food. Wood and coal stoves were never "turned on"; they were used only when economical in time, in labor, and in fuel. This made them less flexible than modern gas and electric stoves, which cooks can use one burner at a time.

City dwellers during the nineteenth century increasingly favored coal over wood: as the forests were cut down and the railroads brought fuel from distant coalfields, wood became more expensive than coal in the urbanizing areas. In 1869, Catharine Beecher wrote that a "city load" of wood was a third of a cord, hardly enough to keep a stove going throughout the winter. She advised three tons of anthracite in the Middle States, and four in the Northern, to keep one fire through the winter. Urbanites less prosperous than Beecher's readers, lacking money and storage space, scavenged fuel or paid dearly for the small quantities they bought. By 1881, even Helen Campbell's manual for country housekeepers assumed that they would use coal rather than wood, although she did mention that "the same principles" applied to wood fires as to coal ones. Coal had other advantages besides cost: it burned longer, and so required much less frequent feeding and fire tending. It also lightened the work: 292 pounds of coal was a lot to carry, but much less than an equivalent amount of wood, a less concentrated fuel.

The pots used on top of stoves, like those used at the hearth, were

The Vollrath Company of Sheboygan, Wisconsin, introduced the first enameled steel utensils at the end of the nineteenth century. These Vollrath workers were photographed about 1924.

almost exclusively made of iron throughout the nineteenth century. Most cooking pots were designed to fit into the stove holes (Sears advised its customers to "be sure and buy the same size as your stove"), and the size numbers may still be seen on the handles and bottoms of most cast-iron cookware. The fit provided direct heat; smaller pots or pots used for simmering could be placed on top of the stove lid. (Adapter rings were introduced early in the twentieth century: "This is a very convenient little device, as the varying sizes of the openings in the cover will be found very useful.")

In 1874, Jacob Vollrath produced the first enameled cast-iron ware in Sheboygan, Wisconsin. Enameled sheet steel did not join the Vollrath line until 1892, because until then the quality of American sheet steel was too poor for enameling. Once it was made practical, sheet steel quickly supplanted the heavier cast-iron for enameled kitchenware, as for stoves and most other industrial products. By 1897, Sears was advertising a full line of "gray enamelled ware . . . formed from a *sheet of steel* enamelled, inside and outside," which cost about three times as much as their stamped-tin counterparts. Enameled ware, with its smooth rust-free finish, must have had wide appeal despite its extra cost. Sears offered thirty-eight separate items, most available in many sizes, ranging from pots to basting spoons, funnels, and soap dishes.

Aluminum, a still more expensive option, appeared on the cookware market at about the same time as enamel. The metal had been imported earlier, but had always been costly; the change came in 1886 with Charles Martin Hall's new refining process. The Pittsburgh Reduction Company (later Alcoa), organized in 1888, promoted aluminum as a material for cooking utensils. Although cheapened considerably by the Hall process (it cost $545.00 a pound in 1852 and $2.25 a pound in 1890), aluminum remained a luxury for some time. The aluminum utensils Sears offered in 1897 cost much more than those made of other materials. A ten-inch

---

Sears's 1897 assortment of cooking pots and utensils. Note that pot sizes fit stove holes.

STOVE FURNISHINGS.

Complete Kitchen Furniture Assortment.

Our facilities for furnishing all sorts of kitchen utensils are unequaled, and in the outfits named below we offer you an assortment which contains not a single article but what is a very necessary part of household furniture. **We handle no seconds.** All our utensils are first quality and guaranteed perfect. When you order your stove from this list be sure to include the assortment that goes with the size wanted.

We have quoted our stoves without furniture, for the reason that many people wanting a stove are already supplied with the necessary utensils.

Order from us and get more for your money than from any other house.

In ordering Stove Furniture be sure and buy same size as your stove.

No. 15984.

1 Copper bottom tin Wash Boiler.
1 Copper bottom tin Tea Kettle.
1 Cast iron Stove Kettle.
1 Cast iron Spider.
1 Wrought iron Fry Pan, 10 inch.
1 4-pint tin Tea Pot.
1 5-quart tin Coffee Pot.
1 10-quart retinned Dish Pan.
2 Black Dripping Pans, 10x12 and 10x14.
1 Tin Bread Pan, 5¾x10¾x3.
2 Common square Bread Tins, 7¾x11¾x1½.
1 Revolving Flour Sifter.

1 Box Grater.
1 Biscuit Cutter.
1 Dover Egg Beater.
1 Doz. 3-inch plain Patty Pans.
¼ Doz. 9-inch tin Pie Plates.
1 14-inch tin Basting Spoon.
1 Cake Turner.
1 Dipper.
1 1-quart tin Cup.
1 Vegetable Fork.
1 Tin Dipper.
1 Flat handled Skimmer.
1 Fire Shovel.
1 Tin Wash Basin.
1 Tube Cake Pan, 10 inch.

Price above assortment, No. 7 or 8.....................$3.50
Price above assortment, No. 9.......................... 3.75

No. 15985.

1 Heavy IX-tin copper bottom Wash Boiler.
1 Iron Stove Kettle.
1 Iron Cover to fit.
1 Iron Tea Kettle.
1 Iron Spider.
1 Fry Pan.
1 Stove Shovel.
1 Nickel plated copper 5-pints Coffee Pot.
1 Nickel plated copper 4-pints Tea Pot.
1 Retinned Preserving Kettle.
1 Cover to fit.
1 Retinned Saucepan.
1 Cover to fit.
1 Muffin Frame, 12 cups.
¼ Doz. tin Pie Plates, 9 inch.
1 Extra heavy retinned Dish Pan.
1 Pieced tin Cup, 1 pint.
1 Galvanized Water Dipper, 2 quarts.
1 Flat handled Skimmer.
1 Vegetable Fork.
2 Drip Pans (give size of oven).

3 Tin Bread Pans.
2 Tin Cake Pans.
1 Doz. assorted Patty Pans.
1 Basting Spoon.
1 Cake Turner.
1 Steamer.
1 Retinned Cullender.
1 Cake Cutter.
1 Biscuit Cutter.
1 Doughnut Cutter.
1 Nutmeg Grater.
1 Large Grater.
1 Patent Flour Sifter.
1 Dover Egg Beater.
1 Covered japanned Dust Pan.
1 Oval hardwood Potato Masher.
1 Wood Potato Masher.
1 Paring Knife.
1 Mincing Knife, double blade.
1 Bread Board.
1 Rolling Pin.
1 Oval hardwood Chopping Tray.
1 Set Mrs. Potts' Sad Irons.

Price above assortment, No. 7..........................$6.00
Price above assortment, No. 8.......................... 6.25
Price above assortment, No. 9.......................... 7.00

frying pan, for example, cost 14 cents in stamped tin, 40 cents in enameled steel, and 84 cents in aluminum. A three-quart preserving kettle, 18 cents in porcelain-lined cast iron, cost 52 cents in aluminum. At those prices, no aluminum ware appeared even in Sears's expensive Complete Kitchen Furniture Assortment, a sixty-four-piece collection of pots, pans, and cooking utensils, "first quality and guaranteed perfect." Aluminum ware was displayed in its own section of the 1897 catalogue, after the iron, tin, and enamel ware.

The copywriter's enthusiasm indicates the severe drawbacks of the more traditional materials. "Aluminum being now nearly as cheap as copper, no one who has consideration for purity, cleanliness, durability, and the other peculiar quality of aluminum ware, should use anything else," said the copy under the headline "Beautiful as Silver—Pure as Gold." It was light; it would not rust; vinegar and fruit acids had no effect on it; it was "pure solid metal all the way through" and therefore "practically everlasting." And it was absolutely pure: free from the salts of tin, free from the verdigris of copper and brass, free from the lead, arsenic, and antimony often used in enamels.

The problems involved in caring for cooking utensils may not seem large to the modern reader who treasures a few well-seasoned cast-iron skillets or carbon-steel knives. In the nineteenth-century household every pot and every knife would rust without proper care. Steel wool was yet to be invented. Metals used in cooking sometimes tainted the food with bad flavors, if not poisons. The extra minutes required for caring for the pots added to the burdensome housekeeping routine. Enameled steel and aluminum offered freedom from some of the burden.

Other cooking utensils were made of crockery, basketry, wood, or tin, all with serious drawbacks: the tin rusted, the wooden ware and baskets absorbed flavors from one food and transmitted them to another, the crockery broke, the wood cracked, and both tin and certain clay glazes could poison the food. Don't put acid foods into red earthenware, warned Catharine Beecher, for "there is a poisonous ingredient in the glazing which the acid takes off." Use stoneware instead, she said. Watch out for high heat with porcelain-lined preserving kettles, which might crack. Don't leave wooden ware outside; it may "fall to pieces."

Mechanical cooking utensils existed in the second half of the century, but few houses had them. Eggbeaters, cherry stoners, apple parers and corers, butter churns, meat choppers—all these and more were patented in large numbers. But mechanical devices rarely appear in lists of necessary equipment for nineteenth-century kitchens; apparently the world never beat paths to the doors of their inventors. In 1869, Catharine Beecher listed none, other than "a mill, for spice, pepper, and coffee . . . needful to those who use these articles"; her eggbeater was a wooden whip. Helen Campbell, writing for country women in 1881, listed "every article required for a comfortably fitted-up kitchen . . . what is needed for the most efficient work." Her list was not brief; it included a dozen popover cups, a dozen custard cups, a dozen muffin rings in addition to a muffin pan and small cake tins, five different sieves and wire baskets, and at least twelve different pots and saucepans, plus frying pans. The Dover eggbeater—that ubiquitous item which Sears later claimed was "celebrated as the best beater made"—was the only mechanical device Campbell listed. Writing to an audience blessed with cherry and apple trees and burdened with preserving their fruit, she warned that "many complicated patent arrangements are hindrances, rather than helps."

Sears's 1897 prices suggest that the mechanical devices certainly hindered the budget, though inflation has made the figures seem small. Apple parers were available for 40 cents and 75 cents, cherry stoners for 60 cents. Meat choppers were $1.35 and $2.35, and a large revolving grater cost $1.20. For $3.50 the 1897 catalogue shopper could purchase the less expensive of two "complete kitchen furniture assortments," including wash boiler, teakettle, stove kettle, tea and coffee pots, frying pans, dishpan, dripping pans, three bread pans, a dozen patty pans, six pie plates, and thirteen other items (including the 9-cent Dover eggbeater and a 9-cent rotary flour sifter). The more expensive mechanical devices assumed

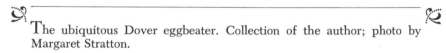

The ubiquitous Dover eggbeater. Collection of the author; photo by Margaret Stratton.

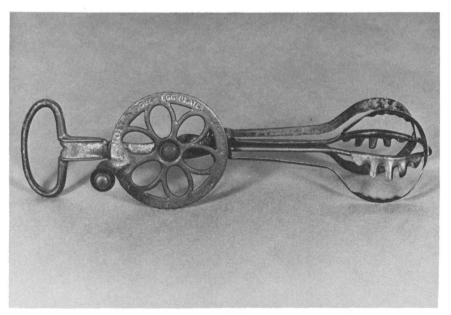

the financial proportions of the modern food processor; the decision to purchase these devices probably was perceived more often as a matter of luxury than of need.

Hannah Lambertson, interviewed in 1974 at the age of ninety-eight, recalled that she got a mechanical butter churn when, in her mid-twenties, she moved back to her father's northwestern Michigan farm after her husband deserted her. "On the farm I had a dasher churn. That's a stone crock, and there's a hole in the cover with a stick goes down inside it—that's your dasher and you churn your cream and get your butter. One time Dad came up from the field and I said, 'Dad, suppose you churn awhile.' And he did. I don't know how many days later it was, but he made a trip to Kalkaska and he came back with a barrel churn that had a hoop on it. I'd just go like this and get my butter. It was faster, you see." Around the time Hannah moved to that farm, Montgomery Ward sold the Star Barrel Churn for $3.00 to $6.00, depending on capacity; a "common dash churn" cost 56 cents to 96 cents.

Most women who churned still pumped the dasher, and most women who stoned cherries or pared apples still stoned and pared by hand. Most homes at the turn of the century still owned only tin and iron pots and pans. During the next few decades, the general expansion of the consumer economy brought the new materials and mechanical devices within the reach of most people. In 1919, even a government estimate of the standard of living for the working poor "at a level of health and decency" suggested some modern kitchen equipment that would have been extravagant in an equivalent estimate twenty years earlier. According to the government investigators, these items—enamelware soap dish, hand basin, coffeepot, teapot, preserving kettle, three stew pans or kettles, double boiler, colander, and funnel; aluminum salt and pepper shakers and measuring cups; a nickel teakettle with a copper bottom; a meat grinder, a flour sifter, and an eggbeater—had all become minimal equipment by 1919. None of those things had existed for most of the nineteenth century.

The cooking process follows the rule for technological improvement in household work during the nineteenth century: the operating principles for machines and devices that would ease household labor were developed long before the century's close. The government granted thousands of patents for kitchen implements and appliances, but until the advent of mass production and a national distribution system, even those inventions that were produced were well beyond most families' budgets. With one major exception (the stove) and one minor one (the eggbeater), American food preparation in 1900 looked much as it had in 1800. Three times daily, women prepared meals for their families, using heavy iron utensils, first at fireplaces, later at stoves. Three times daily, they gathered their households together for food that really was a blessing: the product of long hours in the field or factory joined with the hot labor of the kitchen.

Throughout the day, the family lived in the kitchen. The hot stove, like the fireplace, remained the focus of the kitchen and of family life. Rachel Haskell, whose diary for March 1867 recorded in intimate detail her life in a small Nevada mining town, used a sitting room sometimes after dinner when there were guests, but the kitchen constantly during the day, and often in the evenings: "Tuesday 12th . . . Sat in kitchen all evening finishing the remnant of my baking and reading the book I began previous evening. Boys around me at the table. . . . Wednesday 13 . . . Mr. Haskell at home reading enterprises in kitchen. . . . We are sitting in the kitchen this evening. . . . Friday 15th. We all felt worn out and sat in kitchen. Mr. H. reading 'Sketch book.' I sewing at my sacque. Ella ironing." On Tuesday the 19th, Rachel's husband wrote at the kitchen table all day while she sewed, "our beans boiling all this while with bacon . . . a dish savory enough for Jupiter." The Haskells made a fire in the sitting room after supper that evening; that extra fire was one reason for not leaving the kitchen every night. During the day there was almost always something to attend to at the stove—punching down bread, stirring the boiling beans, or checking the fire. A retreat to the parlor had its drawbacks: after one pleasant evening of games and conversation with company in the sitting room, Mrs. Haskell and her daughter Ella "washed dishes in cold kitchen after every one left. Not so pleasant a finishing for company. . . ."

Although Ella does not appear to have cooked much, she did many other chores, often providing company for her mother Rachel's labors in the kitchen. Vinnie Dickinson, too, washed dishes in the kitchen while her mother cooked; her better-known sister Emily did all the baking for the Dickinson household, producing a constant supply of bread, cake, cookies, and biscuits. Undoubtedly daughters and other women relatives helped with the cooking in many households, whether or not they were allotted a particular specialty like Emily's baking. Cooking was then a social activity in two senses: it took place in a context of people, since families used the kitchen as a sitting room, and it involved others in its labors, especially other women and girls.

In a letter to a girlhood friend, nineteen-year-old Emily Dickinson expressed the emotional payoff for all the work. Her mother was sick in bed, she wrote, but her father and brother "still clamor for food; and I, like a martyr, am feeding them." She rationalized the endless labor, "providing 'the food that perisheth'" by her "desire to make everything pleasant for father and Austin." But it was probably more than mere rationalization. Women had to cook so their families could eat; cooking was their central daily activity. Their lives revolved around this work and around the fireplace or stove. Craft satisfaction—their own pride in what they did—mingled with love at the hearth and the cooking range, compensating (when it all worked and the food was "savory enough for Jupiter") for the heat, the fatigue, and the heavy work.

Industrially produced implements have never destroyed that pride and

The kitchen served as an arena for female companionship. This is Mrs. Nevins and her sister, Madison, Wisconsin, 1897. Annie Sievers Schildauer, photographer.

sense of craft; women continue to act on the belief that the way to a man's heart is through his stomach, and recently men, too, have begun in greater numbers to experience the pleasures of cooking to feed the people they love. Industrialization has, however, reduced the necessity for thrice-daily cooking; hardly any modern families get together for all their meals, and restaurants and supermarkets provide options for buying food that somebody else has cooked. Cooking remains the central ritual of house-keeping, but, like the rest of the housekeeping routine, that ritual endures only in truncated form. The work itself, performed with gas and electric stoves, devices that do the chopping and mixing, and utensils requiring little care, bears little relation to the time-consuming, hazardous, heavy work of the colonial hearth. Most of that change began around the turn of the twentieth century, as mass production and mass distribution brought new implements and new fuels to many people at prices they could afford. The cast-iron stove, the major nineteenth-century technological change in cooking, reduced the hazards and some of the work, but did not eliminate the central tasks of hauling fuel and tending fires. In cooking, as in other household tasks, women still did the work of producing energy in 1900; their daughters would come to consume it.

THREE

The Home Fires

As American industry and commerce began to provide the nation with useful goods for daily survival, the ordinary means of lighting and heating changed during the nineteenth century from home-made candles and wood-burning fireplaces to kerosene lamps and coal heating stoves. The new devices offered better heat and light with less work and less fuel. Still, they made only limited inroads on the natural cycles—the daily cycle of light and darkness, and the yearly cycle of heat and cold that governed life and determined cycles of human activity as long as energy was not a commodity to be bought, but the product of time and labor. Loads of fuel had to be hauled, fires had to be made and tended, and lighting devices had to be filled and cleaned. The regular movements of the earth and the sun continued to define seasonal and daily chores and to restrict human activity throughout the century.

Colonial houses had offered only scant protection from the winter's ravages. Early colonists spent most of their waking hours confined to the "hall" or central room, where the blazing fire served both to heat the room and cook food. Fireplaces in other rooms, generally smaller than kitchen hearths, provided heat only close to the fire. Insulation was unknown; fireplace construction was not yet based on accurate physical principles. Veterans of British winters, milder and shorter than those of the New England colonies, did not know how to protect themselves against the cold. New Englanders shivered through six or seven months of the year; their diaries record their sufferings as ink froze in their pens while they wrote by the fireside, where oozing sap froze at the ends of flaming logs, and basins of water, even when set directly in front of blazing fires, froze solid. Four-poster beds served utilitarian rather than decorative purposes: in unheated bedrooms, heavy woolen bed curtains insulated sleepers, as well as providing privacy. Some colonists enjoyed the luxury of beds preheated with warming pans, usually copper or brass containers filled with hot coals from the fire. British settlers in the Southern colonies encountered milder, shorter winters, but their winter discomfort may have been nearly as great in houses built to accommodate the hot, muggy Southern summers, with more open space, larger windows, fewer fireplaces, and kitchen hearths in separate structures.

In Scandinavia, Holland, and Germany, intense cold and scarce fuel had fostered early development of efficient stoves. Immigrants from those countries who settled in the Middle Colonies brought the molds for casting stoves with them. They had the most comfortable homes in the colonies, with stoves made most commonly of cast iron but sometimes of sheet metal or decorated tile and brick. Although travelers in the German and Dutch colonies noted their comfort and efficiency, these stoves remained ethnic peculiarities until the nineteenth century.

Well before the Revolution, the discomfort of the American winter and the developing fuel shortage in the settled areas encouraged inventors and scientists, the most prominent of them being Benjamin Thompson and Benjamin Franklin, to tinker with heating devices in search of thermal efficiency. Thompson, better known as Count Rumford, an American-born officer for the British in the Revolution and later an administrator in the Bavarian court, developed an accurate theory of heat, contradicting the prevailing notion that heat was itself a substance. In a

A heavy woodbox, photographed on the E. A. Bancroft farm in Hinsdale, Illinois, in 1923 for the Agricultural Extension Department of International Harvester Corporation, Chicago.

paper presented to the British Royal Society in 1798, Rumford maintained that particle motion produced heat. Unusual among physicists for his practical interests, he worked tirelessly on practical applications for his theoretical breakthrough. He invented numerous stoves and smaller cooking appliances, including several types of coffee percolators. Although most of his designs, huge and elaborate constructions for the kitchens of Bavarian nobles or large social institutions like the Munich workhouse or an Italian hospital, required custom installation, his principles influenced a host of other inventors and iron founders in developing more popular cast-iron stoves for individual homes.

Many of those designs, perfected during the first decades of the nineteenth century, adapted Benjamin Franklin's much earlier creation, the "Pennsylvania fireplace" invented in 1742, the first major innovation in a long series of stoves and stove gadgets that eventually brought other Americans to the Pennsylvania Dutch standard of comfort. Franklin's original design, a box formed from cast-iron plates fitting into a conventional fireplace, increased thermal efficiency by using heat that otherwise would go up the chimney; smoke and combustion gases passed through flues that heated the plates, which in turn radiated heat into the room. Concentrated in the small space, the fire used all the air that entered the stove, producing a hotter and more efficient flame.

The open Franklin stove retained a sense of the hearth. Franklin had criticized the Dutch and German stoves because "there is no sight of the fire which is in itself a pleasant thing"; his own designs, and the ones that continued to bear his name until sloppy usage made every cast-iron stove a "Franklin stove," shared the feature of an open fire, having either an open front or doors that could be left open. By the end of the nineteenth century, the fanciest Franklin stoves had translucent mica doors, allowing the sight of muted flickers even when they were closed. "Would our Revolutionary fathers have gone barefooted and bleeding over snows to defend air-tight stoves and cooking-ranges?" asked Harriet Beecher Stowe in 1864. The memory of the hearth, she said, "its roaring, hilarious voice of invitation, its dancing tongue of flames . . . called to them through the snows of that dreadful winter to keep up their courage, [and] made their hearts warm and bright with a thousand reflected memories." The cast-iron enclosure could burn fuel more efficiently than the open hearth, and the expanse of hot metal could radiate more heat into the room, but it had none of the hypnotic quality of the open fire.

Still, because they relieved the bitter cold of winter, providing more heat with less fuel and less work, by the middle of the nineteenth century iron stoves had begun to supplant fireplaces for heating as well as for cooking. Made in small foundries all over the country for local distribution, they came in all shapes and sizes, plain or ornate, often enhanced by the clever innovations of individual craftsmen. By the end of the century, the Franklin stove had been joined by box stoves (rectangular boxes for wood heating, usually with cookholes or boiler holes on top); cannon, globe, or "potbellied" stoves; many versions of cylindrical parlor stoves with various styles of flues, dampers, and grates; and self-feeding base burners, which remained standard working-class household equipment well into the twentieth century.

A few homes possessed central hot-air furnaces, based not on radiation from the stove but on convection; the basement furnace heated fresh air and directed it through ducts to upstairs rooms. At the end of the Civil War, these furnaces, like furnaces that used hot water and steam heat, could be found in the mansions of the developing class of industrial and commercial entrepreneurs. For their middle-class contemporaries, Catharine Beecher's ideal house plan of 1869 connected a basement furnace, Franklin stove, and kitchen range together in a central heating and ventilating system, based on hot-air convection. Beecher believed hot water and steam heat were healthier, but radiator installation was far too expensive. Even this plan was utopian, not a description of her readers' homes, still warmed by fireplaces and free-standing heating stoves, for which she provided directions for safe and economical use. Beecher's earlier plans, published in her 1841 *Treatise on Domestic Economy*, had not even used stoves; there she advocated centrally located chimneys, as exceptional then as the central heating system would be twenty-eight years later, which could prevent heat escaping through the outside walls of the house and warm more than one room per fire. Neither central chimneys nor central heating prevailed until long after Beecher published her plans. As late as 1897, Sears offered no central furnaces; by 1908, thanks to mass production, the new rolled steel, and the national distribution system, the company supplied coal-fired furnaces for both hot air and hot water, along with radiators, valves, and fittings. Customers who sent in their house plans could receive cost estimates and furnace plans; two special supplementary catalogues, "free upon request" and devoted to furnaces, displayed even more than the general catalogue. Central heating became more commonplace during the next two decades. About half the houses in two small Midwestern cities were using central furnaces by the mid-1920s, "although most of the working class still live in the base-burner and unheated-bed-room era."

Except in isolated rural homes, stoves and furnaces ordinarily burned coal. Wood was already scarce in Boston by 1637 and in New York by 1680; almost all colonial towns regulated firewood sales during the eighteenth century. Unscrupulous dealers shorted their customers and charged high prices, the poor shivered with small quantities of charity wood, and the wealthy increasingly depended on coal imported from British mines. Colonial cities treated fuel as a matter of crisis proportions, appropriating money to distribute it to the needy, establishing committees to investigate possible improvements in the supply, and regulating wood gathering on common lands. Soft coal was discovered near Richmond, Virginia, about 1750; by 1820, coal mined domestically constituted about three-quarters of the annual supply, although coal from Newcastle and other British mining areas continued to compete successfully with American coal until water transportation (and later railroads) made it possible to deliver the mineral to the populated East. In the middle of the nineteenth century, the growing household and industrial markets created a demand for coal that raised the mining industry to a central position in the American economy; about 6,800 coal-mine workers in 1840 swelled to 180,000 in 1880, while coal shipments increased about fourteenfold between 1850 and 1880. Even those without stoves burned coal on the hearth, in specially designed grates fitted into their fireplaces.

Unlike town dwellers, who purchased fuel as a commodity even in early colonial times, frontier folks were producers, not consumers, of artificial heat. Men and boys did much of the work of wood heating, felling trees, hauling logs close to the house, and chopping them into manageable pieces; women usually did the final chopping and brought the wood into the house. As more of the population went to live in towns, men's direct and central role in the tasks of heating diminished. Urban consumers of wood and coal had only the final work to do—and that was women's work. Urban men earned the money to buy the fuel, while their wives continued to work much as country women did, tending fires and bringing in the fuel; seasonal cycles continued to dominate urban women's work life as the factory whistle and the clock increasingly defined their menfolks' time.

Stoves, especially those burning coal, required less of that work than fireplaces. Still, they had to be tended: although the most sophisticated (and most expensive) stoves had self-feeding mechanisms late in the century, most heating stoves demanded just as much tending and fuel hauling as cooking stoves. Even the self-tenders tended themselves only between hopper fillings. "Start your fire in the fall," Sears crowed about its Acme Sunburst self-feeding base burner in 1908, "fill the magazine at the top once or twice a day . . . regulate the draft . . . shake down the fire once or twice a day, remove the ashes occasionally, and the stove does the rest. Then, to all purposes you are living in a steam heated house. . . ." A tiny number of Americans *did* live in steam-heated houses, using steam

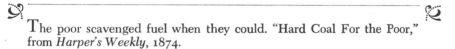

The poor scavenged fuel when they could. "Hard Coal For the Poor," from *Harper's Weekly*, 1874.

produced in central heating plants and sent through underground pipes; although one architectural journal in 1877 called this plan "Communism in Hot-Air," it might be better understood as the ultimate in the general trend: artificial heat itself as a commodity. The vast majority, even those who bought their fuel, had to do some hot and heavy work for their heat, hauling fuel and feeding fires.

Stove users created a raft of new problems. Making their houses as airtight as possible in their zeal for thermal efficiency, they produced

Brochure, front and back covers, Buck's Stove and Range Company, Saint Louis, 1898–99 season. Buck's, one of the most successful stove companies at the turn of the century, offered six new stoves "in addition to the many standard stoves whose sterling possibilities have been so long proven. As our ever increasing trade leads us into new territory, and our wide-awake patrons demand new and different designs for heating stoves; as our own practical knowledge expands with new conditions; and we conquer one by one the difficulties which assail us; it naturally follows that every few weeks a new stove is born or one is remodeled."

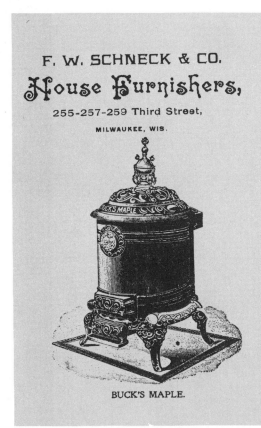

BUCK'S MAPLE.

stuffy and even poison-filled rooms and stayed in them until spring brought relief and fresh air. Sealing up fireplaces and introducing airtight stoves certainly saved fuel, as Harriet Beecher Stowe admitted in her *House and Home Papers*; "it saves, too, more than that; in thousands and thousands of cases it has saved people from all further human wants, and put an end forever to any needs short of six feet of narrow earth which are man's only inalienable property." Carbon monoxide, formed when carbon burns with a limited amount of air, was a by-product of every stove designed to conserve fuel, far more dangerous even than the excessive human-produced carbon dioxide that permeated rooms shut up for winter. Every stove leaked some carbon monoxide; defective ones caused additional problems: too short or tight a flue, cracked pipes, too short a chimney, broken chimney bricks, and many other conditions produced poor drafts and smoke-filled rooms. Furthermore, stoves took in dry cold outside air and heated it, greatly increasing its capacity for moisture. This humidity "it sucks up, like a sponge, from the walls and furniture of a house," wrote Catharine Beecher; introduced into human lungs, it sucked moisture from the rest of the body. She recommended pans of water and house plants (which also added oxygen and used carbon dioxide) to humidify the air. In general, she considered bad ventilation such a serious issue in American homes that she devoted four chapters of *The American Woman's Home* to this "household murder." Providing healthy air was, according to Beecher, both a woman's central duty as mother and wife and her particular problem because—unlike men, who at least got out—women shut themselves in all day.

For all these hazards and all the work, the stove-heated homes of the second half of the nineteenth century remained cold in the winter. Rags stuffed into cracks provided the only insulation. Most rooms were hotter near the ceiling, floors almost universally chilly. Although a very good stove, bought toward the end of the century, might keep a coal fire burning overnight, most people awoke to cold mornings after nights spent in unheated bedrooms. Alice LaCasse, a New Hampshire cotton worker, remembered her family's substitute for the colonial bed-warmer: "We had a big stove in the kitchen and three grills in the ceiling, so in the winter a little bit of heat went up to the second floor but hardly any at all reached the third and fourth floors." The children, who slept in the cold, undressed by the stove, then ran upstairs with hot irons wrapped in towels and stuck them under the covers.

Coal heating in cast-iron stoves did reduce some of the hazards of wood-burning fireplaces. Many real-life counterparts to Jo March of *Little Women* must have scorched their dresses by standing too close to the fireplace trying to keep warm; poor Jo had to play the wallflower at her next party, to hide the burn on her best dress. Worse still, fireplaces had made everybody in the household a possible prey to house fires, apparently so common in 1846 that Beecher gave advice about them in a

section called "Miscellaneous Directions," among the hints for cleaning combs, fixing broken earthenware, and waterproofing gardening shoes. "If a house takes fire at night," she wrote, wrap a blanket around you to keep off the fire; if your dress catches fire, "do not run, but lie down" and roll over until you can reach something (perhaps the edge of the carpet) "in which to wrap yourself tight." "Keep young children in woollen dresses, in winter," ran her most telling advice, "to save from risk of being burnt." Revising the book twenty-three years later when stoves had supplanted fireplaces, she transferred house fires to a chapter entitled "Accidents and Antidotes."

Lighting, on the other hand, remained a source of fire danger throughout the century. Christie Devon, Louisa May Alcott's heroine in *Work, A Story of Experience*, lost her domestic service job by setting her room on fire; she ignored the standard nineteenth-century advice against reading in bed, advice that appeared in housekeeping manuals long after lamps superseded candles. Mrs. O'Leary's cow may be fiction, but the great Chicago fire of October 1871 was not, nor were any of the other urban conflagrations so frequent throughout the century, and so frequently caused by the open flames lighting American homes and sheds.

In the colonial and early national periods candles, of course, provided most of the artificial light; they could be made at home from tallow (animal fat, from deer, moose, bear, or domestic animals), beeswax, bayberry wax, or a combination of these. Camphor, alum, saltpeter, or other chemicals added longevity to rapidly burning tapers. Candlemaking usually followed butchering in the fall, to use the fatty by-products and create a supply that would last through months of long winter nights; women rendered tallow in huge vats with boiling water, dipping six or eight wicks at a time. Hanging from sticks, these cooled between chairs or stools while the next stickful of candles was dipped. Some intinerant chandlers owned tin or pewter molds and went from house to house supervising candlemaking; in other places, neighbors shared the molds or the work itself, socializing at cooperative candle-dippings as they did at quilting bees.

A variety of primitive homemade lamps supplemented candles. "Pine knots," "pine torches" or "candlewood," knots of the turpentine-filled pitch pine, blazed smokily and dropped tar on their stone bases. Grease-soaked rags served the same purpose; Rebecca Burlend, an Illinois pioneer, used such rags. She would have preferred candles, she wrote, but she had neither molds nor tallow; by the light of the rag "we could see to sew and read pretty well," but the rag tended to drown in the melted lard and she broke three saucers from the heat ("a circumstance much to be regretted, as pots of all kinds are dear in Illinois") before she hit upon the plan of using the kettle lid, "inserting the knob or holder into a piece of board to make it stand." In 1841, Beecher gave directions for "floating tapers,"

A good stove could end the hazards and hassles of fireplace heating, and protect the homeowner from inferior stoves' smoke and danger, all illustrated in this ad for the Dubuque.

available in stores but "easily made": a beeswax-coated wick, run through pieces of cork and tin, floated on oil in a small tin cup, especially good for night lights.

Beecher dropped those directions in 1869, because the floating tapers could be bought "very cheap," but retained her 1841 candlemaking instructions; by then candles were "used only on rare occasions, though many families prefer to manufacture into candles the waste grease that accumulates in the household." Candles, too, could be purchased. The candle manufacturers, well established in the colonies, joined in a price-fixing trust in 1761, managed to get themselves protected from import competition by the first American tariff law of 1789, and had "developed into an extensive, mechanical, and relatively complex factory process" by the middle of the nineteenth century. After the Civil War, commercially made candles were so cheap that few families made them; even Campbell's 1881 guide for rural housekeeping gave no directions for candlemaking. More important, candles had by then been supplanted by various kinds of lamps.

Brighter and steadier, oil lamps began to alter daily habits previously circumscribed by the daily cycle of light and darkness. These lamps, consisting of a base, a font for the fuel, a burner through which the wick was pulled, and a chimney, came in many materials and used many kinds of fuel. The Argand burner, invented in 1783, the first major innovation in a long series of inventions for lamps, fed air directly to the flame through a metal tube inside a cylindrical wick. Burned with good sperm oil, Beecher wrote in 1869, it was the best and the brightest, producing a steady white flame. In 1841, she had recommended oil lamps over the more expensive wax candles for economy, and over tallow candles because they "afford a clearer and steadier light, and do not scatter grease." None of the possible fuels—lard oil, cottonseed oil, castor oil, turpentine, or camphene (a distilled turpentine product, sometimes combined with alcohol to make an illuminant called spirit gas or burning fluid)—could match sperm oil, which was increasing in price as whales were killed off. Fortunately for domestic lighting, a new fuel appeared in mid-century: kerosene.

Invented in 1854, kerosene cheapened quickly after the discovery of petroleum in Pennsylvania in 1859; in a world with no gasoline engines, it was by far the most important refinery product. Within a decade, it had superseded other oils "to such an extent . . . that it is scarcely worth while to give any special directions in regard to them." A mixture of liquid hydrocarbons, it came in varying proportions. Good kerosene was relatively free of hydrocarbons that evaporated at low temperatures; if spilled, it produced fewer combustible vapors than the more volatile mixtures. Easily ignited, inferior kerosene imperiled its users; it was hard to fill lamps without spilling some, and worse, a broken lamp full of "poor oil" was "always attended by great peril of a conflagration." By the end of the century, states regulated kerosene shipping; various mixtures came to be called Illinois, Indiana, Michigan, or Wisconsin "legal test," and Sears stated firmly that "we do not solicit kerosene oil trade in the state of Iowa, owing to the annoying inspection laws," though Iowans could buy one oil, the 175-degree fire test, "entirely" at their own risk.

Innovation on burners, lamps, and chimneys designed specifically for the new fuel continued during the second half of the century. Removable fonts eased filling, new kinds of glass made "unbreakable" heat-tolerant chimneys, screwed wick movements made trimming and rewicking less messy, and improved burners cut down on flickering, smoking, and hence chimney cleaning. Most important, the later lamps gave off more light: the earliest kerosene lamps, burning at six to twenty candlepower, could hardly match the ordinary lamps of the turn of the century, which offered sixty to eighty.

Although good oils and good lamps reduced fire danger, oil lighting required considerable care. Beecher cautioned against reading in bed, as dangerous with lamps as with candles; less obviously, she warned that people who attempted economy by sitting too close to the lamp could damage their eyes with excessive heat: "Better burn a larger flame, and keep it at a greater distance." Another economy, turning down the wick to save oil in sickrooms or other situations requiring little light, resulted in rooms full of noxious gases. Excess oil expanded when overfilled lamps were lit, covering the outside of the lamp and greasing "every thing near it." Turned up too quickly, newly lit lamps produced enough heat to crack glass chimneys.

These cautions attended all the tasks associated with lamps, and there were plenty of those: daily chimney wiping and wick trimming, weekly washing of chimneys and shades, and periodic rewicking and dismantling for thorough cleaning with soda, inside and out. Unpleasantly sooty and smelly, these tasks had to be done for decent light: untrimmed wicks flickered, and dirty chimneys or shades dimmed the light. Rachel Haskell, the Nevada housewife and diarist, complained of these operations, calling lamp cleaning "a hard operation always." The best advice domestic writers had to offer—keeping a supply of clean rags and neatly storing lamp supplies away from everything else—could only make the chores slightly more pleasant.

Unfortunately, all lamp soot did not remain in the chimneys or find its way onto the beleaguered housewife's hands and rags. Like the soot and smoke from wood and coal fires and the dust created by laying in winter fuel supplies, it found its way onto every surface in every home. The accumulated grime was so staggering, and keeping up with it on a daily basis so impossible, that even writers who relentlessly repeated that "it is better to keep clean than to make clean" admitted the necessity of spring

—and sometimes fall—housecleaning. Nobody liked this "household earthquake," this "ordeal." "'House' is being 'cleaned,'" wrote Emily Dickinson one spring. "I prefer pestilence." Household advice writers applauded the war on pestilence, but not its common disruptive form. "As generally managed," Helen Campbell wrote in 1881, spring housecleaning was "a terror to every one, and above all to gentlemen, who resent it from beginning to end. No wonder, if at the first onslaught all home comfort ends, and regular meals become irregular lunches, and a quiet night's rest something sought but not found." Another home economist called it "A general housewrecking process . . . an abomination of desolation. It breaks women's backs and causes men to break the Ten Commandments." One Muncie, Indiana, merchant—clearly one of those gentlemen who resented it from beginning to end—recorded a week-long cleaning in his diary for October 1887. It started on a Tuesday morning; by Saturday the upper part of the house "(except our room)" was done, along with the parlors and lower hall. On Monday, he complained, his room was "in the mess."

Admitting that even the most carefully kept house required "a special

The worst of the work of heating and lighting with coal, wood, and oil: the "household earthquake" that chased the men from their homes and obsessed the women. From *Harper's Bazaar*, 1879.

THE HOUSEHOLDER'S ANNUAL MISERY.
"The spring house-cleaning days have come,
The saddest of the year."

putting in order," Campbell offered rules to "rob the ordeal of half its terrors"; fuel could be laid in before cleaning began, and heavy carpets could be taken up in alternate years, the tacks removed and the edges cleaned in the interim. Most of the suggestions, though, fell into the category of hints for lightening the basic tasks—cleaning carpets and heavy draperies, scouring painted walls, mothproofing, washing windows and mirrors, polishing furniture—rather than doing away with them. Put borax in water for scouring paint, she advised; use black pepper on carpet edges and camphor gum on clothes to keep away moths; oil furniture with boiled linseed oil; never use soap on varnished finishes; brighten carpets by "sprinkling a pound or two of salt over the surface, and sweeping carefully" after shaking them out.

Despite the disruption and the colossal labor, spring housecleaning had regenerative qualities. After months of cold weather, seasonal change meant nearly as much to city dwellers as to their country cousins; housecleaning, the annual ritual cleansing of the filthy by-products of nineteenth-century lighting and heating, signaled the onset of spring as much as the first robin or crocus and represented renewed life as directly as the budding trees. Open windows admitted fresh air into stuffy rooms whose occupants, according to Harriet Beecher Stowe, had spent the winter "enervated both by the heat and by the poisoned air," unable to go out because their systems were ruined and they would catch colds, and subsisting on the "daily waning strength which they acquired in the season when windows and doors were open," much as bears subsisted during hibernation on their summer's fat. "No wonder we hear of spring fever and spring biliousness," she maintained; not then attributed to daydreams, these diseases, "the pantings and palpitations of a system run down under slow poison, unable to get a step further," necessitated the many spring tonics and nostrums celebrated for purifying the blood.

Opening windows constituted only part of a more general opening up of space in the spring; as the weather changed and the days grew longer, yards, porches, and additional rooms turned into living space. A colonial woman recorded her relief at the coming of warm weather, when she moved her spinning to a room "where it escaped the espionage of the curious eyes and gossiping tongues that during the winter had at times been excessively annoying." Houses shrank during the winter, as their occupants huddled around fireplaces and stoves, candles and lamps, often confining themselves to one room with the onset of cold weather and staying there until spring. Well into the twentieth century, "Aunt Nellie" wrote in her nationally circulated column about "the common farm practice of abandoning the rest of the house for a three-months retreat in the kitchen"; she assumed that living rooms "must be given up during the winter," but suggested that a young farm couple might heat a "cozy end" of the dining room to give them privacy from their hired hands. Before the turn of the century, city dwellers shared this winter confinement; in

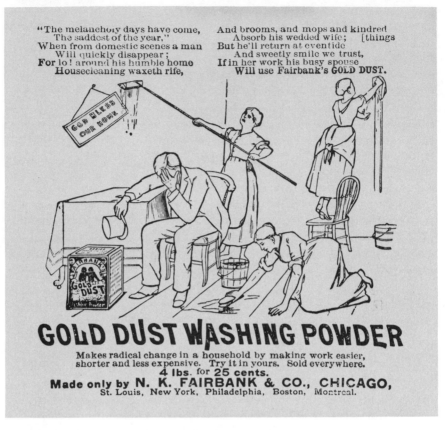

"The melancholy days have come, And brooms, and mops and kindred
The saddest of the year," Absorb his wedded wife; [things
When from domestic scenes a man But he'll return at eventide
Will quickly disappear; And sweetly smile we trust,
For lo! around his humble home If in her work his busy spouse
Housecleaning waxeth rife, Will use Fairbank's GOLD DUST.

GOLD DUST WASHING POWDER

Makes radical change in a household by making work easier,
shorter and less expensive. Try it in yours. Sold everywhere.
4 lbs. for 25 cents.
Made only by N. K. FAIRBANK & CO., CHICAGO,
St. Louis, New York, Philadelphia, Boston, Montreal.

More on the annual misery, from an advertisement in *Harper's Bazaar*,
1893.

households full of relatives and boarders, individual privacy could rarely
be found.

Living in space defined by its focus—the lamp or stove—rather than
framed by walls, dependent on their own talents and interests for their
evening entertainment, people experienced family intimacy later lost in
an age of central heating, electric lights, and television. Margaret Byington, a social worker describing steelworkers' households in Homestead,
Pennsylvania, in 1908, set the nostalgic scene: families gathered around
the grate in the evenings, she wrote, mothers sewing, children playing,
enjoying "those simple festivities which enliven existence in this town.
One mother described happily the evenings with her children: 'My boys
are so musical and the other fellows come in and we all have such a good
sing together, and then Mamie dances the Highland Fling.'" Byington,
who only observed the life of poverty, could romanticize it; she and her

middle-class contemporaries by then enjoyed a life more spacious than the one she studied, thanks to gas and electricity. Those who had to live with the conflict between intimacy and privacy experienced just that. Rachel Haskell's diary, describing the nightly scene as she, her children, her husband, and their frequent visitors gathered around the table looking at maps, reading, writing the journal, sewing, playing games, and making music, gives plenty of evidence for the coziness that must have compensated for the winter's sense of constriction and the lack of privacy. But often the baby was squalling, or the children were making "quite a noisy party" as their father provoked them "by getting the better of their game," while Rachel, annoyed, did her best to attend to her magazine or her neglected diary.

Rachel Haskell cherished her intimacy *and* lusted for privacy, much as modern Americans cherish their privacy yet complain of empty lives in singles apartments and suburban houses designed with a room for every member of the family, each well lit and comfortably heated. They purchase that comfort with gas and electricity; energy itself joined the list of industrial commodities as most Americans connected their homes to those centrally controlled utilities during the first third of the twentieth century.

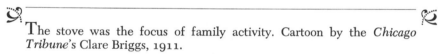

The stove was the focus of family activity. Cartoon by the *Chicago Tribune*'s Clare Briggs, 1911.

Nineteenth-century Americans worked to produce their heat and light, but with increasing help from industry; economic expansion brought more products—stoves and lamps, and the coal and kerosene to burn in them—and brought more people into the money economy, working for wages and producing cash crops to pay for the new products. The wealthy bought more of those products than the poor, the urbanite more than the country dweller, but like other nineteenth-century products, the new heating and lighting devices significantly raised the general American standard of living. By 1900, few Americans lived in the primitive conditions that made winter so intolerable for even the prosperous colonists.

Warm, well-lit homes became part of the American way of life, contributing to what eventually became a national addiction to excessive energy consumption. In a nation now plagued with the political and ecological effects of that addiction, some individuals attempt to revive the devices of the nineteenth century in the new circumstances of the twentieth. "I just spent twenty minutes struggling to saw up three pieces of wood in the rain," one professional woman wrote in an angry note to her husband shortly after they had purchased a wood stove to cut their heating costs in 1980. "While doing that, I figured out that we have devised for ourselves the most labor intensive way of keeping warm that I can possibly imagine. By the time I finished three pieces my back was aching like fury and I was seeing red. Then I hauled it into the house and saw that the whole fireplace area looked like a pig sty. Dirt all over everywhere. No matter how often we brush it up, twenty minutes later, it's dirty." Raised on a farm with wood heat, she was no stranger to the process. "I spent a lot of years living like that," she continued. "I worked real hard to get out of that kind of situation. Now I'm still working real hard to *stay* out of it, but I find myself both working hard *and* living like that. Dammit!" Without suggesting that they jettison the wood stove, she proposed twentieth-century solutions to its problems: rent a chain saw and buy a new vacuum cleaner.

For the society at large, wood represents a resource as scarce as the gasoline for the chain saw and the electricity for the vacuum cleaner; for women as a group, now working "real hard" at full-time jobs and expecting to use their wages to relieve them from some of the burdens of housework, nostalgic solutions for the high cost of energy represent giant steps backwards. Herculean labor and hazardous living distinguished nineteenth-century heating and lighting as much as the intimacy of the family gathered around the lamp and stove. The home fires kept burning only with the constant attention of the women charged with tending them—and for all that, our ancestors had only the flimsiest defenses against winter cold and nightly darkness.

FOUR

At the Flick
of a Switch

Gas and electricity, the new fuels for home heating and lighting, altered family relations not only by changing Americans' sense of household space but by totally revamping their conception of time. Gas and electric heat dulled the distinctions between summer and winter, removing the winter work from household routine—no more wood chopping, fuel hauling, hopper tending, or fire building. Gas and electric cooking made summer meals al-

most as comfortable to prepare as winter meals were; gas and electric light made winter evenings as bright as summer. Seasonal differences, fading at the same time because of food preservation and transportation, and because of the simple fact that an increasingly urban population had less reason to spend time outdoors, held less sway over daily human routines. Artificial light merged night and day; central heat and the new fuels introduced warm winter mornings without work; gas and electric cookstoves with individual burners offered an afternoon cup of tea or warm milk at two in the morning even in the summer. The seasonal differences held no great attraction for people who spent so much time and labor attempting to brighten winter nights and stay warm; the new fuels appealed precisely because they saved all that work. No one complained about moving from private production of energy to consumption of heat and light publicly produced for profit, although few could afford to purchase energy until after the turn of the century.

Painter Rembrandt Peale, who initially installed gas lighting as a brilliant curiosity to illuminate the paintings and stuffed animals in his eclectic Baltimore museum, established America's first gas company in that city in 1816. Along with four other investors, he gained a charter from the city and a contract to lay pipes along the streets and erect street lights; the company built a manufacturing plant that inaugurated American commercial gas lighting in 1817. Propaganda from the whale oil and tallow interests impeded the Baltimore company's progress; twenty years later, only two miles of gas main had been laid. Nonetheless, other cities began to consider gas as a fuel for public use.

In New York, a municipal committee investigated the possibilities for a municipally owned gasworks and built a rudimentary experimental system, eventually concluding that the high costs should be borne, not by the city, but by private investors operating under a city charter. In 1823, the city chartered the New York Gas Light Company and contracted with it to lay pipes and manufacture enough gas to light Broadway from the Battery to Grand Street within two years, and to light other areas at the city's request after five years. Samuel Leggett, the gas company's first president and also president of the Franklin Bank, gathered a board of directors composed of substantial citizens, which offered four thousand shares to the public at fifty dollars each; owing to the board's reputation and the success of gas stocks in London, the issue sold out immediately. By 1830, the company had expanded substantially—its capital, labor force, manufacturing and storage capacity, area of operation, and number of subscribers all boomed—and other groups of investors began to establish competitive firms to challenge its monopoly.

Municipal gas systems were expensive to start; they required all the manufacturing capacity of any industrial concern, plus the distribution systems, the pipes and fittings. The only Americans with that kind of money had made it in commerce and finance; most farmers still operated outside the money economy, the growing class of wage laborers had nothing to spare, and even the few who operated the new manufacturing concerns had only enough to reinvest in their own plants, still dependent themselves on the commercial interests. From the start, bankers and merchants controlled the gas companies everywhere, establishing systems in most major cities during the 1820s and 1830s, and in smaller towns during the next two decades. By the beginning of the Civil War, state legislatures had chartered over three hundred companies to operate in towns of all sizes.

Although the New York company at first manufactured gas from oil and rosin, a method used by some companies until the middle of the century, most gas manufacture until the 1870s used soft or bituminous coal, heated in an airtight furnace to produce "coal gas" (cooled and

Eight of the many nineteenth-century innovations for gas burners, from United States Patent Commissioner Benjamin Butterworth's *The Growth of Industrial Art*, 1888: (1) bat-wing, (2 and 3) Argand, (4) self-regulating, (5) vapor, (6) enriching attachment, (7) flat flame, (8) heating attachment.

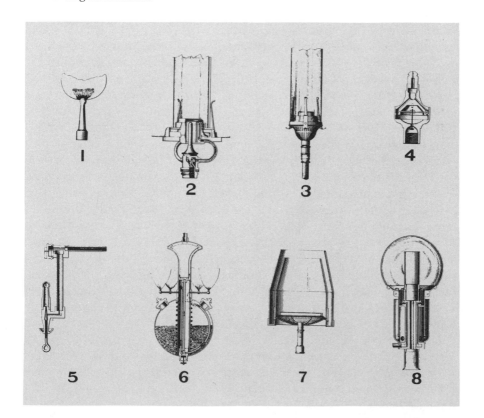

collected in a series of pipes) and its major by-product, coke (which is to coal as charcoal is to wood). Manufactured separately as a fuel for iron-making, coke went to waste as a gas by-product, while the gas went to waste in coke ovens; nineteenth-century ironmakers considered the retort ovens that would save both expensive, the market for gas limited, and retort-oven coke inferior. Coal gas provided unsteady, smelly light at about fifteen to seventeen candlepower.

As improved lamp designs and the new kerosene fuel began to brighten both American lighting and oil's competitive prospects, coal gas became less attractive. Soon after kerosene hit the market, two inventors, French-man Tessie du Motay and American T. S. C. Lowe, independently devel-oped "water gas." This new illuminant, produced by reacting steam with superheated coke or hard anthracite coal, provided twenty-two to thirty-five candlepower when mixed with oil vapors or other gases. First intro-duced in Pennsylvania in 1873, it rapidly supplanted coal gas after 1880; by 1890, America's 742 city gasworks produced more water gas than coal gas.

Natural gas competed with manufactured gas only in limited geograph-ical areas. Thomas Jefferson mentioned a "burning spring" in West Vir-ginia in his *Notes on Virginia,* later dedicated as a park by George Washington; salt-well drilling produced natural gas in 1815 in Charleston and in 1820 in Pittsburgh, but nobody wanted or used the gas. The first intentional gas well, dug in Fredonia, New York, in 1821, provided enough gas for thirty burners, each of two candlepower. Improved by storage systems and lead pipes, the Fredonia well attracted international attention. General Lafayette, touring the United States and greeted at a Fredonia hotel blazing with light at two o'clock in the morning, remarked that he had better leave a place "evidently too near to Hades"; the Ger-man explorer Alexander von Humboldt called Fredonia gas the eighth wonder of the world. But even the Fredonians failed to recognize the commercial potential of their gas, not organizing a company to make improvements until 1858; more important, most of the early producers of petroleum failed to exploit the natural gas that accompanied the oil. A few manufacturers used natural gas during the 1870s, and many more during the 1880s in places near gas fields, particularly the Pittsburgh area. In 1891, the Indiana Natural Gas and Oil Company built the first high-pressure long-distance pipeline, running 120 miles between the northern Indiana gas fields and Chicago. However, natural gas did not outstrip manufactured gas until the 1930s, and even then remained more popular for industrial purposes than for domestic use.

Domestic use provided only a small market for manufactured gas as well, until the end of the century; although gas companies abounded, their product primarily lighted city streets and public places. The simplest fixtures—T-shaped iron pipes (usually with two burners, one at each end of the T) or plain elbows with one burner at the end—provided light for factories, prisons, hospitals, schools, and plebeian saloons. More fashionable bars and stores often used gas pillars, ornamental standards on pedestals or mounted on the bar or counter, with branches at the top capped by burners and shades. One firm, Cornelius and Baker, supplied a wide variety of fixtures for government buildings; by 1859, they had lit nearly all of the state capitols and many rooms in the White House, and had commissions for the United States Capitol and the Treasury Building. These chandeliers and brackets incorporated statuettes representing Produce, Commerce, Liberty, and the like, along with American eagles, buffaloes, corn, Indians, state heroes, and American presidents. The company's apparatus for lighting the Senate and House chambers in the Capitol spaced gas jets so closely that they could all be ignited by a single pilot light—2,500 burners "lighted instantaneously" on the Senate side.

Fixtures in some private homes displayed similar ostentation. A. T. Stewart, owner of the largest dry-goods firm in the world, lit his marble mansion at Fifth Avenue and Thirty-Fourth Street in New York with twelve-light bronze chandeliers, ornamented with porcelain, etched glass shades, and Egyptian Revival heads. Stewart's house, completed in 1869 and generally acclaimed as the finest in the city, predated most other millionaires' mansions, but even the Vanderbilts' "bourgeois brownstone," which they ultimately abandoned for palaces on Fifth Avenue and in Newport, included in 1873 a splendid glass chandelier.

Not everyone who used gas had as much money as Stewart or the Vanderbilts, but only relatively wealthy people could afford the installation cost or the fuel itself before the end of the century. Those who bought it used it almost exclusively for lighting; at the end of the century, gas was still very much a "fuel of the future" for domestic cooking and heating. Despite the many gas companies and gas mains, the fuel might have disappeared quickly when faced with its first serious competition, electricity, during the 1880s, had it not been for the Welsbach burner, or gas mantle, invented in 1885 and first manufactured in the United States in 1887. Thanks to this treated cotton mesh cylinder that created an incandescent light, gas lighting maintained "an increasingly futile rearguard action" until about 1910.

The Welsbach mantle kept the gas companies alive while they established themselves firmly in some localities; at least two early-twentieth-century studies of working people's houses in New York, for example, showed a majority with gas lighting. Meanwhile, the companies devoted themselves to promoting other domestic uses for their fuel, especially cooking. Despite the new mantle, gaslights flickered more than electric ones, required ventilated fixtures, and produced soot; unlike both kerosene and electric lamps, which could be moved around a room, gas fixtures had to be installed permanently. Faced with this obvious

Gas chandelier in A. T. Stewart's mansion, Fifth Avenue and 34th Street, New York City, 1869. Stewart was the nation's leading dry-goods merchant, and his house the first of the sumptuous Fifth Avenue mansions.

competition, the gas lighting companies allied themselves with the gas appliance manufacturers in the National Commercial Gas Association in 1905; this organization applied itself to merchandising the fuel, developing new appliances, training sales personnel, and producing showroom displays and demonstrations. A national advertising campaign, jointly sponsored by gas companies and appliance manufacturers in 1912–1913, promoted many uses for gas; by 1918, its future was assured, despite the serious competition.

This competition displayed itself at the World's Columbian Exposition in Chicago, which opened in May 1893. The exposition, commemorating the four-hundredth anniversary of Columbus's discovery of America, surpassed all the other nineteenth-century world's fairs—London's 1851

Crystal Palace, the 1889 Paris exposition for which the Eiffel Tower was built, and the 1876 Philadelphia Centennial. Within 3 of the 150 buildings of the White City, designed by the most famous architects of the day, model kitchens offered women fair visitors a glimpse of the future. The Women's Building kitchen, primarily used by home economists for twice-daily cooking lectures, contained seats for the audience and a platform with a gas stove and a table. The Electrical Building featured a complete model house, with electric stoves, hot plates ("Dishes are kept hot on the table by dainty, polished electric warming furnaces connected by wires under the table"), washing and ironing machines, fans, dishwashers, and carpet sweepers. Its gas counterpart, located in the Horticultural Building, promised to "delight all housekeepers" with its gas stoves, hot-water heater, refrigerators and coolers, and automatic dishwasher. Most of the delighted housekeepers went home to wood and coal stoves and houses without plumbing; these were the only dishwashers they would see in a lifetime. To them, electric cooking was no more fantastic than gas.

Electric lighting had started in competition with gas. Others had long experimented with arc lights and dynamos; Thomas Edison's major achievement was not the light bulb but a total system "for generating, controlling, measuring, distributing, and utilizing power." Edison, who made his first fortune manufacturing stock tickers for Western Union, had already established the nation's first research-and-development firm at Menlo Park, New Jersey, a well-equipped laboratory and a permanent staff dedicated to full-time invention in an organized fashion, aimed at making "a minor invention every ten days, and a big one every six months or so." When he decided to tackle the problem of incandescent lighting, a decision based on the greater potential financial rewards that lighting held over such possible areas of invention as the telephone and phonograph, he limited the research by fixing the price at the price of gaslight. He could profit only by lowering costs as much as possible, and designed the rest of the system (generators, light sockets, junction boxes, safety fuses, underground conductors, and much more) to do that. The system as a whole, first demonstrated in 1879 and first established commercially at the Edison Electric Illuminating Company's Pearl Street power station in New York in 1882, proved competitive with gas, exactly as intended in its design.

Setting up the system required financing far beyond the research-and-development stage; Edison needed help, and turned to big businessmen for support in forming the Edison Electric Light Company, a forerunner of General Electric. With other bankers and the president of Western Union, J. P. Morgan provided major financial backing for the several Edison companies; his partner served as director and treasurer of Edison Electric Light until 1883; and his New York mansion served as an early demonstration of the Edison system. Morgan himself helped to form

General Electric in 1892, and served on its board until his death in 1913. Henry Villard, the president and financier of the Northern Pacific Railroad, financed some of Edison's early work and created the merger that became General Electric. That merger, combining two of the three large electrical equipment manufacturers (Edison General Electric and Thompson-Houston, leaving Westinghouse independent), represented as well a merger of New York and Boston financial interests. These financiers were important to the merger "because the electrical manufacturers were the first American industrialists not intimately connected with railroads who found it necessary to go to the capital markets for funds in order to build their initial enterprise."

Dominated by these outside financial interests, the board of General Electric continued to exert powerful control over the operations of the salaried managers. The top management, in turn, held tight rein over the middle management, building large central staffs and carefully defining their responsibilities, creating "the basic organizational form used by modern American industrial enterprises." The sales department, with its own vice-president and a manager for each major product, responsible for coordinating its production and marketing, met monthly with the manager for foreign sales and the advertising director to consider "pricing, competitors' activities, market conditions, customers' needs and concerns, and the processing of major orders." Coordination between sales and production departments, central to all modern corporations, was particularly important at General Electric because its salesmen, knowing more about the technical aspects of the equipment than their customers, had frequent contact with them, serving as installers and repairmen; many GE salesmen, like those in other technologically advanced industries, had engineering degrees.

Most of this sales and service force handling GE's early industrial products served the large manufacturers that demanded power-generating equipment. Eventually, however, households joined the electrical industry's consumer market; their ignorance established a similar dependence on servicemen. The new terminology that came along with electrical equipment—watts and amps and volts—could be confusing. Some local lighting companies supplied alternating current, others direct, well into the 1930s; equipment came designed for use with either or both, and voltage varied likewise in different localities and for different appliances. Women's magazines and household manuals explained the terms, suggesting that ignorance in these matters led to misunderstandings about why the toaster burned the toast or why the waffle iron didn't work like Cousin Mary's. In the end, though, the whole thing was a matter for experts. "It is unwise to attempt repairs yourself," advised one article after explaining watts and meter reading. You might treat a slight cold or a small cut, suggested a manual called *The Electric Home*, "but for a real sickness you

Wiring for households in the streets of New York. Drawings by W. P. Snyder from *Harper's Weekly*, 1882.

would call a physician." Likewise, you might wish to fix a cord or socket or change a fuse yourself, "but beyond this consult your electrical contractor or lighting company. They are your electrical doctors." Wires embedded in the walls of the house, like gas lines and plumbing pipes but quite unlike anything common in households before 1900, contributed to this dependence on servicemen.

Ignorance, combined with the genuine dangers of fire and electrocution, engendered fear. Mrs. Cornelius Vanderbilt, who in 1881 went to a costume ball dressed as an electric light, demanded that her Fifth Avenue house's entire new electrical system be removed a short time later because it caused a small fire. Electrical companies that hoped to attract a broader clientele than the Vanderbilts and the Morgans had to counteract such fears in order to establish the new fuel as the competitor Edison had designed it to be. They never did so by explaining the mysteries of the ampere or by addressing fears about fire and electrocution directly; instead, in the budding tradition of the advertising industry that was emerging at the same time, they diverted attention to the product's advantages.

For the first thirty years or so, the only households that could afford electricity could also afford domestic servants. Electricity, its proponents claimed, promised freedom from the ages-old servant problem: electrical appliances could not talk back. A Columbian Exposition guidebook described gracious living in the electric future at the model house in the Electrical Building. A servant answered an electric bell, ushered the visitor into the reception room, and turned on a phonograph, which kept the guest occupied with a selection from *Faust* until the hostess appeared. She kept contact with the servants "by electric calls daintily fashioned." Electricity could, then, serve even those with servants. But it also could dispense with them: "About the time the dinner is over the servant gets angry at something and picks up her 'duds' and goes off in a huff." The fortunate mistress of the home of the future sends her guests to the parlor, "excuses herself for a moment," sends the dishes upstairs on the electric dumbwaiter, does them in the electric dishwasher "in five minutes," and dries them in the electric dish dryer. If the servant is not replaced by the time washday comes, the mistress "need have no fear of breaking her aristocratic back leaning over tubs or ruining her pretty hands by constant soaking in hot suds," but can wash them in an automatic washer that drains and fills for washing, rinsing, and bluing, hang them to dry in front of electric radiators in the garret, run them through the electric ironer, and be "none too tired to go to the opera in the evening."

By 1917, the disappearing servant was commonplace; many of the women who had formed the servant population were taking other jobs instead, the popular press moaned about the servant problem, and a variety of reformers proposed solutions. General Electric joined in. Advertising light bulbs to the middle-class readers of *McClure's*, they sug-

The electric servant, as depicted in a General Electric advertisement, *McClure's*, 1917.

gested that electricity had other uses besides light. "Housework is hard work—and the problem of help in the home is growing more and more acute." Both the work and the problem could be simplified with "electrical servants," dependable for the "muscle part of the washing, ironing, cleaning and sewing." They could cool or heat the house, percolate the coffee, or "do all your cooking—without matches, without soot, without coal, without argument—in a cool kitchen. Don't go to the Employment Bureau. Go to your Lighting Company or leading Electric Shop to solve your servant problem." The first step, buying Edison Mazda light bulbs to save "enough current to operate several electrical appliances without increasing your electric bill," would "light the way to lighter housework." In an ad directed at women short of servants who used electricity only for lighting, the company sold light bulbs but promoted the entire industry.

After World War I, pictures of servants virtually disappeared from advertising for women; most ads depicted housewives doing their own housework. Many new ads treated household tasks as expressions of emotion: a new bride showed her love by "washing tell-tale gray out of her husband's shirts"; a mother cleaning the bathroom sink protected her family from disease. A Muncie, Indiana electric company advertisement of the 1920s suggested that electricity promoted good motherhood. "This is the test of a successful mother—she puts first things first. She does not give to sweeping the time that belongs to her children." Men, ran the ad, were "judged successful according to their power to delegate work. Similarly the wise woman delegates to electricity all that electricity can do. She cannot delegate the one task most important. Human lives are in her keeping; their future is molded by her hands and heart." As live-in servants disappeared from households and electricity entered them, the electric companies suggested that housewives could use the new fuel to save time for more important tasks.

Some of the appliances offered as "electric servants" did save time. The electric iron, first patented in 1882 and first sold in 1893, relieved women of the hot work involved in continually heating heavy flatirons, although carefree ironing had to wait until about 1927 for the adjustable automatic thermostat. Before that, electric irons were either on or off. Immensely helpful and relatively inexpensive, irons became the most popular electric appliances during the 1920s. Fifty-nine percent of the households in Zanesville, Ohio, where interviewers for a market research firm knocked on every door in 1926, had them; 82 percent of that firm's sample of somewhat wealthier families in thirty-six other cities ironed with electricity.

Almost as many had vacuum cleaners: 53 percent in Zanesville and 60 percent in the other towns. Nonelectric carpet sweepers—always dominated by the Bissell company—had literally swept the nation beginning in the 1880s; David Kenney patented the first electric suction cleaner in 1907. The two most popular vacuum cleaner types had both appeared by the time of the Zanesville study: the Hoover, which beat the rug with a power-driven brush, was patented in 1908 and had created a national market by 1919; the Electrolux, the first tank or cylinder type cleaner, imported from Sweden in 1924, sold well enough immediately that by 1931 the company had decided to manufacture cleaners in the United States. Many companies, large and small, sold vacuum cleaners house-to-house; by 1926, an edition of Marion Harland's famous 1871 cookbook, *Common Sense in the Household*, "Revised for Gas and Electricity," maintained that "almost every woman who lives in or near a town of any size" had seen a vacuum cleaner demonstration, "and even the dweller in remote country districts has probably had the automobile of the demonstrator stop at her door."

Electricity, floor care, and the servant question. In 1906, those who could afford electricity or large, fixed vacuum systems could also afford servants like the maid and valet in the Vacuum Cleaner Company ad, published in *Theater Magazine*.

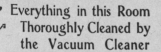

Everything in this Room Thoroughly Cleaned by the Vacuum Cleaner

The dust is drawn from carpets, rugs, chairs, statuary, mouldings, picture frames, cornices, and upholstery of all kinds, through small lines of hose, easily handled, to receptacles in the basement, where it is retained until destroyed.

Dust not scattered about as by the old method of cleaning by broom or carpet sweeper but is actually removed. The small dust particles that ordinarily remain on furniture after sweeping are not present.

Anyone can handle the hose, and the result in absolute cleanliness is the delight of the houseowner. Carpets and rugs cleaned without removal, which renders the annual housecleaning unnecessary.

Your valet or maid can keep all of your garments free from dust, and in spotless condition. The dust that blows on them from the street can be removed at once upon your entering the house.

Think what this means to you: in greater ease, in more economy, and in better health. Germ infected dust removed from the room forever, and you and your children protected from it. You can imagine how improved your condition will be with your house absolutely clean.

The White House, the residence of Miss Helen Gould, the St. Regis Hotel, the Times Building, the Duquesne Club, of Pittsburgh and the Jordon-Marsh Store of Boston, to mention different types of houses and buildings, are all cleaned by the Vacuum Cleaner.

For full information, estimates for installing the plant in your house, building, etc., address Dept. X

The engine may be installed in the basement, and run by electric or other power. It takes up but little room and is easily managed.

Vacuum Cleaner Co.
DAVID T. KENNEY, Pres't.
427 Fifth Avenue, New York

Harland's daughter, who wrote the revision, loved these machines. Their superiority to brooms and carpet sweepers, she wrote, "is at once apparent." The "swiftness and ease" of the work "seem miraculous." "It is like play to see ravelings, lint, feathers and hair and other scraps drawn into the maw of the cleaner and vanish from sight." The numerous attachments made short work of cleaning hangings, tufted furniture, cornices, picture frames, "and remote corners under bureaus and bookcases." Best of all, she wrote, the vacuum cleaner "has in a measure done away with housecleaning. The old fashion of having a semi-annual upheaval," that old household earthquake, when carpets were removed, hangings taken down, pictures and books displaced, "and general misery produced through the household, is no longer essential to cleanliness." Delivered from this "bondage," housekeepers could look forward to the next step: "Not yet has a machine been devised which will mechanically mop up a floor or take china from the shelf and wash it, but it is probably on the way and when it comes it will undoubtedly be run by electricity!"

None of the other small electric appliances sold as well as vacuum cleaners and irons. Hot plates, heating pads, grills, percolators, room heaters, and fans appeared in some households by 1926, but only about a fifth of Zanesville households owned toasters, which far outstripped all these others. The first electric toasters, appearing around 1910, adapted the wire-frame designs long used on top of the stove; GE's 1912 Radiant Toaster, a frame holding one slice of bread, produced a slice a minute, "Crisp, Delicious, Golden-Brown Toast on the Breakfast Table." Automatic toasters, first widely marketed by Toastmaster after 1926, timed the process so that the cook could leave the table. "How many times *each week* do you have to throw out burned slices of toast?" the company asked in a 1927 *Saturday Evening Post* ad. "This amazing new invention" ended that waste and annoyance in "three fascinating operations": drop in a slice of bread, then press two levers (one set the current, the other operated the timer), and "Pop! up comes the toast automatically when it's done, and the current is automatically turned off. The toast is made in a jiffy because both sides are toasted *at the same time*. There is no guess-work."

Other specialized cooking devices, designed for one function alone, appeared on the market in the 1920s and early 1930s; although few families bought them, electric waffle irons, chafing dishes, and coffee makers promised further freedom from the stove and the kitchen. A woman could prepare her family's entire meal at the table, or cook it in the kitchen and keep it warm in the dining room; she could serve her guests and enjoy their company at the same time. By 1934, she could buy even the most highly specialized appliances—egg cookers (with "no moving parts to wear out or to cause trouble"), corn poppers ("useful not only for making pop-corn at Hallowe'en parties and gatherings, but also for roasting chestnuts and freshening nuts"), doughnut bakers (which made four greaseless doughnuts at a time "right on the dining room table"), wiener cookers ("furnished in different sizes and colors to suit one's fancy"), and baby-bottle warmers ("which you can place on your bedside table at night" for two o'clock feedings).

Most of the early ads for electric appliances celebrated their economy: the 1912 GE Radiant Toaster made toast for one-tenth of a cent per slice, the 1909 Hoover Suction Sweeper would "Sweep With Electricity For 3¢ a Week," the 1913 GE Even Heat electric iron promised "Real Economy" over its competitors, even at fifteen cents per "average family ironing," because it ironed faster, "thereby requiring less electricity." Most GE ads promoted the current-saving Edison Mazda light bulbs: "Replace the old-style lamps and you can enjoy using these electrical appliances without any increase in the monthly bills for current." By the 1920s, economy no longer dominated the ads, which now celebrated electricity's ability to relieve women of burdensome chores. "What Every Woman Wants," one utility-sponsored ad stated, was an all-electric kitchen, "A Kitchen Where Work Is Easy!" The 1927 Toastmaster ad used the words "automatic" and "automatically" seven times and noted the "gleaming nickel" finish that made it "an attractive piece for the dining table," but never mentioned economy at all.

As electric service spread to more households, the price of current dropped; in 1912, when about 16 percent of American dwelling units had electric service, a kilowatt hour cost about nine cents, while the 35 percent who had it in 1920 paid seven and a half cents and the 68 percent in 1930 paid six cents. Customers spent more money on electricity, however; as time went on, they installed more lights, bought more appliances, and used more current. The average annual use per customer doubled between 1912 and 1930. Still, most of them limited themselves to lights, irons, vacuum cleaners, and the curling irons that created the fashionable hairstyles of the 1920s. American consumption of electricity in 1930, although greatly increased over the past and still on the rise, suggests that while every woman might well have wanted an all-electric kitchen, it was scarcely more a reality then than it had been at the Columbian Exposition in 1893: the average customer used only 547 kilowatt hours. Customers in 1970 bought thirteen times that much electricity.

Electric service, available in most cities by the turn of the century, spread rapidly in urban areas after World War I. By 1920, almost half of the nonfarm dwelling units in America had electric service; a massive Bureau of Labor Statistics study conducted in forty-two states in 1918–1919 reported that some members of all economic groups had electricity, although poorer households used less current. At the beginning of the Depression, 85 percent of nonfarm dwellings had electric service. Farm homes lagged far behind—only about 10 percent had electricity in 1930—

until after 1935, when Franklin D. Roosevelt created the Rural Electrification Administration. The REA made long-term loans to farmers' cooperatives, state and local governments, and nonprofit organizations, enabling farmers (not individually eligible for the loans) to electrify at minimum cost. By 1941, 35 percent of farm homes had electricity. The REA liberalized the loan policy in 1944; more than half of farm homes were electrified by 1946.

Few dared or bothered to comment on the broad social effects of so fundamental a transition. Once produced by household members who chopped wood, hauled coal, and tended kerosene lamps, energy now became a commodity, something people bought from corporations whose motive was profit. Once burdened by hard work, women could now buy "electric servants" that did the work for them. Once framed by nature, daily life now stood independent of the seasons and the daily movements of the sun. What could it all mean? Were women now at leisure, free to pursue lives in the world outside the household, or to change their roles within it?

One group that did ask those questions, a graduate seminar at Bryn Mawr College in 1925–1926, produced a comprehensive bibliography of books and articles about electricity in the household. The students "established the fact that practically no work has been done on this subject, and that we have no actual knowledge as to the social and economic effects of the introduction of electricity in the home." They found almost no written conjecture on what they understood to be fundamental questions about daily life, except for discussions of electricity and the servant question, a relationship without clarity about cause and effect. They guessed that most of the change lay in the future, for electricity had not yet touched the lives of the unskilled laboring classes; they speculated that electricity might even return production to the home, decentralizing manufacturing by bringing back some of the work that industrialization had removed—a possible revival of home sewing, for example. Without predicting exactly what might happen, the Bryn Mawr researchers knew something would, because of two "relatively recent factors": "first the rapidly declining cost of electric current—and second, the fact that electricity in the near future will be practically everywhere available and in unlimited quantity."

Those assumptions, upon which all discussion of electricity rested until they were shattered during the 1970s, allowed Americans to take electric power and its social effects for granted for about half a century. The Bryn Mawr students correctly predicted that electricity would help free American women from much of the "monotony and drudgery" that they called "so largely the portion of womankind the world over"; their prediction that production would return to the home proved considerably less accurate. In fact, electricity contributed to its further removal, and the industry that produced electric power and electric appliances followed

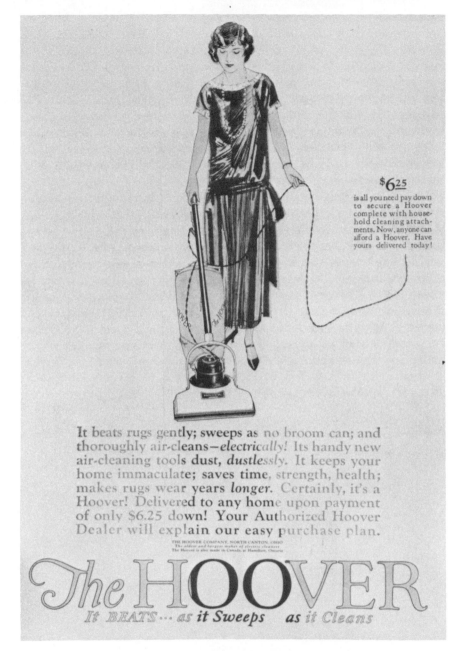

$6²⁵ is all you need pay down to secure a Hoover complete with household cleaning attachments. Now, anyone can afford a Hoover. Have yours delivered today!

It beats rugs gently; sweeps as no broom can; and thoroughly air-cleans—*electrically!* Its handy new air-cleaning tools dust, *dustlessly*. It keeps your home immaculate; saves time, strength, health; makes rugs wear years *longer*. Certainly, it's a Hoover! Delivered to any home upon payment of only $6.25 down! Your Authorized Hoover Dealer will explain our easy purchase plan.

THE HOOVER COMPANY, NORTH CANTON, OHIO
The oldest and largest maker of electric cleaners
The Hoover is also made in Canada, at Hamilton, Ontario

The HOOVER
It BEATS··· as it Sweeps as it Cleans

By 1924, many residents of cities and smaller towns had electricity, and—with the company's installment plan—"anyone can afford a Hoover." Advertised in the *National Geographic*.

the patterns of expansion, centralization, and corporate domination by large investors that characterized the process of industrialization in other industries. Electric power's predecessor and competitor, gas, under the control of local bankers and financiers, had set the majority of American households apart from affluent homes and many public places during the first half of the nineteenth century. Even wealthier investors dominated the electrical industry, initially created and designed to return maximum profits to the financiers, not to free housewives from monotony and drudgery; from the start, the industry promoted dependence on manufactured products and on the experts who understood them well enough to keep them in repair.

Women welcomed electricity and gas in the early part of the century because they no longer had to haul fuel, build fires, and clean lamps; they knew that electric vacuum cleaners and washing machines would relieve them of backbreaking labor. Now, with energy conservation a serious issue for both the nation and their own pocketbooks, American women must evaluate their dependence on extravagant energy consumption and on an industry devoted to wasteful production of unneccessary goods planned for obsolescence. Hooked on power, devoted to the electric can opener along with the electric light, to electric knives and toothbrushes along with vacuum cleaners, and continuing to buy that power and those appliances from the same corporations—now even fewer, larger, and more centralized—American households become ever more prey to the effects of corporate decision making on daily life.

FIVE

Fetch a Pail of Water

Like the new fuels that ended fuel hauling and fire building, indoor plumbing accomplished basic chores that burdened nearly every household task: lugging fresh water into the house and carrying dirty water and liquid refuse out of it. As with gas and electricity, public services came to substitute for private labor, the rich got the services before the poor, the city dweller before the farmer, and consumption replaced productive labor. Nineteenth-

century technological development did not, however, foster the production of any intermediate devices for water. At least wood and coal stoves and oil lamps removed some of the burdens of heating and lighting in households not sufficiently well-to-do for the most advanced technology, but poor women at the end of the century continued to haul water from urban street hydrants much as everyone had hauled it for centuries from streams and creeks. As a result of this lag, and despite a broad range of technological possibilities for getting water and disposing of sewage, indoor plumbing accentuated the class differences that were developing throughout the nineteenth century, as the United States went from a nation of self-sufficient producers to an industrial giant dominated by wealthy individual entrepreneurs and built by their impoverished workers. The bathroom in George Vanderbilt's Fifth Avenue house, built in 1885 when he was in his early twenties, anticipated the bathroom design that was to become standard during the twentieth century; elsewhere in New York City, industrial workers used the ages-old outdoor privies and hauled all their clean and dirty water, while the middle class denoted their intermediate status by rudimentary plumbing systems.

Without indoor plumbing, most women hauled every drop of water they used for cooking, dishwashing, bathing themselves and their families, laundry, and housecleaning; after using it, they hauled it back outside the house, though not necessarily going as far as they had come from the well, the spring, the creek, or the urban hydrant or pump. Heavy work even in the spring or fall, it became unbearable in summer's heat, and in winter women had to crack ice and thaw pumps to get to their frigid water supplies, and empty more chamber pots. Lucky housewives had water close to the house, but none close enough. A North Carolina Farmer's Alliance organizer, talking to the men about finding an issue that could attract women to meetings as "honorary members" in 1886, calculated one wife's mileage. She and her husband (who appeared at the meeting wearing faultlessly white linen) had a good spring, "as good water as ever flowed out of the ground," sixty yards from the house they had lived in for about forty-one years. Water had to be brought to the house eight or ten times on an average day. "Well, suppose we figure a little," said the organizer, producing a pencil, "and we will put it at six instead of eight or ten times a day. Sixty yards at six times a day is 720 yards—in one year it amounts to 148 miles and during the forty-one years that you have been living there it amounts to 6,068 miles—don't you think we could get up some question that would interest the farmers' wives and daughters? Remember too that half the distance is up hill with the water."

The organizer's questions suggest that, although men might help, water tasks were considered primarily women's work; getting others in the household to help could cut down on the labor, but not on the responsibility. "When Ben and the hired men are round see that they fill up the tank," the Curtis farm magazine's "Aunt Nellie" advised her fictional niece Janet during World War I. " 'Watchful waiting' must be your policy— never lug any water yourself, but wait till you can catch Ben or one of the men. See that the last thing at night someone fills it for the morning." This advice applied only to the heaviest work, filling the main tank, which would serve both kitchen and laundry until Ben and Janet could afford a "pressure system of waterworks." Janet still had to lug water from the tank to the hot-water reservoir on the stove, and from there to the dishpan or laundry tubs; a bath was still a major production. Coy "watchful waiting" might go on for a long time during busy seasons on the farm, when Ben and the hired men might well assume that Janet could take care of her own jobs while they did theirs; nor was it a reasonable strategy for women whose husbands worked twelve-hour days in factories. Young children, who could at least bring in a stick of wood at a time, could carry only inconsequential amounts of water; the task required

Fortunate women had water close to their homes; others carried pails from streams, wells, and urban hydrants. Photo taken in the 1920s for the Agricultural Extension Division of International Harvester Corporation, New Jersey.

adult strength, and belonged to the women. Six or eight or ten times a day, they trooped to their wells and pumps and tanks with buckets.

Conservation helped. Modern urban Americans have only to go camping to discover that baths can be forgone, clothing changed less frequently, and dishes cleaned with fewer rinses when water is scarce. Nineteenth-century housewives conserved water at home. "If the washerwoman has to draw water, at a distance from her place of work, or, if she obtains it only by a laborious process, she will be very apt to stint her measure of it," Catharine Beecher wrote in 1841. Clean white clothes required "an abundance and frequent change of water." Even so, Beecher advised using the entire series of waters over and over; two tubs of suds, one boiling tub, one rinse, and a bluing rinse should each be employed first for fine white clothes, then for coarser ones, then for colored clothes and flannels.

Reusing dishwater with progressively dirtier and greasier items had the

Nearly every drop of water carried inside had to go back out again. Household writers agreed that carrying slops—including the contents of chamber pots—was the most disagreeable of household chores. Photo from the 1920s, for the Agricultural Extension Department of International Harvester Corporation, Chicago.

same function; Beecher provided complete directions. A swab, two or three towels, three dishcloths (for those progressively dirtier loads), two large tin tubs (one for washing, one for rinsing), a "large old waiter [tray] on which to drain the dishes," a soap dish, hard soap, a slop pail, and two water pails constituted "a full supply of conveniences." Wire dish-draining racks seem to have been unavailable throughout the century; mentioned neither in Beecher's works nor in Campbell's 1881 manual, none appears in the Sears catalogue as late as 1897. Campbell suggested a "wire dish cloth" for scouring pots, though sand more often did the job. Soap, made at home at the beginning of the century from accumulated waste grease and lye manufactured from ashes, was commercially available even then, from craftsmen and from farm women who sold it at market stands; coming only in bar form, it had to be scraped to be used for dishwashing. Although primarily an urban product in 1860, commercial soap soon prevailed, and housekeeping manuals published after the Civil War rarely included soap-making instructions even when addressed specifically to farm audiences. (Other than regular soaps, only two commercial cleaning agents were advertised before 1880: ammonia and Sapolio, a gritty scouring soap. Magazines and manuals offered hints for cleaning with sand, milk, salt, soda, borax, camphor, lye, vinegar, turpentine, lamp oil, clay, various acids and oils, and mixtures of these things.)

The nineteenth-century dishwashing procedure is basically familiar: scraping, washing with soap, rinsing, wiping, and putting away. The "nicest articles," writers maintained, should be done first, then the greasy dishes, the milk pans and utensils, and finally the pots, roasters, kettles, and gridiron, sure to be sooty from fireplaces or open pot holes in cast-iron stoves. Fresh hot water should be added with each new load. Dishwashing required carrying an enormous amount of water—cold water to the stove, hot water to the dishpans, dirty water outside—even in a house that, like Beecher's ideal suburban home of 1869, had indoor pumps.

These methods survive today where hand washing continues, whereas dishwashers and washing machines destroy the fixed order of procedure and, often, the principle of separating articles by degree of soil. Water conservation itself was a casualty, not of machinery, but of indoor plumbing; it began to go as soon as running water became available. In Philadelphia, for example, water consumption per subscriber doubled between 1823, when the city completed new public waterworks, and 1837; it had more than doubled again by 1850. Although women with faucets in their houses may have reused their dishwater, they could use more dishes to begin with, fill their dishpans deeper, add more hot water as the dishwater cooled, and let some water go down the drain unused, without adding much to their work load. As they learned to waste water, they also began to use it more.

More water induced more washing, which in turn meant cleaner and

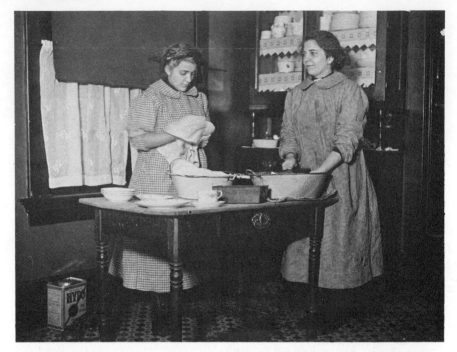

Dishwashing without running water. Photo probably taken in Madison, Wisconsin, about 1910.

healthier people. Baths, at best a Saturday-night luxury with recycled bathwater for most families throughout the century, became a real possibility only with adult-sized tubs and the running water necessary to fill them without breaking backs. Lydia Maria Child, one of the foremost women writers of the period, advocated free public baths in 1844; "the wealthy," she wrote, "can introduce water into their chambers . . . but for the innumerable poor, this is a luxury that can seldom, if ever, be enjoyed. Open bathing around the wharves is of course prohibited; and the labouring man has to walk three or four miles to obtain a privilege so necessary to health."

People who wanted to wash more often could not simply go out and buy running water. Unlike prepared foods or new utensils, indoor plumbing was a matter of public policy as well as private production and consumption; even the urban elite needed large waterworks systems. These municipal systems owed their existence more to pressing public health concerns than to any consumers' needs. The piecemeal sanitary provisions that characterized the colonial period proved insufficient for the long-run needs of developing urban areas; even country people found

Sapolio was a gritty scouring soap, one of the earliest widely distributed commercial soap products. From *Everybody's Magazine,* 1900.

that improper drainage ultimately poisoned their water supplies, and certainly cities could ill afford to slight sewerage and waterworks. Massive technological and financial problems, however, deterred them until necessity forced them to do something. Philadelphia, pioneering public waterworks in the United States, did so only after massive yellow fever epidemics throughout the 1790s.

Benjamin Latrobe, the designer of the Philadelphia systems and several other waterworks, usually considered the first professional architect in the United States, brought to the task a set of skills far beyond architecture, for creating the waterworks presented new technological and organizational problems. As architectural historian James Marston Fitch points out, the project straddled two eras. Working without models and limited to contemporary processes and materials, Latrobe created a concept for a new urban industrial society, based on steam pumps, a culvert from the Schuylkill River to the settlement's edge, and distribution through wooden pipes and street hydrants. He proposed a private subscription plan, believing that construction and operation costs could be met by charges to businesses and households directly connected to the system. This proved to be untrue; in 1811, ten years after the system opened, only 2,127 Philadelphians had subscribed. Most of the city's 54,000 residents continued to draw water from private wells or took it from the system's street hydrants without paying. Although the water system was running heavy deficits, Latrobe had amassed support among the city's merchant elite, who remained committed to the plan. They ultimately sponsored deficit financing of improved works—with a dam across the Schuylkill, water-powered pumps, hilltop reservoirs, a gravity-fed system, surplus capacity for growth, and grounds laid out as the first large urban park in America—fostering eventual financial success and more widespread use of public water by 1837.

Charles Dickens, visiting Philadelphia in 1842, commented that the city "is most bountifully provided with fresh water, which is showered and jerked about, and turned on, and poured off, everywhere." Americans marveled at public waterworks as much as their foreign visitors; Lydia Maria Child published a paean to New York's Croton Aqueduct in a discussion of beautiful things about the city appearing first in the *Boston Courier* around the same time as Dickens's *American Notes* and later collected in a highly successful book. Often asked how she, "so deeply enamoured of nature," could live in New York, she replied that beauty might be found even in the city, on the noble avenues, in the lovely verandas, in the music of the Philharmonic Society and the Italian Opera —and in Croton water. "To me, there is something extremely beautiful in the idea of that little river, lying so many years unnoticed among the hills"; like Shakespeare's genius, unappreciated by his contemporaries, the river's powers were now finally "brought to all the people, a perpetual fountain of refreshment." Even the most avid modern New Yorker, asked how to find beauty in Gotham, would scarcely choose the waterworks for such celebration; yet Child and Dickens made accurate assessments of the systems that were to make possible the expansion of the cities themselves.

Smaller cities followed the lead of Philadelphia and New York; by the time of the Civil War, 136 cities—probably all towns with greater than 10,000 population—had some kind of public waterworks. Many of these rudimentary systems provided no purification and served only a few sub-scribers. Prairie towns dug town wells near rivers and hired tank wagons to haul the water around town, filling private barrels; eventually they dug hilltop reservoirs or mounted supply tanks in high places to send water through pipes by gravity. By the end of the century, the 136 towns with waterworks had grown substantially in population, and another 3,060 towns had established water systems (probably all places of 2,500 popula-tion or more); as a result, close to half the country's population enjoyed the benefits of public water of some description. Municipal responsibility for public supply, however, did not imply municipal concern for indoor plumbing within households until the Progressive period of reform at the very end of the century; urgent public health concerns had created a

"Thawing the Pump," a cartoon by Clare Briggs, 1912.

demand for public waterworks, but once the epidemics subsided so did
any effort to bring the benefits of the new technology to the poor. Most
households in cities with public water had no fixtures at all within their
homes; most of those with fixtures had only a single faucet.

Nor were cities quick to take strides in drainage and sewage disposal
equivalent to their water-supply efforts. In 1855, more than a half-century
after the Latrobe waterworks inaugurated public water supply, Chicago
began to design "the first comprehensive sewerage project of the country,"
but did not install the first sewer until nine years later. In 1866, only one-
eighth of the city had sewers. Although the tunnel system emptied thirty
feet below lake level, water contamination plagued it from the start.
Usually administered separately from water systems, sewage disposal
lagged behind water provision throughout the century in towns of all
sizes, until the efforts of public health reformers in the later decades made
it a recognized municipal concern, worthy of significant monetary appropriations; about one-third of Boston's total city budget in the last third
of the century, for example, went to sanitary projects. Speculators and
subdividers of that city's suburbs extended the provision of sanitary services to the middle classes, grading streets so that the city would do the
initial sewer work before the subdividers erected houses. Despite the
appropriations and the reformers' concerns sewage remained a problem.
"During the century . . . the old oaken (bacterial) bucket that hangs by
the (contaminated) well has given place to various methods of supplying
water by the use of vessels or pipes that will not decay, from sources of
water that may not become contaminated," Boston reformer Edward
Atkinson told those gathered for a three-day celebration of American
technology commemorating the centennial of the United States patent
system in 1891. Progress in sewage disposal and drainage, however, "has
not kept pace with this more abundant supply of water"; Atkinson urged
this as an "important field for future invention."

Manuals on drainage and sanitation stressed the defective engineering
of even the largest cities' systems; sewage passed through porous brickwork walls, contaminating the earth around them and often leaking into
people's cellars. Improper sewer ventilation, the books claimed, was an
even greater problem; poorly designed and improperly installed house
fixtures were said to leak "sewer gas," which at least one architectural
historian represents as a mythical substance attributable to Americans'
uneasiness about connecting their homes to public systems of any sort.
Certainly the sanitation writers of the 1870s and 1880s colored their discussions of effective drainage with lurid accounts of disease-ridden pipes
and contaminated dwellings, and entrepreneurs capitalized on public
fears with a variety of services and devices. One of these, the earth
closet—advocated by Catharine Beecher, the judges at the 1876 Philadelphia Centennial Exhibition, and sanitary writer George Waring—did

away with plumbing entirely; Beecher called it an alternative to the expense of plumbing installation and "the almost inevitable troubles and disorders of water-pipes in a house." The Centennial judges, too, commented on the inadequacies of the water closet, and Waring celebrated the earth closet's production of good fertilizer. But whatever its advantages, the earth closet's time never came, because of problems getting and disposing of the dry earth, especially in cities. Although Waring maintained that the refuse would be inoffensive and the job of the person charged with removing it unobtrusive, "the chance to get rid of human wastes through an invisible network of pipes was too attractive for most people to resist."

Most people did not yet have access to that invisible network. Women carried liquid refuse outside—dirty dishwater, cooking slops, and of course the contents of chamber pots, "the most disagreeable item in domestic labor," according to Catharine Beecher and no doubt to most of her readers, especially those caring for the sick and the aged. Some

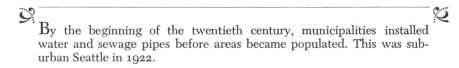

By the beginning of the twentieth century, municipalities installed water and sewage pipes before areas became populated. This was suburban Seattle in 1922.

human waste went directly outside, deposited in outdoor privies. The privies were said to cause terrible physical irregularity; with paths blocked by snowdrifts or hanging vines, people (especially women) deferred "their visits to the privy until compelled by unbearable physical discomfort" and allowed themselves "to become so constipated that days and sometimes weeks will pass between stools." Waring attributed the problem to feminine modesty and ignorance; probably it had as much to do with the awkwardness of fashionable women's clothing.

Throughout the second half of the century, a broad range of technological possibilities created an equally broad range of sanitary facilities in American households. Water could enter the household in buckets filled at private wells or springs, rivers or streams, or street hydrants, through pipes connected to public water mains, or in barrels filled by water-hauling carts. An individual household, even in a metropolitan area, might have no running water at all, or it might have a complete system with water closet and hot water in both tub and sinks. At the beginning of the Civil War, toilets and bathtubs were still luxury items; city water departments charged extra for them, above the normal water rate. Four years after the war ended, Catharine Beecher established them as the ideal for the middle-class home; the house plans in her *American Woman's Home* (1869) called for indoor plumbing, unlike the ideal plans in her 1841 *Treatise on Domestic Economy*.

The earlier plan grouped all water-using activity near the back door; these "back-door accommodations" included the kitchen sink and a bathing room, supplied by a system involving a well, a pump, and a reservoir. A two-compartment privy—not equipped with water closets—sat at the very back of the house, across from the woodpile and ashbin; "keeping the window open, and the door shut, will prevent any disagreeable effects in the house." The considerably more complex plan Beecher proposed a quarter of a century later linked running water throughout the house; it provided for two water closets (one centrally located on the second story, the other in the basement near the laundry area) and a second-story bathroom supplied by a garret reservoir, filled by means of a forcing pump in the cellar. Beecher's descriptions of both of these truly ideal plans contain hints about the more common practices of her readers. "The water-closets," she wrote in the 1869 version, "must have the latest improvements for safe discharge, and there will be no trouble. They cost no more than an out-door building, and save from the most disagreeable house-labor."

At the end of the century, Sears catered both to those with indoor plumbing and those with none. In 1897 they offered sinks, washbasins, and urinals fitted for plumbing, but no bathtubs or water closets; toilet sets—the matching pitchers and basins available today in antique stores—came either with or without slop jars and covers. Robert and Helen Lynd, the sociologists whose seminal study of "Middletown" (Muncie, Indiana) set the standard for community studies, maintain that in 1890 only about one-eighth to one-sixth of Muncie families "had even the crudest running water—a hydrant in the yard or a faucet at the iron sink. . . . For the most part, Middletown pumped its water to the back door or kitchen from a well or cistern. By 1890 there were not over two dozen complete bathrooms in the entire city." Plumbing was only slightly more common in larger cities: the United States commissioner of labor's 1893 report found that 53 percent of New York's families, 70 percent of Philadelphia's, 73 percent of Chicago's, and 88 percent of Baltimore's had access only to an outside privy.

The major development during the second half of the century came, not in plumbing for the very wealthy (who had complete systems all along) or the poor (who had none until after 1900), but in the changing middle-class concept of minimal equipment as plumbing became affordable. Harriet Beecher Stowe, for example, went to considerable trouble and expense to get "water privileges"—a sink with a pump—installed in the house she rented in Maine during the summer of 1850. She bought two large oil hogsheads from the local cotton factory to use as cisterns, but discovered when they were delivered that there was no way to get them into the cellar. "In days of chivalry," she wrote her sister-in-law, "I might have got a knight to make me a breach through the foundation walls," but those days were over, and the hogsheads, "standing disconsolately in the yard, seemed to reflect no great credit on my foresight." Finally she found "a real honest Yankee cooper" to take the hogsheads apart and reassemble them in the cellar. Then followed a month of negotiations with her neighbor and landlord John Titcomb, "a very clever, but (with reverence) somewhat lazy gentleman" not particularly interested in installing Mrs. Stowe's sink. "How many times I have been in and seated myself in one of the old rocking-chairs, and talked first of the news of the day, the railroad, the last proceedings in Congress, the probabilities about the millennium, and thus brought the conversation by little and little round to my sink!"

Landlords were no more generous about sanitary facilities in 1907, when social worker Margaret Byington studied the lives of workers at the Homestead, Pennsylvania works of United States Steel as part of the Pittsburgh Survey, a massive project undertaken by the charitable Russell Sage Foundation. Middle-class expectations, however, had changed considerably: Mrs. Stowe had demanded nothing more elaborate than one sink with one faucet supplied by a rainwater cistern, whereas Margaret Byington was appalled by back-porch water faucets and outdoor privies. A shortage of rental housing put Homestead property owners "in a position to disregard the desires of the tenants" and to rent "unimproved dwellings at profitable rentals without having to put them in good order."

An urban hydrant, southeast Washington, D.C., 1942. Office of War Information photo by Gordon Parks.

Only four of sixty-six families paying less than $5.00 a week in rent had indoor toilets; only seventeen of the fifty paying less than $3.00 even had running water. Byington, who intended to demonstrate the falsehood in "the oft repeated declaration that [these] people would not live better if they could," insisted that her facts showed their desire for houses "which in size, sanitation, and conveniences would make a normal and efficient life possible." Standards of normalcy and efficiency had changed since Mrs. Stowe's time; by the beginning of the twentieth century indoor water closets and kitchens with sinks, still luxuries to urban industrial workers and to most rural people, constituted minimal standards for a decent, normal life to a middle-class social worker.

Byington was only one of an army of social workers, sociologists, and reformers (the distinctions between these terms were blurry at that time) who attacked the problems of the poor during what has come to be known as the Progressive Era. In large cities with diverse industrial bases and in small company towns like Homestead, they trooped into the homes of the working class and the dependent poor to study their "living conditions" and "standards of living," hoping to discover a way to extirpate the vermin and the overcrowding that most of them understood as the seamy

Plumbing remained a matter of class well into the twentieth century. Here a coal miner's wife carries water from Bertha Hill, on Scott's Run, in West Virginia, 1938. Farm Security Administration photo by Marion Post Wolcott.

side of American capitalist development. In New York and Chicago as in Homestead, they kept finding that "how the other half lives" (to use the words of Jacob Riis, one of the most influential urban reformers) was terrible, especially with respect to the outrageously poor sanitary conditions. Only one of twenty-five families in the poorest group of New York workers studied by Robert Coit Chapin had a bathroom. Chapin's study, another Russell Sage project conducted in 1907–1908, specifically excluded charity-dependent families, limiting observation to families with earned income and both spouses living; only 20 percent of the entire group studied had a bathroom, only 31 percent a toilet within their apartments. By 1919, middle-class expectations had been extended even to the dependent poor; in a report prepared for the Committee on Relief of the Chicago Council of Social Agencies, social worker Florence Nesbitt set a firm standard for sanitary facilities. "There should be toilet facilities in good condition with a door which can be locked, for the use of the family alone; running water in at least one room in the house besides the toilet," she wrote. "A bath room is highly desirable and should be included wherever possible."

Well into the twentieth century, indoor plumbing remained a matter of class: the rich had it, the poor did not. The ones in the middle benefitted increasingly from the new municipal policies and from the greatest influence on the diffusion of plumbing to individual households: the industrial production of plumbing parts, which increased substantially at the end of the century. Plumbing was a luxury by its very nature as long as its manufacture as well as its installation maintained a craft status. For it to spread even to the middle class, the industry had to adopt modern methods and take its place among the industrial giants; as it did so, plumbing reached further down the income scale, bringing a former luxury to the working class. As New Hampshire cotton worker Ernest Anderson recalled many years later, he "felt just like a millionaire" upon moving to a corporation-owned tenement with modern conveniences; "we didn't have to run outside."

Many people must have felt like millionaires during the first three decades of the twentieth century, as indoor plumbing became commonplace. Sears, which in 1897 offered no bathtubs fit for plumbing fixtures, urinals but no flush water closets, and only kitchen sinks, pictured a full line eleven years later. Three complete outfits—bathtub, "closet" (toilet), and "lavatory" (sink)—ranged from $33.90 to $51.10; each fixture could be purchased separately in several styles, made of white enameled cast iron or the cheaper enameled sheet steel. The tubs had feet, since the process for mass-producing double-shelled enamel built-in tubs cast in one piece was introduced only in 1915 or 1916.

With mass production, standardization, and the installation of fixtures where before there had been none, production of enameled sanitary fix-

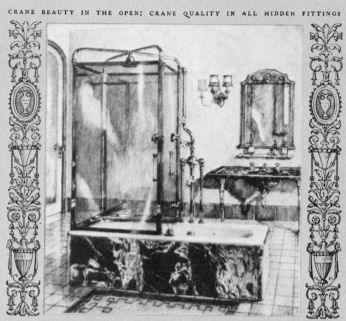

CRANE BEAUTY IN THE OPEN: CRANE QUALITY IN ALL HIDDEN FITTINGS

CRANE CRYSTAL SHOWER INCLOSED IN PLATE GLASS. SHOWN WITH TARNIA BATH SET IN BLACK AND WHITE MARBLE

THE ease with which the combined *Crystal* Shower and *Tarnia* bath can be adapted to any arrangement you desire is a great advantage in planning your bathroom.

They can be set in five positions: in a right or left corner, in an alcove, against a wall with ends free or entirely in the open, as illustrated above.

Inclosed on three sides in plate glass, the *Crystal* shower admits light and air freely, and eliminates clinging curtains yet is splash-proof.

Crane fixtures, sold only through plumbing and heating contractors, include styles within reach of all. Write for our book of color schemes, "The New Art of Fine Bathrooms."

CRANE

GENERAL OFFICES: CRANE BUILDING, 836 S. MICHIGAN AVENUE, CHICAGO
CRANE LIMITED: CRANE BUILDING, 386 BEAVER HALL SQUARE, MONTREAL

Branches and Sales Offices in One Hundred and Forty-eight Cities
National Exhibit Rooms: Chicago, New York, Atlantic City, San Francisco and Montreal
Works: Chicago, Bridgeport, Birmingham, Chattanooga, Trenton and Montreal

CRANE EXPORT CORPORATION: NEW YORK, SAN FRANCISCO, SHANGHAI
CRANE-BENNETT, LTD., LONDON
Cᵉ CRANE: PARIS, NANTES, BRUSSELS

Crane bathrooms of the mid-1920s: An advertisement for elegant fixtures from the *National Geographic*, which in 1925 had the limited audience appropriate to the ad.

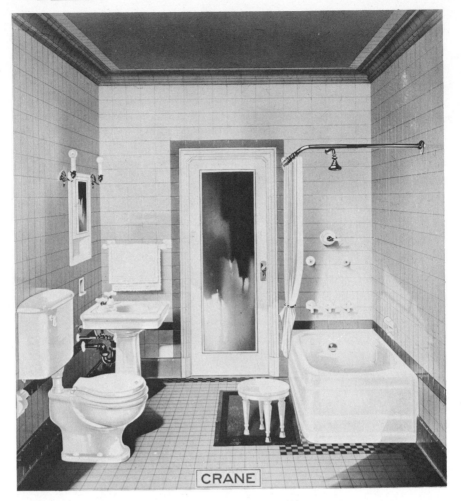

Crane bathrooms of the mid-1920s: Sketch for the bathroom for a more typical United States home, about 1927.

tures boomed after World War I, more than doubling between 1921 and 1925. By the late 1920s, surveys indicated that indoor plumbing had left the luxury category. In 1926, 91 percent of all the houses in Zanesville, Ohio, had running water; 61 percent had complete plumbing systems. Only about 7 percent of the small wage earners studied by the Chicago Department of Public Welfare in 1925 still had to go outside to use the toilet, although many had to leave their apartments to use a shared bathroom. Many of their bathtubs had only a cold-water tap, and frozen pipes rendered all facilities useless for long periods; conditions for these stockyard, railroad, factory, and service workers, 44 percent of whom were black and 17 percent Mexican-born, had improved only slightly over those for workers of the previous decades. Urban-rural differences continued to matter as well; the President's Conference on Home Building and Home Ownership reported that 71 percent of urban families surveyed and 33 percent of rural ones had bathrooms in the late 1920s.

As in the nineteenth century, money and access to public water continued to determine individual families' plumbing well into the twentieth; the range of possible water sources and available fixtures continued to be broad, and wealthier people living in more expensive urban housing had more complete plumbing systems. Still, the class nature of indoor plumbing shifted further down the income scale during the new century's first decades, and most people had running water by the time the Depression slowed economic expansion. They bought their fixtures and paid city water departments for their water; like food and energy, water had become a purchased commodity, controlled by municipal decisions and those of the manufacturers who produced plumbing parts on a mass scale. As with those other commodities, industrial production raised the American standard of living, providing people the means for cleaner, healthier bodies, clothes, and houses.

Technologically feasible for nearly a century before most people could afford it, indoor plumbing, and the mass production that made it possible, changed American household routine. Permitting women to stay inside their houses, it both softened the harsh effects of the seasons and deprived housewives of the interaction with their neighbors that they had found around the well, the hydrant, and the spring. They lost that social life along with the staggering burden of water-related work that had dominated their days as they hauled clean water into their houses and lugged slops out of them, hoisted buckets and basins to and from hot stoves, and maintained the household supplies of water for drinking, washing, and laundry.

SIX

Blue Monday

O f all the household chores that depended on hauling water and building fires to heat it, laundry earned the most complaints from nineteenth-century housewives and the writers who advised them. Rachel Haskell, the Nevada diarist, called it "the Herculean task which women all dread" and "the great domestic dread of the household"; she complained of her aching back and "hands too tender to sew" and "thought I should not attempt to do this another week but suppose when the day comes shall do so rather than send clothes up town." Nearly every writer of household advice made the same point: laundry should not be a one-woman job. Catharine Beecher called it "the American housekeeper's hardest problem" and advocated its removal from household routine, despite her general stance promoting housework as women's "proper profession." From all available evidence— how-to manuals, budget studies of poor people's households, diaries—it appears that women jettisoned laundry, their most hated task, whenever they had any discretionary money at all. Although their solutions varied, even women of limited means sought relief in the form of washerwomen, commercial laundries, and mechanical aids.

Without running water, gas, or electricity, even the most simplified hand-laundry process consumed staggering amounts of time and labor. One wash, one boiling, and one rinse used about fifty gallons of water—or four hundred pounds—which had to be moved from pump or well or faucet to stove and tub, in buckets and wash boilers that might weigh as much as forty or fifty pounds. Rubbing, wringing, and lifting water-laden clothes and linens, including large articles like sheets, tablecloths, and men's heavy work clothes, wearied women's arms and wrists and exposed them to caustic substances. They lugged weighty tubs and baskets full of wet laundry outside, picked up each article, hung it on the line, and returned to take it all down; they ironed by heating several irons on the stove and alternating them as they cooled, never straying far from the hot stove.

Without miracle fabrics, washing machines, or detergents, getting clothes really clean was a complicated process, described in almost identical detail by Catharine Beecher in 1841 and Helen Campbell forty years later as the "common mode of washing." Sort the clothes first by color, fabric, and degree of soil, they suggested, and soak them overnight in separate tubs full of warm water; with few soaps or washing fluids, overnight soaking saved "considerable labor." The next morning, drain off that water and pour hot suds on the finest clothes. (Beecher suggested wringing them out from this first suds bath, then throwing them into another tub of hot suds, but one wash water was sufficient for Campbell.) Wash each article in that suds bath, rubbing it against the washboard. Wring them out, rub soap on the most soiled spots, then cover them with water in the boiler on the stove and "boil them up." (Beecher suggested "moving them about, with the wash-stick, to keep them from getting yellow in spots" during the boiling. Although Campbell, like everybody else, recommended some boiling, she emphasized that a short scalding would suffice; "long boiling does not improve clothes.") Take them out of the boiler, rub dirty spots again, rinse in plain water, wring out, rinse again in water with bluing, wring very dry, dip the articles to be stiffened in starch, and wring once more. Hang clothes on the line until perfectly dry.

Woman washing clothes outside, between Charleston and Gauley Bridge, West Virginia, 1938. Farm Security Administration photo by Marion Post Wolcott.

And while that load is on the line, *repeat the entire process* on progressively coarser and dirtier loads of clothes.

It took all day. Monday was traditional because most people changed their clothes on Sunday and the operation could be eased by washing "before dirt has had time to harden in the fiber of the cloth." Campbell hinted that Tuesday might be better because it allowed for preparation on Monday, saving Sunday as a day of rest; otherwise the tubs could be filled on Saturday night and warmed on Sunday night with just a bit more hot water, in preparation for a Monday washing. Although some women may have rebelled at the tradition—one California woman recalled that her mother "said she'd wash on the day she wanted to, so she did"—most, at least in towns, found a whole community of women outside on Mon-

The evolution of the washing machine, from Benjamin Butterworth's *The Growth of Industrial Art*, 1888. The model shown in #8 was the most popular, imitating the hand and washboard by rubbing the clothes between two curved surfaces.

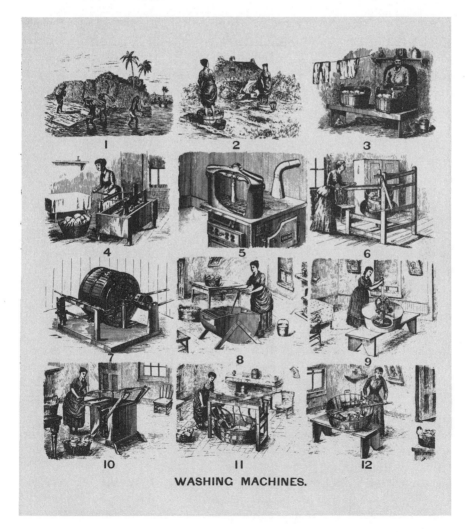

WASHING MACHINES.

days, gossiping in groups "awaiting their turn at the pump" and hanging laundry on adjacent lines, displaying (and competing about) their skills and their pride in their craft. Every other household chore suffered on washday; washday meals consisted of whatever was easiest, and a good husband would "eat a cold dinner on washday without grumbling."

Ironing usually consumed the day after washday. First the dry clothes had to be dampened: Campbell suggested either sprinkling them with the hand or "shaking over them a small whisk-broom which is dipped as needed in water." Rolled in a cloth and left to sit for one to twelve hours (depending on the kind of material and the person giving the advice), they awaited ironing. Three to six irons, each rubbed with beeswax and wiped before each use, stayed hot on a piece of sheet iron set on a hearth "free from cinders and ashes," or, later in the century, on a stove; cast-iron stoves must have saved many a woman from the irritation and extra work of clothes soiled by sooty irons. Every iron fresh from the fire had to be tried on a piece of paper or spare cloth to be sure that it would not scorch the cloth. Large articles were ironed on tables, covered with a woolen ironing blanket and then a linen or cotton ironing sheet; for smaller items, both Beecher and Campbell recommended a bosom-board, which raised the fronts of shirts from the regular ironing surface, and a skirt-board. "This," wrote Beecher in 1841, "is a board five feet long, two feet wide at one end, tapering to one foot and four inches wide at the other," the large end resting on a table and the small one on a chair; "it saves much trouble, in ironing the skirts of dresses, and enables the ironer to do them quicker and better." By 1894, Montgomery Ward offered three different folding ironing boards: one standard kind that came in six sizes, one "adjustable to standing or sitting position," and a third that could double as a stepladder. Fluting, crimping, and ruffling irons for fancy work were available as early as Beecher's 1841 book.

Beecher's and Campbell's descriptions provide a picture of an ideal laundry practice. Undoubtedly many women economized with fewer soakings and rinses, but the many additional hints for particular stains and particular fabrics suggest that this might be done only at the cost of having dirty clothes, for even the complicated ideal procedure left some things less than immaculate. Without miracle fabrics, ironing was more than an optional finishing touch; heavier irons, weighing eight or ten pounds, made the work go faster and "would really get the pressing done." Even the most pared-down version of the laundry routine demanded an enormous amount of hard, hot, heavy work—hoisting the irons, hauling heavy tubs full of hot water and wet clothes, rubbing, wringing, and bending down for clothes to hang on the line. The burden was severe in both heat and cold: in summer, when the temperature exacerbated the heat from the laundry, and in winter, when frigid conditions often made the water hauling and the hanging intolerable. No wonder Rachel Haskell complained of her aching back and raw hands; no wonder she considered paying for help with the laundry even though her daughter Ella did the ironing.

Laundry help came in three principal forms, all of them illustrating significant trends in the history of housework, and in the history of work in general. More hands, the first and most obvious, could mean either an unpaid helper like Ella or a hired laundress. The most common kind of domestic servants throughout most of the nineteenth century, laundresses worked either "in" or "out"—that is, either at their employers' homes or their own—even for families in no financial position to afford general houseworkers. The second option, the commercial laundry, evolved from the individual laundress who worked for many families in her own home. Industrialization of laundry work, like the industrialization of other processes, spawned technological advance; most of the labor-saving laundry devices—the third form of relief—first appeared in commercial laundries, later being marketed for home use.

Laundresses who "came in" to their employers' homes tended to be the poorest of the women who did laundry for pay; they sacrificed the independence of working in their own homes, usually because they lacked the equipment to do so. They hired themselves out to well-equipped households that could afford such specialized servants, usually extremely wealthy families that already had a general household servant. Working women preferred laundry work to general housework because it generally did not require living in; they could live where and with whom they chose. Precisely these objections to domestic service induced many women to opt for longer hours, harder work, and lower pay in factories.

More commonly, women who made money doing other people's laundry took it into their own homes. Colonial newspapers ran advertisements from women who offered fine laundering, starching, dyeing, and cloth-glazing services to fashionable ladies. By the middle of the nineteenth century, independent laundresses catered to a much broader clientele. In the West, they served single men of all classes. One woman wrote from California in 1854 that a friend could make her fortune in dressmaking, or do quite well taking in laundry: "Just as much as you can do all the time cash down when they take the cloths the is a lady lives close by me that take in washing . . . she makes from 15 to 20 dollars a week washing when she has all she wants to do so you can see that women stand as good chance as men." Despite the inflated prices in the gold fields—fifteen or twenty dollars a week did not go far—there were customers galore and an independent living to be made; one Nevada woman reminisced that "the washing was too much for me, and wore me out very fast, but I could not give it up just yet." Back east, taking in laundry offered a way for women to earn money without leaving their homes and their small children; it also provided a way for other women (and not necessarily wealthy ones)

Wringing clothes—a task mechanized, then electrified, and finally eliminated. This is John Eshe's daughter, posing in 1923 for a home economics exhibit sponsored by the Agricultural Extension Division of International Harvester Corporation, Chicago.

to purchase a hand with their housework without hiring a full-time domestic servant.

Women who took in laundry had even more autonomy than those who worked in their employers' homes; working under their own supervision, they made independent decisions about starting, stopping, and timing their work and about the details of the work process, what kind of soap to use or how hot the water should be. They could fit laundry work into their own household chores, or even—like Mary Mathews, a widow with a small child who made money teaching, sewing, and taking in laundry during the 1870s—into other paid employment. "I got up early every Monday morning," she later wrote, "and got my clothes all washed and boiled and in the rinsing water; then commenced my school at nine." At noon and after supper she sewed, often "till twelve and one o'clock at night. . . . Tuesday morning I had my clothes on the line by daylight, and my breakfast ready." She starched at noon Tuesday, ironed "as many of them as I could" after school, and finished the ironing at night. "Then I had the rest of the week to sew in. . . ." She used all the money she saved from this grueling schedule to invest in stock, and later in a boarding-house, where she worked just as hard, doing laundry for twenty-six boarders, sewing sheets and pillowcases, and making repairs, again "working every night till twelve and one o'clock."

The individual laundress's autonomy eventually faded in the workplace

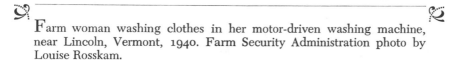

Farm woman washing clothes in her motor-driven washing machine, near Lincoln, Vermont, 1940. Farm Security Administration photo by Louise Rosskam.

of the commercial laundry, almost unknown in 1860 and a major employer of female industrial labor fifty years later. Like shoemaking or clothes production, laundry went through the seemingly inevitable stages of economic development, as it progressed from home industry through the craft stage represented by the individual laundress to the industrial operation performed in the commercial laundry, where entrepreneurs could profit from economies of scale and the division of labor. Catharine Beecher noted this economic process in 1869. Soap and candles used to be made at home, she wrote; now they had entered the craft stage—"we buy soap of the soap-maker, and candles of the candle-factor"—and laundry could be put there, too. "How would it simplify the burdens of the American housekeeper to have washing and ironing day expunged from her calendar!" If all the money that each family spent on equipment, fuel, and soap "were united in a fund to create a laundry for every dozen families, one or two good women could do in first rate style what now is very indifferently done by the disturbance and disarrangement of all other domestic processes in these families." This suggestion, antithetical to the rest of Beecher's work, may be taken as testament to the trials of home laundry for the nineteenth-century housewife. Her major mission, "redeeming woman's profession from dishonor," as she put it, elevated the status of housework by training middle-class women to do their own work well instead of entrusting it to domestic servants. Apparently she believed that middle-class women would never give up their servants if they had to do the laundry.

Beecher's solution to the laundry problem took clothes washing from the home-industry stage to the craft stage. "Cooperative Housekeeping," a series of articles by Melusina Fay Peirce published in the *Atlantic Monthly* in 1869 (the same year *The American Woman's Home* appeared), took both the suggestion and the analysis of the industrial development of housework to further extremes. Peirce believed that resources should be pooled in formally organized cooperative societies, which would hire the "one or two good women" who actually did the laundry as regular employees of the women whose laundry they did. She proposed a woman-controlled transition, not from home production to a crafts stage, but to the industrial production of clean clothes.

Peirce herself directed the laundry in the short-lived experiment of the Cambridge Cooperative Housekeeping Society, a group of elite women in Cambridge, Massachusetts, which she organized within a few months after her articles appeared. The society lasted less than a year after the laundry and the store opened (the proposed cooperative kitchen never did); only twelve of the forty member households actually patronized the operation. Peirce later attributed the failure to "HUSBAND-POWER which is very apt to shut down like an invisible bell-glass over every woman as soon as she is married."

A more successful group of cooperative laundries later harnessed "HUSBAND-POWER" by exploiting the husbands' own cooperative efforts; some Midwestern dairy cooperatives utilized the water supplies and the steam plants already operating in their creameries to do laundry for the cooperating families. At the Milltown Cooperative Creamery Company in Wisconsin, fifty families' loads of clothes could be washed in forty-five minutes, dried, and ironed with mangles. "So far," wrote the *Wisconsin Agriculturalist* in 1914, "nothing has been shown in disfavor or opposition to the plan."

In 1914, however, the dairy cooperatives' laundries were simply a rural equivalent to the well-established and widespread urban commercial laundry industry. Although the first power laundries appeared in the 1830s in Troy, New York, washing only the detachable shirt collars for which Troy was famous, the commercial laundry industry remained in its infancy until after the Civil War, expanding rapidly throughout the rest of the century. They generally laundered only men's shirts, collars, and cuffs ("bachelor bundles") and flatwork; primarily hotels and boarding-houses patronized the flatwork services, although some individual house-holds sent sheets and tablecloths, especially if they had no washtubs large enough to hold them. By the first decade of the twentieth century, social workers who investigated family budgets found that even some of the poorest people in the urban slums sent out some of their wash, presum-ably because they lacked the equipment for washing large items in tene-ment apartments or doing an adequate job on men's collars and cuffs. In 1909, power laundries grossed over $100 million, an average of $5.30 per American household, or about 10 cents per week. These figures, of course, include the hotel and boardinghouse laundry; most families spent much less. A Russell Sage Foundation study published that year found that 60 percent of the 391 New York City workingmen's families studied spent at least some money on laundry service. About three-quarters of these fami-lies spent less than the 10-cent national average, the proportion who spent more increasing as income rose. The report's author, Robert Coit Chapin, proposed 5 cents weekly in his model budget, providing at least for collars and cuffs (although these constituted "Sunday best" for workingmen, who usually went collarless), and occasionally, for the heaviest family linens.

With this widespread use, commercial laundries became a major source of jobs for the single women who had always composed a part of the industrial work force. Unlike the work of individual laundresses, theirs had all the earmarks of industrial labor: they had definite hours, deter-mined by their bosses; they worked in commercial establishments, not at home; they labored in groups, not alone. Supervised closely by a boss, they worked not as "laundresses" but as stackers or folders or pressers, as industrial establishments subdivided the craft for reasons of efficiency. Commercial laundry workers lived like factory workers; no longer could

Washing day, Pacific coast, 1908, from Clifton Johnson, *Highways and Byways of the Pacific Coast*.

An avenue of clothes washings between 138th and 139th Street apartments, just east of Saint Anne's Avenue, The Bronx, New York City, 1936. Farm Security Administration photo by Russell Lee.

women combine paid laundry work with other moneymaking activities or with their own housework and child care. Movement from the craft stage to the industrial stage, therefore, destroyed a major arena for married women's paid work.

Laundry did not pass through the stages of economic development in precisely the same way as shoemaking or clothes production; unlike those industries, commercial laundries provided a service, not a product, and (partly because they rarely did a family's entire washload) they eventually found themselves in competition with another industry that did offer a product: washing machines. Ironically, the commercial laundries' success had spurred the technical innovation that resulted in labor-saving devices for the home; like the processes for canning food, those for machine washing, invented for commercial use, reached the household only belatedly. The earliest clothes-washing machines imitated the motion of the human hand on the washboard, using a lever to move one curved surface over another, rubbing clothes between the two surfaces, each ribbed like a washboard. Based on longstanding British precedents and first patented in the United States in 1846, this type of washer survived as late as 1927, when it appeared in the Montgomery Ward catalogue as "Our Famous 'Old Faithful,'" and in the Sears catalogue as "The Quick and Easy Washer." While this rubbing principle was certainly time-tested, commercial laundries found it unsuitable, since each article had to be fed individually through the machine. Their large-scale laundry operations prompted entirely new principles for washing-machine design: steam cleaning, agitating the clothes in soapy water, and containing the wash within two concentric cylinders.

The thousands of patents issued for washing machines during the nineteenth century described all of these principles, and some that never caught on at all. Most of these machines never washed a shirt, for they were never produced. Although most of the machines that actually existed operated in commercial laundries, home machines began to appear immediately following the Civil War. The Union Washing Machine and Clothes Wringer, advertised in the *Atlantic* in 1866, would fit any tub; its makers claimed it would wash "without soaking, rubbing or boiling."

Most models, however, dispensed only with the rubbing; the few who owned them saved little time and not much labor. At the end of the century, Sears and Montgomery Ward each offered four washing machines. The Anthony Wayne, the Western Star, the Sears Electric (so called for its electrically welded wire hoops), and Ward's New Combination Washer all circulated soapy water through the clothes with hand-cranked agitators, after an overnight soaking and an initial boiling, and before a regular rinse and a bluing rinse. They cost $2.50 to $4.25. For $5.50 at Sears and $6.00 at Ward's, customers could buy Cline's Improved Steam Washer, with the "decided advantage" of "a faucet attached to the

boiler for removing the water without lifting the boiler from the stove."
The only model based on the concentric-cylinder principle, this machine
contained a cranked cylinder that turned inside the boiler sitting on top of
the stove. Sears printed directions for the Anthony Wayne and Western
Star models in the catalogue, calling for as much water hauling as Beecher's and Campbell's hand-washing directions. Sears also offered six wringers at $1.30 to $3.00, one expensive one celebrated for its ball-bearing
arrangement ("Turns with half the strength required for others") and
another a combination wringer and bench ("With the ordinary tub
wringer it is about as much work to hold the tub as to turn the wringer").
The highest-quality washboard still cost 20 cents.

The catalogue instructions for using the machines recommended both
soap and a special Anthony Wayne Washing Fluid with appended recipe
(potash, salts of tartar, ammonia, and hot water). Most women used
caustics of various strengths—lye, sal soda, lime, and borax—and rinsed
the clothes carefully in several changes of water to keep them from developing holes. Craftspeople, as Beecher suggested, sold soap during the
middle of the century as the soap industry developed and home manufacture died out. Bluing and starch, on the market commercially in the
1870s, were more easily and more commonly homemade. The same national market that developed prepared foods developed the cleaning-
products industry at the end of the century, spurred by the expanding
distribution system and by the growing industries—meat packing and
cottonseed-oil manufacture—of which soap was a by-product. Before the
turn of the century, several brand-name general-purpose soaps (Ivory,
Sapolio, Gold Dust, and Borax) had wide distribution; many lesser-
known soaps appeared on the market in limited geographical areas. Until
Lux Flakes (advertised for delicate fabrics) appeared in 1906, all soaps
marketed specifically for laundry came in bars, to be cut up or scraped
before use. Rinso, the first granulated general laundry soap, introduced in
1918, preceded many other brands that appeared in the early 1920s.

The granulated soaps were developed for use in electric washing machines, which first appeared for home use around 1914, causing an immediate expansion of the washing-machine industry. The earliest models
of the "wringer machines" still available, these nonautomatic machines
reduced labor more than time; although the operator no longer had to
crank the machine (and could even leave the room while the laundry
agitated), she had to start and stop it, add soap, add and remove water,
and put each item through the wringer. For those with the required
plumbing (often hot running water as well as cold) and draining facilities, electric machines lightened the washday burden: water running into
one tub eliminated all the heavy lifting, and electrically powered agita-
tion did away with hand cranking and washboard scrubbing.

Because of these advantages and the concurrent expansion of electricity

Ironing with flatirons, from a Kingsford's Oswego Starch advertising card. Salesmen for most late nineteenth-century consumer products offered such cards, often depicting scenes unrelated to the product.

and plumbing, electric machines caught on quickly, expanding the washing-machine industry as a whole and nearly exterminating the hand-cranked versions. In 1921, seven years after their first appearance on the market, 70 percent of 416,000 new washing machines were electric; by 1929, on the eve of the Depression, 84 percent of the 1,134,000 new machines were powered by electricity. The washing-machine industry boomed, producing in 1929 more than six times the value of the machines manufactured in 1914; measured in constant dollars, this figure accounts for inflation. Although by no means universal at the end of the 1920s, electric washers had stopped being oddities; more than a quarter of the nonfarm households with electricity had washers.

In response to this competition, commercial laundries began to offer a greater variety of services after 1915. "Damp wash" came back from the laundry with flatwork ironed and wearing apparel damp; "flat ironed" laundry was all run through the mangle; "rough dry" instructions returned the flatwork ironed and the wearing apparel starched and dry; "economy" or "fluff dry" wearing apparel was dry but not starched; and "finished family wash," the traditional commercial laundry service, sent everything back ready to wear. The laundry owners' trade association dispatched speakers to women's luncheon clubs to celebrate the benefits of these services; one such talk emphasized the scientific research that had produced superior methods at commercial laundries and the freedom "from a task which lessens woman's ability to guard the true interests of her home—the health and education of her children and the unwearied companion-

Happy "laundry girls" posed for Kirkman's Borax Soap, 1891.

HAPPY · LAUNDRY · GIRLS.

"Do we look cheerful? Washing clothes is pretty hard work generally, but if you use KIRKMAN'S BORAX SOAP according to directions, it's really wonderful how it lightens labor and, besides, it makes the clothes as sweet as a rose and as white as snow."

ship and encouragement of her husband." Likewise, the washing-machine manufacturers pitched their advertisements against the power laundries. At least twice, in 1927 and 1933, the two trade associations negotiated agreements to cut down on unscrupulous advertising attacks on each other's members.

Commercial laundries eventually lost the competition; economist Heidi Hartmann attributes the washing machine's victory to several important economic factors. Although the commercial laundry industry started out with more firms, more employees, and higher total receipts, she writes, it "remained highly decentralized, geographically dispersed, and relatively small scale." In the washing-machine industry, "concentration appears to have increased over time," as firms grew and production centered in the industrial Midwest. Controlling patents through holding companies, the largest washing-machine manufacturers used that power and their market position "to extract direct financial benefits from other firms, to encourage mergers, and to maintain prices." The many small power laundries remained technologically backward: 6,776 small commercial laundries, employing an average of 38 people in 1929 and taking in an average of about $77,000 each, simply could not adopt new methods as easily as 65 closely situated and aggressively controlled washing-machine manufacturers, which had an average of 153 employees and took in an average of $1.4 million each. Nor could the commercial laundries centralize in imitation of their competition; providing a frequent service rather than a product, they had to remain small and close to their customers. Nobody cared where their washing machines were made or how long they traveled from the factory to the store, whereas commercial laundry customers wanted their clothes back soon. Unable to benefit from new technology, economies of scale, and centralized production, commercial laundries raised their prices during the 1920s, as the price of washing machines fell. Commercial laundry service for home use, Hartmann maintains, peaked in 1929, although the industry continued to grow thanks to dry-cleaning services and to increased industrial laundry use. Washing-machine production and sales grew much faster, even during the Depression; after World War II, when the automatic washer was introduced, the washing machine achieved unquestionable victory.

This victory seems on the surface to present a unique situation in the history of industrialized housework, and a raw deal for the housewife, who might have been relieved of laundry chores forever had commercial laundries won the competition. A job once performed at home, substantially commercialized before 1929, heading out of the household, bound for the social realm like weaving and soapmaking and all the other traditional household skills, went back home. Once again, the individual housewife—this time using her own washing machine or hauling her wash to the laundromat instead of sweltering with the old-fashioned washboard and boiler—did all the laundry, unable to take advantage of the economies of scale and division of labor recommended in Beecher's and Peirce's proposals as early as 1869. The general trend from home industry through the craft stage to industrialization is such a fundamental feature of the last two centuries of capitalist economic development that it is hard to imagine another such example of a task returning to the household once it had left it. Yet the image exaggerates the facts, since commercial laundry service actually supplemented home washing. The victory for home laundry products—and not for housewives—demonstrates more about the normal processes of a capitalist economy than it contradicts.

Although nearly everybody sent *some* laundry out during the first three decades of the twentieth century, most women still did most of their wash at home. In 1919, a government investigation establishing a "minimum level of health and decency" for a worker's family added its weight to the bulk of complaints about the impossibility of this chore for the individual housewife in an unmechanized household. "It would seem unreasonable," the analysts wrote, to expect a housewife to do all the laundry herself, on top of all the cooking, cleaning, sewing and mending, and marketing. "Expenditure in assistance with laundry work may not be considered possible in the family of an industrial worker," but "from the standpoint of health" they recommended it. Acknowledging the "almost universal" practice of sending the husband's collars and cuffs to the steam laundry, they advocated hiring an assistant for $104 per year rather than increasing the laundry order. Power laundries simply never competed for the whole family washload.

For the women who laundered at home, the electric washing machine was a heavy financial investment that could cut their labor substantially and reduce their dependence on hired help. Like other industrial products, washing machines—and eventually, clothes dryers—altered daily and weekly routine, depriving housewives at the same time of the compensations of their arduous work. No longer gossiping at the hydrant or competing over the clothesline on Mondays, modern women draw water and dry their clothes in the isolated privacy of their own homes, on any day they like; others lug their laundry to the commercial laundromat, choosing if they can the hours when the laundromat is least crowded and they will not have to compete to use the machinery. Like other industrial products, the machines helped to raise the standard of living; more people have more clean clothes with less work than ever before, a change benefitting poor people more than those who have always had the money for help with the laundry. Modern equipment has clearly released women from the woes of Rachel Haskell, who wore herself out weekly. Even though standards of cleanliness rose with the active intervention of advertising, the advantages balance the stupidity of guilt about "ring around the collar."

Advertising helped to increase housewives' dependence on the organized economy, substituting repairmen and the factory workers who made commercial laundry products and synthetic fabrics for the old-style independent washerwoman. Without the new products, the machines were either useless or inferior to traditional laundering; caustics and bluing and soaking and boiling worked better than detergents and machines on natural fabrics. Home laundering—which encompassed not only the washing-machine industry but those that produced detergents, textiles, electrical parts, and plumbing supplies—demonstrates the interconnections between segments of the economy that facilitated its continual expansion; that expansion depended also on the waste of labor and raw materials involved in producing a mass of individual machines, each of which sits idle most of the time.

In providing a way out of the nineteenth-century laundry dilemma, American corporations and their investors naturally gave more weight to their own profits than to the possible advantages of commercial laundry

Real laundry workers at an unidentified laundry, possibly in Boston, around 1905. Currier photo.

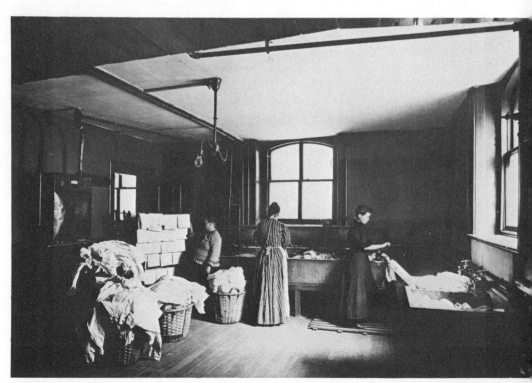

Star Steam Laundry.

LINDOW BROS., Props.

417 GRAND AVENUE, OPPOSITE PUBLIC LIBRARY.

TELEPHONE 1509.

Mark _H39_   Milwaukee,_____   _Dec 5 1891_

Mr _____ _Hinckley_ _____

Bill _30_

PRICE LIST.

..... Shirts. Plain...10c ....

...... " Fancy, or with collar.......15 to 25c ....

...... Collars ....3c ....

...... " Cape or Fancy...................3 to 8c ....

...... Cuffs, per pair..............................5c ....

...... Handkerchiefs..............................3c ....

...... " Silk....................................5c ....

...... Undershirts....................................8c ....

...... Drawers ....8c ....

...... Socks, per pair ....5c ....

..... Night Shirts..................................10c ....

...... Overalls........ ....10 to 15c ....

...... Jackets.................................10 to 15c ....

...... Towels ....3 to 8c ....

..... Sheets..... ....8 to 10c ....

..... Vests.................................15 to 25c ....

...... Coats...............................20 to 50c ....

....

....

....

" Promptness and First-Class Work," our motto.
NO CLAIMS ALLOWED UNLESS MADE WITHIN ONE WEEK, AND ACCOMPANIED BY OUR ORIGINAL LIST.

BREITHAUPT & SONTAG, Printers, Cor. E. Water and Mason

Laundry list, Milwaukee, Wisconsin, 1891.

service for the housewife. The washing-machine industry consisted of large firms, centrally organized, which could and did settle in the Midwestern heartland of heavy industry, taking better advantage of economies of scale, technological advances, and the division of labor than the smaller companies of the commercial laundry industry. Many small individual machines offered more profits than a few large industrial ones, and established a greater dependence on the expanding consumer economy. Individual home-laundry machines were neither the sole nor the inevitable industrial solution to that "most trying part of domestic labor"; rather, with household electricity and the electric machines that provided genuine competition to commercial laundries, home laundry offered the more advantageous area of investment to profit-seeking investors and manufacturers.

Laundry is not the only activity initially commercialized as a mass service and later individualized and isolated for greater profit and economic growth; mass transportation has given way to individual automobiles, and mass entertainment in vaudeville and movies to private television reception. Yet despite the individual benefits of televisions and cars and washing machines, consumers suffer from the personal effects of isolation in both work and play, increasingly conscious of the social effects of corporate inattention to ecological questions. As Beecher and Peirce pointed out over a century ago, commercial laundries offered an application of the industrial principles of economies of scale and the division of labor that could have saved on women's work time, on water and the energy that goes to heat it, and on the labor time and raw materials that go toward producing equipment usually left sitting idle. But socially provided laundry could not succeed in an economy that depended on growth and rewarded socially wasteful decisions for their profitability.

Neither commercial laundries nor washing-machine manufacturers, however, offered equally advantageous substitute employment for the women who took in extra laundry to make money during the nineteenth century. These women, practicing their trade as most craftspeople did before industrialization, could work at home, caring for their children or attending to other household tasks while the wash boiled or the clothes dried on the line; free of bosses, they could set their own pace and step outside for momentary relief from the heat. Commercial laundry work had all the hallmarks of other industrial labor; most of the women who worked in laundries before 1900 were single, like most women factory workers. Married women who wanted to make money at home had other options: producing farm products to sell at market, sewing for other women, doing piecework for manufacturers, and taking in boarders. Like laundry, these options contracted around the turn of the twentieth century, as factory production and factory-style labor conquered more areas of traditional life.

SEVEN

A Stitch in Time

While most other household tasks remained in the home throughout the nineteenth century, the processes of making clothes—spinning and weaving cloth, and designing, cutting, and sewing garments—moved to the factory during this time. American industrialization started in the New England textile industry; that industry's story, as its classic history puts it, "is the story of the industrialization of America," for it "brought the factory sys-

tem to the United States and furnished the laboratory wherein were
worked out industrial methods characteristic of the nation." First spinning, then weaving, then clothing manufacture progressed through the
stages of economic development, from home production for home use
through the independent crafts stage to industrial manufactures, affecting
all classes of people long before the century's close: almost everybody
could and most people did buy ready-made fabric and men's clothing.
Producing clothes for the family, once grueling, never-ending productive
labor that was compensated in part by a mission of love, a sense of craft
satisfaction, and the sharing of a community of women, now became a
task of consumption. By 1900, industrialization had cheapened textiles,
altered the standard of living, relieved most women from the burden of
making their husband's clothing, and provided them with a tool—the
sewing machine—for making their own and their children's clothes and
for earning money.

Throughout the colonial period and the first years of the new nation,
women made most of the nation's cloth in their homes. They cultivated
fields of flax and raised sheep. In the laborious prespinning processes, they
used tools and methods dating back to Biblical times, shearing their
sheep, carding their wool, harvesting, soaking, pounding, and combing
their flax, producing long parallel fibers that could be spun. On spinning
wheels made and sold by local or itinerant craftsmen, they drew out the
fibers, twisting them together into a continuous thread and winding it
onto bobbins; they warped their looms (more expensive and less common
than spinning wheels) and wove the yarn into homespun wool, linen, or
the combination linsey-woolsey. Coarse and unbleached, or finely spun,
carefully dyed, and closely woven, these fabrics covered their beds and
(cut and sewed by hand) kept their bodies warm. As late as 1810, Secretary of the Treasury Albert Gallatin estimated that two-thirds of the
clothing and house linens nonurban Americans used—and almost everybody *did* live outside cities—was "the product of family manufactures."

Independent craftspeople made some of the remainder or specialized in
some part of the process; most towns, for example, had carding mills
where women brought their wool to be carded by machine, usually paying the miller in wool. Housewives who sold yarn or cloth they did not
need became independent craftspeople, selling at market, on consignment
at shops in town, or to weavers who bought homespun thread and sold
finished cloth. Other weavers took in yarn and sold only their services,
returning the fabric to the woman who spun the yarn; itinerant weavers
carried their looms and brought news and gossip from house to house.
Others established themselves in towns, with permanent shops, apprentices, and sometimes additional employees. Seamstresses designed, cut,
and sewed women's and children's clothes; the most fashionable were
called "mantua-makers" well into the nineteenth century, probably after
mantua silk, as the mantua itself (a loose gown) had long since passed

out of fashion. Their work arrangements varied: some did only the designing and cutting, leaving all the sewing or just the finishing to their customers, and they might work at home, come into their customers' homes,
or (like other town craftspeople) run large establishments with hired help
or apprenticed labor. Men's tailors usually worked in shops, sometimes
alongside the women's clothiers, and made the whole garment. Most
artisans lived near or above their shops and most apprentices lived with
their masters and mistresses; they worked indefinite hours, divided be-

Flax wheel, Mount Pisgah, North Carolina. Photo by William A. Barnhill.

tween their craftswork and their housework. Except in the largest towns, craftspeople usually farmed, practicing their craft in the winter or squeezing it in between farm chores. Full-time professional craftspeople acquired status in their communities; they handled money (although they often also took barter), erected large buildings to house several workers, supervised other people's work, and operated in their trades independent of the farmers' seasons, the slaves' overseers, and the hired laborers' bosses.

So did the merchants who sold imported textiles, the third alternative to homespun and weavers' cloth. Most Northern farmers, frontier folk, and slaves wore simple clothes made of homespun, but finer and more expensive imported fabrics prevailed wherever people had the money and valued fashion. Town dwellers, North and South, and Southern planters' families paraded in fashionable garments cut from English cloth. England depended on the colonial market for its manufactured goods, importing tobacco, indigo, ships' timbers, and (in the later period) cotton from the American colonies, thereby providing the colonists with the money to buy finished products. The mother country imposed a variety of laws, taxes, and regulations designed to suppress colonial manufactures and maintain this dependent relationship, including restrictions on importing the new textile machinery that was creating the English industrial revolution during the decades before the American colonies declared their independence.

By law, this machinery—James Hargreave's spinning jenny (1767), Richard Arkwright's water frame (1769), Samuel Crompton's spinning mule (1779), and Edmund Cartwright's power loom (1785)—could not leave England, nor could designs and drawings that showed how to build it, or even skilled textile craftsmen who carried that knowledge in their heads. Enthusiasts for American manufactures smuggled designs when they could, first for spinning machinery and, beginning in 1814, for weaving machinery as well; these early entrepreneurs established factories while waging an ideological battle, spearheaded by Alexander Hamilton, maintaining that manufacturing should become the basis for American economic and social well-being and that the government should enact policies to protect and promote it.

The first successful American factory, Samuel Slater's Rhode Island spinning mill established in Providence in 1790, depended on women's and children's labor; entire families hired themselves out, lived in company housing, and worked for wages paid in credit at the company store. Because Slater's firm sold finished cloth, it also used the "putting-out" system: independent hand weavers, working in their own homes and shops, took Slater's yarn on consignment, selling it back to the company as finished textiles. "Putting out," a distinct stage in the development of nearly every industry, had different characteristics at different times and

in different industries. Some craftspeople owned their own tools; some
had to buy the raw materials from the manufacturer or from a shopkeeper
who acted as the manufacturer's middleman; others used tools and raw
materials provided by manufacturers: but putting out always meant that
they worked under their own supervision in their own homes and shops.
Eventually manufacturers would establish central shops where they could
supervise the work and the workers; Slater did so in 1809. These central
shops brought together workers using hand tools, not machinery, for
weaving.

In 1814, Francis Cabot Lowell of Boston established the first American
textile factory, bringing workers together to make cloth, providing them
with both spinning and weaving machines, and paying them money
wages. Lowell's Boston Manufacturing Company eventually gained fame
for its paternalistic management model; the company hired the unmarried
daughters of New England farmers, reassured their parents by housing

By the Civil War, industrialization had reduced household textile manufactures to economic insignificance; the women who worked in the
earliest mills were being replaced by male immigrant workers.

POWER LOOM WEAVING.

these young women in supervised boardinghouses, and even sponsored a mill girls' literary magazine, *The Lowell Offering*. Other companies followed suit. Relatively well educated, these young women usually came to millwork for a limited period between school and marriage or teaching (one of the few respectable paid employments for women); their independence away from home balanced the long hours in the factory and the boardinghouse restrictions. Lucy Larcom, who later became a teacher and writer, remembered the independence, the broadening outlook that the women gained from leaving the confines of their farm families, and the "incalculable help" of finding themselves among other young women, "all of us thrown upon our own resources, but thrown much more upon each others' sympathies." However unusual among nineteenth-century industrial workers, the Lowell women were the first American wage workers—except sailors—"who left their homes in order to maintain them," the forerunners of the modern mobile industrial labor force.

Working conditions in the mills worsened as the industry expanded. Lucy Larcom remembered the oppression of her machine as well as the feminine camaraderie: "The half-live creature . . . was aware of my incapacity to manage it, and had a fiendish spite against me. It was humiliating." Lowell's first strike, in 1834, protested wage cuts. Followed by strikes at other mills, it signaled the end of the model manufacturing community. Intolerable conditions, low wages, and other opportunities forced and lured the young women out of the mills, to be replaced by people who came even farther from their homes: Irish immigrant men and women, who flocked to the company boardinghouses with their entire families, especially after the 1846 Irish potato famine. Desperate to eat, they accepted the long hours and poor conditions and hired out their children. Lowell and the other textile towns became the first real American factory towns, where entire families lived, worked in the mills, and raised their children to do the same.

By the time the immigrants arrived, the textile industry had passed through all the basic stages: home industry, independent crafts, putting out, central shops, and factories. Some women continued to spin and weave at home, but the "family factory" was disappearing fast. Not surprisingly, household manufacture died slowest in the South, where slave women made slave clothing, and on the frontier, where cash was scarce and cloth hard to obtain, except on occasional trips to the far-flung frontier stores. By the eve of the Civil War, textile production had left the home. Homespun clothed only inhabitants of the backwoods and the Appalachian South. As a factor in the American economy, household textile production was "practically nil," producing, compared to factories, a negligible amount of yardage.

With the help of their daughters and other female relatives, housewives continued to transform that yardage into clothing. "Have to do my sewing by snatches," complained Rachel Haskell, who finished some pants for her son, made herself a grey sacque trimmed with plaid ("It is real Scotchy") and a long nightgown, cut and sewed a flannel shirt for her husband, and began the "everlasting" work of designing and making a fancy dress for her daughter Ella to wear to the Oddfellow's Ball, during the month she kept a diary in 1867. Ella did some sewing, too, including a "frock of some old plaid" for the baby. Mothers taught their daughters to sew early, so they could help with the gargantuan task of producing and maintaining an entire family's wardrobe; they divided the labor according to skill, the daughters stitching the plainer clothes (like the baby's frock) while the mothers attended to more complicated projects.

Rachel and Ella spent many evenings mending worn clothes, for laboriously made garments served as long as possible; "I finished my sacque and entered it to live therein till its last days arrive," Rachel wrote. Although factory production had cheapened textiles considerably, they remained expensive enough to promote conservation by mending, making scraps into patchwork, and converting old clothes, like the large-size socks (presumably full of holes) that Rachel made into smaller ones for her boys. Catharine Beecher told her middle-class readers to extend the lives of their silk dresses by "ripping out the sleeves when thin, and changing the arms and also the breadths of the skirt"; Eliza Farrar devoted two full pages of *The Young Lady's Friend*—the most popular etiquette book for young women of the mid-nineteenth century, addressed to girls who could afford Paris fashions—to darning. Even the wealthy conserved cloth.

Families who had money hired seamstresses to help with the clothing, but only rarely to do the whole task; usually seamstresses fashioned and cut the dresses, leaving the actual needlework to the women of the family. Catharine Beecher suggested that novice sewers should "get a dress fitted (not sewed) at the best mantua-maker's," then take the basting out, lay the pieces flat on paper, and trace patterns for future use. Emily Dickinson's family hired several different seamstresses, often at the same time. Some came to live with the Dickinsons for a few days, while others worked in their own homes; some were married, others were single; some were friends or neighbors, others the Dickinson letters mention only for their sewing. Their work always supplemented the Dickinson women's sewing; although Emily's sister Vinnie once complained that she ran "an express" between three seamstresses' houses, the sisters commented often on their own sewing chores and regarded the seamstresses' work as assistance.

Seamstresses like these operated as independent craftswomen, not servants. Even those who lived in their employers' homes established their own independence by working for many families, coming to each for a few days or a week several times a year. They expected good treatment and demanded respect, decent lodgings and food when they lived in, and address by title, Miss or Mrs. As in other crafts, ambitious seamstresses established permanent shops, called themselves tailors (for men's clothes) or mantua-makers (for women's), and employed assistants, producing fashionable custom-fitted clothing for the very wealthy.

Even those women of means who bought finished clothing at the mantua-maker's did some needlework. "A woman who does not know how to sew is as deficient in her education as a man who cannot write," *The Young Lady's Friend* told its fashionable readers. Women who understood plain sewing, Eliza Farrar claimed, could decently reward others who sewed for them, and would have "a resource against want" in case of "a reverse of fortune." She criticized the frivolous and distracting fancy needlework and embroidery that more commonly occupied her readers, who found patterns and ideas in women's magazines and traveled everywhere with their workbaskets.

W omen rarely gathered in groups without sewing, and rarely sewed by themselves. More than any other household task, sewing filled spare moments and provided social activity. These women, of the Emil Gaetz family, gathered in Atlanta, Idaho.

Women would get together to sew; even women with servants and seamstresses left their homes in the afternoons to join their charitable sewing circles. A fashionable Philadelphia woman, Mrs. Trollope claimed, left home at eleven in the morning, clad in fine clothes, to sew with "seven other ladies, very like herself." She "produces her thimble, and asks for work; it is presented to her, and the eight ladies all stitch together for some hours," talking of Liberian missions, handsome young ministers, who wore what to church, and the profits from their last sale, until three in the afternoon. Women without that leisure sewed together less often, but did get together regularly for quilting bees—"quilting frolics," Mrs. Trollope called them, noting that "they are always solemnised with much good cheer and festivity." A well-established American tradition by the 1820s when Trollope visited the United States, the quilting party had functioned as an important women's social activity in both the Northern and Southern colonies. When women got together under less formal cir-

Dakota farm women and children at a quilting party about 1885. Left to right: Myrtle Robinson, Liza Histness, Gertrude Pendroy, Susie Pendroy, Lizzie Pendroy, Mrs. McKay, Alzie Allern, Jessie Robinson Pendroy, Sarah Pendroy, Lulu Pendroy, and—under the quilt—Beatrice Pendroy.

cumstances, too, they sewed and talked about sewing, showed off their work, and exchanged ideas, methods, and hints. Going to town with her husband one Saturday, Rachel Haskell "called on Mrs. Mack. Learned a new way of making a tidy of serpentine braid and cotton thread. Enjoyed talking with a lady." Sewing was linked with adult feminine companionship among women of all classes, but most sewing was done within the family circle. Rachel Haskell's call on Mrs. Mack broke a routine marked by evenings around the lamp, where she usually sewed while her husband and children read, played games, or made music. Louisa May Alcott's four "Little Women" sewed sheets together for their aunt, lightening the burden of the "uninteresting sewing" by adopting "Jo's plan of dividing the long seams into four parts, and calling the quarters Europe, Asia, Africa, and America . . . they talked about the different countries, as they stitched their way through them." Even the fashionable *Young Lady's Friend* advised girls to do their own mending and darning, and to help their mothers with their fathers' and brothers' shirts and stockings, in a family group; the men could read aloud while the women worked "during the long evenings of winter."

As a labor of love, sewing offered other rewards. Some women—certainly not all—loved the craft itself, taking pleasure in a good fit, straight seams, even stitching, and colorful patterns, and displaying their handicraft privately to the women with whom they sewed, or publicly at country fairs and contests. Rachel Haskell never wrote about her pride or pleasure in sewing, yet the many hours she spent on Ella's ball dress—planning it in bed one night when she couldn't sleep, sewing on it for days, taking it apart and redesigning it, and sewing some more—suggest that even though it eventually became in her mind "the everlasting dress," she wanted it perfect for Ella.

As time went on, fewer women bestowed such tangible symbols of their love on adult men. Always excluded from the sewing circles and quilting bees, men increasingly wore clothing made in the public world, not the private; the ready-made clothing industry developed earlier in men's clothing, and men's wear dominated the industry throughout the nineteenth century. In 1890, women's wear accounted for less than one-fourth of the value of all factory-made clothing. Always a women's activity, home sewing became an activity *for* women and children during the second half of the century; men no longer entered the sewing circle even to try on a half-finished pair of pants or to have their say about the fabric and style of their clothes. Women's clothes remained the product of the private home and the independent seamstress, although paper patterns, which "made it possible to sell the *design* of a garment separately from the garment itself," brought international fashion even to the frontier home by the mid-1870s. Advertised in and distributed by women's magazines like *Godey's Lady's Book* and *Demorest's Illustrated Monthly*

Magazine and Mme. Demorest's Mirror of Fashions, the paper patterns partially standardized women's clothes long before women's ready-made clothing appeared in great quantities.

Men's ready-made clothing manufacture, like other industries, operated at first on the putting-out system; women sewed for manufacturers in their own homes. The army set up an "immense Government Tailors'

Demorest's Illustrated Monthly cover for December 1875. *Demorest's* paper patterns, included with every issue, helped to create standardized women's fashions before ready-made women's clothes.

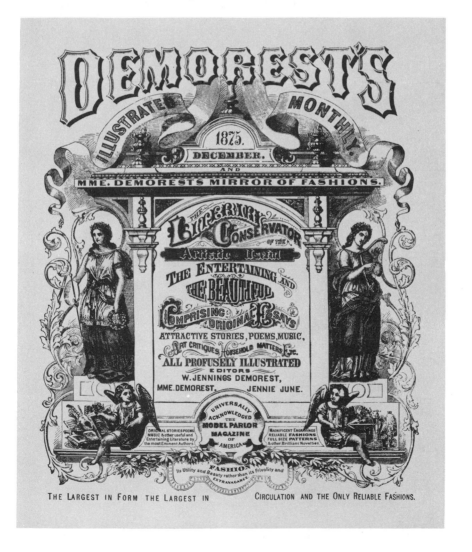

Men's shirts were among the first ready-made clothes to achieve near-universality. This lithograph appeared originally in color, 1874.

Shop" for uniforms at the beginning of the War of 1812, buying and cutting out the fabric, then hiring the sewing out to "windows and other meritorious females" in Philadelphia, an early large example of what became known in the trade as the "outside shop." Sewing women submitted references and samples of their work, then left cash deposits that guaranteed manufacturers the return of the finished clothes. Sometimes the deposits represented the full value of the materials, a severe hardship for most working women, and occasionally manufacturers kept the money, claiming unsatisfactory work. Both manufacturers and the contractors and subcontractors who entered the industry around the 1840s paid piecework wages and established deadlines for the work, encroaching on the seamstresses' independence even without direct supervision.

Successful tailors and mantua-makers set up the first "inside shops," hiring workers to make garments for the custom trade. Conditions in these shops, suggested *The Young Lady's Friend*, might not be apparent to the "young belle" who ordered her dress from "the flourishing head of a fashionable establishment" without thinking "of the pale and lean girls who are to do the work," their "aching sides," "throbbing temples," "smarting eyes," and "toil-worn fingers" exploited by employers anxious to please wealthy customers. Some custom tailors extended their operations to supply the early demand for ready-made clothing, using their employees during the slack season to make extra cloth into garments that could then be sold to unknown customers. For the most part, however, inside shops did custom work, or cut garments to be sewed outside by women at home, until the 1850s.

Although ready-made manufacturers in the early nineteenth century advertised to all classes and prated about their fashionable garments, they sold mostly to the lower classes. Sailors, itinerant laborers without wives, and slaves whose masters considered it more profitable to buy them clothes than to employ slave women in making them constituted the early market for ready-made; the poor also wore secondhand clothes, sold at retail in Eastern cities and shipped in quantity to the South and West. These people could not afford to care about style or fit; they wore what kept them warm.

Poor fit plagued the industry until after the Civil War, when the demand for uniforms in large numbers, standard patterns, and—most important—standard sizes spurred the Union Army to collect body measurements of more than a million conscripts, "providing for the first time a mass of statistical data regarding the form and build of the American male," later released to the clothing industry. Before the war, manufacturers had relied on a variety of proportional systems based on the principle that one measurement on a man's body provided the key to the rest; few of them dared to advertise good fit, even those who boasted of their beautiful fabrics and wide variety of fashionable styles. Fitting sys-

tems with numbered sizes developed during the second half of the century, but even then ready-made clothes often fit poorly; arm bands controlled the length of shirt sleeves, for example, until measured sleeves appeared in 1911.

Technological change had its first impact on the ready-made industry and for that matter, on sewing in general, during the 1850s. Although Elias Howe's was the fifth American patent for a sewing machine, and although another inventor later sued him, claiming to have been the first to design a machine that made a lock stitch with an eye-pointed needle, his 1846 patent became the prototype for most later machines. More skillful as an inventor than as a businessman, Howe eventually made his fortune, not by manufacturing or marketing his machine, but by suing other manufacturers and forcing them to do their business under his license and pay him royalties. Eventually he joined with them in the first patent pool, the Sewing Machine Combination, which controlled the industry by owning all the patents. Many other industries eventually adopted this form of business combination, which was attacked in anti-trust legislation after 1890.

The Combination ended the highly competitive "sewing-machine war" among manufacturers, all anxious to control a market that appeared almost immediately. Clothing and shoe manufacturers, of course, quickly perceived the sewing machine's value and bought most of the early machines; in 1862, about three-quarters of the sewing machines in America served manufacturers in inside shops. Throughout the 1850s, as sewing machines came on the market, the clothing industry expanded rapidly, although it was so small to begin with that, even with this great rate of change, it stayed small until after the Civil War. Because the manufacturers bought machines that were beyond the means of most seamstresses, the new invention initially created larger inside shops, balancing the proportion of inside and outside workers in the ready-made industry. Because larger manufacturers could buy more machines than smaller manufacturers, the invention killed off small companies or forced them to merge with each other; between 1850 and 1860, while capital investment in the clothing industry doubled as the manufacturers filled their shops with sewing machines, the number of manufacturers decreased by 11 percent. And because the new, larger inside shops employed more workers, the machine promoted a greater division of labor; most hand sewers had worked on a garment from start to finish, while in the new mechanized inside shops they sewed one or two seams and then passed the work on.

Sewing-machine manufacturers understood that housewives and private seamstresses constituted a huge potential market for their product that could not be tapped without some new financial arrangements. Women and their husbands still made most products in their homes during the 1850s; even the cast-iron stove—the one prevalent "consumer durable"—cost very little compared to a sewing machine, with its many precisely made moving parts. *Godey's Lady's Book* suggested that "ten families in each country village" buy a sewing machine together, each using it "in an agreed period" and then passing it on—a solution to the high price obviously repugnant to sewing-machine manufacturers, who preferred to sell ten machines to ten families. Isaac Singer's partner Edward Clark came up with the manufacturers' solution only ten years after Howe's first patent. In 1856, Clark introduced the installment plan to American business: five dollars down and the rest in monthly installments of three to five dollars, including interest to the company. Singer's sales nearly tripled during the next year, although the company was criticized for its high interest rates and for repossessing machines nearly paid for. The next year, Clark created another marketing innovation, the trade-in

The sewing machine transformed both home sewing and the clothing industry; many women bought machines to sew for manufacturers. This interior view of the Singer company's central office on Broadway, New York City, appeared in *Frank Leslie's Illustrated Newspaper*, 1857.

"The Female Slaves of New York: 'Sweaters' and their victims. 1. Scene in a 'sweater's' factory. 2. The end. 3. Scene at Grand Street Ferry." From *Frank Leslie's Illustrated Newspaper*, 1888.

allowance, offering fifty dollars "for old Sewing Machines of any and every kind in use"; sales again rose by nearly half in one year. Singer's competitors quickly adopted the new selling techniques, and the industry invested its new profits in production machinery that allowed sewing-machine manufacturers to halve the consumer's price by 1859.

Lower prices and new techniques brought sewing machines to women who could barely afford them; in 1860, the *New York Daily Tribune*, attacking Elias Howe's colossal royalties when he applied for a patent renewal, claimed that "the principal sale of sewing machines is to the poor needle-women, widows and orphans, those who by toiling day and night barely gain the bread for starving relatives and themselves." Although the *Tribune* exaggerated about overall sales—still primarily to manufacturers—it emphasized an essential point about the early machines: women bought them not only to make clothes for their families but also to provide themselves with incomes. Mary Mathews, worn out from taking in laundry and teaching school in Virginia City, Nevada, during the 1870s, invested thirty dollars in a sewing machine; "I could get plenty of sewing," she wrote, happy to quit the work that "was breaking me down too much." In addition to the independent seamstresses like Mathews, women bought machines to use as outside workers for manufacturers, who until about 1880 continued to employ large numbers of women working in isolation at home. By 1880, these women did finishing work instead of making the entire garment. The new machines and the new selling techniques helped to retain the putting-out system in the clothing industry long after it had disappeared in other crafts.

These outworkers, usually immigrant women with families, shared the wretched lives of most industrial workers of their day. When women hired seamstresses privately to provide a service, the seamstresses could set their own prices and hours. They might develop personal relationships with the women for whom they performed this intimate task. Mary Mathews took sick while working on Mrs. Judge Rising's sewing; she sent her son with the work she had already finished, and he returned home with a basket of food. "I considered it very kind of her," Mathews wrote, "for I was an entire stranger to her, only having done a little sewing for her. She also paid a good price for it." The manufacturers' outworkers, in contrast, sold their labor to profit-making concerns. Like the many women who did piecework at home for cigar manufacturers, artificial-flower companies, and other industrial concerns, they became dependent on their employers, who owned and marketed the goods, set the piecework rates, established quotas and deadlines, and often rented to them the places where they both lived and worked. The putting-out system, in its earliest phases a way for manufacturers to employ skilled craftspeople who often maintained their independence and control over both their labor and their product, became, in the outwork of the late nineteenth century, an extreme form of exploitation, though one with certain ad-

vantages for poor women who had children to tend and could only work at home.

When the putting-out system did disappear in the ready-made industry, it was replaced, not by large factories, but by small shops—often called sweatshops for their intolerable working conditions—run by contractors and subcontractors. Manufacturers still bought the raw materials, designed the clothes, and marketed the final product; some supervised the cutting process in inside shops. Contractors, often immigrants little better off than their employees, rented lofts or used their own tenement apartments; they bought sewing machines on the installment plan and acquired raw materials on credit from the manufacturers. They recruited and supervised teams of about ten workers—family members, boarders, new immigrants from their villages in the old country—whom they organized on the "task system," assigning a work quota to the whole team rather than paying individual workers by the piece, but dividing the work itself into minute tasks. By the turn of the twentieth century, most ready-made clothing came from these small shops employing fewer than ten immigrant operatives working under contractor supervision.

Garment workers in a sweatshop at 40 East Broadway, New York City, 1908. Photo by Lewis Hine.

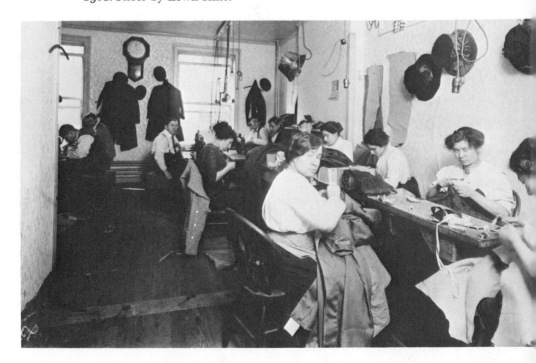

Meanwhile, improved sewing machines, cutting machines, pressers, and buttonholers increased each worker's potential output and set the ready-made industry in a position to extend its market to women's wear. The value of factory-made women's clothing, less than one-third that of men's in 1890, skyrocketed to almost half a billion dollars, twenty million more than men's wear, by 1914. In 1919, a government report estimating a "minimum standard of health and decency" for a worker's family assumed a "considerable amount of sewing at home," but by no means all of it; the hypothetical wife made no clothing for her husband, no underwear, only some garters for a twelve-year-old son, her own housedresses, and most of the clothing for two smaller children. In one Midwestern industrial city where 1910 newspaper advertisements had rarely shown women's dresses but featured yard goods prominently, the head of the fabric department of the largest department store said in the mid-1920s that the department sold "only a fraction" of the amount sold in 1890. Nearly two-thirds of the working-class women in that city spent six hours per week or fewer on sewing and mending.

By 1900, when this ad appeared in the *Ladies' Home Journal*, the ready-made industry had begun to conquer its last markets—women's wear, children's clothes, and underwear.

Making clothing—so long a source of craft satisfaction for women of all classes, an activity that brought women together and justified their socializing, an endless task that occupied spare moments and discouraged idle hands at all times—now became a hobby. Women so inclined still sew for pleasure, or to increase their wardrobes for less money; since they buy their fabric and patterns and sew on machines, their task is hardly comparable to the arduous labors of preindustrial home production. Few choose to sew their families' entire wardrobes; mending and darning, essential adjuncts to laborious handcrafts, have become virtually lost arts. Home economics classes teach girls—and now boys—the tasks that daughters once learned at their mothers' knees, apprentices at the trade that practically defined womanhood. Department stores define newfangled seasons, offering woolen dresses and corduroy jackets in the heat of August as if preparation for winter still took months.

As the *New York Tribune* predicted at the end of the 1850s, "the needle will soon be consigned to oblivion, like the [spinning] wheel, and the loom, and the knitting-needles. . . . People will have more work done, will dress better, change oftener, and altogether grow better looking. . . . The more work can be done, the cheaper it can be done by means of machines *—the greater will be the demand.* Men and women will disdain the soupçon of a nice worn garment, and gradually we shall become a nation without spot or blemish." Industrial production of clothing, the classic example of the removal of production from the home, raised the standard of living; first factory-made textiles, then sewing machines, finally ready-made clothing for both men and women did create demand, enabling even working-class people to change their clothes and discard the "nice worn garment." The growing economy of "a nation without spot or blemish" flourished on the production of natural fibers and petrochemicals necessary to produce closets full of unworn clothes; women found it easier to discard the standardized products of industrial production than the personalized results of countless hours spent in traditional handcrafts.

The process of economic expansion multiplied the businesses, machines, and products, meanwhile also expanding the proportion of people who worked for the entrepreneurs. Throughout the nineteenth century, as spinning, weaving, and sewing moved to the factories, some women, especially unmarried ones, moved with their work, but clothes production continued to offer a substantial number of married women a source of income that they could earn at home, directing their own work. The triumph of women's ready-made clothing during the first two decades of the twentieth century doomed the independent seamstress; her work represented one of the last opportunities for women to earn the money they spent on the new mass-produced goods without leaving home to participate in the system as wage workers.

EIGHT

The Boarder

Current debates about the American family often rest on the assumption that new kinds of family structures—single-parent families, single-person households, unrelated adults living together—are replacing the nuclear family, which in turn supposedly replaced the extended family. In fact, unrelated adults have often lived together. The extended family of popular literature, with many generations and many branches of a family tree inhabiting the same

house, has always been comparatively rare in America. For the first several generations in the colonies, married children set up their own households on subdivisions of their parents' property; relatives served also as neighbors, and strong kinship ties stretched the borders of the family beyond the individual household and the borders of the household beyond the walls of the house. This "nuclearized semi-extended" family offered both privacy for the nuclear group and continuing intimate bonds with other blood relations.

Population growth broke down that pattern. Farmland could only be subdivided so many times. Eventually those who wanted to continue an agricultural life-style had to move, opening up new territory and exchanging extra produce or raising barns with neighbors who were not kin. Others moved to towns, where population growth extended commercial and crafts activity, creating opportunities to work for pay. As apprentices and servants, many new town dwellers lived with their bosses; others paid for lodgings in private families or moved in with city cousins whom they might never have known in childhood. Work opportunities expanded even further in the mid-nineteenth century as towns became manufacturing centers, and those who came to town to take advantage of them, both from the American countryside and from Europe, needed places to live. They found them with people unrelated to themselves.

By the middle of the nineteenth century—the supposed heyday of the nuclear family, and the period when popular literature first began to celebrate it—few Americans lived only with relatives throughout their lives. Although apprenticeship was disappearing with the crafts system, the other options were expanding; many people either had boarders in their own homes, or boarded with other people's families, or lived in boardinghouses, at some time in their lives. Besides providing living space for a mobile population, boarding offered a source of income to women with small children and household duties who could not or would not go out to work. Not every woman liked to sew, and those who ran boardinghouses or took boarders into their apartments and houses could make money even more independently than seamstresses, although boarders compounded their work: more people dirtied more laundry and ate more food. Boarding brought strangers into the household, often as intimate companions, making the nineteenth-century nuclear family no more nuclear than its fabled predecessor was extended.

Boarding—paying money to live with someone else—makes sense only in the context of wage labor: boarders must have money to pay for their lodgings, which they must earn elsewhere in the community. All kinds of strangers in the home (apprentices, distant relatives, servants, and boarders) extended families beyond the nuclear group. But apprentices worked for room and board and education, servants worked for room and board and sometimes cash, and relatives might or might not work and might or

CHAPTER III.

OF BOARDING WITH A PRIVATE FAMILY.

ERY often, when circumstances compel an individual to find eating, drinking, and sleeping accommodation among strangers, he compromises the Boarding - House question by securing lodgings with a private family. Probably he entertains a wholesome distrust of the Establishments to which our book is devoted, perhaps hopes for a nearer approach to domestic felicity for eschewing them. If prudent, however, he will religiously avoid such tenements as put forth advertisements offering "all the comforts of a home" at low, or indeed any prices. For, as few persons receive boarders from inclination, it logically follows that the resources of those who are unable to cater for more than *one* must be very limited, and it is more than probable that they are simply cannibals, desirous of

Boarding provided young workers with places to live and their landladies with income. This page from Thomas Butler Gunn's *The Physiology of New York Boarding Houses*, published in 1857, suggests that boardinghouses were better than boarding with private families, but the rest of the chapters—each devoted to a different kind of lodgings—lampooned established boardinghouses as well.

might not pay. Boarders, by definition, paid. Historians have discovered them in many societies where landless transients encountered opportunities to earn money working for others: an eighteenth-century Austrian manor, a nineteenth-century North American commercial city, an industrial town in rural Lancashire in 1851, mining towns in the American West, and the immigrant communities of industrial America.

The transition from barter, crafts, and agricultural self-sufficiency to industrial wage labor affected all of American society during the nineteenth century—and seemingly all of American society boarded. Descriptions of these living arrangements filled travel accounts written by visiting Europeans, who naturally stayed in places for transients and formed most of their impressions from the transient population. One historian suggests that by 1860, enough people boarded to give visitors "the idea that nearly all Americans lived in hotels or boarding-houses." Many hotels, beginning with Boston's Tremont in 1829, provided accommodations specifically for permanent guests; the "American plan," almost universal in American hotels during the 1850s, included meals with the price of lodging, a response to permanent hotel living among "fashionable" people. Cheaper accommodations could be had in boardinghouses, often former mansions abandoned by wealthy people for places farther from town; major city directories listed over a hundred of these houses, and every small town had at least one.

Another alternative, firmly established by the 1850s, was boarding and lodging with families in their private homes. In one North American city, 56 percent of the families kept boarders in either 1851 or 1861, and undoubtedly even more at some time in between, since most of the boarders, young single people or elderly ones, tended to move in and out of households without staying long. Middle-class and even wealthy families took boarders into their homes, maintains historian Michael Katz, in order to keep "a close check" on the young single men of the town. Often these men boarded with their employers' families, but worked outside the household, at the employer's commercial establishment.

The major reason why even middle-class families took in boarders, however, was to make extra money. Of the various money-making options open to women, boarding offered a good chance to "make money and not lose social class," according to "Money-Making for Ladies"; this article, published in *Harper's* magazine in 1882, was addressed to "that numerous class who, while not obliged to enter the ranks of recognized working-women, yet feel the need of increasing a limited income" to buy Christmas presents, new silk dresses, and "various comforts and belongings of civilized life." The article stressed gentility: women who baked pies for sale should hire someone else to go around the city selling them; women who shopped on commission should do it quietly, for friends. Boarding received more attention than any other single option. Setting up a boardinghouse, the article pointed out, "is probably as harassing an occupation as can well be found, especially with the risk of hiring a large house and furnishing it for the purpose." Women who already had some room to spare, however, might reasonably decrease expenses by taking in boarders —not without difficulty, "but money can not be made in any way without effort of some kind." Certainly many genteel people sought lodgings in decent homelike atmospheres with pleasant furnished rooms and good cooking.

Most written comment on middle-class and upper-class boarding, to the end of the century, showed less enthusiasm for the practice, especially when it concerned women boarders. Frances Trollope scorned boarding as a way of making women insignificant; it was not very easy to say what they did in boardinghouses, she wrote, "but I believe they clear-starch a little, and iron a little, and sit in a rocking-chair, and sew a great deal. I always observed that the ladies who boarded wore more elaborately worked collars and petticoats than any one else." *Ten Dollars Enough*, a

Some boarders found lodgings through newspaper advertisements like these from the *New York Times*, Sunday, May 1, 1892.

Summer Resorts.

GRAND UNION HOTEL

Saratoga Springs,

WILL OPEN JUNE 14.

For information regarding rooms, terms, &c., apply to J. P. Caddagan, Plaza Hotel, New-York.
WOOLLEY & GERRANS, PROPS.

LONG BEACH HOTEL,

ON THE ATLANTIC,

WILL OPEN JUNE 21.

TO RENT FOR THE SEASON—JUNE TO OCTOBER—A FEW FULLY-FURNISHED COTTAGES, WATER AND GAS INCLUDED.
NEW-YORK OFFICE, GRAND HOTEL, BROADWAY AND 31ST ST., NEW-YORK.
CHAS. E. HITCHCOCK, Manager.
No change of proprietorship has or will take place this season.

Boarders Wanted.

NO EXTRA CHARGE FOR IT. Advertisements for THE TIMES may be left at any American District Messenger office in this city, where the charges will be the same as those at the main office.

THE UP-TOWN OFFICE OF THE TIMES.

The ONLY up-town office of THE TIMES is at 1,269 Broadway, between 31st and 32d Sts. Open daily, Sunday included, from 4 A. M. to 9 P. M. Subscriptions received and copies of
THE TIMES for sale.
ADVERTISEMENTS RECEIVED UNTIL 9 P. M.

1—MADISON AV., 105.—Second floor front room; quiet, select house; transient or permanent; references.

5TH AV., 437.—Mrs. Beach, for years 307, has handsome suite of rooms; private table; house and appointments strictly first-class.

21ST ST., 33 EAST. — Handsomely-furnished rooms, with board; reasonable rates; references.

21ST ST., 145 EAST (GRAMERCY PARK.)— Cool rooms; generous table; everything first-class; privilege private park; references.

27WEST 34TH ST.—Second floor; large, handsome room, with board; references exchanged.

33D, 10 EAST.—Desirable second-floor rooms, singly or en suite; strictly first-class accommodations; references.

47TH ST., 8 EAST. — Handsomely-furnished suites; single rooms; families; gentlemen; appointments first-class; references.

47TH ST., 16 TO 20 EAST.—Second floor, front, and fourth floor, back; superior table; references.

47TH ST., 16 TO 20 EAST.—Second and fourth story square rooms; superior table; references.

book of articles reprinted from *Good Housekeeping*, went through thirteen editions between 1886 and 1897; primarily a cookbook in the form of a novel, the book presented recipes in an unusual narrative style that explained how to time an entire meal by working on more than one recipe at a time. Heroine Molly's husband Harry Bishop, a young Harvard graduate disowned for marrying her instead of "the rich Miss Vanderpool his mother had looked out for him," earned too little to buy a house, so they had to board. Molly, feeling insignificant, attended cooking classes, practiced at a friend's house, read "everything she could find about housekeeping," and finally managed to convince Harry to try the experiment of renting a cottage from friends while they went to Europe. *Ten Dollars Enough* naturally ended with the best of all worlds: a baby, a house of their own, and a junior partnership in the family firm, Harry's father having been won over by Molly's good housekeeping.

The book's author, Catharine Owen, participated in a symposium on boarding published in the *North American Review* in 1889; five writers, including Marion Harland (author of the best-selling *Common Sense in the Household* and then editor of *Home-Maker* magazine) and Maria Parloa (an original teacher at the Boston Cooking School), asked "Is Housekeeping a Failure?" and came to the unanimous conclusion that even if it was, boarding was worse. Boardinghouses simply were not homes. So many untrained women, afraid to manage households, boarded that "it would seem that a far larger number of people are boarding than keeping house," but at great expense: children suffered, vain women prized luxury and gossip above their families, and unwholesome food and surroundings stifled everyone. Only better training in economical housekeeping could solve the problem.

Rose Terry Cook, author of numerous short stories, made the major argument vivid. "The family is an institution of God," she wrote, "the archetype and foundation of all human government." The kinds of people necessary to that government, "good citizens, noble women, patriots and saints . . . do not spring from the social hot-beds of hotels and boardinghouses; they grow in the fair fresh gardens of home, the only trace left to us of that beauteous and fruitful field wherein the first family of earth were set." Individuality, the quality those people most needed, could be nurtured only in private. "People who eat by contract and in herds, and whose very bed-chambers are not secure from prying eyes and intrusive feet," Marion Harland added, "soon begin to dress, look, talk, and *think* for the vulgar many, rather than the beloved few."

Although the *North American Review* symposium primarily addressed boarding as a problem of the wealthy living in hotels or large boardinghouses, its arguments typified late-nineteenth-century glorification of home and family. Similar arguments about privacy and wholesomeness, and similar suggestions for home economics training, appeared in the literature about the "lodging evil" among the working class and particularly among immigrants. For these people, boarding was a standard pattern, "a natural institution," as one Jewish immigrant to New York recalled, "particularly in the early years when most immigrants came without their families." Because boarding represented an option for transient groups in a mobile society, it made particular sense for the largest transient group of all, the participants in the transatlantic labor market that developed in the second half of the century.

Immigration, the solution to a longstanding labor shortage, fueled American industrial growth; about twenty million people immigrated to the United States between 1870 and 1910, creating a population one-third foreign-born or first-generation American. Without land, without much money, and often without skills applicable in their new country, foreigners and their children took what jobs they could get; although a few found professional and managerial jobs, and slightly more worked in agriculture, the masses huddled overwhelmingly in the lower strata of industrial work. Some manufacturers recruited workers in Europe, a practice legal until 1885, when prevoyage contracts became void, but companies employed labor agencies or sent their own agents to recruit on the docks in New York City, hoping to entice those who had come to walk streets made of gold. In time, immigrants developed their own networks and channels of communication about employment opportunities; companies worked with priests and rabbis, heads of fraternal organizations, and other immigrant leaders to ensure a steady labor supply. Those information networks transmitted information about living arrangements; boarding itself kept the information flowing and helped with the adjustment process. Immigrants found homes for their friends and relatives from the old country through the people they worked with; they found jobs through the people they lived with. Boarding with fellow immigrants, they could eat familiar foods and speak their own language.

In Pennsylvania steel towns, one-third of immigrant workers were single, and three-quarters of the married men who had been in America less than five years had wives still abroad. Because the steelworkers' wage would not support a family of five with the barest necessities, workers with families supplemented their incomes by taking in these people as boarders. This pattern appeared all over the country throughout the century, in immigrant communities of all sizes and all nationalities, and among populations working in all industries. At any one time, 25 to 50 percent of the mostly immigrant industrial working class had boarders, statistics that underplay the phenomenon, since families without boarders at the time of a census taker's or social worker's visit often had them a year later. Nearly all working-class people lived with nonrelatives at some stage of their lives, either in their youth, when they boarded, or in their later years, when they took others in.

Boarding arrangements varied from household to household, and even within an individual household, where boarders might pay different amounts for different accommodations. "A star boarder slept on a folding bed," one man reminisced about New York's Lower East Side. "But I knew a printer who every night unscrewed a door, put it on two chairs; he couldn't pay as much as the one who had the bed." Food accounts could be divided in many ways: the total food bill for the family divided by the number of boarders plus the household head, totally separate food accounts for each boarder, or separate accounts for meat and other special foods. By 1921, according to one study of immigrants in Chicago, identifying terms codified the arrangements: "boarders" paid fixed sums for room, board, and sometimes laundry; "lodgers" paid amounts that varied with household or individual food expenditures.

Whatever the specific arrangements, the work fell to the women. Immigrant women from preindustrial European cultures, accustomed to hard work and to having an economic role, adapted their American work patterns from those they had known in the old country; they divided the labor of supporting and running the household with their factory-worker husbands, as they had always divided it with men working in the fields. At least one such woman made the connection herself, as reported by a federal Children's Bureau investigator in 1915: "Mother aged 35 years; 6 births in 12 years; 4 live births and 2 still births. All live born died in first year. . . . SAYS SHE HAD ALWAYS WORKED TOO HARD, KEEPING BOARDERS IN THIS COUNTRY AND CUTTING WOOD AND CARRYING IT AND WATER ON HER BACK IN THE OLD COUNTRY. . . . Father furious because all babies die; wore red necktie to funeral of last to show his disrespect for wife who can only produce children that die."

Women like this jeopardized their health and their children for one main reason: money. "Taking lodgers," as social worker Margaret Byington put it, "is not giving a home to a friend from the old country nor letting an extra room; it is a deliberate business venture on the part of a family to increase the inadequate income from the man's earnings." Over and over, social workers like Byington, investigating working people's living conditions at the turn of the century, found that they took in boarders in response to the combination of low wages and high rents. Some studies showed that workers with more money took fewer boarders; one found that steelworkers of the same nationalities took fewer boarders where rents were low; another demonstrated that higher family incomes among working people usually came from lodgers and often paid for moves to better, higher-priced housing. The lodging question, suggested the New York State Conference of Charities and Correction, was actually a question of wages and rents: families kept lodgers "necessarily . . . to meet additional expenditures."

Women, especially those with husbands and children, had few other

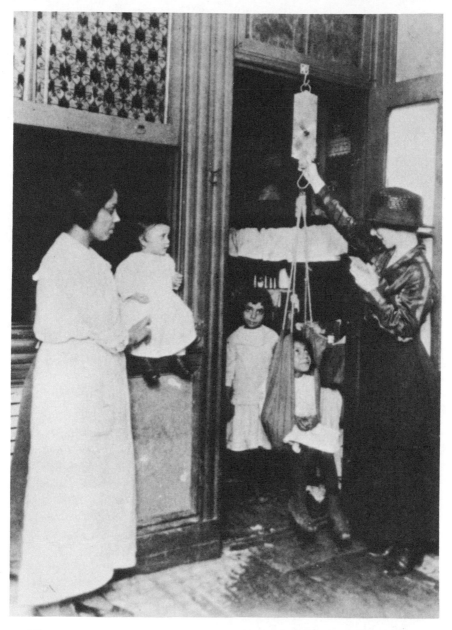

Boarding was a "natural institution" among immigrants, who arrived in the New World without places to live and with few household goods. They crowded into big-city tenements, alarming urban reformers and social workers. Here a welfare worker visits tenements in New York City.

job options. Pennsylvania steel mills and Western mines hired only men; elsewhere, women often found outside employment impossible. Yvonne Dionne's mother, who worked in a Manchester, New Hampshire cotton mill for a while, left her small children in the care of the eldest. "My sister wouldn't stay in the house," Yvonne recalled years later. "She'd go outside to be with her friends. One day, I tried to reach the kettle to take it off the stove, and I dropped it and burned myself and one of the babies. My mother never went back to the mills after that." Maria LaCasse, another Manchester resident, worked in the mills before her marriage, and peri- odically after that "when things would get too hard and my father didn't have any money," according to her daughter Alice. "My father didn't really want her to work. That was a big issue because she always wanted to go in and earn a little money. But the minute she said she wanted to work, there would be a big fight. He'd say, 'No, you're not going to work. You're going to stay home.'" Maria LaCasse did stay home, and took in boarders, renting rooms to other workers from the mills.

Other opportunities for earning money at home were limited for many women by the turn of the century. Those who needed money but could not take jobs outside the home could, if they lived in the country, keep chickens and grow large enough gardens to sell eggs, produce, and pre- served foods at the markets; this option was closed to women in large cities and most industrial towns, where small plots might at best produce enough food to supplement the meager paycheck. Tenement dwellers could not establish themselves as independent home-based washerwomen because they had sinks and washtubs barely large enough even for their own tablecloths or sheets; by the turn of the century, as noted earlier, the power laundry had in any case obliterated the option of taking in laun- dry at home, and most independent laundresses worked in their employers' homes. Nor could immigrants easily take in sewing as private seamstresses; their English was often poor and their acquaintance with wealthier women usually limited, and most employers expected seamstresses to live in while they did their work. In some towns, clothing manufacturers and other industrialists offered piecework to be done at home, making women dependent on the contractors who set prices, deadlines, and other condi- tions on the work. Taking in boarders offered more independence than most of this home work, and it was in many places the only available employment for women who wanted to make money while staying at home to care for their children.

It did add to the household work load. More people ate more food, dirtied more dishes, and made much more laundry; boarding arrange- ments always included washing bed linen, and often clothes as well. Only the relatively wealthy owned labor-saving devices to make that work easier; in Homestead, for example, Margaret Byington found that a few steelworkers' homes had gas ranges, water heaters, ironers, or cheap hand- cranked washing machines to "lighten the tedious task of keeping clothes clean in a smoky mill town," but the homes of the poorest families did not. These were the ones who "found it necessary to increase their slender income" by taking in boarders. Women who kept boarders with separate meat accounts often cooked separately for each person in the house; sometimes they fried different kinds of meat in one pan, "each with a tag of some sort labeling the order." These women, in other words, ran restaurants, and did not simply add people to a regular family mealtime routine; some boardinghouses actually functioned as restaurants, where nonlodgers ate along with the lodgers and the family. Boarding involved administrative work as well, to cope with often complex household accounts.

Women served often as surrogate mothers, wives, and sisters for their boarders. Cora Pellerin, thirteen years old when her mother and father returned to their Canadian farm in 1914, begged her mother to leave her in New Hampshire to work in the cotton mill. "My mother said, 'If I can find a good boardinghouse, I'll let you stay.' So she found a family-style boardinghouse that would take me, my sister, and my brother. . . . The woman who kept the boardinghouse said to my mother, 'As long as they mind me, you don't have to worry. If they don't mind me, I'll write you and let you know.' " The woman had six children of her own; the Pellerin children joined the family. Boarders often joined the family—and then some; the tale of the boarder and the faithless wife appears often in immigrant fiction and probably was standard in immigrant reality as well, especially when wives stayed in Europe for several years before joining their husbands in America. Boarding bred intimacy; people lived in close quarters, and the extension of housework's compensations often accompanied the extension of its burdens.

That intimacy distressed middle-class housing reformers, whose efforts to change overcrowded immigrant housing conditions created laws limiting the number of people who could live in a given space, brought pressure on city boards of health to enforce those laws, and generated designs for model tenements. Overcrowding was a genuine problem, especially in New York; Manhattan had the densest population in the world in 1894, a statistic that translated into unbearable existence in the tenements. One immigrant later described "a two-room apartment on Allen Street containing parents, six children, and six boarders. On Saturdays, since the father was a cantor, the apartment was turned into a synagogue. Two daughters took in dresses to sew at home. One boarder, a shoemaker, worked in the apartment. 'The cantor rehearses, a train passes, the shoemaker bangs, ten brats run around like goats, the wife putters in her "kosher restaurant." At night we all try to get some sleep in the stifling roach-infested two rooms.' " In one Yiddish novel of the period, three boarders tried to stave off increased overcrowding: they offered to pay more so they would not have to share their room with a fourth.

Nonetheless, as their landlady pointed out to her rabbi husband, who

had objected to the boarders in the first place, overcrowding paid the rent. "Only millionaires can be alone in America. By Zalmon, the fish-peddler, they're squeezed together, twelve people, in one kitchen. The bedroom and the front room his wife rents out to boarders. If I could cook their suppers for them, I could even earn yet a few cents from their eating." From the reformers' standpoint, morality, comfort, and physical health demanded enforceable laws to limit overcrowding. As urban historian Roy Lubove points out, "The best interests of the immigrant and the community, as the housing reformer defined them, did not always coincide with the immigrant's definition of those same interests."

Most reformers operated, not on the notion that boarding *caused* overcrowding, but that it constituted overcrowding by definition; like those who campaigned against upper-class boardinghouses and hotels, they cherished the privacy of the nuclear family. The United States Bureau of Labor's 1910 report on the condition of woman and child wage earners, for example, worried about privacy both for women boarders and the families with whom they lived. Women boarders socialized with the families, the report stated; close quarters made privacy inpossible, and "the lodger or boarder becomes practically a member of the family." Rather than viewing this as potentially supportive for everyone involved—especially for single women working in large cities—the report suggested that this intimacy was a problem. Lawrence Veiller, the dean of housing reformers, more explicit about the potential breakdown of morality in close quarters, called boarding "fraught with great danger to the social fabric of the country. It means the undermining of family life; often the breaking down of domestic standards. It frequently leads to the breaking up of homes and families, to the downfall and subsequent degraded career of young women, to grave immoralities—in a word, to the profanation of the home." Charles Henderson, a professor at the University of Chicago, addressing a 1902 home economics conference, applauded tenement-house legislation as a "fight against a lapse into primary communism, a clear-eyed and unflinching determination to save and purify the monogamic family." By gathering people not biologically related to each other into a household, boarding supposedly created a much larger problem: large numbers of people living in households neither nuclear nor private.

Like defective plumbing and dark rooms, overcrowding genuinely alarmed well-meaning reformers who wanted to upgrade sanitary conditions, but their ultimate argument—its destruction of family privacy—aimed at establishing and reinforcing individualism among the labor force. People who both lived and worked together enjoyed an intimacy that united them, making them more likely to resist their employers; homes full of boarders furnished safe places for workers to plan strikes or sabotage or simply to offer each other support. Employers knew that

friends and relatives working together could and did help each other
make factory work more bearable. At the Amoskeag cotton mill in New
Hampshire, where workers helped each other meet quotas during speed-
ups and switched employee passes so they could substitute for each other
or take turns going to work, the management attempted to keep relatives
and friends from the same ethnic group from working together in the
same workroom. Although boarding arrangements helped employers by
serving as employment networks, their intimacy posed a serious threat
during a period when most industrial workers, vastly overworked and
underpaid, toiled under miserable conditions without union contracts.

The reformers who attacked overcrowding and the practice of boarding
that caused it suggested that the dangers extended beyond the interests of
particular employers, to the society at large. Social workers grouped at
Chicago's Hull House, America's first settlement house, maintained that
the problem was order, and that social order could not be achieved without order on the individual level, impossible in overcrowded conditions.
One Hull House resident wrote, "One room for everything except sleeping
—cooking, washing, caring for the children, catching a breath for the
moment—means no repose, no calm, no opportunity for planning that
order which is the law of the well-governed home." Jane Addams, the
group's leader, maintained that "men of executive ability and business
sagacity have found it to their interests" to organize workers at their jobs,
but not at home; instead, workers lived in large groups where "the chaos
is as great as it would be were they working in huge factories without
foreman or superintendant." This chaos, she claimed, cramped their ideas,
extinguished their "desire for higher social pleasure," and excluded them
from "the traditions and social energy which make for progress." In other
words, according to the social workers, social progress and the orderly
organization of society at large depended on an orderly home life for the
working class, to be achieved through regulation.

While agreed on the goals, housing reformers disagreed on the correct
means to combat overcrowding and institute order. They were caught on
the horns of a dilemma: enforcing laws against overcrowding required
public intrusion into private life. Lawrence Veiller, secretary of the National Housing Association, maintained that adequate inspection would
"require an army of inspectors" and involve "an invasion of the privacy of
the home, which is repugnant to American institutions." Veiller told the
Second National Conference on Housing in Philadelphia in 1912, where
much of the discussion concerned inspection, that laws should hold landlords rather than tenants responsible. Laws charging the tenant could not
be enforced: people lied about their boarders during the day, boarders
left by the fire escapes during night inspections, and even when inspections produced evidence of overcrowding, tenants could pull judges'
heartstrings. "Why they should always have been 'widows,'" Veiller said,

describing the scenes in court, "I have never been able to find out, but widows they were." A woman accused would bring "all of her own children, and—some borrowed from the neighbors for the occasion. She would shed copious tears and between sobs would explain to the judge that all of the men found in her rooms were 'cousins' or friends of the family who were just there for a night or two, while they were looking for work."

Thomas Jordan, Boston's chief Department of Health inspector, answered Veiller at the conference. Jordan, who inspected tenements at night with a policeman after a preliminary visit by one of his staff, claimed that the horrendous overcrowding, often worse than the day inspector thought, could end only with night inspection. "We find people

Two officials of the New York City Tenement House Department inspect a basement living room, around 1900.

sleeping in all sorts of conditions. Cot beds that have been stowed away in closets are brought out; chairs are used for putting mattresses on; even the kitchen range is used to put mattresses on." People took in lodgers out of greed, not poverty: they managed to meet their bail and pay fines when caught. "About the fire-escapes," Jordan continued. "The only time I ran across that was last winter, and I can assure you that the men who did it that night won't try it again in a hurry. . . . We knew what they were doing—could see that they were going out by the fire-escape. There was one big fat fellow who got stuck on the fire-escape, he couldn't go either in or out; we had to pull him in through the window. We saw that the men were not more than half-dressed. It was an extremely cold night, so I said to the police officer, 'I guess we had better sit down here a little while and rest ourselves. We are in no hurry.'"

Like other Progressive Era reformers, those concerned with housing committed themselves to public solutions for problems that they believed to be the individual reflections of society's ills. Although few of them shared Jordan's sadism or his belief that greed rather than poverty lay at the root of the problem, they all agreed that boarding was a social issue, with social solutions. They glorified home and family, and worried about intruding on privacy in order to save it, but stressed the links between the private household and the larger society, proposing public support for housing construction and laws to prohibit overcrowding. In the short run, their efforts failed: studies conducted in the 1920s indicate that poor women, especially from ethnic minorities, continued to earn money by caring for small numbers of boarders in their homes. A commission in California found boarders in 11 percent of skilled typographers' households and 22 percent of semiskilled streetcar workers' homes; among small wage earners in Chicago, 43 percent of Mexican families, 42 percent of black families, and 28 percent of native white families took in boarders.

Boarding was nevertheless on the decline. With every census after 1910, fewer women described themselves as boardinghouse keepers, relative both to other women's occupations and to the population as a whole. That decline coincided with the disappearance of other options for making money at home without bosses: seamstresses competed with the ready-made clothing industry, laundresses with the power laundry and with washing machines. Increasingly, women who needed money had to leave home to work; freed from at least some of the arduous and time-consuming labor of traditional housework by new fuels and indoor plumbing, and attracted by new opportunities in the expanding service and clerical sectors of the economy, married women began, at first in very small numbers, to go out to work in supervised jobs.

In joining the organized labor market, married women created more demand for household products; they spent less time at home but retained primary responsibility for housework, and they had money with

Employers often provided lodgings for employees. This was the board-inghouse for employees of the Quaw-Gunder Lumber Company, Edgar, Wisconsin, 1894.

which to buy the new goods and services. An expanding economy pro-duced ever more things with ever more value, while growing numbers of women joined their brothers and husbands as direct participants in the money economy, both as workers and as consumers. Constantly decreas-ing household size—partly brought on by the decline of boarding—aided that expansion; while the population more than doubled between 1910 and 1970, the total number of households more than tripled, average household size dropping from 4.8 people to 3.1 people. Simply put, the more households, the more demand for household goods; every home needed its own stove and coffeepot, and eventually (at least according to the advertisements) its own washing machine and electric can opener.

Economic expansion, of course, ground to a halt between 1929 and

1932, to be restored by government spending on New Deal programs and decisively revived by World War II; after a brief postwar slump, it began again, halted by cyclical recessions and reactivated by the Korean and Vietnam wars. Residential construction boomed after World War II, contributing to the postwar recovery and creating new kinds of places to live, from the massive suburban housing developments of the immediate postwar period to the singles apartments of the 1970s—few with room for boarders. To meet the rent or the mortgage, to pay for the stove and the washing machine, more women—denied the home-based paid-labor options of the nineteenth century—went out to work.

People continue to live with relatives and friends during short periods of transience, but boarding (and the intimacy that accompanied it) has disappeared from most American life-styles. The statistical trend toward smaller households expresses numerically an increasing preference for privacy, not merely for the family, but now for the individual as well. Urban group housing and apartment sharing, the closest modern approximation to the boardinghouse and the shared tenement, more often represent a purely economic relationship; although a few communes and collectives share nightly meals and child rearing, most roommates eat the majority of their meals as individuals, and many keep separate food supplies. They sleep in separate rooms, and wake in time for work at different jobs for different employers. Unrelated adults now live together, not in overcrowded tenements where they become "members of the family" or large boardinghouses where they share their complaints about the landlady's cooking and the boss's labor policies, but in houses where they share only the rent, or apartment buildings where they share only each other's noise. Without the woman who earned her living by cooking the boarders' meals and doing their laundry, people who share houses and apartments often simply share real estate. That woman, like the seamstress, the laundress, and the full-time domestic servant, has left the household to earn money working for business and industry.

Mistress and Maid

While women who needed money increased their work load by taking in boarders, those who had it attempted to lighten their burdens by hiring servants. Live-in domestic service, before plumbing and the new fuels the only possible help for the trials of housekeeping, offered single women their largest source of paid employment. Hired by households for their services, not by entrepreneurs who could make profits from their labor these women engaged with their employers in personal, informal, and occasionally intimate relationships, regulated by the personalities of mistress and servant, rather than by the constraints of industry and profit. Unlike seamstresses, laundresses, and boardinghouse keepers, who were usually married and relatively independent, domestic servants were generally single women who lived in their employers' homes, always on call and subject to their mistresses' whims. By the end of the century, many single women who could find factory work chose it for its freedom, producing a shortage of servants that plagued mistresses who did not yet consider the new household technology an adequate substitute for full-time maids. Another group of Progressive Era activists, like the housing reformers intent on bringing home life into the twentieth century, attacked traditional domestic service as old-fashioned and unbusinesslike; their arguments emphasized the rational labor relations that characterized the world outside the home. With factory-provided goods and business-provided services, and with new kinds of domestic service, those rational labor relations eventually came to dominate household work as well.

"You can't get good help nowadays" is an old refrain; nineteenth-century travelers' accounts, domestic manuals, and women's magazines abounded in discussions of the "servant problem." Finding a good servant —a family retainer like *Little Women*'s Hannah, who had lived with the March family for sixteen years "and was considered by them all more as a friend than a servant"—rivaled finding a needle in a haystack. According to the literature, most servants put on airs, stole from their employers, left their positions without notice, and performed their duties without skill or care. Bad servants came and went, so mistresses seeking the elusive good ones often found themselves without help for short periods. Literary complaints rarely concerned price or the difficulty of finding someone to try out; in fact, they offer the impression that nobody went without servants for long. This literature—written by and for the urban middle and upper classes, a tiny segment of nineteenth-century American society—suggests a mammoth treasure hunt, with every housewife in the United States combing huge haystacks in search of the few precious needles.

In fact, domestic service was never so common as the literary evidence would suggest. In 1870, the first year the United States census listed occupations for women of all ages and races, one woman listed herself as a domestic servant for every 8.4 families in the population. Most prevalent in urban areas (where people had more money to spend), in the South (where many black women would work for low wages), and in places with large immigrant populations, domestic service embodied one possible solution—but by no means a universal one—to the cares of nineteenth-century housekeeping. For most of the century, servants cost less than the technological solution; indeed, most of the homes with gas lighting, plumbing, or electricity belonged to the very wealthy, who could

BRIDGET.—"Indade, Misthress Smith isn't in the House. She tould me to tell you so, this very minit, when she set her eyes on you."

PEGGY.—"Please, Ma'am, Cook is dressin' for the ball to-night, and says would you lend her a brooch, and a pair of bracelets, and a scarf, and a wreath.

Two major aspects of the "servant problem"—from the standpoint of the employer—may be seen in these cartoons from *Harper's New Monthly Magazine*, 1857. The series was entitled "The Miseries of Mistresses."

afford staffs of servants as well. People of limited means—that is, most people—employed household help in emergencies. The small middle class that could afford one servant but could not afford technology began to grow at the end of the century, as professional work opportunities expanded and businesses hired middle managers. This middle-class growth created a demand for servants at the very time when industrial expansion was creating new factory and office jobs that competed for the potential servant population and supplied new household products, utilities, and services that could do some of the work of servants at a competitive price. Yet despite the new technology, the demand continued; despite the demand, the "servant problem" remained, as full-time, live-in domestic service declined steadily.

Foreigners, especially the Irish, had predominated among domestic servants throughout the nineteenth century. Of 2,164 applications for employment received in 1825 by the employment registry of New York's

Society for the Encouragement of Faithful Domestic Servants, 59 percent came from Irish women—twenty-one years before the potato famine forced mass emigration from Ireland. Eight percent of the applicants had immigrated from other countries, mostly England, Scotland, and Wales; 21 percent were "people of color"—three years before New Yorkers emancipated their slaves; and only 12 percent were "American" in the society's designation, that is, free, native-born whites. At the end of the century, a study conducted in thirty-nine states and three territories found 60 percent of women servants foreign-born, 17 percent black, and 24 percent native white. Again, the Irish formed the largest group among the immigrants. Few other groups arrived in America with so many women; few others came so totally impoverished and therefore compelled to

Until the early twentieth century, when white women could get factory and office work and large numbers of blacks began to migrate to the North, most Northern servants were immigrants. "Welcome to The Land of Freedom," from *Frank Leslie's Illustrated Newspaper,* 1887.

send the entire family out to work. Many employers preferred English-speaking Irish women to other immigrants.

Although the women who applied for positions as domestic servants confronted few of the "No Irish Need Apply" signs their menfolk encountered, they suffered under a kind of social discrimination that became part and parcel of the mistress-servant relationship. Besides maintaining an employment registry, the New York Society for the Encouragement of Faithful Domestic Servants—established "to teach them that the way to become *respectable* is by *respecting themselves*, and by acting well the parts which Providence has assigned to them"—offered premiums to servants who stayed on a job for a long time. It also tendered "friendly advice to servants": don't leave a job, "except on such account, that in distress, or death, you will think you did right"; don't ask for too much money; "keep your temper and tongue under government"; and keep busy, "for Satan finds some mischief still for idle hands to do." The undemocratic character of this advice did not go unnoticed; an article in the Unitarian *Christian Inquirer*, later reprinted in the *Workingmen's Advocate*, declared that "the society appear to think that there is a certain species of mankind, born for the use of the remainder; and they talk of improving them as they would a breed of horned cattle." A writer in the *Mechanics' Free Press* maintained that a society to encourage faithful employers would be quite as proper.

Some of the discrimination applied specifically to Irish servants; "Bridget" and her sisters became stock characters in popular discussions of the servant problem, and imitations of Irish dialect laced nativist attacks like "The Miseries of Mistresses," a series of cartoons published in *Harper's* in 1856 and 1857. Sarah Josepha Hale, who recommended in 1844 that American servants "be careful to do by their employers as they will want *help* to do by them, when their turn to keep domestics shall arrive," thought that for the Irish, domestic service itself offered social mobility. If Irish servants would only "acknowledge their ignorance," she wrote, and if "benevolent and sensible ladies" would only instruct them in needlework and cooking, they could "always have good places and good pay," buy themselves nice clothes, and "lay up money." "And what a privilege and a blessing it is to a poor Irish girl, who has only lived in a hovel, with scarcely an article of furniture, save the pot 'to boil the praties,' to be instructed in household work!"

Instruction, patience, thoughtfulness, and mutual respect could, Hale maintained, pay off in good service. Catharine Beecher agreed, suggesting the Golden Rule as the ultimate test of employers' complaints; for example, she urged "every mistress of a family who keeps more than one domestic to provide them with single beds, that they may not be obliged to sleep with all the changing domestics, who come and go so often." Yet Beecher and Hale consistently campaigned for the abolition of servants.

Hale published some "hints about help" that implied that in a democratic society, mistresses had no right to expect compliant household help: "It is a tax which the rich must pay for their exemption from labor, to endure the vexations which those who perform the service will inflict upon them." Nobody, she claimed, could expect "to be freed from both labor and care." American democracy, added Beecher, prevented the formation of a servant class "who mean to make domestic service a profession to live and die"; without such a class, American women who maintained "an unsuspected spirit of superiority, which is stimulated into an active form by the resistance which democracy inspires in the working-class," would always have trouble with their servants.

Most powerfully, these mid-century domestic writers argued that women belonged at home, doing their own housework. "The most delicate lady," Hale wrote, "unless her ill health were the pretext, would scarcely boast of retaining a hired housekeeper to perform her duties." Only frivolous, superficial, showy women "despise and neglect the ordinary duties of life as beneath their notice. Such persons have not sufficient clearness of reason to see that 'Domestic Economy' includes every thing which is calculated to make people love home and feel happy there." Women who hired help to perform their own duties shirked the primary responsibility of their sex. Beecher's major goal, "redeeming woman's profession from dishonor," could only be served by breaking the pattern wherein rich women "will have large houses, many servants, poor health, and little domestic comfort, while they train the children of foreigners to do family work." Paying foreigners to do housework "dishonored" the American housewife who did it without monetary compensation, during a period when the money economy was achieving greater dominance.

The writers' campaign against domestic service failed; the urban middle-class audience they addressed expanded in the second half of the century, while black emancipation from slavery and continuing immigration enlarged the population of possible servants. Domestic service continued, especially in urban areas; in 1890, the fifty largest cities had about 18 percent of the total population and 32 percent of the domestic servants. Servants remained the largest group of employed women in every census until 1940, and within the occupational breakdown, private household service remained the largest. Still, after 1870, the status of domestic service relative to other women's occupations declined steadily and significantly; other jobs began to open up, first in manufacturing, later in stores and clerical work, and many women without skills preferred them to household labor. Half of all working women in 1870 were employed in "private or public housekeeping"; fewer than one-third were so employed by 1890, and fewer than one-sixth in 1920. (The trend reversed after that, owing not to a revival of private domestic service but to the expansion of commercial food and lodging services.) By the turn of

From the Parlor to the Kitchen.

Sapolio can be used in all sorts of cleaning. If you use it to clean marble, or to scour a tin pan or iron pot you will find it equally valuable. Sapolio is one of the articles which in this age so shorten the amount of time and effort expended in labor. Your house-work will be reduced one-third if you use SAPOLIO constantly. Beware of any article offered you as a substitute for SAPOLIO.

ENOCH MORGAN'S SONS CO.

NEW YORK.

"Your housework will be reduced one-third," reads the ad copy, but the woman in the picture is a maid, not the buyer of the product. From *Peterson's Magazine*, 1891.

the century discussions of the "servant problem" no longer focused on quality; it had become primarily a problem of quantity.

A variety of organizations and individuals looked for solutions to this new servant problem; unlike their predecessors, they advocated domestic service reform rather than its abolition. These reformers often worked under the auspices of larger organizations that took an interest in the general questions of women's employment and the protection of working women. Women's clubs, state and federal departments of labor, and college alumnae associations sponsored studies of domestic service; the YWCA established a national commission on household employment; the Legal Aid Society published a handbook for servants and employers. The Domestic Reform League of Boston's Women's Educational and Industrial Union was probably the most influential of the many local groups formed to consider and attack the problems. Domestic reformers set up employment bureaus, designed sample contracts, established training schools for servants, published reports, and organized conferences and lectures. From Lucy Salmon's book *Domestic Service* to the briefest pamphlet, their documents, published between 1897 (the year of the league's birth and of Salmon's book) and about 1920, display a striking thematic unanimity. They defined the problem underlying all others as the unbusinesslike nature of traditionally organized domestic service, and their solution was to rationalize it.

Under nineteenth-century conditions, domestic service shared few of the attributes of the factory, store, and office work that came to dominate paid employment as the United States industrialized. Servants lived with their employers; they rarely had contracts; they were on call at all times instead of working definite hours; and they received pay partly "in kind" (room and board), not solely in money. Rationalization, the reformers claimed, required conformity to the principles of capitalist industry; domestic service would not survive at all unless it adopted those principles.

Despite the long hours, low wages, and unhealthful conditions of factory work, single women of the largely immigrant working class preferred it to housework. Women simply did not want to enter domestic service. Reformers reported not only a shortage of servants but the refusal of unemployed women to accept positions as domestics, although housework was a relatively well-paid occupation, especially since room and board supplemented wages. Lillian Pettengill, a Mount Holyoke graduate who became a servant in order to write a book about her experience, reported that she enjoyed good health and relatively high pay, working for the most part in decent surroundings; nonetheless, she wrote, domestic service presented "perplexities real and puzzling," for which solutions must be found, if anyone were to take the job.

The first was social stigma. Lucy Salmon—Vassar College's first history professor, who wrote *Domestic Service* with the aid of Carroll D. Wright, pioneer social statistician and commissioner of the United States Bureau of Labor—pointed to the characteristic manifestations. The very word "servant," she wrote, had come to denote social degradation. Servants wore uniforms, not, as in some professions, to indicate their own professional status, but to establish the social status of their employers. Their employers addressed them by their Christian names. Daily contact reinforced servility, since employers seldom introduced a servant to guests and often denied her "the common daily courtesies"; the servant "takes no part in the general conversation around her . . . speaks only when addressed, obeys without murmur orders which her judgment tells her are absurd," and obeys even the whims and commands of children. Gail Laughlin, in a report to the United States Industrial Commission on the Relations and Conditions of Capital and Labor, cited a survey of shop and factory workers and the testimony of the head of a charitable employment bureau in New York "who meets on an average some 1,500 or

The maid's uniform was a distinguishing mark that reformers, and the servants they interviewed, considered one of the degrading aspects of the job. Photo from Homedale, Idaho, early twentieth century.

1,600 shop and factory workers yearly, and who has suggested domestic service to many of them as a substitute for factory work." The feeling that domestic service implied social inferiority was "practically universal," Laughlin maintained, describing one working girl's ostracism at a settlement-house club after she took a cleaning job. "A teacher or cashier, or anybody in a store, no matter if they have got common sense, don't want to associate with servants," one shopgirl told the president of the New Century Working Woman's Guild. "Young men think and say, 'Oh, she can't be much if she hasn't got brains enough to make her living outside a kitchen.' You're just down, once for all, if you go into one."

The most important material objection, the indefinite working became an issue because differences between families—their size, the size of their house, the presence of other servants, and the demands of the employers—led to vast differences in the nature of the employment from one family to another. "To a young woman therefore seeking employment," Salmon wrote, "the question of working hours assumes the aspect of a lottery—she may draw a prize of seven working hours or she may draw a blank of fourteen working hours." Even if the actual working hours were not excessive, servants were expected to be on call at all times, generally with the exception of one afternoon and one evening off per week. Hours of service were relatively long in comparison to other kinds of employment, wrote Laughlin, but the lack of "absolutely free time" evoked a greater objection. The worst of it was that domestics worked in the evenings and therefore could not visit places of amusement or join working women's clubs. "My first employer was a smart, energetic woman," one former servant reported. "I had a good room and everything nice, and she gave me a great many things, but I'd have spared them all if only I could have had a little time to myself."

The arguments about hours went hand-in-hand with arguments about lack of independence. Employers, for example, interfered with servants' work and personal habits rather than allowing the worker to do a set task independently. Domestic service allowed for no independent home life;

Most mistresses refused to allow their domestic employees any visitors, perhaps believing that their kitchens would resemble this scene from "The Miseries of Mistresses," *Harper's New Monthly Magazine*, 1856.

"Who is them Fellows, did you say, Mum? Them Gentlemen's my Cousins, Mum, jist dropped in to kape me company, Mum!"

employers regulated the number and character of visitors. "The domestic employee can neither accept nor give an invitation to supper," Salmon pointed out; "she cannot offer a cup of tea to a caller; she does not ask a friend to remain to dinner, except perhaps at rare intervals a mother or sister." She could eat as much as she wanted, but could not share it. Servants could not socialize, could not go out, could not meet men. Employers might claim that they desired, above all, trained, efficient maids, but, wrote one reformer in a YWCA commission bulletin, "Do they not desire something else just a little more, namely a willing, self-effacing, tractable girl who will do as she is told and is on tap, so to speak, at any time of the day or night?"

Factory labor might be unhealthful; it might bring lower wages than domestic service; it might be harder work; its hours might be longer. But the factory worker could choose her own home—with her own family, as a boarder, or in a working-girls' home—and lead her own life there. She worked a certain number of hours for a certain amount of money and did not have to negotiate the quality of the dollar as she might have to negotiate the quality of wages paid in room and board. The work itself was defined and systematic, and employers did not change tasks arbitrarily. In domestic service, on the other hand, "it is the person who is hired and not, distinctively, the labor of the person," Laughlin wrote. The "underlying cause" of the servant problem, the "contract" that demanded a servant "to be at all times subject to the call and direction of the employer" rather than to perform "certain specified services," demanded revision.

Other reformers agreed. The YWCA commission bulletin of 1915–1916 contrasted the relationship of "mistress and maid" with that of "employer and employee." "When employers adopt for their households a business basis," it said, "systematizing the work, regulating the hours, granting the worker sufficient time and freedom to live a normal life among her own people, then both educators and girls will be more than glad to do their part in meeting the demand for trained service." Domestic service would finally "meet the fundamental requirements of a good job"—and in modern society, those requirements were established by factories and businesses. Some reformers offered an explicit historical analysis. I. M. Rubinow, a government statistician writing in the *Journal of Political Economy* in 1905, blamed "the survival of mediaeval terms of contract" for the problems of modern domestic service. Ida Tarbell, already famous for her critical *History of the Standard Oil Company* when she wrote about domestic service for the YWCA commission bulletin in 1916, agreed. American housewives, she claimed, lived "back in the eighteenth century, and not in the eighteenth century of revolutionary France, and revolutionary America, but the feudal eighteenth century."

Tarbell's article, "What a Factory Can Teach a Housewife," recommended that women study how manufacturers held on to their employees and adopt the spirit and methods of industry. Lillian Pettengill put the question on an individual basis: "A dinner ordered at half past six is a business engagement with the cook, and should be honored as such." Lucy Salmon devoted ten pages of her book to the relationship of business principles and domestic-service reform; every type of work except for housework, she claimed, benefitted from concentration of capital and labor, from specialization, division of labor, association and combination among both employers and employees, technical training, profit sharing, and women's increasing independence. Household employment must move "into the current of these and other industrial and social tendencies." The rhetoric of the domestic-service reform movement repeated the point incessantly: domestic service must be rationalized according to well-developed principles of capitalist industry.

The first step was a written contract, which, wrote Laughlin in the United States Industrial Commission Reports of 1901, should delineate specific tasks and fix definite hours; although emergencies might arise as in any other occupation, a contract could establish hours for "ordinary circumstances." Reformers who actually worked with domestics and their employers proceeded more cautiously. Boston's Domestic Reform League in 1903 provided a sample contract that specified wages and prescribed a trial week but did not delineate hours or duties; likewise, in 1908 the Legal Aid Society of New York, in a small handbook designed to educate domestics about their legal rights and duties, suggested a monthly contract with a trial week that obligated an employer to pay the domestic worker a wage and "to supply her with lodging and sufficient and wholesome food," but said nothing about hours or duties.

Employment offices offered one means of supervising domestic employment and spreading the idea of the contract. Charitable institutions maintained these offices for women who sought industrial and shop jobs as well as service positions; other agencies were run for profit or—as is clear from the Legal Aid handbook's delineation of employee rights—as covers for white-slaving. By 1907 the Domestic Reform League employment office, established ten years earlier, processed well over 15,000 applications per year from employers and employees; breach of contract, whether verbal or written, immediately debarred both employers and employees from further use of the office.

The league's bulletins measured supply and demand, showing an increased emphasis on day labor for hourly wages as opposed to resident domestic service. Although employers continued to apply for resident domestics, the employment bureau could fill only 29 percent of those applications; nearly twice as many employers applied for resident domestics as there were women registered to work on a live-in basis. Day labor prevailed only in commercial establishments at the turn of the cen-

"Standard"

PORCELAIN ENAMELED
Baths & One Piece Lavatories

Will guarantee the comfort and sanitation of your home

"Standard" Porcelain Enameled ware is the indispensable equipment for a modern home; always moderate in cost no matter how simple or elaborate. Its snow white, seamless, non-porous surface is a constant assurance of health, its beauty a source of comfort and satisfaction to all the family, and its installation in your home is a small investment, which not only quickly earns its cost through daily use, but considerably increases the value of your house, if at any time you should want to sell or rent.

Our Book, "MODERN BATHROOMS," tells you how to plan, buy and arrange your bathroom, and illustrates many beautiful and inexpensive rooms, showing the cost of each fixture in detail, together with many hints on decoration, tiling, etc. It is the handsomest booklet of its kind, and contains 100 interesting pages.

The ABOVE INTERIOR, No. P-27, costing approximately $90.00 — not counting piping and labor — is described in detail among the others. FREE for six cents postage.

CAUTION: *Every piece of "Standard" Ware bears our "Standard" "Green and Gold" guarantee label, and has our trade-mark "Standard" cast on the outside. Unless the label and trade-mark are on the fixture, it is not "Standard" Ware. Refuse substitutes—they are all inferior and will cost you more in the end.*

Standard Sanitary Mfg. Co. Dept. 34 PITTSBURGH, PA.

Offices and Showrooms in New York: "Standard" Building, 35-37 West 31st St.   London, England: 22 Holborn Viaduct, E. C.

This ad, from *Life* in 1905, was one of many during the period that showed servants without explanation or apologies, and without suggesting that manufactured products would substitute for domestic help.

tury, but not because of any shortage of potential workers: the bureau filled 93 percent of its day-labor orders.

Although reformers called for removal of the restrictions that came with living in, they approached day labor cautiously. The Massachusetts Bureau of Statistics of Labor, expressly seeking to determine "whether present domestic difficulties could be alleviated by having a part of the housework done by persons living outside the house and coming in by the day or hour," addressed the employers they surveyed with prudence. "Of course, such an arrangement could not be brought about suddenly"; if it happened at all, it would come "as a result of slow change and growth and could only be perfected by adapting houses and methods of housework to meet the change." Lucy Salmon, who maintained that "a very large part of the work of the household" could be done with day labor, dismissed it in fewer than two pages, while devoting sixteen to the adaptation of profit sharing to the household.

This caution apparently derived from the reformers' belief that employers resisted day labor. Jane Addams, the founder of Chicago's Hull House, ascribed that resistance to selfishness, narrow social ethics, and backwardness. The housewife who relinquished resident service, Addams wrote, "would be in line with the industrial organization of her age. Were she in line ethically, she would have to believe that the sacredness and beauty of family life . . . consist . . . in sharing the corporate life of the community, and in making the family the unit of that life." Addams's argument, nearly identical with her argument about keeping boarders, stressed the connection between the household and the larger society and the individual housewife's responsibility for social progress.

Social progress, and conformity of the household to principles established in the social world, depended on making domestic service like other jobs: hourly work implied payment in money rather than in kind. Employees in tobacco and shoe factories, Rubinow pointed out in his *Journal of Political Economy* article, no longer received "the privilege of unlimited smoking" or "partial payment in shoes," nor should the servant accept meals as payment just because she prepared them. "Like the industrial worker, the domestic servant may require payment for her labor in units of universal value—money, with the privilege of spending it according to her own taste." This reform, he maintained, would finally end the "strongest manifestation of the social inferiority of the servant": her eating separately from the family, in the kitchen. The only other way to cure that ill would be to bring her to the table, but "the objection to placing a total stranger at the family table—a stranger possibly little cultured and ill-mannered—is a perfectly legitimate one." Paying her money and sending her to eat at her own home at the end of the day solved everyone's problems. Although sympathetic to the servants' plight, most of these reformers shared the employers' prejudices and class outlook; their pri-

mary concerns were with social order and the solution to the employers' "servant problem." Day labor, rationalizing domestic service according to business principles, conformed to established social principles and offered the only possibility for luring resistant working women into household work. "The new way is coming," wrote Pettengill, "and its coming will be the dawning of housekeeping's golden age. Non-resident household labor may never be universal, of course, but it is bound to be general."

Curiously, the reformers paid little attention to the most significant trend developing during the years they wrote, and the one that may have most influenced the eventual triumph of day labor: the increasing predominance of black women in domestic service. As domestic service declined in importance for American women in general, the number and proportion of black women servants increased, especially in Northern cities. Part of a general black migration from Southern tenant farms to Northern ghettos at the beginning of the century, many black women moved specifically to take jobs as domestic servants, recruited by employment agents who traveled around the South offering them transportation and jobs upon arrival. They took the places both of immigrant women (decreasing in numbers as immigration declined after World War I began) and of native white women whose other job opportunities expanded with the development of office and shop work. Black women, about a third of all servants in 1900, constituted nearly half the servant population in 1930. Because racial discrimination denied them other work, black women became a servant class: most black women wage earners worked as servants and laundresses, and more servants and laundresses came from the black community than from any other ethnic group. They worked because they needed the money, and most of them could expect to work for most of their lives, since black men earned even less than working-class native or immigrant whites. Unlike working-class white women, who throughout the nineteenth century had tended to work outside the home only before marriage and then to supplement their husbands' earnings by taking in extra housework, black women, as slaves and as freedwomen, had always worked in other women's households; they had learned long before to combine marriage and outside employment. In 1920, 33 percent of married black women worked, as opposed to 6 percent of married native and 7 percent of married immigrant white women; put another way, black women made up 35 percent of the married women working, while the population was 10 percent black. The increase of black women among the servant population, then, created a similar increase among married women servants in general.

Married women, of course, preferred day labor; they could work elsewhere all day but return to their own houses and husbands and children. Arriving in the North when white women were finding new job opportunities in the expanding sales, clerical, and service sectors of the econ-

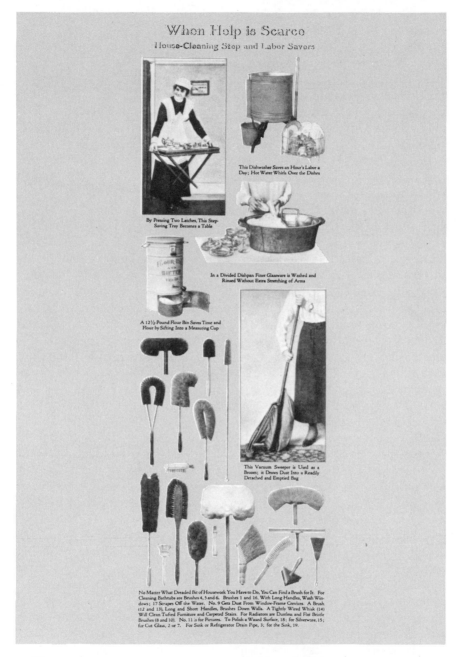

When Help is Scarce

House-Cleaning Step and Labor Savers

This Dishwasher Saves an Hour's Labor a Day; Hot Water Whirls Over the Dishes

By Pressing Two Latches, This Step-Saving Tray Becomes a Table

In a Divided Dishpan Finer Glassware is Washed and Rinsed Without Extra Stretching of Arms

A 12½-Pound Flour Bin Saves Time and Flour by Sifting Into a Measuring Cup

This Vacuum Sweeper is Used as a Broom; it Draws Dust Into a Readily Detached and Emptied Bag

No Matter What Dreaded Bit of Housework You Have to Do, You Can Find a Brush for It. For Cleaning Bathtubs are Brushes 4, 5 and 6. Brushes 1 and 16, With Long Handles, Wash Windows; 17 Scrapes Off the Water. No. 9 Gets Dust From Window-Frame Crevices. A Brush (12 and 13), Long and Short Handles, Brushes Down Walls. A Tightly Wired Whisk (14) Will Clean Tufted Furniture and Carpeted Stairs. For Radiators are Dustless and Flat Bristle Brushes (8 and 10). No. 11 is for Pictures. To Polish a Waxed Surface, 18; for Silverware, 15; for Cut Glass, 2 or 7. For Sink or Refrigerator Drain Pipe, 3; for the Sink, 19.

By 1918, many readers of the *Ladies' Home Journal* had to do their own "dreaded bit of housework," and few had dishwashers to save an hour a day.

omy, many black women with families accepted low wages for part-time, nonresident domestic service, which they offered to employers on a take-it-or-leave-it basis. The employers took it, although many would doubt-less have preferred the compliant, tractable, full-time white "help" they could not find. Exhorted by reformers to consider non-resident services, more housewives could now do so by substituting products and utilities for people, as electricity, plumbing, prepared foods, and mass-produced goods opened the possibility of a middle-class life-style without full-time domestic help. Bridget, the stereotyped full-time, live-in servant of the nineteenth century, left the scene, replaced by Beulah, the part-time black maid of the twentieth.

The transition to part-time domestic service failed to create the "golden age of housekeeping" the reformers promised; with the exception of day labor, their proposals did not gain general acceptance. Maids negotiated verbal agreements with their employers about hours, but few signed writ-ten contracts delineating specific duties; payment in kind (usually lunch and old clothes) continued to supplement the defined hourly wage; the social stigma survived, exacerbated by racism. Nor did many servants benefit from the twentieth-century legislation that served other workers: legally exempt from some benefits (such as minimum wages and occupa-tional safety regulations) because they worked for private households that employed only one person and did not engage in interstate com-merce, maids were illegally deprived of others—notably Social Security—by many unscrupulous employers. Mistress and maid continued to share intimate space without defined obligations on either part, their relation-ships still wholly dependent on their personalities. Employers "don't care anything about you," complained Roena Bethune, a black household worker interviewed in 1977. "They don't want to know nothing about your background; they don't even want to know what's going on in your home. All they want to know is what you are doing for them." No indus-trial worker, with defined obligations to an employer specified by con-tract, expects that kind of caring.

Although many domestic employees continue to hire themselves out to private families, some now work for the new professional housecleaning services. Almost nonexistent at the beginning of the 1970s, dozens of these services were listed by major city Yellow Pages in 1980, usually small companies with several employees who worked for a one- or two-person management. "Our well-trained employees work under maximum super-vision," claimed one in Seattle; no longer need the housewife seeking help trouble herself with training, references, supervision, wage negotiations, or ambiguous relationships. "I am a broker of household technicians," declared Coralee Kern of Chicago, whose franchised Maid-To-Order business employed three hundred domestics in five cities in 1978. "Today people need trained professional domestics just as they need a plumber or electrician. That's what Maid-To-Order is all about." The firm charged seven dollars an hour, paying domestic employees roughly half of that, depending on their length of employment. The rest went to management, to expand the business or to keep as profit. Kern's claim that people need "trained professional domestics" echoes those of the domestic reformers at the turn of the century; businesses like hers go beyond the reformers' intentions to put domestic service "on a business basis." The new house-cleaning services *are* businesses, establishing formal relationships with employees, training them, paying them hourly wages like other workers, sending them home at the end of the day, and making profits off their labor. For the employees, wage labor—not simply labor hired on terms "like" wage labor—has at last replaced the medieval terms of contract criticized so long ago.

The virtual disappearance of full-time domestic service during the twentieth century provides yet another demonstration of the effects on daily life of the general trends of economic development. Increasing numbers of industrial products and services substituted for women's arduous labor at home; growing numbers of individual workers began to work according to the rational principles established by business. With day labor, domestic service, for so long the major employer of women's labor, began to "meet the fundamental requirements of a good job," freed from the oppressive requirements that came with living in. With mass production, domestic service became an adjunct to standardized, dependable products; the housewife at last assumed the primary responsibility for her housework that Catharine Beecher and Sarah Josepha Hale had assigned her in the mid-nineteenth century. Increasingly, however, the modern housewife combines that responsibility with paid work outside the home, whereas the nineteenth-century writers made their assignment as part of a more general effort to elevate women's status without removing them from their "proper sphere," the household.

TEN

Redeeming Woman's Profession

As the American economy developed during the nineteenth century, so did the distinctions between the nature of women's work and that of their husbands. While men went off to work in factories and businesses, formidable household labor and small children made it difficult for women without domestic help to leave home to earn money. In a society increasingly dominated by money and profit, their arena—the household—stood apart: full-time housewives earned only their subsistence in food, clothing, and shelter, laboring to maintain their families while their menfolk worked for wages to produce profits for business. Factory workers spent their days closely supervised, their labor hired for definite hours and carefully timed. Women who worked at home, even those earning money from boarders, laundry, or sewing, regulated their own time, oriented to the task rather than the clock. They could choose what they thought needed to be done, not what the boss dictated; they could chat with friends while they worked or suspended a task to comfort a crying baby or stir the soup. Like Rachel Haskell, who sewed at night while she entertained guests, they intermingled labor and social life, while their husbands distinguished between "work" at the factory, store, or office and "life" at home.

Working alone or in very small groups, women could not share their husbands' political activities; while workers' organizations and unions gained strength and workplaces became arenas for political discussion, no industrial organization could penetrate the home. Because married women were isolated and unorganized in their households, class became a less important distinction for them than for their husbands and brothers, despite important class differences *between* households. Although money could buy both domestic help and an ever greater number of products and services to lighten housework, so that by mid-century a few women acted as home administrators and socialites while the vast majority toiled endlessly, gender was the crucial distinction within any individual household as men went out to work and women stayed home.

The "ideology of separate spheres," which codified these distinctions, first began to appear in popular literature around the 1820s, at the same time that the early capitalists organized the first factories. In the poetry, fiction, and sermonizing that filled the women's magazines, religious literature, etiquette books, household manuals, and sentimental gift books of the industrial revolution, the message came in two parts. First, in a developing urban industrial society, only the home could preserve certain crucial values. An article appearing in the *Ladies' Magazine* in 1830 contrasted the *"sanctuary of home,"* where "sympathy, honor, virtue are assembled," with "the scenes of business and pleasure," where "the *heart* is sensible to a desolation of feeling." Outside the home, "we behold every principle of justice and honor, and even the dictates of common honesty disregarded, and the delicacy of our moral sense is wounded; we see the general good, sacrificed to the advancement of personal interest." Men, who operated in this sullied milieu, the new industrial order, needed a haven, a place where they could find love in an unloving world, stability amid geographic and economic mobility, religion in an increasingly secularized culture, purity in the midst of immorality and the cult of mammon, and submissiveness since they were no longer their own

economic masters. Fortunately, these virtues could be found in Woman and in her "sphere," the Home.

The second part of the "separate spheres" message, of course, was that women belonged at home; Lydia Maria Child expressed it in her popular manual *The American Frugal Housewife*, which first appeared in 1829 and went through thirty editions by 1842. "What a lesson is taught a girl in that sentence, '*Let her enjoy herself all she can, while she is single!*'" Child wrote. "That one pernicious sentence teaches a girl to consider matrimony . . . a necessary sacrifice of her freedom and her gaiety." Instead, women should consider "domestic life as the gathering place of the deepest and purest affections; as the sphere of woman's *enjoyments* as well as of her *duties*, as, indeed, the whole world to her." Only women's virtues—which one historian has characterized as "purity, piety, submissiveness, and domesticity," adding up to a "cult of True Womanhood"— could preserve that gathering place in an unpure and unaffectionate world; women must appreciate their duty to preserve the haven.

One obvious paradox in the separate-spheres ideology arose from the fact that men and women lived together in the same houses; the home might be "the whole world" to women, but their menfolk had another, and commuted between the two. In the world outside the home, a "vast wilderness" where men stood "naked and alone surrounded by savages," as popular author John Todd wrote in *The Student's Manual* (1835), they needed "the useful 'rivalry' and the 'pressure' of frightening competition," which could not be found at home. Men's very participation in that world necessarily sullied them and beset them with temptation. "How then could men dare to leave home at all to pursue careers in American society?" wonders historian Kirk Jeffrey, who calls this the "commuting problem." "Or if they did leave, even for a few hours a day, what would happen to their wives and families when they returned?"

Popular writing for young women trained them to wonder the same thing. Taking premarital virginity for granted, Eliza Farrar, author of *The Young Lady's Friend*, the most popular etiquette book for unmarried women, taught girls how to avoid physical contact: "Be not lifted in and out of carriages, on or off a horse; sit not with another in a place that is too narrow; read not out of the same book; let not your eagerness to see anything induce you to place your head close to another person's." Even thoughts about men should be treated with a "wholesome dread," since they led to "entanglements" and "snares"; girls should consider masculine company "dangerous," and must "stifle their preferences to death," turning their thoughts "resolutely to something else." Young women should keep their brothers entertained at home in the evenings with "innocent amusements," since "so many temptations beset young men, of which young women know nothing." In short, morally superior young women must distrust masculine motives, which issued from a sphere that they did not inhabit.

Eventually, however, these young women would join with men in the paradoxical institution of marriage, ideally a glorious bond of intimacy, a "perfect union." The atrocious loveless marriage must be avoided even at the cost of seven weeks like those described in "Fragments from a Young Wife's Diary," a story in *Harper's*: "I have been married about seven weeks. . . . I do not rave in girlish fashion about my perfect happiness— I do not even say I love my husband. Such words imply a separate existence—a gift consciously bestowed on one being from another. I do not feel thus: my husband is to me as my own soul." This perfect union could hardly be achieved with beastly men, and the sexual expression of married souls obviously ran head-on into the ideal of purity. Women—on the one hand chaste, on the other controlled by their reproductive organs, which dominated their emotions and established their social roles—could never depend on the perfect union, since they could never depend on their husbands. Women alone possessed the morals, the ideals, the principles, and the consciences, and they must nurture and guard those virtues in the home.

Paradoxical in itself, the separate-spheres idea could not endure because the spheres were not separate; although women might be denied entry into men's sphere, the home existed to educate and rehabilitate those who operated in the outside world. The qualities that defined the ideal wife—dependence, gentleness, emotionality—destroyed the ideal mother, who performed heavy housework duties and prepared children for the demands of the outside world. And even the ideal mother was only clearly fitted to raise her girl children; boys might benefit from a mother's love, but too much of a good thing could ruin their ability to deal with the jungle outside the portals of home.

Although the writing about women's sphere contained rhetoric hostile to the developing economic order, it merely promised a haven from it, thereby justifying submission to the system that increasingly dominated American life. In the decades after such rhetoric appeared in popular literature, more men left home for significant parts of the day, towns and cities grew, and an ever greater proportion of the population forsook the primarily self-sufficient agricultural life-style. The preindustrial housewife, equal partner in an agricultural enterprise based on the sexual division of labor, lost ground to the new housewife, who stayed at home while her husband went off to make money. Although this new housewife had plenty of arduous work to do, she did not "work" in the terms of the new society; she worked at home, supervising and timing herself. The ideology of separate spheres, which undertook to soften the harsh effects of the new industrial life by providing a safe sphere of retreat, retained a certain reality throughout the nineteenth century. As long as most married women stayed home, building fires and hauling water, directing their own never-ending activity, the idea that they inhabited a separate sphere represented a genuine distinction between the traditional household and

Advertising, like this lithograph for the Domestic Sewing Machine, suggested that industrial products could enhance and preserve the virtues of the domestic sphere.

traditional working life on the one hand, and the leading sectors of the new industrial society on the other.

Still, as the economy developed during the second half of the century, writers on household affairs had to confront two new problems. First, the separation of the spheres began to blur. Although few women could afford the plumbing and gas that eventually relieved housewives of so much grueling and time-consuming labor, most bought factory-made textiles, soap, candles, and other products by the end of the Civil War; economic development encroached on productive work in women's traditional sphere. This contributed to the second problem: housework was losing status. As the economy expanded and more families spent money earned from industrial work on the new machine-made products, money and goods assumed greater importance; as half the society became accustomed to wage labor in the developing American industrial economy, the independent home-based work of the other half began to look like something other than work. Unpaid housewives, working without machines and repeating endless tasks like cleaning and making fires that generated no tangible products at all, seemed less important to the new society than wage-earning industrial producers.

It therefore fell to those who wrote about domestic affairs to "redeem woman's profession from dishonor." The phrase is Catharine Beecher's; her writing best demonstrates the paradoxes of mid-century domestic advice. Although others perceived the same problems and suggested similar solutions, Beecher's many books and articles, among the most popular of the household-instruction manuals, offer a coherent theory of household management and a complete guide to nineteenth-century housework. Beecher's mission, to assert that women could and should find self-respect within their traditional sphere, led her into contradictory positions as she attempted to adapt ideas about that sphere to the new demands of the industrial world outside the home.

In order to establish the honor of woman's profession, Beecher devoted considerable effort to glorifying housekeeping, attempting to convince her readers that their daily duties, although possibly tedious and distressing, constituted important work, assigned to them by Nature and God. She based her entire system of domestic economy on the "Christian family state"; the housewife ("minister of the family state") fulfilled her most important duty—that owed to God—by doing her housework and teaching her children to work together for the good of all. Considerations of the next world aside, the housekeeper made an infinite number of critical daily decisions, matters of life and death, in providing her family with healthful food and surroundings.

Making these decisions presented an unending intellectual challenge; an advertisement for *The American Woman's Home*, which Beecher published with her sister Harriet Beecher Stowe in 1869, offered this argu-

ment: "There is no housekeeper so expert but she may learn something from others whose experience has been different, and particularly from those who have made the art of housekeeping a scientific study." And a scientific study it was. The housekeeper, Beecher claimed, should be a jack-of-all-sciences—architecture, pneumatics, hydrostatics, calorification, floriculture, horticulture, animal husbandry, botany, hygiene, physiology, domestic chemistry, and economics, to name but a few. Whereas men specialized, women's work involved duties of an infinite variety; understanding the scientific processes behind those duties provided a constant intellectual frontier.

Without physical exercise, all this intellectual work would be unhealthy; luckily, housework offered opportunities for that, too. Beecher cited her own life as example: ten years of study and teaching had ruined her health; she had regained it by doing domestic labor. Women would "constantly be interested and cheered in their exercise by the feeling of usefulness and the consciousness of having performed their duty" if they did "useful domestic exercise at home" instead of walking "for the purpose of exercise." God, who "made woman to do the work of the family," had so formed her body "that family labor and care tend not only to good health, but to the *highest culture of mind.*"

Patriotic duty joined the moral and religious. Democratic custom, Beecher said, rested on the principle that the virtuous of all classes must work. Only aristocrats scorned domestic work; by doing their own housework, women who could afford servants upheld the most fundamental American standards. Domestic work further served patriotic goals by attending to the future leaders of America. "You," Beecher exhorted her readers, "are training young minds whose plastic texture will receive and retain every impression you make; who will transmit what they receive from you to their children, to pass again to the next generation, and then to the next, until a *whole nation* may possibly receive its character and destiny from your hands! No imperial queen ever stood in a more sublime and responsible position. . . ."

Housework, then, could be "redeemed from dishonor" only if the women who did it fully understood the importance of their duties. Another part of Beecher's strategy, adapting household practices to the new demands of the outside world, rested on the proper use of time. She devoted an entire chapter of *The American Woman's Home* to early rising, necessary to patriotic living because American democracy depended on the principle that work was a virtue and indolence an aristocratic vice, and "indispensable to a systematic and well-regulated family" because children and servants, rising early, could not be supervised by sleeping mothers and mistresses. Public benefits supplemented the private ones; early rising "has a relation to the general interests of the social community." Beecher argued that people "employed in business and

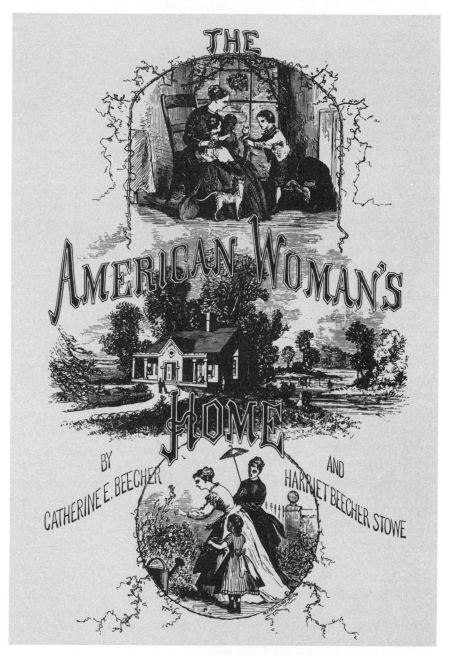

The sphere of woman, as depicted on the title page of Catharine Beecher's most popular manual, *The American Woman's Home*, published with her sister Harriet Beecher Stowe in 1869.

labor" had to rise early, and all their meals and appointments must be regulated accordingly. "Now, if a small portion of the community establish very different hours," she wrote, "it makes a kind of jostling in all the concerns and interests of society. The various appointments for the public, such as meetings, schools, and business hours, must be accommodated to the mass, and not to individuals." Different as it might be from the rest of the world, women's sphere must adapt to its demands, and Beecher provided her readers with ways to establish routines compatible with those outside the home.

Household labor must be designed with regard for efficiency. Along with her philosophy of domestic life, Beecher offered women plans for the orderly management of their households in her numerous manuals and cookbooks. She insisted that the many and various obligations of housekeeping made such plans fundamental to good domestic work: "There is no one thing more necessary to a housekeeper in performing her varied duties, than a *habit of system and order*. . . . It is wise, therefore, for all persons to devise a systematic plan, which they will at least keep in view, and aim to accomplish, and by which a proper proportion of time shall be secured for all the duties of life." She suggested explicit weekly schedules, apportioning all the tasks of the household so that everything would get done on a regular basis: Monday, preparing for the week; Tuesday, washing; Wednesday, ironing; Thursday, ironing, mending, folding clothes, and putting them away; Friday, sweeping and housecleaning; Saturday, arranging things and putting them in order. Sunday she reserved for religious duties.

Systematic living further required that there be a place for everything and everything in its place. To this end, Beecher described plans for ordered closets to store washing, ironing, sewing, and kitchen supplies, and plans for entire houses designed to save time and steps; she published these plans in *Harper's* as well as in her books. "In many large kitchens," she wrote, "half the time of a cook is employed in walking to collect her utensils and materials, which all might be placed together." Architectural historian James Marston Fitch calls Beecher's ideal house, as it appeared in *The American Woman's Home*, "a true machine for living": "every cubic inch has been carefully analyzed and organized for a specific purpose." Decades ahead of her time, Beecher designed cabinetwork "of astonishing modernity" and created the ideas "for that free-standing, middle-class suburban house which Frank Lloyd Wright was to bring to esthetic perfection, thirty or forty years later."

Although Beecher did not articulate the notion of running households like businesses, as later writers like Christine Frederick and Lillian Gilbreth would, her new systems pointed in that direction. She sometimes relied on other kinds of rationales; a chapter entitled "Economy of Time and Expenses," for example, maintains that "Christianity teaches that, for all the time afforded us, we must give account to God; and that we have no right to waste a single hour." Whatever the rationale, Beecher's "habits of system and order" copied the organization of work that industrialization had brought to the world outside the home. Such habits thus brought women's sphere more in line with that of men, enabling women better to adapt household routines to the pace and the practices of their husbands' lives, and to establish their self-respect in a world that increasingly valued efficiency above more traditional values.

Orderly habits, Beecher maintained, should be taught to young women at school. Earlier writers had called for better domestic education; Lydia Maria Child had recommended it as the solution for domestic troubles in

Catharine Beecher's plan for rationalizing the cooking area. From *The New Housekeeper's Manual*, 1873, a manual nearly identical to *The American Woman's Home*, in which this page also appeared.

"Shake Hands?" a popular painting by Mrs. Lilly M. Spencer that was reproduced in engravings as well as this 1854 lithograph, shows the unrationalized kitchen that Beecher wanted to reform.

The American Frugal Housewife, first published in 1829, though she suggested domestic apprenticeship, not school training. Young girls, Child wrote, "should spend . . . two or three years with a mother, assisting her in her duties, instructing brothers and sisters, and taking care of their own clothes." Beecher, on the other hand, wrote that domestic apprenticeship had failed. Because mothers "have not been trained themselves, and so can not teach *properly*," the schools must take over. "Institutions should be established where women will be trained to be scientific, healthful, and economical cooks; to be intelligent, loving, and careful nurses of young children; to be skillful seamstresses and mantua-makers. . . ." No mere theorist, Beecher established domestic education in her role as headmistress of the Hartford Female Seminary.

Although Beecher believed that women were essentially and necessarily domestic creatures whose school training should be directed solely toward their future domestic duties, she did not advocate training solely in home economics; good household management required cultivated taste and imagination and trained minds as well as household skills. Minds could be trained, however, without neglecting domestic education. "Young women," she wrote, "are taught to draw mathematical diagrams and to solve astronomical problems; but few, if any, of them are taught to solve the problem of a house constructed to secure pure and moist air by day and night for all its inmates by safe methods." Domestic problems, relevant to life, made more sense than abstract ones; young girls could more easily understand stove design, for example, than "the first problems of Geometry—for which they will never have any practical use, while attention to this problem of home affairs will cultivate the intellect quite as much as the abstract reasonings of Algebra and Geometry."

Beecher believed that her dreams of domestic order could never be realized until schools trained girls to do domestic work, but an educational system run by men had not provided this training. Women must therefore become professional educators, although it meant leaving the home; they might also work in "womanly" professions like sewing and nursing. She never suggested that a woman might prefer a profession to marriage, or that employed women might work outside "the branches included in woman's profession"; rather, they should be trained for professions "in case" they did not marry or their husbands died. Nor did she accept the implications of her own unconventional life: Beecher interpreted her teaching and writing as "womanly," but her teaching assumed women's domestic role; she called intellectual activity ruinous to mental and physical health, but (after the death of her fiancé when she was twenty-one) she never attempted to find a husband or to establish the lifestyle for which she claimed God had designed her body and mind. She suggested that single women could become matriarchs by adopting orphans, but never did so herself.

If recommending professions other than housework constituted widening women's sphere, Beecher did so cautiously; she carefully avoided identification with radicalism, insisting that women and men existed in separate spheres, and that women's work must harmonize with their basic female natures. The remedy for women's problems, she wrote, "is not in leading women into the professions and business of men, by which many philanthropists are now aiming to remedy their sufferings, but to train woman properly for her own proper business and then to secure to her the honor and profit which men gain in their professions." Her writings offer a striking contrast to the rhetoric and philosophy of the early women's rights movement, with which she consciously and actively disagreed. No amount of analysis can reconcile her rhetoric with most of the Declaration of Sentiments and Resolutions passed at the first women's rights convention in Seneca Falls, New York, in July 1848; this document, modeled on the Declaration of Independence, called for women's suffrage and for "the securing to woman an equal participation with men in the various trades, professions, and commerce." Elizabeth Cady Stanton's eighth resolution for the declaration challenged Beecher's central tenets: "*Resolved*, That woman has too long rested satisfied in the circumscribed limits which corrupt customs and a perverted application of the Scriptures have marked out for her, and that it is time she should move in the enlarged sphere which her great Creator has assigned her." But Beecher would have agreed that man "has endeavored, in every way that he could, to destroy [woman's] confidence in her own powers, to lessen her self-respect, and to make her willing to lead a dependent and abject life." She sought independence and self-respect for women, shared the women's movement's distrust of men, and asserted women's superiority: in those senses, Catharine Beecher may be seen as a quasi-feminist. But she was adamant that women had their own sphere and should remain in it.

Without the proper training that would bring women to a position of supremacy in their own sphere, housekeeping was a life of trials, fraught with domestic discontent. This malaise, described variously as bad temper, irritable depression, and despairing feelings of worthlessness, discouraged housekeepers and burdened their families. It therefore became a subject for manuals otherwise concerned with the details of daily household routine. *Miss Beecher's Housekeeper and Healthkeeper*, her final compendium of domestic advice, much of it reprinted from *The American Woman's Home* and other books, contained two such chapters, entitled "The Preservation of Good Temper in the Housekeeper" and "Comfort for a Discouraged Housekeeper." In both, Beecher, trapped in the framework of "separate spheres," in a self-contradiction advised submission, self-delusion, and retreat from her systematized ideals. By Christian law, she wrote, the woman must obey the man, "head and chief magistrate by the force of his physical power and requirement of the chief responsibility." This did not present a problem in a loving marriage; with no love, "the only dignified and peaceful course is for the wife, however much the man's superior, to 'submit, as to God and not to man.'" Although she directed her primary efforts at reform of marriage, that is, the establishment of families founded on love and Christianity in which women would reign, she advised morally superior women to submit to their physically superior husbands and to Christian law.

Submission imbued Beecher's rules for the preservation of temper; although her rules incorporated her advice about making plans and building systematic habits, she implied here that order was a mere ideal, to be sacrificed for the sake of good temper. Housekeepers, the rules maintained, must prepare themselves for inevitable interference with their plans, which should be made "in consistency with the means at command, and the character of those around." A woman with a "heedless husband" could not make the same plans as others, but "must aim at just as much as she can probably attain, and no more" so as to escape disappointment. Readers who wanted to maintain good temper should refrain from angry tones, with perfect silence if necessary, remembering that God was responsible for whatever happened, and trusting "the power of religion to impart dignity and importance to the ordinary and petty details of domestic life." Beecher, the pioneer designer of household habits of system and order, recommended that frustrated readers submit to chaos, if necessary, as God's will.

Even more astonishingly, Beecher advised self-delusion. The rules for good temper imply that she knew that housework made her readers unhappy and that her attempt to elevate it in their minds was an uphill battle. She justified Rule One, to regard household duties as "dignified, important, and difficult," not by making an argument for their dignity, importance, or difficulty, but by maintaining that "the mind is so made as to be elevated and cheered by a sense of far-reaching influence and usefulness," and that a woman who believed her work insignificant had little to "sustain and invigorate" her. Rule Two similarly appealed to a good frame of mind: "Again, a housekeeper should feel that she really has great difficulties to meet and overcome." Although she contended elsewhere that housework *was* difficult and dignified, Beecher did not stress that point of view in the chapters devoted to domestic malaise; here, instead, she advised housekeepers to make themselves *believe* that it was so.

"Comfort for a Discouraged Housekeeper" began with an assurance that "you really *have* great trials to meet; trials that entitle you to pity and sympathy." Because women were as unprepared to run households as to "take charge of a *man-of-war*," the blame for this "very painful and difficult situation" rested with their elders. Then came the advice—redefine duty: "The next word of comfort is, the assurance that you *can* do *every one* of your duties, and do them well, and the following is the method by which you can do it. In the first place, make up your mind that it never is your duty to do any thing more than you can, or in any better manner than the best you can." Make a list, Beecher wrote, "of all the things that need to be done in your whole establishment. Then calculate what things you find you *can not* do, and strike them off the list, as what are not among your *duties*." After cutting the list, assign priorities: select "certain things that you will *persevere* in having done *as well as they can be done,* and let these be only so many as you feel sure you can succeed in attempting. Then make up your mind that all the rest must go along as they do, until you get more time, strength, and experience." In this way, she concluded, "you will have the comfort of feeling that in *some* respects you are as good a housekeeper as you can be, while there will be a cheering progress in gaining on all that portion of your affairs that are left at loose ends."

Contrasting with almost all of Beecher's other writing, this "word of comfort," the last chapter of her book, involves a striking concept of duty; after 450 pages on the manifold duties and obligations of domestic life, on house plans and hints for system and order, she assured her readers that they could handle their responsibilities well if they in fact deducted difficult tasks from their definition of duty. In one sense, the chapter did reflect Beecher's tone elsewhere: she wanted her readers, however incompetent, to be orderly. They were to discover and inventory their incompetence in an orderly fashion. Positing the elevation of women's work in the home as the only way to elevate women's status within the ideology of separate spheres, Beecher's quasi-feminism led her into paradoxes when she tried to give advice for domestic discontent.

Catharine Beecher's paradoxical commitment to the concept of separate spheres also contradicted developing tendencies in American society, which she acknowledged in *The American Woman's Home*, written in 1869 for an audience of consumers. The book contains sparse chapters on gardening and care of domestic animals, certainly not sufficiently detailed for anyone attempting to live off the land. It includes some directions for making household items, mostly incomplete or intended solely for decoration. Beecher endorsed specific factory-made products for the home: heating and cooking stoves, ventilation systems, and the earth closet. Most important, she recognized that the removal of production from the home constituted the coming force in American domestic life; analyzing the transfer of soap and candle production from the home, and pointing to its extension to baking and laundries in France, she recommended industrialized laundry service, with hired labor, "to solve the American housekeeper's hardest problem." "It should be an object," she wrote, "to exclude from the labors of the family all that can, with greater advantage, be executed out of it by combined labor." Nor should that labor be combined in a communal or cooperative plan; indeed, writing in *Harper's*, Beecher explicitly denounced communal housekeeping as utopian communities practiced it. While married women's work might leave their sphere, to be done by hired labor in the industrial world, the women must remain in their private homes tending to their mission as "ministers of the family state." Although she observed the trends of mid-century industrial life, Beecher did not transcend the challenge they presented to the ideology of separate spheres.

At about the same time *The American Woman's Home* appeared, an obscure visionary named Melusina Fay Peirce published a series of articles in the *Atlantic Monthly* that used a similar analysis to propose cooperative housekeeping. Like the more popular Beecher, Peirce adapted an extreme statement of the ideology of separate spheres to the new trends appearing at mid-century; unlike Beecher or any other contemporary writer, she proposed the ultimate rationalization of domestic

---

Nineteenth-century household writers had to confront the profound transformations of industrialization and urbanization that made subsistence farmers into anachronisms by the end of the century. This is the Legacy family, French Canadian immigrants to Washburn, Wisconsin, 1895, in a photo made for W. A. Henry's *Northern Wisconsin: A Handbook for the Home-seeker.*

labor: removing both married women and household functions from the private home and making worldly work part of all women's lives. That work, she claimed, would be done in a new and proper women's sphere. In the past, she said, production ruled the feminine sphere; even women of royalty superintended meat salting, brewing, spinning, and weaving, compounded medicines, and did fine embroidery. Now only some women produced: any woman with servants belonged to the "immense feminine host" that had "sunk from its former rank of manufacturing producers into that of unproductive consumers," parasites who lived off a society to which they did not contribute. Only children, the aged, and the infirm had this right, she maintained; healthy adult women did not.

The change could be blamed on men and their machines. "Hitherto," Peirce wrote, "men have allowed us at least to make up . . . the fabrics they sell us. But this last corner of our once royal feminine domain they are determined now to wrest from us. They have invented the sewing-machine, and already it takes from us not far from five hundred million dollars' worth of sewing annually. Our husbands are clothed entirely from the shops, and in all the large dry-goods firms they have marshalled the pale armies of sewing girls to ply the wheel from morning to night." Now ready-made women's garments appeared, and fashions so complicated that only professionals could make them; "necessary" articles of clothing had become so numerous that "no woman who does all her own sewing can do anything else." To save themselves time and trouble, women bought clothes, putting profit in the storekeeper's pocket, "made on the wretched wages of his seamstresses"; meanwhile, young women learned nothing of sewing, "and in fifty years the needle will be well-nigh as obsolete as the spinning wheel."

Women could neither rely on men to remedy this situation nor hope to retreat and recapture their former sphere of manufacture. Educated women, who should produce with their brains, could appropriately supervise working-class women in food and textile production, but they lacked the capital to start manufacturing enterprises. Retail trade, on the other hand, required little strength and such eminently feminine characteristics as taste; the true and fitting feminine sphere, it served other women, increasingly responsible for retail purchasing. Taking retail trade "back" from men would give women money to buy things for themselves, support colleges and churches, pay working women decently, and make themselves credible in a society that respected only money. If women assumed this function, men would be released for their own natural vocations, agriculture and production; male degeneration, both physical and moral, stemmed from their participation in distribution. Women could take over retail trade, lifting themselves from their parasitic status, as an extension of the small beginnings they could make in cooperative housekeeping societies.

Peirce offered this analysis in her first *Atlantic* article; the second article presented a model constitution for a cooperative society, with proposals for the physical plans and organization of a cooperative laundry, sewing room, and kitchen. Her individual mind could only propose vague plans, she pointed out; the cooperating housekeepers themselves would have to work out the details. The last three articles sketched her vision, the "probable effects" of cooperative housekeeping once many women in many places adopted the scheme. It would revolutionize retail trade, agriculture, and the relations between town and country. It would revamp women's work, ending the servant problem, making inroads on prostitution, raising standards of housework, and freeing talented women to pursue other professions. Women's common interests would then appear, awakening interest in "universal womanhood suffrage"—separate from manhood suffrage—which would establish all-woman legislatures to regulate retail trade. Eventually, women thus awakened would establish feminine bureaus of charity, medicine, and education, women's newspapers, and a new kind of women's art. The vision took the notion of separate spheres to previously uncharted frontiers, anticipating separatist feminism by a full century.

In flowery prose, Peirce blamed men for women's problems. "Back, sirs, back!" she wrote. "For shame! this unmanly intrusion into the women's apartments. Vast numbers, in the guise of clerks and small shopkeepers, have so long played at the spinning Achilles and Hercules that they have quite forgotten their natural vocation, and have degenerated. . . . To make their imitation of the self-degradation of the Oriental monarch complete, nothing is wanting but the *chignon*, crinoline, and train,— which by law they should be compelled to wear,—as they stand measuring ribbons and tapes so daintily to their women customers. . . . Give us the yard-stick, O heroes, and let us relieve you behind the counter, that you may go behind the plough and be off to those fields where truest glory is to be won in wresting from Dame Nature her treasures of golden grain and sweet-smelling hay. Thus, each in a fitting sphere, shall we make a good fight for the world."

Peirce's use of the separate-spheres ideology is illuminated in this passage. She blamed men for being degraded, not because of base natural tendencies or the taint of the outside world, but because they had assumed women's economic functions, thereby making both sexes unfit for modern life. The sphere, for her, became not a physical setting but a sphere of economic activity. Cooperative housekeeping, removing middle-class women from the home and improving working conditions for working-class women, would bring all their labor within the feminine sphere of activity, which would include charity, health, education, and distinctly feminine arts as well as retail trade.

To achieve her dream, Peirce wrote, women must make their sphere more like the masculine one, by understanding that cooperation and the division of labor had brought about the advance of civilization and that women, too, must learn to work together in order to go forward. They would resist because they tended toward "willful independence," most of them "happier to reign . . . supreme in the little corner some man allots to her, than to be secondary to any in the spacious palace we might build in combination." Still, that happiness was "that of the savage, who is equally undisciplined and prone to petty jealousies"; if women continued to choose individual happiness over united action, "fundamentally we shall belong to the same category as savages." She attacked Beecher's brand of domestic feminism: reigning supreme at home amounted to savagery. Although she won no substantial following, Peirce best perceived the trends of her time, not only the trend from production to consumption in household work but the profound contradiction between the increasingly

Domestic writers increasingly addressed their audience of consumers explicitly. Readers shopped at markets like the Lexington Market, Baltimore, a nineteenth-century market still in operation.

social aspect of men's work in production and the privatism of women's work in the home.

Had she stuck to her visionary role, Peirce might have avoided the most obvious paradox in her scheme, but she tried to be a realist as well, perceiving her plan as an organizational device. Cooperative housekeeping, the first step on the ladder leading to women's emancipation and full participation in society, also represented a concrete step individual women and their neighbors could take immediately. Small-scale cooperation, the tiny beginning of a complete reformation that would take a generation or more, must begin realistically. Because husbands controlled the purse strings, Peirce proposed in her model constitution that a council of husbands "have absolute power of veto in all the moneyed transactions of the society." Fifteen years later, writing about the failure of her own experiment, the Cambridge (Massachusetts) Cooperative Housekeeping Society, she had changed her tune: the husbands had amended their wives' constitution, only one example of a general obstacle. "I regret to believe that there *is* a 'lion in the path,' and a very real one—and he is nothing less than that HUSBAND-POWER which is very apt to shut down like an invisible bell-glass over every woman so soon as she is married, and affectionately say to her, 'My dear, thus far shalt thou go and no further.'"

Unlike most of her contemporaries, including most of the political feminists, Peirce advocated removing women as well as their work from the home. Indeed, the home would be a changed place under her plan. New houses could be designed with neither kitchens nor laundry facilities; the cooperative would assume those functions instead. Even more important, she advocated a major change in the function of employment in American women's lives: they would work for pay throughout their lives. The associations would use no voluntary labor, paying salaries commensurate with prevailing male pay rates. Working-class women could join the societies by paying membership fees in installments, and work there, directed by middle-class women, laboring finally under decent conditions for decent wages. Let the societies declare that "it is just as necessary and just as honorable for a wife to earn money as it is for her husband. . . . Then alone shall we begin to walk in self-respect, and the poor, wronged workwoman throughout the world to raise her drooping head." Cooperative housekeeping would combat the prevailing argument for underpaying working women, that women constituted an unstable work force who left their jobs to marry.

Peirce's comments on working women provide the key to her attack on the system; she opposed women's oppression under capitalism as it had developed, but not capitalism itself. She perceived that capitalist methods of efficiency, developed in large enterprises using the division of labor, could apply to a cooperative enterprise but made little sense in the context of the private household. Habits of system and order could not re-

form women's work without an organized force like cooperative housekeeping, which would "swallow up" all the disorganized individual households. Nor could women be emancipated until they, like men, labored for wages in a social setting and throughout their lives.

With capitalism came classes. Many of Peirce's contemporaries addressed women as if they were a separate class; as long as few married women left their homes to work, writers could and did write as if they shared the same class status, whatever their economic status. Thus Beecher, advocating the abolition of domestic service, recommended that married women all bear the same relationship to their society. Peirce, on the other hand, wanted all women to work out of the home; she recognized that some would be employers and some employees, some would be directed and some would do the directing.

Despite their differences, both Peirce and Beecher attempted to respond to new societal trends within the old ideology of separate spheres.

Mid-nineteenth-century consumers bought products previously sold only by artisans and craftsmen. Industrialization replaced the miller relatively early; flour was one of the earliest products to be mass-produced and widely advertised.

By mid-century, capitalist industry was beginning to affect many women's housework, with manufactured textiles and other household products, and with increasing numbers of husbands obliged to operate on schedules determined by their activity in the outside world. Yet as long as housework remained a full-time job, married women lived in a realm that really was different from the rest of the society, where the producer worked alone for her family, without boss or time clock or profit motive. The ideology remained an accurate statement of the differences between most women's lives and those of their husbands, but it was becoming a less accurate and more paradoxical description of the relationship of women's work to the world, and could no longer meet the requirements of any serious writer on household affairs who carefully observed new trends in American society. Beecher and Peirce took a set of ideas already paradoxical and attempted to bring them up to date: Beecher tried to find a way for women to reign supreme in their traditional private sphere; Peirce, to find a new sphere for her sex, still separate but public.

The ideology of separate spheres left a strong legacy, evident in the "feminine mystique" of the 1950s, in the exhortations of the New Right to "save the family" during the late 1970s, and even in the women's liberation movement's abandonment of private domestic issues for more tangible political and economic goals: all of these suggest that the private sphere of everyday life, traditionally guarded by women, may be considered the independent province of individuals who can act in their own interest to provide themselves with emotional satisfaction. In fact, the reality of separate spheres had already begun to fade more than a century ago when Beecher and Peirce wrote. Not only do the modern versions of the ideology preserve distinctions long outdated, but, in their concentration on consumption and motherhood as the fundamental activities of women in the private sphere, the "feminine mystique" and New Right varieties incorporate the thinking of writers on household affairs who at the turn of the century abandoned the separate-spheres idea and defined new roles for women and household work. For fifty years, the connections between the spheres had been assuming greater importance as more households consumed more industrial products and produced more labor for the expanding labor market. The assertion that women were a separate and unified group, standing in a different relation to society than men, had been losing credibility. Class had come to the fore as a dividing principle, obvious with the massive importation of immigrant industrial labor, with the great wave of labor activity that began in the late 1870s, with substantial depressions in 1873 and 1893, and with the increasing participation of women as workers in the organized economy. By the turn of the century, writing on household affairs reflected all of these trends.

ELEVEN

The Business
of Housekeeping

Catharine Beecher's attempt to elevate the
status of women within their own sphere
endured primarily in its influence on the
movement for domestic education; her
written instruction in domestic matters
and her promotion of domestic education in the
schools made her the primary early figure in that
movement. During the last three decades of the
nineteenth century, other women promoted domestic education in other arenas, establishing courses

in domestic work in colleges, urban cooking schools, and public elementary and secondary schools. Coalescing in the home economics movement at the turn of the century, the new domestic education abandoned the concept of separate spheres so central to Beecher; the mainstream home economists placed new emphasis on the connections between the household and the larger society, at the same time that more extreme writers promoted the application of business efficiency principles to the individual household or the total industrialization of housework.

The first plan for organized domestic education, adopted by Mount Holyoke Seminary at its founding in 1837, kept tuition costs down and school spirit up by requiring students to do the dormitory housework. Mary Lyon, the seminary's founder, called the domestic work system the school's "little appendage," claiming that it instilled camaraderie among students who worked together for the common good. Mount Holyoke offered no formal coursework in home economics. One of the earliest land-grant schools, Iowa State College, which adopted the Mount Holyoke plan in 1869, required each woman student to work two hours a day in the dining room, kitchen, or pantry, and supplemented that work three years later with the first college home economics instruction. The Iowa State program aimed to train housewives. Mary Welsh, its founder, said later that it had "done real service to the young women of the state," teaching them manual skills and respect for manual labor, and adding "dignity to that part of their life work hitherto considered as menial drudgery." This practical expression of Catharine Beecher's goals became the fundamental principle underlying all the home economics programs that constituted women's education at the many Western and Midwestern state colleges founded after the Morrill Land Grant Act of 1862. Lou Allen Gregory, the first professor of domestic science at Illinois Industrial University, agreed with Beecher that women's education "must recognize their distinctive duties as women—the mothers, housekeepers, and health keepers of the world—and furnish instruction which shall fit them to meet these duties." Her school aimed to offer women a "liberal and practical education, which should fit them for their great duties and trusts, making them the equals of their educated husbands and associates, and enabling them to bring the aids of science and culture to the all-important labors and vocations of womanhood."

If the educated homemaker was the natural helpmate for the educated farmer who graduated from the Western land-grant colleges, she was not, apparently, the ideal mate for the urban Ivy Leaguer. Women's colleges, attempting to establish liberal arts curricula comparable to those of the prestigious men's colleges, eschewed coursework in domestic affairs; Bryn Mawr's president maintained that there were "not enough elements of intellectual growth in cooking or housekeeping to furnish a very serious or profound course of training for really intelligent women." By 1902, when

a committee on home economics in colleges and universities reported its findings to the Fourth Lake Placid Conference on Home Economics, state agricultural and mechanical colleges and some state universities dominated home economics education. The prestigious state universities shied away from the subject; Cornell, Wisconsin, and California offered only courses in hygiene. Thirteen women's colleges offered a total of eight courses related to home economics, five of them in personal hygiene. At a few elite coeducational institutions like the University of Chicago, students could take such advanced courses as Household Technology (Chicago) or Sanitary Chemistry and Biology (MIT).

At about the same time that the land-grant colleges were beginning their home economics programs, urban reformers instituted cooking schools in conjunction with their other efforts on behalf of working women. The first one began in 1874 as a cooking class at the Women's Educational and Industrial Society of New York's free training school for working women. Two years later, teacher Juliet Corson opened the New York Cooking School in her home, responding to requests from wealthy women who wanted to take her course. Corson taught a children's class for mission-school students, a "plain cook's class" for hired cooks and workers' wives, and a Ladies' Class for "those who desire to combine some of the elegancies of artistic cookery with those economical interests which it is the duty of every woman to study." The Ladies chose their menus, paid for them, and kept the cooked food; the mission children ate but did not pay; the plain cook's class charged tuition, but Corson turned nobody down for inability to pay, supported by a charitable board incorporated in 1878.

Within a few years, noted cooking schools established in Boston and Philadelphia adopted a similar class-segregated model. The Boston Domestic Reform League School of Housekeeping, established in 1897 as a solution to the servant problem, offered three elaborate curricula. Employers of domestic servants met twice a week for three months to learn "House Sanitation, Chemistry of Foods, Domestic Economy, and the Principles of Housework, Cooking, Marketing, etc." Their daughters could enroll in the Course for Young Women, a full-time live-in program aimed at educating future housewives and women who wanted to work in settlement houses. Pupils in the free Course for Employees paid for their education in service, doing their own housework and the housework of the Young Women; the five-month formal course was followed by a three-month probationary period as a private domestic servant.

Charitable and reform influences dominated the third important group of domestic educators, those who worked in the public schools. Massachusetts educators, the first to promote manual instruction for both girls and boys, celebrated sewing instruction for young women for "encouraging habits of carefulness and industry; developing a taste for quiet, regular employment; furnishing a resource against idleness; and adding largely to the power of self support." Working-class girls, many with shiftless or employed mothers, could make their own clothes while gaining skills to make money and the disciplined habits appropriate to good industrial workers.

Early cooking schools offered courses for wealthy ladies, as well as for professional cooks and the children of the poor. This picture appeared in George Augustus Sala's *America Revisited*, published in London in 1882.

Like the housing and domestic service reformers, the public school reformers connected their individual efforts with larger social questions.
Some perceived home economics education as a means of intervening in
working-class home life. The Worcester, Massachusetts superintendent of
schools declared that he introduced elementary sewing into the Worcester
public schools as a "reformatory power through the homes of our schoolchildren," because sewing, "indispensable to the tidiness and decency of
home," added to "household comfort." Public school cooking classes
offered a way to teach thrift, nutrition, cleanliness, and American ways to
the poor through their children; Jane Addams, America's first settlement
worker, suggested that "an Italian girl who has had lessons in cooking at
the public school, will help her mother to connect the entire family with
American food and household habits." It worked, according to Irving
Howe, who has pointed out that immigrant Jews in New York, who ate
few vegetables "except for horse-radish, carrots, cabbage, and beets,"
came to regard lettuce and tomatoes as " 'good for the children'—the cult
of the vegetable being transmitted to the immigrant kitchen by both the
Yiddish newspaper and the American school." Emily Huntington, a welfare worker who combined the new kindergarten with the new home
economics in "kitchen garden" programs, used carefully organized lessons
and miniature housekeeping equipment to teach "poor children how to
make their homes more comfortable." Part of a more general manual-
training movement designed to produce good workers for industrial
life, public school home-economics programs served also as a reform
measure of direct intervention into working-class households through the
children.

Such intervention, like other Progressive Era reform efforts, operated
on the assumption that social progress depended on public attention to
matters formerly considered private. Public attention required organization; participants in the various domestic education programs came together after 1899, first in a series of annual conferences on home
economics held at Lake Placid, New York, and, in 1908, in the American
Home Economics Association. A wide variety of people and organizations
made up the home economics movement, involving its participants in
other reforms. Home economists functioned in settlement and relief work,
government bureaus and commissions, public school reform, the women's
suffrage movement, the temperance movement, organized attempts to
Americanize immigrants, and many other causes and activities of the
Progressive period. Activists in these movements served on the boards of
each other's organizations, as speakers at each other's conventions, and as
resources for each other's principal interests.

Those who concentrated on domestic education, who were active participants in organizational life, defined home economics as a field for full-
time professionals who would interact with men as professional peers in

all of those organizations and activities. Indeed, two of the original offi-
cers of the American Home Economics Association *were* men. The
women in the movement concentrated on their professional lives; those
who married did so late in their careers, and few of these had children.
Ellen H. Richards, the first woman to receive a degree from MIT, the
founding spirit of the Lake Placid conferences and first president of the
association, married at thirty-three and remained childless. Isabel Bevier,
the association's first vice-president, did not marry; Mary Davies Swartz
Rose, a professor of nutrition at Teachers College, Columbia, married at
thirty-six and had her only child at forty-one. These women, participating
in organizations full of other women like themselves, interacting with
men as colleagues, established a field that expressly connected the private
household with public institutions. They thus developed a notion of
women's professionalism that departed from the older conception of
separate spheres.

Professionalism required the creation of a hierarchy within the home
economics movement, according to Henrietta Goodrich, director of Boston's School of Housekeeping, who at the Second Lake Placid conference
in 1900 presented an elaborate plan for teaching home economics on all
levels, from kindergarten to graduate school. Trade schools for training
servants would depend on "common adoption of business principles in
dealing with the worker, recognition of the worker as an independent
entity [and] the real organization of housework as a trade." College
home-economics programs would require courses in the sciences, in economics ("emphasizing the economics of consumption"), in sociology
("including a study of the home as the organized social unit"), and in
personal and public hygiene. Existing professional schools of architecture,
medicine, divinity, and engineering would include "something of home
economics" in their curricula.

The keystone of the system, "The Professional School of Home and
Social Economics," would join the other professional schools in the universities, establishing research laboratories and training several levels of
professional home economists. It would offer four separate programs leading to master's degrees: for home economics teachers, social workers,
sanitary inspectors, and institutional nutritionists. In addition to the master's degrees, it would confer the Ph.D. for "original investigation in the
line of applied science . . . only where marked ability and evidence of
originality have been shown, at the end of not less than three years of
resident study"—a level of analysis, Goodrich maintained, that required
laboratory facilities. Home economists would thereby be able "to increase
the body of exact knowledge, to formulate and classify the unwieldy
material that we have already collected," tasks that "must be accomplished
before we can claim a true science of home economics, or dignify its
applications as 'professions.'" Real professions had real graduate schools

Manual training for young women at the Wisconsin Industrial School for Girls, 1884. Industrial training was one of the early sources of the home economics movement.

that granted advanced degrees, and they had, therefore, ranked educational hierarchies.

Professional home economists expressed some confusion about the housewife's place in this hierarchy. In Goodrich's plan, the professional school offered a Course for Home-Makers, which conferred a certificate rather than a degree; she apologized for including this course, with its lower entrance requirements and easier courses, in the professional school, "but in its aim, as fitting young women for the profession of home-making, it is professional." Incorporating it in the professional school offered "economy of administration and equipment." Lucy Salmon, the domestic service reformer, who claimed that a professional school was the only thing that could "turn the household into the channels where every other occupation has made advancement," suggested that housekeepers themselves take postgraduate courses in home management. Colleges offered courses in hygiene, but physicians went to medical school; college courses in constitutional law did not amount to legal training; and "professional training and investigation must supplement home and collegiate instruction in the case of the housekeeper." Julia Lathrop, the first head of the Federal Children's Bureau, thought that housekeepers should "study their families and their children" as a contribution to the full-time professionals' research; the "profession of carrying on households" would then "be constantly stimulated by research and . . . part of a great new work of discovery," while young housewives would find their lot not narrow but "enormously broadening and stimulating." Although the home economists called housework a "profession," they did so grudgingly; only the efforts of the full-time researchers and teachers made it so.

The relationship between the housewife and the home economist represented only part of a more general issue for the movement, the relation-

Home economics class in a well-equipped "laboratory," about 1925, Burlington, Wisconsin—probably one under the University of Wisconsin Agricultural Extension Service.

ship between the home and the larger society; the home economists believed the two were inextricably intertwined and had identical interests. Ellen Richards, interpreting the goals of the movement to the Sixth Lake Placid Conference, claimed that home economics aimed at material simplicity, to "free the spirit for the more important and permanent interests of the home and society." In order to bring the home and the society into harmony, Henrietta Goodrich told Lake Placid participants, people must think of the home as "something more than the idea of personal relationships to individual homes. Men must admit consciously that the home is the social workshop for the making of men. No home, however isolated, can escape the social obligation that rests on it, i.e. responsibility for the quality, fineness, and strength of the men and women who are its output." The household and the social world, then, were not equal partners, nor was the outside world a threat to the domestic sphere; home economists, formulating an ideology of home life compatible with industrial conditions, saw the home as but one link in the larger chain, and their own field as an element in the whole of social progress. The development of home economics, Goodrich told the 1900 Lake Placid Conference, was "in line with the great social and industrial forces of the day," "in the direct line of progress," and its success was therefore inevitable, "for the laws of progress 'are of one with the laws of morals' and of life."

Progress required scientific rationality. Ellen Richards, the leader of the movement, interpreted its goals: "HOME ECONOMICS STANDS FOR: The ideal home life for today unhampered by the traditions of the past. The utilization of all the resources of modern science to improve the home life." Graduate-level research, essential for professionalism, could free the home from the shackles of tradition. Secretary of Agriculture James Wilson, applauding the initial efforts of home economists in 1897, compared the field to medicine and engineering: formerly empirical arts based on practical skills, those disciplines now based practice on scientific principles. "Today no doctor or engineer is fitted to pursue his profession until he has drunk deep at the fountains of science"; home economics, too, must adopt those principles. Goodrich included the social sciences as well as natural science; her professional school for social service would emphasize "scientific investigation of social phenomena, and practical application of scientific principles to the bettering of present conditions of living"; the "vagaries of sentimentality" that characterized old-style philanthropy must be replaced with the "law and order" of the new social science and the new social work.

Both kinds of science, social and natural, could be applied to a major goal of the movement, educating women to be good consumers; from the start, home economists encouraged educated consumption by studying and teaching food values and textile qualities. Juliet Corson took her New

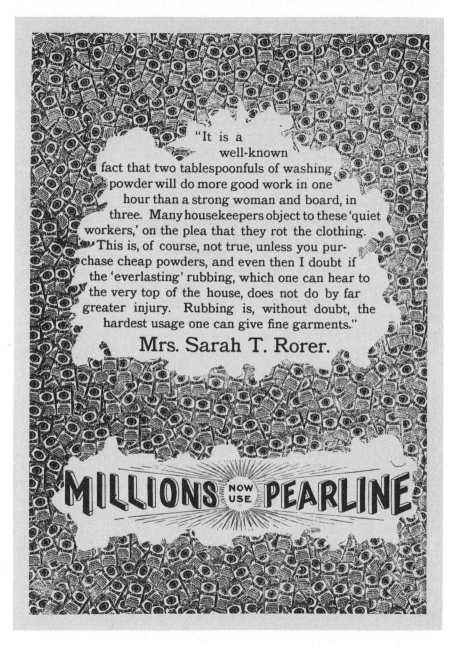

"It is a well-known fact that two tablespoonfuls of washing powder will do more good work in one hour than a strong woman and board, in three. Many housekeepers object to these 'quiet workers,' on the plea that they rot the clothing. This is, of course, not true, unless you purchase cheap powders, and even then I doubt if the 'everlasting' rubbing, which one can hear to the very top of the house, does not do by far greater injury. Rubbing is, without doubt, the hardest usage one can give fine garments."
Mrs. Sarah T. Rorer.

MILLIONS NOW USE PEARLINE

From the start, home economists worked with businessmen to promote the products of industry. Mrs. Rorer was the founder of the Philadelphia Cooking School and culinary editor of the *Ladies' Home Journal*, where this ad appeared in January 1898.

York Cooking School classes to the public markets, where she taught her pupils about freshness, quality, and prices. Later home economists worked with social workers to teach poor families—usually from European peasant backgrounds—how to use money, often requiring them to keep written budget accounts. Florence Nesbitt, a home economist for Chicago and Cleveland public relief organizations, told social workers that they must translate scientific principles from the language of the researcher into that of the impoverished homemaker, whose limited budget necessitated an understanding of food values and dietary standards. Her own book for poor women stressed wise buying, a combination of economy and value. Home economists emphasized education for consumption on the college level as well; women who took home economics in college without intending to become full-time professionals in the field should concentrate on learning how to consume, according to Caroline Hunt and Alice P. Norton, two leading home economics professors, at the University of Wisconsin and the University of Chicago. "We are all consumers," Norton declared, "and everyone will acknowledge the desirability of training in intelligent use of commodities." The movement's clearest acknowledgment, of course, came in their choice at the first Lake Placid conference of a name for their discipline: "home economics," they claimed, was "a broader term than household arts or any term previously used." Broad or not, it stressed the new order: the primacy of social science and the trend from production to consumption.

One practical expression of the new link between the home and the economic world, the link between home economists and businessmen, became an issue because not all home economics graduates could be expected to teach; in order to expand their field, home economists had to discover other opportunities for their students. The first generation— primarily professors of home economics, consultants to governmental and charitable agencies, and writers on domestic affairs—had only indirect business ties at most, but they courted the business world to get financial support for their charitable work and to expand the job options for their pupils. Those efforts paid off by the 1920s, when the business world began to employ women with home economics degrees. Utility companies in particular, attempting to expand their business and to calm public fears, put home economists to work, demonstrating and giving instructions for new equipment.

Defining a practical function for their discipline and for household work in the new consuming society, the home economists often made direct comparisons between the home and business, a business analogy found throughout their literature. "In many ways the business of housemaking is the most important one in the world," Florence Nesbitt wrote in her housekeeping manual for poor women. "To carry it on successfully requires no less thought, study and work than the merchant or mechanic gives to his business." This terminology, the *business* of housekeeping, the *profession* of housework, infused the movement that sought to apply "thought and study" to domestic work. Its ultimate expression appeared among the writers who stressed home efficiency and scientific management in the household.

Taken to its logical extreme, "putting the home on a business basis" led to attempts to apply the principles of Frederick Winslow Taylor and his scientific management movement. Taylor, the first modern management consultant and the first efficiency expert, formulated the central ideas of twentieth-century factory management: separating manual from mental labor, and breaking up each into specialized tasks for the purpose of increasing the efficiency of each worker, defining and timing each task and determining the "one best way" to do it. Because Taylor's principles dominated business management discussions at the turn of the century, adopting business principles was tantamount to adopting Taylorism. The critical differences between business and households—the household had only one worker and no profit motive—disconcerted but failed to daunt the household efficiency experts who attempted to apply Taylor's factory methods to the private home.

People interested in home economics used the term "efficiency" as they did other business terms—incessantly, and often quite broadly. In 1906, the joint Committee on Home Economics of Boston's Association of Collegiate Alumnae and the Women's Educational and Industrial Union announced a $100 prize for the best essay from a college sociology or economics student on individual and social efficiency. Books with titles like *Increasing Home Efficiency*, *The Efficient Kitchen*, and *Efficiency in the Household*, while employing the factory analogy, often used "efficient" as a synonym for "good"; some writers employed such titles for tracts on the relationship between home and society.

Others showed an intense interest in applying to household life the scientific management techniques that had been successful in factories and offices. To be sure, the household efficiency experts suggested some far-fetched schemes. Probably few American women painted grids on their floors and walls so that they could conduct time-motion studies of dishwashing, or even used the more practical "pin or string plan" suggested by Lillian Gilbreth, mother of the *Cheaper by the Dozen* children and partner with her husband Frank in extending scientific management beyond Taylor's original formulations. Following this plan, a child followed Mother around with a ball of string, unwinding it to measure the distance she traveled; a scale drawing of the workplace, with pins at the places where Mother turned, would show if she had wasted motions by retracing her steps. Despite the few converts to such schemes, eventually home economists and the women they taught did adopt many of the central principles of the household efficiency movement.

The most coherent statement of those principles may be found in the work of Christine Frederick, the movement's central figure, who first published her system in the *Ladies' Home Journal* in 1912, and later in two books, *The New Housekeeping* and *Household Engineering: Scientific Management in the Home*. She created a career as a "household engineer," studying scientific management in factories, investigating her friends' homes, and ultimately turning her own Long Island home into an "experiment station" for testing household equipment. Frederick's writings about households used business terms; most striking, she consistently called both domestic servants and housewives "workers." She frequently employed analogies to factories and offices: she justified the use of schedules, for example, by their use in a ball-bearing factory, an "immense organization employing thousands of clerks," and in many other businesses where workers had "time off."

Scheduling, central to Frederick's system, compelled provision of regular rest periods: "Its whole idea is simply, *plan what you are going to do, do it, and then rest*; instead of not knowing what you are going to do, resting or stopping when you feel like it, and never knowing when you are going to get done." Plans—for time, for space, for using food and other consumer products—dominated her thinking; unlike Taylor and the other factory scientific managers, she could not assign mental and manual tasks to individual workers, for most households had only one, but she did differentiate between the two kinds of tasks. All mental labor should be done in advance: kitchen equipment, for example, should be grouped to meet the order of work. Her diagrams of planned and unplanned cleaning in identical houses showed the reader how to save steps. She offered schedules for days, weeks, and years. Meals, planned one or two weeks ahead with every ingredient on a purchasing sheet, would concentrate on a single process to economize on time and tools: everything in any given meal should be boiled, or baked, or fried. The inexcusable leftover would be replaced by the essential "planned-over." *Household Engineering* was not an inappropriate title for the book that gave details for all these plans.

Planning, arranging for "peak-load" times in advance, by reducing confusion reduced fatigue. *"Today,"* wrote Frederick, *"the woman in the home is called upon to be an executive as well as a manual laborer.* Just to be a good worker and keep on working until you drop is not sufficient—or efficient either. The more planning, the more brains, the more management, a woman puts into her housework, the less friction and the less nervous energy she will have to expend." Her plans went beyond the "habits of system and order" Catharine Beecher had proposed half a century earlier; she made a genuine effort to separate planning from execution, mental from manual labor, a direct borrowing from Taylorism and the factory model of efficiency.

In the few households with servants, Frederick wrote, books of rules should set down in black-and-white directions for every task; the mistress was to write the book and the servant to perform the manual labor. But even the vast majority of servantless households needed written directions for every task, "just as in industries we have written rules for the way this piece of work or that should be done." Frederick called these written directions, which specified methods, tools, and time, "standard practice"; she pointed out that successful cooking had long depended on such definite instructions: "the reason why our meals are so often better cooked than our rooms are cleaned, is almost solely because there have been no written directions or 'practice' for the latter, while there was for the former. There cannot be a properly cleaned room if some one step is forgotten." She published standard-practice directions for bedroom and bathroom care, for cleaning several rooms on one floor, bread making, dishwashing, and dressmaking; her laundry chapter offered five "standard practices," each applicable to different equipment. Like recipes, the plans were separated into steps, so detailed that even modern readers, unfamiliar with the equipment and ignorant of the unwritten rules, can understand them. Frederick advised each individual housewife to modify

---

Good and bad planning of kitchen equipment, from *Household Engineering*, by Christine Frederick, 1920.

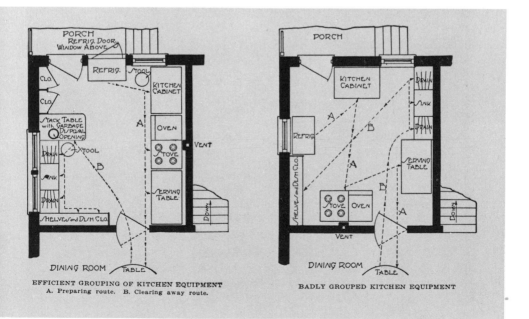

EFFICIENT GROUPING OF KITCHEN EQUIPMENT
A. Preparing route.   B. Clearing away route.

BADLY GROUPED KITCHEN EQUIPMENT

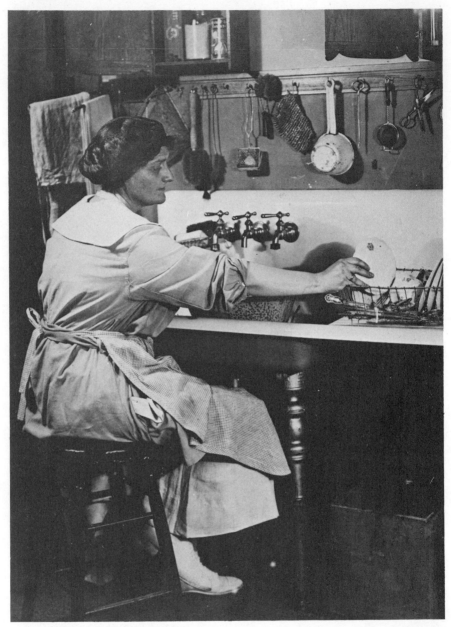

With good planning, everything could be within arm's reach, according to Christine Frederick and the home economists who adopted less extreme versions of her efficiency plans. Photo from International Harvester Corporation, Agricultural Extension Department, Chicago.

or combine the rules to suit her own conditions and then to write down *her* own standard practice, with its appropriate time schedule.

Frederick's notion of "standard practice" in the household serves as an illustration of the fundamental difference between her household engineering and true scientific management. Taylor's factory system rested on the contention that there existed "one best way" to do any particular job, to be determined "scientifically" by breaking it into its component tasks and analyzing each one; with many workers, each doing a task in the "one best way," employers could make the most of their labor dollars, for profit from workers' labor constituted the employers' incentive in hiring the efficiency experts and adopting their methods. Like the scientific managers in industry, Frederick did maintain that every household chore could be analyzed into distinct tasks and that the housewife-manager should conduct time and motion studies to determine the "one best way," but unlike her industrial teachers, she confronted two features of household work that she had no intention of challenging or changing. Women worked alone in private homes, without any clearly defined equivalent to the profit motive. With one worker, why break the job into discrete tasks? With one worker and no profit motive, why save time in the first place? Without the profit that impelled manufacturers to adopt new technology, housewives worked under various technological conditions; how, then, to "standardize" the tasks?

In such circumstances, true scientific management was impossible. Moreover, housekeeping consisted of many tasks done at different intervals, and all subject to interruption; dishwashing might be broken into individual motions, timed and standardized, but housekeeping as an enterprise could not be. Frederick argued that this very feature necessitated scheduling: "If a woman were doing nothing but the same thing without interruption from morning until night, there would be no use for a plan of work. There is only need of a plan when there are several pieces of varying work to be done at different hours with different tools. Then it becomes essential to arrange these varying tasks in order and on time, so that the worker may proceed with the least amount of friction and effort." Taylor, who analyzed tasks far more specialized than housework, aimed not to "arrange" varying tasks but to divide them, assigning them to different workers, standardizing each one, and setting the worker to do "the same thing without interruption" with as few tools as possible.

Differences between households, arising from family tastes, house plans, and labor-saving devices, forced Frederick to abandon the "one best way" idea to which she paid lip service. Time and again, she maintained that individual circumstances lay at the core of good planning. Houses should not be run according to "*arbitrary standards*, set up by friends or the community." Nobody else could or should tell the housekeeper what to do; she should follow "whatever methods conduce to the efficient management of her particular home, regardless of tradition, or what is supposed to be the 'proper' way." Frederick sacrificed the "one best way" to privacy and individual choice for the housewife, who functioned both as worker and as manager. Taylorism, based on profit making and efficient management of hired labor, specifically denied workers their individuality and control over their work; the factory scientific-management literature contained no formulations like "*What is the best order only the individual worker can determine for her individual case.*"

Frederick concluded *Household Engineering* with a discussion of how to use the time saved by good management, the central issue for a proponent of efficiency with no profit motive. "*The real object in saving time and effort,*" she wrote, "*is to enable the homemaker to have leisure time* to devote to interests *which are more important than the mere mechanics of living.*" Women should not organize their housework to save time as an end in itself; instead, a "definite purpose and plan" for their leisure time would give them the incentive "*to subordinate housekeeping routine to the attainment of the higher ends of personal and family happiness and success.*" She listed specific suggestions in "Ten Things To Do in Leisure Time." A woman could learn more about housework through reading or courses; she could study her husband's business "so that she can aid, sympathize and be a comrade in his work," supervise her children's work and play, take time for grooming and physical exercise, or cultivate her mental life—reading, "making personal thought-out decisions on the problems of life, ethics, immortality, philosophy of life, etc." The hundred best books of the world could be read in three years at the rate of half-an-hour a day saved from housework; housewives could read general magazines catering to "the larger human interests of the world of both men and women," which offered broader cultivation than the narrow women's magazines. Because women would enjoy doing these things, they would adopt efficiency methods to save time for them, and develop the "right mental attitude." This demanded that they understand housework as an interesting and stimulating problem to be solved.

Although the list of things to do in leisure time included volunteer charity work, pursuing a "business, hobby or interest beyond housekeeping," and staying abreast of a premarital profession to prepare for possible widowhood, the "right mental attitude" did not, in Frederick's opinion, permit a preference for paid employment. "Our greatest enemy," she wrote in the *Journal of Home Economics*, "is the woman with the career," who feels "weighted down" by housework. Women with "the intelligent attitude of mind" understand "that home making is not drudgery," that it is just as stimulating and interesting and artistic as "any of the fields in which women are running with eager feet because it expresses their wonderful individuality." Let those women express themselves through home decoration, stimulate themselves by studying nutrition and planning balanced meals for their families, and interest themselves in caring for their own children instead of going "down on the East Side" to "take care of Annie Bolowski." Social work and art, while they broadened the mind and offered incentives for adopting efficiency methods, must not be allowed to become substitute careers for women.

Christine Frederick shared with Catharine Beecher a passion for organization and an interest in labor-saving devices, but they based their ideas on fundamentally different principles. Beecher explicitly argued against most of Frederick's suggestions for filling leisure time, which she never wanted for her readers to begin with. She never suggested that women should understand their husbands' businesses; she proposed that housework itself provided physical exercise; she discouraged women from worrying about "the problems of life, ethics, immortality, philosophy of life, etc." or engaging in any intellectual activity other than that contained within housework; she held no brief for hobbies and interests "beyond housekeeping." Above all, the "larger human interests of the world of both men and women" was a concept foreign to her, for she held to the notion of a world composed of separate spheres for men and women. Writing half a century later, Frederick, like the mainstream home economists whom she influenced, applied her organizational passion to a household situated in a new world of merging spheres.

That new world also produced the ideas of Charlotte Perkins Gilman, who challenged what Frederick took as given: the single woman worker in the private home, and the lack of any clearly defined equivalent to the profit motive. Freed from the trap of separate spheres that had made Melusina Fay Peirce's ideas seem so far-fetched, Gilman proposed industrialized housework, which could benefit from the specialization, the division of labor, and the profit motives that had characterized American manufacturing to date. She was, above all, a sensitive social observer and the best prophet of her time; her predictions described twentieth-century trends that were only in the first stages when she wrote.

Although the popular press maligned Gilman's personal life—her divorce from an extremely supportive husband, her subsequent friendship with him and the best friend whom he later married, and her yielding her daughter to them—Charlotte Perkins Gilman received much positive attention for her ideas. Her books ran through many editions and her articles appeared in a wide variety of journals and magazines. Best known for *Women and Economics*, which appeared to rave reviews in 1898, she became a popular lecturer. Women's clubs, suffrage groups, labor unions, and other reform organizations sought her services through lecture agent Major James B. Pond, who also promoted Mark Twain, Julia Ward Howe, William Dean Howells, and Thomas Nast, among other famous speakers. Active in reform circles, she forged close ties with Progressive

Era thinkers and activists; for a time she lived at Hull House with Jane Addams, and home economist Helen Campbell was a close friend and occasional housemate.

Although she had connections with socialists, not socialism but feminism and evolutionary thought formed the main theoretical currents in Gilman's work. *Women and Economics* analyzes the historical evolution and the social effects of a crucial difference between humans and other animals: "We are the only animal species in which the sex-relation is also an economic relation." Evolution had brought about this state of affairs, now outmoded and crippling to women; its cure involved directing the future evolution of the capitalist system, not a direct challenge to capitalism. She based her evolutionary thought on the theories of Lester Frank Ward, one of the first and most important American sociologists, whom she called "quite the greatest man I have ever known." Ward believed that society could and should direct its evolutionary development through social planning; his "gynaecocentric theory" asserted that women were the basis of the human race, and their emancipation "the only sure road to the evolution of man."

These ideas infused Gilman's *Women and Economics*. A study of women's dependence on men, the book maintained that monogamous marriage, originally "the form of sex-union best calculated to advance the interests of the individual and society," had resulted in the overdevelopment of "sex-distinction," the female characteristics that ruled relationships with men. For the human female, sex distinction had become "not only a means of attracting a mate, as with all creatures, but a means of getting her livelihood, as is the case with no other creature under heaven." Women had become economic parasites. Nevertheless, Gilman retained her untrammeled belief in progress. She berated those who venerated the old, who "worshipped backwards," who maintained that things acquired "imputed sanctity by the simple flux of time." Clocks were better than hourglasses, sewing machines surpassed bone needles; people who failed to appreciate progress held back any further progress, "warped and hindered" progressive change. Conscious direction of that change involved recognizing and promoting what was already under way; the mastery of the future required shaping the evolutionary course by distinguishing unacceptable atavisms from progressive steps toward a better future. Capitalism, in other words, was a given; women must utilize the best features of capitalism—like organization and the division of labor—for their own advancement and the consequent advancement of the whole society.

Gilman applied this point of view to her ideas about household work, presented in part in *Women and Economics* and greatly expanded in *The Home: Its Work and Influence*, published in 1903. This book did not share its predecessor's success; even the good reviews equivocated. Apparently the explicit steps required to shape social evolution, detailed in *The Home*, presented more of a threat than the theoretical treatise had done. In fact, the steps Gilman advocated in the new book represented nothing more than the practical consequences of her theoretical stance, applying to the work remaining in the home the lessons of the work that had left it.

Like many other domestic writers beginning with Catharine Beecher and Melusina Fay Peirce, and including the early home economists who were her contemporaries, Gilman recognized the fundamental historical tendency that had turned women from producers into consumers; unlike most of them, she understood that the process was continuing, as yet incomplete. Domestic industry, she claimed, was not a particular *kind* of work but a *stage* through which all kinds of work passed: "All industries were once 'domestic,' that is, were performed at home and in the interests of the family." Arguing against those who considered the home a unique institution apart from others, she intended "to give a general impression of the continual flux and growth of the home as an institution, as one under the same laws as those which govern other institutions." Those laws of social progress, stifled in the home because of veneration of the past, were perfectly clear: "The savage works by himself, for himself; the civilised man works in elaborate interdependence with many, for many." Home industry, still in a savage stage, had moved as far as it had only thanks to outside influences from the development of manufacturing; to move the household in a progressive direction, the fundamental principles that had guided industrial progress must be applied to home life.

Those principles—association, organization, specialization, division of labor, and profit incentives—formed the basis of progressive change in industry. Disorganized solitary workers unmotivated by profit could never advance at home. "What would shoes be like if every man made his own?" asked Gilman. "What would houses be like if every man made his own? Or hats, or books, or waggons. To confine any industry to the level of a universal average is to strangle it in its cradle. And there, for ever, lie the industries of the housewife."

Women working alone attempted to practice too many occupations at once; it cost more time, more strength, and more money to feed, clothe, and clean humanity that way than it would cost if the principles of progress were applied. It constricted the progress of the work itself, leaving methods elementary except insofar as modern utensils and furnishings, provided by world industry, had improved them. Working within the family and for the family reduced women to "no other ambition, no other incentive, no other reward . . . no room for growth."

The problem, then, lay in the very nature of work privately done in separate households, and the solution was to remove it from the home; application of the principles of industrial evolution to household work meant, literally, industrializing housework. Gilman criticized the waste of private housekeeping—repetition of labor and waste of plant: "We have to pay severally for all these stoves and dishes, tools and utensils, which, if properly supplied in one proper place instead of twenty, would cost far less to begin with." The private household was an anachronism: feudal lords kept fools and poets and cooks, while modern people, patronizing the theater and reading the public work of free poets, still cooked privately. "There is," she wrote, "nothing private and special in the preparation of food; a more general human necessity does not exist. There must be freedom and personal choice in the food prepared, but it no more has to be cooked for you than the books you love best have to be written for you." For better food, and for women's freedom, food preparation must be industrialized; "If we are willing to receive our water from an extra-domestic pipe—why not our food?"

Gilman pointed to the progress that had already begun; many of the initial processes of food preparation had left the home by the time she wrote. "Our housewife does not go out crying, 'Dilly-dilly! Dilly-dilly! You must come and be killed'—and then wring the poor duck's neck, pick and pluck it with her own hands; nor does the modern father himself slay the fatted calf—all this is done as a business." She applauded prepared pickles, preserves, and breakfast foods, delicatessens, and bakeries; she mentioned three companies that supplied hot cooked food ready to eat. The result of cooking as a business had been social progress; food was becoming better, more hygienic, more nutritious, and cheaper, and with a minimum of effort, of expense, and of social and private waste.

But what would women do once industry took over housework? Gilman hoped they would join men in the social world of production; sexual equality would come when men stopped supporting women, the over-developed sexual prisoners of a parasitic economic relationship. Sexual equality, the philosophical theme of *Women and Economics*, was the end toward which she pointed her specific proposals in *The Home*. Women must not abstain from the work of the world; the laws of social evolution require that they follow men out of the house, as cooking must follow shoemaking. If people live their lives "in their true arena, the world, that world will grow to have the sense of intimacy, of permanent close attachment, of comfort and pleasure and rest, which now attaches only to the home." Reverence and love, transferred to the world, "will have its natural, its inevitable effect, and make that world our home at last."

Gilman was a first-rate prophet, the most far-sighted domestic theorist of her time. Like Melusina Fay Peirce a half-century earlier, Gilman predicted a world where men and women both would work and where industry would take over housework. Caught in the ideology of separate spheres, Peirce's predictions suffered, but Gilman, like her contemporaries in the home economics movement, perceived that industrial progress and economic expansion had outdated the separate-spheres concept. While the home economists remained committed to the private house-wife working in the private home, Gilman's insistence on moving women and their work into the realm of social production allowed her to recog-nize the importance of small beginnings. Few married women yet worked outside the home, while the restaurant business was still merely an ad-junct to home life, serving mostly travelers, itinerants, and single male workers. Gilman used her evolutionary viewpoint to extend those trends into the future: she understood that women's employment in industry could release them from parasitic dependence on men, and that the in-dustrial preparation of cooked food could fit as neatly into the capitalist industrial system as fast-food restaurants and factory-prepared frozen meals eventually did.

Unfortunately, some aspects of those trends escaped Gilman's accurate prophecy: they do not all add up to the human liberation she predicted. Oblivious to the compensations of craft satisfaction that women lost as they became consumers of the standardized products of industry, she also failed to consider the compensations that would fall by the wayside as capitalist notions of efficiency were applied to cooking, mothering, and loving—the functions that remained in the household when she wrote. Celebrating industrial progress as the source of better products, she dis-counted the effects of the profit motive as the primary stimulus for production; manufacturers never decided what to produce solely on the basis of human need, and they used advertising to create demand for wasteful products that would penetrate intimate life. Anxious to have significant numbers of women assume jobs in industry and business so they would not be dependent on men for their support, Gilman ignored the dehumanizing aspects of most of those jobs and the likelihood that women would fail to achieve equality in status and pay working in the world of business. As it happened, Charlotte Perkins Gilman's predictions came true, but not until the 1960s and 1970s, when economic necessity and new ideas about women's roles brought many married women into the still expanding labor market, their work at home supplemented by fast foods and profit-making day-care centers. In the interim, full-time housewives assumed new roles, their tasks in the private household over-seen by experts from the public world.

TWELVE

When the Bough Breaks

Recognizing the trend represented by the new packaged foods, Charlotte Perkins Gilman advocated industrialized cooking and the abolition of the private kitchen; similarly, recognizing the trend represented by public kindergartens and national attention to scientific child rearing, she recommended the abolition of the private nursery —without, of course, describing her proposal as "industrialized" child care. Gilman demonstrated startling consistency for her day, for most of her contemporaries who concerned themselves with children, devoted both to the private home and to public progress, offered mothers contradictory advice backed by the claims of science and the power of public programs and the new mass media. They countered Gilman's claim that child rearing must leave the home like weaving and chicken killing; they maintained that children constituted the fundamental purpose of home. They thus established the dilemma of motherhood in the twentieth century: the isolation of the mother in a partially private sphere thoroughly dominated by public life.

Gilman's extreme position on child rearing represented the logical extension not only of the social trends she observed but of her own position that domestic labor was a phase rather than a kind of work; as other productive tasks had left the home, so must child rearing, for the sake of its own development. She paid lip service to the fundamental importance of children; with housework "fast disappearing into professional hands," she wrote, "the idle woman has but one excuse—the babies." If babies' best interests were served by keeping mothers at home, then stay at home they must: "No other call, no other claim, no other duty, can be weighed for a moment against this all-important service—the care of the little child." In fact, home baby care served no one's best interests; indeed, it prepared children for a distorted version of adult life if it did not kill them in the process.

Gilman built her case in a chapter of *The Home* entitled "The Child at Home," beginning with the assertion that children's education, "the most important process of human life," stifled their development when attempted in the modern home by modern homebound mothers. Healthy children needed to live in houses designed for their own needs, not "built and furnished for several mixed and conflicting industries"—cooking and sewing, sweeping and washing, sleeping and adult entertaining, and "incidentally, in the cracks and crevices of all these varied goings on, to 'bring up' children in." Homebound mothers, whose "arrested development" made them submit to the distortions of fashion in their own clothing, confined their children in clothes designed according to their "barbaric taste," disfiguring them and hampering their freedom "with heavy masses of stiff cloth, starched frippery, and huge, nodding, gaily decorated hats that would please an Ashantee warrior." Learning nothing in the isolated home about scientific feeding, yet cut off from the primitive instincts of the animal mother, proud women relied on "the infallible power of 'a mother's love' and 'a mother's care,'" thereby weakening or murdering their babies with improper food, imprisoning them in houses badly built even for adults, and thus exposing them to sewer gas, carbon dioxide, bacteria, dust, and fire. Gilman backed her argument with evidence "collected from one newspaper in one city during one year"— among them "Mother and Baby Both Badly Burned," "Choked in

Mother's Arms," "Child's Game Proved Fatal," "Accidentally Killed His Baby," "Escaping Gas Kills Baby"—thereby demonstrating her point that modern motherhood and modern home life imperiled children's lives.

Children who managed to survive all these hazards, furthermore, learned "facts of life" that could never fit them for adulthood. Mothers, who spent half their time procuring and cooking food, reinforced their children's savage instincts without really pleasing them or teaching them hygienic principles; mothers and servants who ran kitchens without joy or pride could hardly inspire children to "grow up with a burning ambition to be a cook." "Hour after hour, day after day," children watched their mothers devote themselves to an endless round of cleaning, sewing, and mending, and came to assume "that life, this deep, new, thrilling mystery of life consists mainly of eating and sleeping, of the making and wearing of clothes." Homebound mothers, who did nothing else, could teach nothing else; fortunately the child eventually went to school to learn "something of social values" and had a father who was "a real factor in society."

Professionals knew what mothers did not. "A newborn baby," Gilman

Charlotte Perkins Gilman criticized the "barbaric taste" of women who dressed their babies in "starched frippery." Photo of E. R. York's baby, taken during the 1890s, Seattle.

wrote, "leads a far happier, healthier, more peaceful existence in the hands of the good trained nurse" than when "left on the trembling knees of the young, untrained mother." Others proposed training the mother, a socially wasteful solution, or objected that the professional nurse would not love the baby. "What if she does not?" Gilman replied. "Cannot the mother love it *while the nurse takes care of it*? This is the whole position in a nutshell." Loving mothers brought children to doctors without shame, and eventually sent them to school; they could just as well "depend on equally skilled assistance" in caring for healthy children under age five. Babies and young children in good day nurseries, designed specifically to meet their needs and staffed by excellent professionals, grew up happier and healthier; Gilman cited only a French example, pointing out that most American data concerned sick babies in pauper hospitals and lonely ones in asylums, not the ideal healthy, happy baby whose intelligent, active nurse supplemented the mother's love with "calm, wise, experienced professional care."

Public nurseries offered the best child care, Gilman claimed, because child care, like any other task, developed best in the social sphere. Day nurseries and kindergartens, public education, playgrounds, and scientific pedagogy and child study—all implying that children must be recognized as "citizens with rights to be guaranteed only by the state" rather than as their parents' private property—marked civilized nations. They offered children at least a chance of survival: "the home-love and care of the Armenians for their children is no doubt as genuine and strong as ours, but the public care is not strong and well organized, hence the little Armenians are open to massacre as little Americans are not." Domestic child care, domestic protection, and domestic education limited those fields as surely as domestic cooking and domestic shoemaking limited theirs; according to Gilman, the laws of social evolution required that tasks develop beyond the private household stage, for the better organization and quality of the work itself.

Charlotte Perkins Gilman directed all her proposals about housework and child rearing toward one goal: women's emancipation from parasitic economic dependency on men, which she believed they could achieve only by leaving the private home and becoming "real factors in society" who as a matter of course earned wages for work performed in social settings. At the time she wrote, women were beginning to work for wages in increasing numbers, but only foresighted social critics like Gilman could perceive the implications of the nascent trend. Others noticed only the oppression of the impoverished women who worked out of sheerest desperation and the pride of the new college-educated women who worked to proclaim their freedom and their devotion to society. Neither the poor nor the educated and affluent considered their participation in the labor force a necessary part of their status as adults.

Small children have always tended to be underfoot; the nineteenth-century mother, without nursery schools or manufactured playpens, and laboring under a heavy workload, included their care with the rest of her activities. From *Harper's New Monthly Magazine*, 1890.

Most women who could afford to do so stayed home, but the options for earning money there disappeared during the first years of the twentieth century; dressmakers and seamstresses working outside factories decreased by 47 percent between 1910 and 1920, laundresses working outside of laundries by 25 percent; 19 percent fewer women reported their occupations as boardinghouse and lodginghouse keepers. The married women who had relied on income from these occupations began to leave home to look for work, although still in small numbers. Married women were joining the labor force faster than single women; they began to take the factory jobs traditionally held by single women, the new part-time domestic service jobs, and the new jobs in clerical, sales, and service fields that developed along with mass production and mass distribution.

These new jobs, and the new sectors of the economy where they occurred, distinguished the general expansion of the labor force during the two decades before the Depression of the 1930s. The working-age population grew 39 percent while the nonagricultural labor force grew 49 percent; in other words, a larger proportion of working-age people worked for wages at nonagricultural jobs. Industries that relied on manual labor employed fewer workers in 1930 than in 1910 (agriculture), expanded very slowly (forestry and fisheries, mining, and domestic service), or expanded at about the same rate as the economy as a whole (manufacturing and construction); meanwhile, employment boomed in finance and real estate, professional service, government, education, trade, personal service, and transportation and utilities. These industries had the greatest demand for workers in the job categories that expanded more than the general nonagricultural 49 percent: service workers outside private households (62 percent expansion), sales workers (74 percent), professional and technical workers (88 percent), and clerical workers (118 percent).

As women went out to work, they went into the expanding industries and job categories, especially in the lowest ranks. Their labor-force participation increased more than that of men, in the economy as a whole and in all the growing job categories. Clerical work showed the greatest expansion in every sense: the number of clerical workers more than doubled, the number of women clerical workers more than tripled, and women accounted for well over half the numerical increase. In other words, women served the expanding economy by moving into the new sectors as wage workers, while industrialization reduced their household work load and closed off the old-fashioned independent options for earning money at home.

Mothers resisted outside work whenever they could. As Gilman pointed out, orphanages provided the only professional child care in America, an unattractive example and not open to the children of working mothers in any case. Although washing machines eventually eased the burdens of mothers with babies in diapers, and although the new consumer market offered manufactured diapers, toys, baby foods, bottles, and infant furniture, no technological device could comfort a crying infant or answer a toddler's questions. Jobs in the outside world exerted no attraction for most mothers; in 1920, half the employed married women worked at one of four low-paying, low-status jobs (semiskilled factory operative, domestic servant, farm laborer, and laundress), and most of the rest served in the lowest-ranking jobs of the new clerical, service, and sales sectors. These women worked because they needed the money; caring for their

own children in their own homes held many more satisfactions than stacking other people's sheets in a hot commercial laundry or sewing a seam on an endless pile of trousers. Most of all, women loved their children and believed that motherhood was important work.

Others shared and promulgated that belief, at the beginning of "The Century of the Child," a phrase coined by Swedish writer Ellen Key as the title of a book that appeared in English in 1909 and became a best-seller in America. Like Gilman, Key maintained that "the line of progress is tending towards a new society, where all will be compelled to work and all will find work," but she proposed that motherhood be defined as work. In Key's new society, "people will regard the maternal function as so important for the whole social order" that mothers with small children would receive pay "from society" for a fixed period while their children required full-time care. "The mother," Key declared, "is the most precious possession of the nation, so precious that society advances its own highest well-being when it protects the functions of the mother." Her American contemporaries used similar rhetoric without endorsing her scheme to reimburse mothers for their all-important societal contribution; home economists used Catharine Beecher's argument about the importance of housework resting ultimately on its function for training future generations, while President Theodore Roosevelt told a child welfare conference that motherhood "is more worthy of honor and is more useful to the community than the career of any man, no matter how successful." Cowardly, selfish women who shirked their duties as mothers, the president averred, earned the same contempt as men who failed to do their duty in battle when their country called. Another speaker at the same conference told of glory even greater: "The keeper of the gates of to-morrow is the little child upon a mother's arms," she told the assemblage. "The way of that kingdom which is to come on earth, as in heaven, is placed in the hands of a child, and that child's hands a woman holds." In the overblown rhetoric of the child welfare conference, every child was a potential president or a potential messiah.

The reformers who promoted child welfare, like other Progressive reformers, sought solutions in the public sphere; although their rhetoric celebrated motherhood, they advocated public assumption of responsibility for children. Like the home economists and the housing and domestic service reformers, they turned public attention toward matters formerly private; they declared new, rational, "scientific" solutions in the interests of the society at large, and defined those interests as identical with those of the modern household, no longer isolated in the private sphere. Unlike Beecher, who had much earlier declared children's importance as the citizens of the future, turn-of-the-century activists worked in their settlement houses, their meetings, and their newsletters to design programmatic public applications of that obvious principle, campaigning for public playgrounds and against child labor, serving the causes of public kindergartens, compulsory education, and public health campaigns. Those who set themselves up as expert advisers to mothers used the sanction of these programs, sponsored by governments on all levels and by major philanthropic agencies, to dispense child-rearing advice both to the middle-class mothers in the process of acquiring plumbing and appliances and to the working-class mothers who were losing their home-based economic alternatives.

The new child-rearing advice relied as well on its claims to be a science, taking its theories from the new fields of psychology and child study, which proclaimed themselves scientific disciplines as they began to or-

---

Around the turn of the century, babies—like food and housekeeping in general—became subjects for experts, who extolled science and rationality and introduced new devices. This baby incubator was part of an exhibit at the 1909 Alaska Yukon Pacific Exposition in Seattle.

The Baby Incubator

ganize on a professional basis. G. Stanley Hall, the leading figure of the child study movement, the founder of the *American Journal of Psychology*, and a cofounder of the American Psychological Association, led the way both in establishing psychology as a laboratory science and in advancing theories about children's minds. Born savages, Hall claimed, children recapitulated human evolution, developing civilized traits as they grew. He encouraged mothers to keep "life books" on their children, recording "all incidents, traits of character, etc., with frequent photographs, parental anxieties, plans, hopes, etc." and to form child study groups, where they could compare their progress as mothers and their children's evolution as civilized beings. Although many of his theories failed to gain converts, Hall maintained his influence as a promoter both of scientific psychology and of scientific motherhood.

Truly scientific motherhood, however, required that mothers not merely study their children but read and follow the advice of scientifically trained experts. The most popular of these experts, Dr. Luther Emmett Holt, originally wrote his book *The Care and Feeding of Children* as a textbook for nurses; he dedicated its third edition to "The Young Mothers of America," in testimony to its immediate wide circulation among them. Addressing the National Congress of Mothers in 1899, Holt compared motherhood to farming; the farmer who wanted to raise the best grain or cows would study "the reports of the best scientific work on these subjects by experts who make these matters their study under government supervision," whereas mothers too often took "instinct and maternal love" as their guide. His book on child care both popularized the new scientific research (especially with regard to infant formulas) and provided firm guides for mother and infant behavior to replace instinct in both.

The mothers who read Holt's book, and the even more popular Children's Bureau publication *Infant Care*, whose author, Mrs. Max West, derived many of her precepts directly from Holt, learned that babies must be regulated and disciplined from an early age. "Babies under six months old should never be played with," Holt wrote, "and the less of it at any time the better"; this rule might "seem hard," Mrs. West added, "but it is without doubt a safe one" because babies need rest and quiet, and the physical stimulation that makes them laugh also makes them "irritable and restless," which "may result in nervous disturbance of the baby and upset his regular habits." Regular habits of eating and sleeping should begin at birth; the experts provided schedules, telling mothers both what should happen at any given time of a given day and how those schedules would change as the child grew older. Toilet training should begin at two or three months, placing the infant on a bowl "at exactly the same time every day" and, if necessary, using a suppository "in order to start the movement and to indicate to the baby what is wanted"; such early training, Mrs. West admitted, requires "much time and patience . . . but in the end the habit thus formed will be a great saving of trouble . . . and of untold value to the child, not only in babyhood, but throughout the whole of life."

Bad habits must be discouraged explicitly. Holt suggested fastening splints to an infant's elbow to prevent thumb-sucking, while Mrs. West preferred pinning or sewing the baby's sleeve "over the fingers of the offending hand," setting the hands free "now and then, especially if he is old enough to use his hands for his toys, and at meal times, to save as much unnecessary strain on his nerves as possible." For masturbation, she wrote matter-of-factly, "the treatment consists in mechanical restraints A thick towel or pad may be used to keep the thighs apart, or at night the hands may have to be restrained by pinning the nightgown sleeves to the bed, or the feet may be tied one to either side of the crib." Other contemporary child-rearing books contained patterns for making mechanical restraints, recipes for bad-tasting ointments, and recommendations for commercially manufactured thigh spreaders and aluminum mittens.

The Children's Bureau pamphlet justified all this regulation and discipline by citing its good effects on both parent and child. For the mother, it reduced work "to a minimum," providing her with "certain assured

Aluminum mittens, recommended by early twentieth-century child-rearing experts to discourage thumb-sucking and masturbation.

periods of rest and recreation," just like Christine Frederick's schedules for dishwashing and sweeping. Meanwhile, it trained the baby "in a way which will be of value to him all through life"; babies who learned bad habits would only have to unlearn them later, "at great cost of time and patience to both mother and babe." As some historians have pointed out, this approach to child rearing not only regulated babies as if their development corresponded to industrial production, but treated them as future workers who had to learn habits that would prepare them for life in an industrial context.

The baby's future in the world outside the home raised the most difficult issue for the new child experts: on the one hand, responsibility for the child's future gave motherhood its status and importance, but on the other, mothers had to learn to let go so that children could adapt to the world. The *Infant Care* pamphlet counseled both positions. Mothers should nurse their babies, since human milk suited human babies better than artificial feeding. Babies should take their airings in yards or on porches under maternal supervision, rather than in carriages pushed by older children or "some person not altogether competent"; nursemaids habitually neglected children in their care, harming them physically or crippling them emotionally in ways that could "persist to the child's harm for many years." At the same time, "a conscientious young mother is very apt to defeat her own ends by staying at home too constantly and watching over her baby so incessantly that she grows pale and nervous and begins to worry," thereby depleting her milk and making her baby sick. "Healthy babies are better off with a judicious amount of 'letting alone,'" and mothers could well be absent for some part of every day, if they left "a responsible person" in charge.

The experts supported the possibility of nonmaternal infant care in part because its principles underlay their claim to expertise. If mother love sufficed, if maternal instinct knew best, there was no place for the experts or the books they wrote. They appealed first to the value of their scientific knowledge, as Holt did in urging mothers to compare themselves to farmers seeking advice on animal husbandry and grain cultivation. To seal their own status, they made mother's love into a problem, the source of overstimulation and undernourishment. As a government pamphlet on older children put it during the twenties, "the very love of the mother for her child may be the 'stumbling block' that prevents her from successfully fulfilling the obligations of her parenthood. This love is invariably associated with excessive worry, anxiety, and, at times, definite fear which prevent the most intelligent approach to many problems of childhood." Experts who recommended tying infants to their beds and carefully described the sounds of cries of pain so that mothers would ignore cries for unscheduled feeding, human contact, or other "indulgence" could hardly afford to celebrate mother's love.

The child-rearing experts of the Progressive period followed in a long tradition of printed child-rearing advice; by its very definition, all such advice posited that the future of the world rested with children, that children's early years affected their personal futures, and that experts knew something mothers didn't. Lydia Maria Child began her 1831 treatise, *The Mother's Book*, by asserting that national character ("the heaviness of the Dutch and the vivacity of the French") derived from infant care: "The Dutch keep their children in a state of repose, always rocking, or jogging them; the French are perpetually tossing them about, and showing them lively tricks." Like William P. Dewees, whose 1825 *Treatise on the Physical and Medical Treatment of Children* she recommended for its technical advice on foods and diseases, Child maintained that mothers needed help from books; she filled her manual with examples of mothers whose instincts had proved inadequate for their task. Even a mother's instinct for fondness was not entirely trustworthy, Child wrote in her first chapter: "mothers are sometimes fond by fits and starts —they follow impulse, not principle." Readers might learn "principle" from books.

Although printed child-rearing advice was not new, the experts of the Progressive period wielded far greater power than any of their predecessors; their readers were the first generation of mothers to raise children "by the book." Child's book, although popular for its day, sold few copies in 1831 in comparison to its end-of-the-century successors, which benefitted from modern printing and distribution methods. Mass-circulation magazines popularized G. Stanley Hall's scientific theories on the nature of children and published articles based on Dr. Holt's rigorous child-rearing advice. Mrs. West's *Infant Care*, the Government Printing Office's best-selling publication of 1914, cost a quarter, bringing it within the means of the masses. Government agencies and charity programs sanctioned the new experts' ideas; home economists spread them to young women in college courses; social workers taught them to poor women at settlement houses and on home visits; nurses learned them in school and passed them on to new mothers who now delivered their babies in hospitals; social activists discussed them in child welfare conferences. No previous experts had had the opportunity to influence so many mothers.

The experts' influence was further enhanced as traditional means of support and instruction disappeared in the first decades of the twentieth century. Thousands of miles from her own mother and grandmother, the young immigrant mother depended on the social worker to teach her about child care; even native-born women often lived far from their parents and, told by the books to disregard their own instincts, could hardly trust those of their mothers, who continued to hold to old-fashioned methods in other areas of housekeeping. Traditional groups of women who met to do housework and might discuss child rearing had been supplanted by isolated work with industrial products. Women who bought ready-made clothes no longer gathered in sewing circles; those

The turn-of-the-century experts defined child rearing as a discrete task, separate from the rest of housework. Few early nineteenth-century housewives would have had time for the practices they recommended. From *Harper's New Monthly Magazine*, 1871.

who could afford to waste scraps of manufactured cloth held fewer quilting parties; washday gatherings at the well or hydrant died as indoor plumbing made washing an indoor task. Midwives, the traditional experts on infant care, delivered only about half the babies born in 1900; by the Depression, many states had outlawed their practice, and elsewhere the medical authorities harassed them and limited their authority, declaring them dirty, ignorant, meddlesome "relics of a barbaric past." Perhaps inexperienced mothers, blinded by terror and love, *have* always needed counsel; perhaps, as Gilman claimed, human mothers had long since been cut off from the instincts that told animal mothers how to care for their young. The experts' power nonetheless rested not so much on their scientific superiority as on the mothers' isolation in the private sphere.

The authors of the new child-rearing advice exploited the isolated mother's insecurity. Basing their advice on scientific claims, they wrote in terms far more precise and authoritative than were to be found in previous child-rearing literature. Holt published charts prescribing exact quantities of milk and feeding intervals for infants of different ages, and a series of formulas with varying proportions of milk, milk sugar, lime water, boiled water, and barley gruel, to be changed every few weeks as the baby grew; even breast-fed babies, Mrs. West maintained, should be weighed before and after each nursing to determine how much food they got. Room temperature for the new baby should be 65 degrees; bathwater for the colicky infant should be 100 degrees; a soda bath "required" two tablespoons of baking soda to a gallon of water. Infants should get cows' milk from Holstein cows rather than Jerseys or Guernseys for the "more nearly proper percentage of fat." Mothers must forsake their instincts not only for books but for scales and thermometers and charts. New terminology—vitamins, protein, bacteria, and the like—added intimidation, especially for immigrant mothers who learned the new child rearing from social workers, themselves "scientifically" trained in the new schools of social work and home economics departments.

Supposedly scientific psychological theory backed the specifics of schedules and restraints. If a new mother had difficulty letting her child scream until its scheduled feeding time, the experts assured her that its psychological well-being for a lifetime depended on just that. Middle-class mothers who joined child study groups and read women's magazines learned that the advice about regulation and lifetime habits rested on theories developed by Harvard professors in laboratory experiments. Lydia Maria Child, on the other hand, had backed the advice in *The Mother's Book* seventy years earlier with mere common sense: its "leading principles" came from "the standard works on education" and from "frequent conversations with an intelligent and judicious mother." She frequently taught by example: one mother told her child he could have no mince pie but gave it to him when he screamed, eventually sending him to bed with a whipping and a stomach ache, while another (who "managed her family better than any woman I ever saw, or ever expect to see again") sent a crying daughter to bed without supper "for the good of the child." This example taught principles later authorized by psychological theory (don't reinforce bad behavior, act consistently), but Child appealed only to common sense and "good management," and the details she described always suggested that the general principles should be followed as guides in varying situations, not as recipes for lifetime development.

Probably no turn-of-the-century mother followed Holt's advice to the letter; infants defy regulation, as Anna Noyes discovered. Noyes, who raised her son with Holt's book "at my right hand," and in 1913 published her own detailed account entitled *How I Kept My Baby Well*, attempted Holt's methods and recorded her baby's first twenty-five months with splendid precision, but relied ultimately on love and common sense. She tried to toilet-train him at three months, but it took twenty months for his bowel movements to stabilize at a proper twenty-four-hour interval; she attacked his thumb-sucking with quinine, adhesive plaster, cardboard, hand-holding, slaps, and pinches, "but he soon got over all the hurts inflicted and the bad taste in his mouth, and became most efficient in freeing this thumb from bondage." Finally, at twenty-five months, he had fallen asleep several times without his thumb in his mouth, "so we are making progress there. He seems so reasonable about many things that I am hoping his sensibleness will help out in the breaking up of this habit," which had deformed neither thumb nor mouth. Love and common sense, in other words, won out over "the book," even for a mother ready to sacrifice instinct to science.

Anna Noyes read the books but acted on her own ideas: suspecting, for example, that vomiting indicated overfeeding even though everybody told

Unlike many other tasks, child care defied mechanization, except in the imagination. This fanciful invention appeared in the *American Agriculturist*, 1863; much later, Rube Goldberg drew a similar device.

her that all babies throw up, she cut down her son's food and increased the time intervals between feedings ("until at one time he was one-sixth the *time* which Holt prescribes"), keeping her eye on the scales to be sure he continued to gain weight. "Our grandmothers knew" that whatever kept a baby well was best for that baby, "and practiced it long before tables of averages were so much as dreamed of," she decided. "Any unprejudiced, normal person could, after a few moments for reflection, sum up the evidences of health in a baby"—clear skin, sound sleep, sparkling eyes, good appetite, pink cheeks, thoroughly digested food, and steady growth. The experts disagreed. "An inexperienced mother is often greatly at a loss to know whether a baby is properly thriving or not, and may be unduly alarmed at small matters, or may not understand the serious nature of certain conditions," said Mrs. West, providing an identical list of indicators with an appended collection of "points in a normal development"—ages at which babies laugh, sit erect, hold their heads up, walk, and talk. A mother's love, it seemed, distorted her vision; to the experts, an inexperienced mother could not be an unprejudiced, normal person who could see babies for what they were.

The child-raising experts of the early twentieth century both recognized and helped to establish the dilemma that has plagued motherhood ever since. Unwilling to turn this important task over to the public as Gilman proposed, or to reward it with money as Ellen Key recommended, they left it to be done without pay by women working in private households now invaded by industrial products and scientific advice. The independent work of mothers at home remained in some ways similar to that of women of the past: they could put down their ironing to appreciate an intimate moment with a child, or pause on a walk in the park to talk with other mothers. They had time, if they chose, to cook and sew and decorate their houses with handmade goods, garnering the satisfactions of those crafts and of working for their family's love. Yet as women joined the organized labor market during the decades before the Depression, the differences between motherhood and paid labor developed into problems. Mothering produced nothing tangible, whereas even sales workers—obviously not "productive" in the old sense—brought home paychecks. Full-time paid workers came home to recover from their jobs and to provide themselves with the essentials of survival, welcoming the products that freed them from the arduous labor of producing those essentials. As adulthood came to be identified with the economic independence that paid work offered and that gave people the means to buy things, mothers came to be excluded from the activities of other adults. They met each other in groups organized around their children's activities, not around their own adult work, as the sewing circle had been. Social life organized around spending money at movies and restaurants offered no place for small children, thereby excluding and isolating mothers even further.

Yet even in its isolation, the private work of motherhood was increasingly dominated by the outside world. The turn-of-the-century experts brought the values of the factory and the business to motherhood: rationality, science, discipline, and individual accommodation to the social order. They proclaimed that motherhood was significant, but in terms that served industrial goals: good mothers established regular habits that made good workers. With their scientific charts and rationales, they degraded the traditional practices and values of the sewing circle and the midwife. Caught between the satisfactions of caring for their own children in their own homes and the messages from the outside world that invaded their lives, twentieth-century mothers became susceptible to the experts' opinion that mother's love did indeed constitute a problem and to the new messages of consumerism. As the national market expanded, the advertisers claimed that good motherhood required good purchasing, both of products for the children and of ones that would save mothers time to devote to mothering. The private households of the nineteenth century had kept their privacy, uninvaded by television, radio, or even very many magazines or newspapers. As those media developed during the twentieth, under the influence of their advertisers, they created new desires and even new needs for manufactured goods—and for money.

The need for money to maintain home life brought women into the labor market as a matter of course by the 1970s, making the mother at home into a status symbol and bringing guilt and fear into the decision to bear children. Women who held jobs before marriage or before their children arrived experienced the supervised oppression of most outside jobs. Sally, a Boston housewife interviewed in the late 1970s, remembered her years of office work with displeasure: "They used to clock us. They used to watch us, and monitor our work. You only had so much time to go to the bathroom." Caring for her children at home, she said, "I am the boss here and I don't have to answer to anyone what I do all day. I don't have to ask to go to the bathroom. I can cook whatever I want. I can do the wash when I want to." Yet with a husband working at two jobs so she could stay home, she felt unfree there as well. Once he arrived home to find her taking a nap: "I heard the door shut and I jumped up. As though he'd caught me. . . . I feel guilty if I do something strictly for myself, because I think sometimes just being here is a luxury." Nor could Sally and her contemporaries expect to stay home forever; at best they might hope to do so until their children started school, and they pinned those hopes on finding men who would earn enough and stay with them long enough so they could do that.

As women have come to expect that they may leave the labor market during their childrens' preschool years but will return to it eventually, the years at home have become fearful ones. How will they get back, competing with men and with other women who have histories of consistent employment? The rising divorce rate suggests that the decision and the timing may not be theirs and that they may become the sole or major financial support for their children; it compounds the fears, for husbands who encounter working women at their jobs might withdraw both financial and emotional support for those who stay home. Deprived of the nineteenth-century options for earning money at home, those who go out to work confront guilt and fear from other sources: like the turn-of-the-century New Hampshire millworker who took in boarders after her child got burned in an older sister's care, they worry about finding safe child care. Nor is safety the only criterion: they remain concerned for their children's psychological well-being, and for the values of intimacy with which they were raised and which they cannot necessarily find in child-care facilities organized primarily for profit. Competing with men for jobs that are often oppressive, earning money to buy products that merely promise satisfaction, they perceive child care as a woman's responsibility, shoulder the burdens of two jobs that often conflict, and feel guilty.

That guilt is partly a legacy of the early twentieth-century child-rearing experts' definition of motherhood as a discrete task, established by them as a response to industrialization that would keep mothers in the private sphere. Early in the nineteenth century, women cared for their children in the interstices of their burdensome household work, giving them household chores to perform as they grew, including the care of younger brothers and sisters. Sometimes the best a busy mother could offer her infant, Lydia Maria Child wrote in 1831, was "a smile, or a look of fondness . . . now and then" or an endearing call from the next room. As children grew, they could be expected to help: "Even very little children are happy when they think they are useful. 'I can do *some* good, can't I, mother?' is one of the first questions asked." By the end of the century, almost no one made textiles or sewed men's clothes, and the new utilities and manufactured products were firmly established among the urban middle classes. Poor women sewed more than rich ones, and farm wives produced more food than city women, but industrialization had affected even their work, and promised to continue to eradicate these differences. As businesses took over productive work, housewives began to have time to devote to child rearing as a distinct and definable task: nobody who spent two whole days doing the laundry would have had time for all the charts and measurements recommended by the turn-of-the-century experts. Nor could she have attended to the other new duty of the formerly private sphere, the work of buying things.

THIRTEEN

Selling Mrs. Consumer

As mass production removed productive work from the private sphere, mass marketing and mass distribution introduced a new task and a new pastime: buying things. A new kind of consumer, courted by new kinds of advertising, purchased new kinds of goods at new kinds of stores. American consumerism is a historical phenomenon: at one time nonexistent, it became pervasive; the wholesale transformation of most Americans' daily life from near-subsistence farming to mass participation in the money economy both as workers and as consumers, like any other long historical process, proceeded piecemeal. Many seemingly unconnected events, each in itself of minor historical importance, combined over the two centuries to produce a changed world; although this complexity defies precise dating, an enormous transformation occurred during the few decades on either side of the turn of the twentieth century. Advertisers came to see women as their audience; home economists taught women how to shop and how to plan for shopping; new, interrelated products like washing machines and soap powders appeared on the market, each encouraging the use of another; mail-order houses, department stores, supermarkets, and chain stores, emphasizing impersonal relationships between buyer and seller and dominated by large corporations, replaced small shops, country stores, and public markets. By the time of the Great Depression, which delayed the full expression of the new trends, consumption was established as the new task of the private sphere, now completely dominated by the public.

As long as households produced most of the goods they used, consumption in the modern sense of the word meant little. Until the middle of the nineteenth century, farmers bought things, but not much and not often; a trip to town or to the country store at the crossroads was an occasion. City people produced as much as possible. Often men did the shopping; handling money clearly belonged within their sphere, the world outside the home. "The smartest men" in Cincinnati, wrote Frances Trollope in the 1820s, "and those of the 'highest standing' do not scruple to leave their beds with the sun, six days in the week, and, prepared with a mighty basket, to sally forth in search of meat, butter, eggs, and vegetables," returning home for breakfast, which their wives prepared in their absence. Few cookbooks or manuals of household advice before the last decades of the century offered any instruction whatever in buying things —no charts distinguishing chuck from rump, no directives on bulging fish eyes and fresh-looking gills, little guidance on quality in food or fabrics or household equipment. As Catharine Beecher revised her successive comprehensive housekeeping manuals, she added increasing amounts of consumer advice, finally writing a chapter entitled "Marketing and the Care of Meats" for her 1873 *Housekeeper and Healthkeeper.* "Every young woman, at some period of her life, may need the instructions of this chapter," it began, indicating that women with trustworthy servants sent them to market, although even they "should have the knowledge which will enable them to direct their servants what and how to buy." Beecher admitted that thousands of her readers were "obliged to go to market," but evidently those who could avoid such indelicate activity in the world outside the home would do so.

With trustworthy servants in short supply by the end of the century,

with husbands working long hours in factories, and with households increasingly dependent on manufactured products, women of all classes began to assume the function of buying household goods. In 1891, readers of *Printer's Ink*, a new weekly journal for the advertising industry later to become *Advertising Age*, encountered a series of arguments among advertisers on the issue of women consumers. Nathaniel C. Fowler, Jr., a newspaper publisher soon to found the Fowler School of Advertising, began the controversy by asserting that women made the purchasing decisions and that advertisers ought therefore to direct their campaigns at them. Even goods used exclusively by men, he said, sold better when advertised in women's magazines; he had experimented with this concept many times, "until I believe I have a right to claim that the experiment has passed into fact." Nonsense, responded William H. Maher, citing his advertisements for scissors and cutlery in the *Ladies' Home Journal*, which cost more than they paid in sales receipts, and in the *Farm Journal*, which "with rates about the same, pays me well and has always paid

Peddlers, eventually doomed by railroads and crossroads stores, brought a variety of goods to isolated nineteenth-century households. Wood engraving from *Harper's Weekly*, 1868.

well." Women, more timid than men about ordering anything but seeds by mail, rarely even wrote business letters; men, in any case, controlled the purse strings. "In selling cutlery," Maher wrote, "where one woman orders a knife for a man one thousand men will order knives for women, and ten thousand men buy for themselves where one woman orders for herself." Fowler defended himself three weeks later, claiming that he had been "overwhelmed with opinions unconditionally substantiating the ground which I attempted to assume." Maher, "one of the shrewdest advertisers in the country," had based his singular reply on the fact that men's names appeared on the cutlery firm's orders: "He seems to be of the opinion that because men order these things the advertisement is read by the men, not the women." Fowler felt this illustrated a limited under- standing of marriage: "Is Mr. Maher a married man? Has he brothers [who are] married? One would almost suppose he knew nothing of the links of the chain of matrimony, that he never had experienced that delightful thrill which comes to every married man when his wife, kissing him on the doorstep, says, 'My dear, be sure and order so-and-so for me from Mr. Somebody.'" Within a few decades, nobody would debate who decided what scissors to buy, although advertisers would carry on iden- tical arguments with regard to major purchases such as houses, automo- biles, and large appliances.

The advertisers attempted to attract whoever did the deciding. Al- though their ultimate decision to advertise most products to the woman consumer undoubtedly bolstered the development of the consumer role, creating that role and establishing a new function for the household in the world of mass production and mass distribution was, for them, a means to their clients' financial ends. The home economists, on the other hand, consciously created and defined a place in the new economic order for the private home and for the married women who stayed in it. From the start, they taught educated consumption. When Juliet Corson took classes from her New York Cooking School to the Fulton Market, she paraded them around the stalls to point out high-quality poultry ("the best is plump, fat, and nearly white"), fish ("Lobsters and crabs must be bright in color and lively in movement, like these"), meat ("Good mutton is bright red"), and vegetables ("Roots and tubers must be plump"). For those who con- sulted cookbooks instead of taking classes, writers introduced instructions in written form, emphasizing food values in the new scientific terms: calories, vitamins, and protein. Issues of quality intersected with issues of cost. "Economizing on food," wrote Florence Nesbitt in a manual on low- cost cooking, "is a most dangerous thing to try unless the housekeeper has an understanding of food values. She must know what foods are necessary for the health of her family and in what food materials she gets the most for her money, to be able to decide where it is wise and safe to cut and where unsafe." Social workers who translated scientific principles of

At the turn of the century, when this photograph was taken in Santa Ana, California, many kinds of food merchants offered home delivery.

housekeeping to poor women while they oversaw their spending of relief money often required them to keep written budget accounts, providing "uncolored facts as to how the money has gone and what has been secured for it"—and an examination procedure to test their progress. Although they held no such financial power over their students, home economics teachers in public schools and colleges likewise linked quality with price and encouraged careful shopping and conscious budgeting.

Household engineer Christine Frederick took careful shopping and conscious budgeting to their extremes, as she had done with efficient use of time; again, her ideas are important because more moderate home economists adopted her general principles and taught them to millions of women, and her statements of those principles provide their most straightforward exposition. Every large business, Frederick pointed out, employed "persons called 'purchasing agents,' who are trained, informed on market conditions, and able to buy to the best advantage for their particular firms," thereby saving thousands of dollars. Housewives, who spent family funds, must similarly learn about market conditions (when to buy and what to pay) and make their decisions according to their particular needs, family incomes, and express goals. "In other words, every woman running the business of homemaking must *train herself* to become an efficient 'purchasing agent' for her particular firm or family, by study, watchfulness, and practice." This new role offered housewives a truly managerial position in the modern household that stood at the intersection of the previously separate spheres; even those who failed to plan

A Charles Schneider Baking Company delivery man, Washington, D.C., 1942. Office of War Information photo by Howard Liberman.

their dishwashing must plan their purchases or else fail at the "entirely new responsibilities" that replaced the work of the old-fashioned household where women made soap and candles, wove and sewed, and produced food for daily and future use.

The modern household purchasing agent, like her factory counterpart, oversaw an extensive record-keeping system; budget records, of course, predominated. Frederick, writing the textbook version of her ideas in 1920, carefully distinguished between "household accounts," recording expenditures after the fact, and her "budget system," based on annual planning in advance. Husband and wife must sit down together to assess their financial situation and determine the family goals; "otherwise it would be just as if a ship were to start on a voyage without a port toward which to sail. The budget is to the family what a charted course is to the navigator with a settled harbor in view and definite sailing directions to guide." The family could then apportion expenses among shelter, food, clothing, operating expenses, savings, personal luxuries, and "advancement" (education, music, books, church, charity, and vacations—luxuries that benefitted the entire family): "typical divisions for all incomes." Instead of spending their money "just as each need seems to arise—$30 for food one month, $20 the next, 'squeezing' down the food some other month because the entire family needs winter clothing," they could account for all needs throughout the year. The object of such annual planning, Frederick maintained, "is not so much *skimping, economy* or *saving,* as it is *proportionate, balanced spending.*" Although Frederick offered possible apportionments for six income levels, ranging from $600 to $2,400 a year, she emphasized that budgets must be designed by and for individual families, based on their temperaments, social and professional standing, locale (climate and proximity to markets), and size, as well as on income.

Once made, the budget was to be followed; household accounts provided a record of success or failure. Frederick outlined two account plans, one to be kept in a notebook, the other in a card file, both based on simplified versions of double-entry bookkeeping, to be totaled daily and balanced weekly or monthly. Monthly checks against the annual budget helped to avert financial disaster by discouraging long-term extravagance in every category, while the budget records for any given year furnished information for even better planning for the following year.

The good household purchasing agent maintained many other kinds of records besides the household accounts. Each person in the family should be described on a clothes card, listing all sizes, to be carried on shopping trips: "How many times has one seen a 'bargain' in men's shirts which could not be bought because we did not 'remember' whether the neck size was 14 or 15-½!" Every bedsheet should be marked with indelible ink, indicating the size, a number for the particular sheet, and the date of purchase, keyed to a card listing the cost and size of each sheet and the firm from which it was purchased, markings that told "how long that quality at a given price wore. . . . If a sheet has worn badly, why purchase the same grade and price of the same concern?" Canned-goods storage records should show the sizes of cans, prices of purchase, and quantity on hand; "then, as a can of peas or peaches is used, it should be crossed off the list, so that at a glance the number of cans on hand of any particular product can be seen without poking around the storage and actually counting the cans." Armed with this record, the purchasing agent could make up her shopping list.

These budget and purchasing records were only part of an elaborate household filing system that kept track of addresses (social and commercial—one card per address), medical data (three cards for each family member: a medical card with dates of vaccination and childhood diseases, a dental card with dates and costs of fillings, and an oculist card with dates of eye examinations and glasses prescriptions), household storage records, gifts given and received, purchase and repair records, inventories of valuables, and recipes. Bills and receipts, too bulky to keep in the card-file box, resided in an alphabetically arranged partitioned pasteboard box; large envelopes held clippings, pamphlets, and appliance instruction booklets, each recorded in a subject card file for reference.

All these files and papers should be permanently arranged in a home office, or "business corner." "One thing that contributes to being business-like," Frederick maintained, "is to have the right 'business' atmosphere." Like the busy executive who needs a place to keep his papers, the home-maker "needs an 'office' corner, no matter how humble, where she can go to plan her menus, write out her orders and make up her accounts." A few shelves and a table will suffice to "increase her system and pride in the 'business' end of housekeeping"; in other words, housewives must separate their manual from their mental labor in space as well as in time, elevating the mental labor to its prime position in the new world of the consumer.

Lest the reader think that all this filing might be time-consuming, Frederick assured her that the reader's customary haphazard system took more time: "Think of the hours you spent 'hunting' for an important address which you must have immediately. Think what an amount of energy you waste running around the house for a commercial receipt that you are 'sure you paid,' when the collector calls for his bill." The filing system took time, but "*its results are 80 per cent more efficient.*" Even more to the point, women must not think that manufactured products relieved them of responsibilities; they must spend time on consumption itself, keeping track of purchases and becoming trained, educated consumers. "In other words," Frederick wrote, "some of the time saved by having these articles manufactured outside the home must be taken by the housekeeper in learning to *understand how to buy commercially made products.*"

Frederick thus placed consumption in the category of a household

U ntil the combination store after the 1920s, shoppers purchased all of their meat, fresh produce, and groceries in separate stores. Butcher shop, operated by Phil Hof (right), Boscobel, Wisconsin, around 1900. Sam and Herman Hof are behind the counter.

task, specifying its performance more carefully than the home economists who preceded her, and anticipating the popularizers who communicated the idea through the women's magazines during the 1920s. An article on shopping for linens in the *Ladies' Home Journal* in 1928 stated the historical case that Melusina Fay Peirce had made clear in 1869: "A woman's virtue and excellence as a housewife do not in these days depend upon her skill in spinning and weaving." But whereas Peirce, and later Charlotte Perkins Gilman, fretted about women's consequent status as parasites, the *Journal* crowed about the new world of consumption, where "an entirely different task presents itself, more difficult and more complex, requiring an infinitely wider range of ability, and for these very reasons more interesting and inspiring."

The *Journal*'s pep talk on inspirational consumption flew in the face of truth: women bought machine-made products because they made life easier, not more complex, interesting, or inspiring. A character in *Bread Givers*, a Yiddish novel of the period, described her Old World dowry: pillows full of down plucked by hand, embroidered sheets and towels, curtains that took her a whole year to knit, and a hand-crocheted table-cloth in all the colors of the rainbow. "It was like dancing sunshine lighting up the room when it was spread on the table. . . . There ain't in America such beautiful things like we had home." "Nonsense, Mamma!" her daughter replied. "If you only had the money to go on Fifth Avenue you'd see the grand things you could buy." "Yes, buy!" repeated the mother. "In America, rich people can only buy, and buy things made by machines. Even Rockefeller's daughter got only store-bought, ready-made things for her dowry. There was a feeling in my tablecloth—" That feel-ing, the feeling of craft satisfaction, disappeared with all the new products, and the supposed interest and inspiration of consumption never replaced it.

Time spent on consumption tasks did replace time spent on other household tasks. Probably few women elevated consumption to the level Frederick recommended; few established the elaborate files and records and devoted hours solely to planning. Sociologists' studies from the 1920s onward, however, indicate that women continued to spend about as many hours doing their housework as they had done before, substituting extra hours spent with children and in shopping and managerial work for the arduous labor of the old-fashioned laundry and kitchen. Indeed, unlike the old-style work, consumption was an expandable task: nobody would eat without a fire in the fireplace or stove, and the laundry had required a certain amount of water hauling, but consumption, the new women's work, never ended at all. The thrifty housewife could always go to yet another store for yet another sale, clip yet another coupon from yet an-other magazine, read yet another article about yet another kind of appli-ance. It was the perfect task to occupy the full-time housewife while increasing numbers of married women went off to work outside the home. The time studies suggest that employed women devoted considerably less time to housework than full-time housewives; they probably more often called on other family members to help, and substituted industrial prod-ucts and services for their own labor, but they also had less time for consumption. People still had to eat and the laundry still got dirty, but the employed woman would more likely ignore the fact that peaches cost four cents less per pound at the store down the block.

By far the most potent and pervasive force fostering the new consumer role, advertising shaped the concepts in the interests of business. As large firms combined the methods of mass production and mass distribution to create and control a national market, they linked the activities of the consumer housewife to their own through advertising. The small mer-

©1918
CLARENCE SAUNDERS

The first of the supermarket's innovations, self-service, was introduced at this Piggly-Wiggly store in Memphis, Tennessee, 1916.

chants and tradespeople of the old economic order had advertised in newspapers since colonial times; the advertising industry itself began to develop in the 1850s, with advertising agencies that promoted products on local levels. After the 1880s, national agencies worked with the sales departments of the developing national manufacturers; then as now, the manufacturers hired the ad agencies and ultimately controlled the content, location, and volume of their advertising.

The manufacturers' new products required advertising to create demand: consumers did not know they wanted or "needed" products they had never seen. Furthermore, many of the early manufactured consumer goods—packaged cereals, cigarettes, canned foods, and the like—had low unit costs; because manufacturers could not increase demand by lowering the already low price of a package of oatmeal or a can of soup, they had to concentrate on ways of selling more of them to increase their profits. Advertising therefore developed in tandem with mass production: both the ads and the products appeared before the turn of the century and developed consistently, but without infiltrating most people's daily lives until after World War I. Along with the new products, the advertising industry boomed during the 1920s: magazine advertising revenues more than tripled between 1918 and 1929, to become a $200 million business on the eve of the Depression, while commercial radio, inaugurated by KDKA in Pittsburgh in 1920, offered an entirely new and increasingly popular medium for promoting the new products and for connecting the private household with the outside world.

As the industry developed, its techniques changed; the relatively straightforward advertising of the turn of the century gave way during the 1920s to ads that established corporate products as solutions for fearful individuals in a hostile world. Woodbury Soap equipped women with beautiful skin to meet people "proudly—confidently—without fear"; a baby-food ad suggested the infant death rate ("If we only had the nerve to put a hearse in the ad, you couldn't keep the women away from the food," the ad agency head told the copywriter); and numerous ads promoted terror of the new corporate diseases—" 'sneaker smell,' 'paralyzed pores,' 'vacation knees,' . . . 'underarm offense,' and 'ashtray breath.' "

By the 1930s, the real world of economic depression was fearful enough, and the ads began to state directly the most fundamental message of consumerism: money *can* buy love. In one 1933 issue of *Good Housekeeping*, the message went out to both single and married women. "How This Vacation Romance Was SAVED" told the story of a woman who met a "terribly attractive" man with a "grand speed boat" on the beach; sure that he liked her too, she thrilled to his request for the first dance at the yacht club two days later—"and then . . . for some reason or other, he faded way. *What's wrong?*" Fortunately friend Betty stepped in to suggest "Luxing underthings every night, because without Lux you risk perspiration odor," and the heroine ended up in the speed boat. Thrifty housewife Margery similarly saved her marriage with French's mustard: although husband Frank used mild words about the cheap kind she bought ("Don't serve this mustard, darling. It tastes terrible. It'll spoil the supper"), his cartoon face suggested that she'd better borrow some French's from the nextdoor neighbor if she wanted to hold on to him.

Few *Good Housekeeping* readers danced at yacht clubs in 1933, and advertisers eventually dropped the direct line for a more subtle approach, but the advertisements and the national media that provided them with a vehicle set standards even for women who could never quite take the ads seriously. First mass-circulation magazines and radio during the 1920s, and later television during the 1950s, brought the outside world directly into the formerly private home, suggesting how other homes differed. One elderly California woman remembers that her youth was without "advertising on a mass scale," without "*I Love Lucy* or a television," without even "an awful lot of magazines to compare ourselves with." No outside

agency informed her family about how others lived. "So we could care less if we didn't keep up with the Joneses." Who knew what the Joneses did or how they lived?

The Joneses, women learned as the new media spread the word, dropped the old ways of housekeeping in favor of the new products; readers of that same 1933 *Good Housekeeping* issue got the message in several different ways. A well-dressed young woman walks into her mother's cartoon kitchen to find her stirring laundry in a wash boiler set on top of a gas stove. "Mother, it's simply stifling in here!" says the daughter. "How can you stand it?" Old-fashioned mother replies with old-fashioned ignorance: sure it's hot, but "I need this wash . . . How else can I get the clothes white?" Next washday's cartoon shows them using Rinso: "Millions now 'take it easy' on washday! Instead of scrubbing for hours in a sweltering kitchen—instead of torturing themselves still further by boiling the clothes—they just *soak* everything in Rinso suds." Franco-American took the opposite approach in a canned spaghetti ad: equating age with wisdom, the company claimed that many mothers told their newly married daughters never to "think of cooking spaghetti in your own kitchen!" because delicious, nourishing Franco-American spaghetti had made it "a waste of time and energy" and even of money to do so. Gerber's baby foods spoke directly to the young mother who could now tend her baby instead of its food. "It isn't necessary to cook and strain vegetables at home" because Gerber makes better baby food: "You can't, with ordinary home equipment, prepare vegetables as safe, as rich in natural food values, as reliably uniform as the ready-to-serve Gerber products." Advertising copywriters might disagree on the particulars of the strategy, but they commonly debunked the old-fashioned methods. If the old ways were better, why would anybody buy new products?

Inventing and advertising new products formed the crux of the new corporate strategy of the twentieth century. The National Biscuit Company, for example, formed in 1898 as a merger of three regional companies, at first followed old policies. "In the past," the company stated in its 1901 annual report, "the managers of large industrial corporations have thought it necessary, for success, to control or limit competition"; National Biscuit therefore attempted to fight its competitors or buy them, but soon met "disaster" in a "ruinous war of prices" that left them with no purchasing capital. The company therefore "turned our attention and bent our energies" to a new strategy—tightening internal management, centralizing mass production, developing the marketing department, "and above all things and before all things, to improving the quality of our goods and the condition in which they should reach the consumer." Imitating Quaker Oats and Pillsbury Flour, National Biscuit stopped producing bulk crackers for the cracker barrel and invented the "Uneeda Biscuit," advertising its brand name to the consumer until packaged crackers re-

42   LADIES' HOME JOURNAL   February, 1932

ARE *Domestic Hands* A BADGE OF MARRIAGE ?

Her poor bewildered husband simply can't understand the change that has come over Helen since their marriage last June.

She used to love to go to parties and to give them. But now, she never wants to go anywhere and she hates to have people come into their home.

When old friends drop in unexpectedly she is so queer and so self-conscious. It was actually embarrassing the other night when Tom brought Ted Graham home for dinner without warning. And after he had gone there was another of those awful weepy scenes.

The real trouble with Helen of course is a bad case of Domestic Hands.

Unaccustomed to housework before her marriage, she simply has not learned that it is easily possible to have lovely, soft white hands and still get along without a maid.

A Soothing Pure-as-Milk Lotion that Keeps Hands Young

No matter how much housework you have to do, you can easily avoid the embarrassment of Domestic Hands and the inferiority complex that goes with them. All you need do is smooth Hinds Honey and Almond Cream into them two or three times each day. The results will amaze you.

Within a few days' time even hands pitifully roughened by neglect grow softer, whiter and more attractive. You see the improvement almost at once.

Don't Take Chances with Questionable Lotions

The delightful caressing texture of Hinds comes from the mildest and finest skin-softening emollients—a special secret of its half-century tested formula. Avoid imitations, many of which simulate Hinds cream-like texture by the addition of gummy thickening agents that do not benefit the skin. Don't take chances—insist upon the original Hinds Honey and Almond Cream.

Get Hinds from your druggist today—your hands will *show* their appreciation. We'll gladly send a generous sample, free, if you will write the A. S. Hinds Co., Dept. B-18, Bloomfield, N. J.

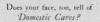

A photographic representation of inferiority complex caused by Domestic Hands. Interpreted by Anton Bruehl.

Does your face, too, tell of *Domestic Cares?*
TRY THESE NEW HINDS BEAUTY AIDS

Because days crowded with household cares so often leave signs of tiredness and neglect, Hinds decided to do for faces what they've always done for hands . . . make them smooth as velvet, lovely and youthful. Try this simple, amazingly inexpensive treatment:

HINDS CLEANSING CREAM This cool, fragrant cream liquefies 2 to 3 times faster than ordinary creams, floating out dirt without stretching pores. 40c and 65c a jar.

HINDS TONING CLEANSER This stimulating new cleanser dissolves pore residue, so pores shrink back to normal size. 65c a bottle.

HINDS TEXTURE CREAM A greaseless softening cream to make the skin satin-smooth. 40c a jar.

If your druggist cannot supply you, write to A. S. Hinds Co., Dept. B-18, Bloomfield, N. J.

HINDS
honey and almond
CREAM

Domestic Hands, one of the new corporate diseases. This may be the only "representation of inferiority complex" ever photographed. From the *Ladies' Home Journal*, 1932.

placed the bulk kind. Thanks to this strategy, food processing, like other consumer-goods industries, established its pattern for the twentieth century, dominated by a few large firms whose marketing, manufacturing, purchasing, and accounting departments were all controlled from a central office.

Brand names, these corporations claimed, operated as guarantees of quality. Some home economists, following Christine Frederick, agreed. The educated consumer, Frederick had said, understood the difference between price and value, the frauds perpetrated on the unwitting, the sanitary standards ignored at the open markets, the adulterants found in many manufactured foods, and the deceit about weights and measures so common among those who sold bulk foods. Only a trademark—"some kind of label, emblem or other *means of identification* bearing the manufacturer's name, place of factory, weight, size, or other words leading to rapid identification on the part of the consumer"—could protect her. "All 'bulk' goods," she wrote, "are open to the same criticism—namely, that they are *unidentified*, and thus the consumer is unable to tell the quality in advance, and thus has no means of safeguarding her purchase." Brand names ensured quality standards, accurate weighing, and sanitary conditions; mass production and wide distribution of brand-name products made prices competitively low. Advertising made mass production possible, meanwhile raising quality, Frederick claimed, "since it does not pay to advertise a poor product"; by bringing so many wonderful products onto the market, and by supporting the printing costs of magazines and newspapers, advertising had raised the standard of living. "Since most advertised articles are also trademarked articles," she concluded, "they insure the consumer guarantee, identification, and time-saving shopping." Within a few years, in 1929, Frederick would demonstrate her alliance with the manufacturers by writing a book for them entitled *Selling Mrs. Consumer*.

Other home economists, particularly those who worked with the poor, saw the matter differently. Florence Nesbitt of Chicago's city relief department began the chapter "Economy in Buying" in her 1915 manual for poor women with a section on the "work of others": "If someone else bakes your bread, cakes or pies, cooks your meat, cans your vegetables, makes your jelly and jam, pays for advertising these things and then sells them to you, you must pay him well for all his work." Bulk cornmeal, for example, cost $2\frac{1}{2}$ cents a pound; "a business firm packs the same sort of cornmeal, puts it into a package, names it, advertises it and sells it for 5 cents a pound." Another firm processed the corn into flakes, raising the price to 16 cents a pound for a similar quantity of food. Nesbitt recognized that mothers who worked outside the home might have difficulty finding the extra time that economizing sometimes took, but in a chapter addressed to that problem, she recommended fireless cookers (the insulated version of today's crock pot) and programs that organized the children to help; apparently she believed that prepared foods simply cost too much to be used by people of limited means.

Even poor women who followed Nesbitt's advice and avoided packaged foods discovered soon enough that they could not avoid all manufactured goods; once they entered the consumer market, their wants turned into needs. After the mother in *Bread Givers* began to take boarders and the daughters got jobs, they started to fix up the house, buying a table "so solid it didn't spill the soup all over the place," a secondhand looking glass, "regular towels" to use instead of old rags, a new soup pot, and plates and utensils "so we could all sit down by the table at the same time and eat like people. It soon became natural, as if we were used from always to eat with separate knives and forks instead of from the pot to the hand as we once did." As they got used to having things, they began to want more: "We no sooner got used to regular towels than we began to want toothbrushes. . . . We got the toothbrushes and we began wanting toothpowder to brush our teeth with, instead of ashes. And more and more we wanted more things, and really needed more things the more we got them." The immigrant family had discovered American standards and incorporated them into their expectations. The toothbrush and toothpowder provide a good example of the interrelationships among manufactured products: nobody would buy appliances without the electricity or gas to run them, and home laundering machines eventually depended on new kinds of detergents that most effectively washed the new kinds of fabrics.

All the new manufactured goods appeared on the shelves of new kinds of stores. Mass retailing began with the urban department stores that appeared almost simultaneously in many cities during the 1870s, but even the largest of these remained primarily local, except for those like Marshall Field's of Chicago, which did much of its business wholesaling to country storekeepers. At the end of the century, those country stores felt the competition of the first national retailers, the mail-order houses. Montgomery Ward, founded in 1872 and supported by the largest national farmers' association, the Grange, marketed a wide range of goods by mail from its inception. Its first serious competition came in the 1890s, when Sears, Roebuck & Company, originally a watch and jewelry concern, began to expand, surpassing Ward's sales around 1900 by taking on nearly every product line that existed—a move so successful that the firm nearly went under from too many orders. It was saved by drastic reorganization of the order-filling process. "The new system," writes historian Alfred Chandler, "permitted the filling of over 100,000 orders a day. That involved as many transactions as most traditional merchants in pre-railroad days handled in a lifetime."

During the years before the Depression, Sears and Ward, suffering

Industrial products filled staple cupboards like this one, belonging to Mrs. Paul Minnich of Lancaster County, Pennsylvania, 1938. Farm Security Administration photo by Sheldon Dick.

from the decline of the rural market, established retail outlets; in doing so, they essentially imitated their newest and greatest competitors, the chain stores. The variety chains, beginning with Woolworth's in the 1880s, followed the lead of the grocery chains. By 1865, when the Great Atlantic and Pacific Tea Company added a grocery line to its tea business, it operated 26 stores; over the next fifteen years it expanded to 100 stores all over the Northeast and as far west as Saint Paul, Minnesota. Other chains followed before the end of the century: Grand Union in the 1870s, Kroger in the 1880s, and Jewel Tea in the 1890s. The most rapid growth for grocery and variety chains came during the first decades of the twentieth century. By the end of 1913, A&P had 585 stores; it opened 1,600 more in 1914–1915, another 2,600 before the end of 1919, and 11,500 during the twenties. The number of food chains doubled during that time, and the number of stores they operated multiplied nearly eightfold. Because the chains had trade margins (overhead and net profit) lower than the independent grocers, they charged lower markups; people from lower-income groups patronized them, while their wealthier neighbors continued to use the credit and the personal service the independents offered their trusted customers.

The original chain stores bore little resemblance to the modern super-market; clerks served customers in stores that specialized in groceries, handling no fresh meat or produce. In 1912, John A. Hartford of the A&P introduced cash-and-carry "economy stores," small operations with low overhead, run by one clerk, offering no delivery service and carrying no credit accounts. Four years later, a Memphis entrepreneur named Clarence Saunders opened his first Piggly-Wiggly store, introducing the turnstile and the idea of self-service with great fanfare; Piggly-Wiggly operated 2,660 stores at its peak. Self-service spread during the 1920s, along with the combination store, which handled fresh meats and produce as well as groceries. In 1930, Michael Cullen opened his first King Kullen store in Jamaica, Long Island, and with it the era of the modern super-market; Cullen, who called himself "the world's greatest price wrecker," emphasized high-volume selling with low markups, running splashy ads in local newspapers. "Cheapy" supermarkets, located in empty factory and warehouse buildings and featuring drugs, auto accessories, clothing, hardware, soda fountains, and other variety store goods along with food, spread throughout the East during the Depression. These huge new stores and their low prices quickly ate into the business of the chains, which began to close their small stores and open their own supermarkets during the middle thirties.

Each one of the supermarket's innovations destroyed the personal rela-tionships that had prevailed at the independent grocery, the country store, and even the stall at the larger public market. Customers and storekeepers stopped bargaining about prices and making credit deals;

Customers leaving the Giant food shopping center on Wisconsin Avenue, Washington, D.C., 1942. Farm Security Administration photo by Marjory Collins.

delivery men stopped coming around the neighborhood; one-stop shopping and self-service cut the number and altered the quality of the interactions the housewife had with the people she bought from. No longer dependent on daily shopping thanks to home refrigeration, women now went to stores with narrow check-out aisles and no room to stand and chat with the clerks. At first the combination store retained the custom-service butcher and the produce man, but eventually they too fell prey to prepackaging and to the cheaper, more detailed division of labor that has characterized work in the twentieth century. The supermarket fit the new task of consumption as the home economists defined it. The trained consumer studied and planned at home for the goods she would need and went to the store ready to buy; armed with the advice of experts, she needed no guidance from the butcher or the grocer.

In fact, she received her guidance not from experts on the products but from experts on selling, advertisers not merely in league with the manufacturers but dependent on them for their livelihood. Under that guidance, the new task of the private sphere became a pastime of a sphere private only in rhetoric. The corporations dominated consumption—apparently the exercise of free, private, individual choice—with the products they offered and the methods they used to sell them.

Industrialization replaced the arduous productive work of the nine-

Supermarkets and chain stores made the Mom and Pop grocery an anachronism. Last days at the Behnke store, Milwaukee, Wisconsin, 1960.

teenth-century household with products that raised the standard of living and made life easier for many people by the 1930s; the large, centralized concerns that manufactured those products invaded daily life with their advertising, creating new needs to establish economic demand. The very activity of buying came to represent happiness, and perhaps indeed to produce it, if only temporarily. The new consumerism declared that things that cost money had more value than those that did not; it even revised the seasons, as January white sales and end-of-summer clearances defined the time of year as tasks like spring housecleaning and laying in the wood for winter once did. The expandable task of consumption, like the other new task of motherhood capable of taking up whatever time the new products released, became ever more necessary as families adapted their daily lives to manufactured existence.

FOURTEEN

Quick and Easy

The many events of the pre-Depression transition period established a new set of household attitudes and expectations: between about 1910 and 1929, Christine Frederick and the home economists taught women how to save and value their time; American industry gave most of them the utilities that enabled them to begin doing so; changes in the occupational structure offered new kinds of opportunities in the outside world and

closed off old ways of making money in the private household; and the motherhood and consumption propagandists established new definitions for the work of a private household now dominated by and part of the public sphere. By the time the factories shifted to civilian production after World War II and the economy began to recover after a decade and a half of depression and war, these events had prepared American households, both materially and ideologically, for a new era dominated by the consumer mentality, by the growing expectation that women would work outside the home, and by a new ideal of convenience in housework. A mixed bag of household products appeared after the war: many of the initial ones, like automatic washers, saved substantial amounts of time and labor but left women isolated within the household with less control of their own work processes; most of the later ones, like microwave ovens, offered only limited benefits, wasted individual and societal resources, and reinforced the notion that married women held the ultimate responsibility for the maintenance of their households.

By the middle of the Depression, almost everybody in large cities used the standard utilities. In Cleveland, where the Federal Real Property Inventory of sixty-four cities did its most complete study in 1935, 98 percent of the homes had electric lights, 96 percent had plumbing that included a toilet, and 89 percent had both hot and cold running water. Economic and geographic differences still prevailed, although the federal rural electrification program had begun to make inroads on the latter; more and better equipment could be found in owner-occupied homes than in rental units, and more in large cities than in small towns and rural areas. In general, however, the utilities had laid their lines and connected them with a substantial proportion of American households before the war, creating the technological preconditions for the mechanized home; once they had the utilities, families could buy the appliances that went with them.

Among the major appliances, families usually purchased cooking stoves first; 95 percent of Cleveland homes cooked with gas or electricity in 1935, although a quarter of them continued to use wood and coal heating stoves. The more expensive heating furnaces usually came next. In other words, people bought first the appliances that took fullest immediate advantage of the utilities: once they had electric lights and running water, they looked to the appliances that would end fuel hauling and fire tending forever. A few complained: recently, one elderly California woman, remembering the day her parents bought a gas stove and relegated "that old wood-burning thing" to the barn, recounted her grandmother's distress. She "just felt terrible. She knew just how to put a piece of wood to make it that much hotter. Or not to put in the piece of wood if she had an angelfood cake in the oven." Most people, however, rejoiced as they stopped producing their heating and cooking energy and started to consume it.

Fewer people bought mechanical refrigerators before the war; refrigerators cost more than stoves, and provided fewer advantages than did the gas and electric heating and cooking devices. Manufacturers began a massive selling campaign for refrigerators in the early twenties; the industry's advertising expenditures, about $45,000 in 1923, grew twentyfold in the next five years, peaking at around $20 million in 1931—about $5 to $10 per refrigerator. Depression-era women's magazines advertised few stoves, washing machines, or other large appliances except refrigerators, which the manufacturers promoted in language that assumed the superiority of the electric refrigerator over the icebox. General Electric praised the beauty, performance, and "world-renowned record of trouble-free service" of its Monitor Top refrigerator in posh *House Beautiful* in 1930: *"These* belong to the refrigerator that *you* are going to want for *your* home," the company promised, stressing the machine's low price and the easy GE time payment plan even to these wealthy readers, without assuming that they already owned refrigerators. Electrolux, Frigidaire, Crosley, General Electric, Kelvinator, Norge, and Westinghouse all placed refrigerator ads in the July 1934 *Good Housekeeping*; the magazine had apparently solicited these advertisements to go with an article entitled "About Refrigerators," since other issues around the same time had two or three refrigerator ads rather than seven. The companies competed with each other's features—how much ice they could freeze how fast, special drawers and compartments, door latches, automatic inside lights; only two of the ads suggested the refrigerator's advantages over the icebox, neither of them mentioning iceboxes explicitly or using the direct put-down of old-fashioned ways that characterized many ads for cheaper products like soap powders and baby foods. The article answered many questions about refrigerator operation: "At what temperatures should various foods be stored?" "How should various foods be placed in the refrigerator?" "Should all foods be covered when they are stored in an automatic refrigerator?" "How often should a refrigerator be defrosted?" "What should I have to pay for service on my refrigerator?" "How much does it cost to operate an automatic refrigerator?" Like the ads, it implied that potential purchasers wondered, not whether refrigerators surpassed iceboxes, but how to afford them, which one to buy, and how to use it best once they owned it.

Despite the campaign, it took ten years for the manufacturers to sell their first million refrigerators. In Zanesville, Ohio, in 1926, less than one-half of 1 percent of the families owned refrigerators; five years later, market researchers for Time, Inc., found them in 16 percent of Appleton, Wisconsin homes but commented that "in the U.S. as a whole, the refrigerator industry has yet to sell as much as 10 percent of the families." The Appleton researchers, who prepared a detailed study of refrigerator sales in the city, found a direct correlation between refrigerator buying and income: families in the group earning over $10,000 a year bought nearly

AUGUST 1930

More and more you'll find the

MONITOR TOP *imitated*

*But its amazing record of trouble-free service . .
that belongs to General Electric alone!*

A mere glimpse of it through the open window—and you recognize it. *A General Electric*—modern in design as this electrical age itself! The aristocrat of all refrigerators—as distinguished in its appearance as it is in its matchless performance. Little wonder they seek to duplicate the individual beauty of the Monitor Top. But the sealed-in-steel mechanism of the Monitor Top—and its world-renowned record of trouble-free service—are beyond all imitation. *These* belong to the refrigerator that *you* are going to want for *your* home. The General Electric!

Prices are now as low as $205 at the factory, and most people buy on our easy time payment plan. For an illustrated booklet, write Section Q-8, Electric Refrigeration Department, General Electric Company, Hanna Building, Cleveland, Ohio.

Join us in the General Electric Program, broadcast every Saturday evening on a nation-wide N. B. C. network.

GENERAL ⊛ ELECTRIC
ALL-STEEL REFRIGERATOR

ELECTRIC LEMONADE 5¢

Refrigerator manufacturers mounted a massive ad campaign throughout the Depression, offering easy terms even to the readers of posh magazines. From *House Beautiful*, 1930.

six times as many refrigerators between 1929 and 1931 as families in the group that earned under $2,000; among those in all income groups who bought refrigerators during those early Depression years, richer families bought larger refrigerators. Thanks to its aggressive advertising campaign and despite the Depression, the industry sold ten million refrigerators during the thirties; according to one writer, 10 percent of American families owned them in 1930, 56 percent in 1940.

Although refrigerators did not save much time or labor, they had obvious advantages: owners could make ice cubes for drinks instead of chipping ice from the block, floors stayed cleaner without those drips from the ice and the drip pan of the icebox, and food got and stayed colder. Refrigerated food stayed fresh longer, reducing some cooking by extending the life of leftovers, and relieving the housewife of the necessity of daily shopping. Because middle-class women bought refrigerators around the same time that supermarkets phased out the personal service of the small-store butcher, grocer, and produce man and the delivery service that brought the store to the home, automatic refrigeration, by ending daily shopping and even the iceman's visits, isolated women at home. Although many stores, especially in suburban areas, already had parking lots and catered to a drive-in trade, few families owned more than one car, most husbands took it to work, and few women had yet learned to drive. Poorer women experienced less isolation; most did not yet own refrigerators or automobiles, and those who lived in cities shopped daily.

The electric washing machine competed with the refrigerator for the consumer's dollar both during the war and after it, when converted factories rushed to fill orders coming from people who finally had both money to spend and products to buy. After the war the manufacturers offered a totally new product, the automatic washer; for the first time, appliance manufacturers sought to convince consumers not simply to buy a major electric appliance but to move up from an old-fashioned appliance to the newest and latest kind, replacing machines that worked perfectly well. After mounting steadily throughout the thirties, production boomed with the new machines; the washing-machine industry manufactured about three times as many machines in 1947 as in 1939.

Automatic washing machines had numerous advantages, Westinghouse pointed out in the seven pages it devoted to the automatic washer in a forty-eight page "Home Laundering Guide" issued in 1944, before the company even had the machines to sell. "Some day soon . . . you'll be free from the drudgery of Washday!" the section began. "Come 'V Day' . . . the hard work of clothes washing will be done for you . . . automatically in the new Westinghouse Laundromat." The company had test-marketed the machines before the war in fourteen communities; owners of the 25,000 sold had "thoroughly tested and proved" the Laundromat's "stam-

ina" for more than two years. This new machine "reduces clothes washing to three simple steps—'put 'em in—set the dials—take 'em out.' For the Laundromat is *automatic!—it fills itself with water, washes, rinses, spins the clothes amazingly dry and shuts itself off."* The company's italicized sales pitch appealed even to the owner of an electric washing machine, who had to fill the washer and the rinse tubs with water from the tap, start and stop the washer, lift the clothes and run them through the wringer, rinse by hand, and wring again. A machine that ended wringing made ironing easier, reduced the number of "torn off buttons or broken fasteners" and therefore the mending pile, and eliminated one serious household hazard. A machine that started and stopped itself, filled and drained itself, and spun the clothes "amazingly dry" obviously saved time and labor in this most onerous and traditionally time-consuming household task.

Over the long run, the automatic washer probably restructured rather than reduced laundry time. As the Westinghouse pamphlet boasted, it ended washday—"an entire new day has been added to your week"—by making the laundry into an "'odd-moments' job—with little time and no hard work involved." Now women could "wash any time, whenever you get a load." At first, most women had to follow the "odd-moments job" with a considerable amount of time and labor, hanging every load of clothes on the line, taking them down, and ironing them. Westinghouse included the clothes dryers they hoped to sell in their model floor plan for the new-age laundry. Eventually, by allowing women to wash "whenever you get a load," the automatic washer, the dryer, and the synthetic fabrics that ended ironing probably increased the weekly household laundry load. Encouraged by advertisements for these machines and for the detergents, fabric softeners, bleaches, and static reducers they used, Americans began to make quicker decisions about what to throw in the hamper. No individual laundry load caused as much fatigue or took as much time as hand-done laundry or even the nonautomatic washing machine; the automatic washer really did permit women to put dirty clothes in and take clean ones out. But it changed the laundry pile from a weekly nightmare to an unending task, increasing the size of the pile, the amount of water and fuel and laundry products most households used, and possibly even the housewife's working time, which was now spread out over the week.

The automatic washer sealed the fate of the power laundry. During the twenties, studies done in California had showed that income determined both how much laundry people sent out and what kind of equipment they used for washing at home. Among a group of semiskilled workers' families in the East Bay Area, about 60 percent sent some laundry out, but the small size of their laundry bills made it "evident that even in these families the wife did the bulk of the washing"; only 14 percent of these

THE *Laundromat* makes possible these ADDED BENEFITS

No more "washday" in your week

Wash any time, whenever you get a load. Laundromat makes it an "odd-moments" job— with little time and no hard work involved.

More time for other duties or doings

An entire new day has been added to your week. And you're never "tired out" from doing the washing.

Saves sending the laundry out

No laundry bills to pay, no waiting for clean clothes; no searching for lost articles.

Easier ironing, less mending

No stubborn wringer wrinkles to make ironing more work. No torn off buttons or broken fasteners.

Brighter, more cheerful homes

You can splurge with color, decorate with washables. Laundromat makes it easy to keep them clean.

The automatic washer almost literally added a day to the housewife's week. This Westinghouse pamphlet, published in 1944, promised the new machines after the war. (Westinghouse went out of the major appliance business in 1975.)

The job the automatic washer eliminated. Mrs. Ferguson wringing out clothes, Point Pleasant, West Virginia, 1943. Office of War Information photo by Arthur Siegal.

women had washing machines of any kind to make the work easier. Their neighbors on the Berkeley faculty both sent more out and owned more machines: 78 percent sent some laundry out, especially flatwork (sheets, tablecloths, and other linens) and men's shirts, the former especially heavy and difficult to wring and hang, the latter especially difficult to iron. Many of them did the remaining wash by machine; 70 percent of the faculty families owned these nonautomatic washers. Both the women who washed entirely by hand and those who had washers got rid of as much laundry as they could afford to have done commercially. Family expenditures on sending laundry out peaked in 1929; recovering somewhat after World War II but never returning to pre-Depression levels, they dropped off during the 1950s and 1960s as the automatic washer and clothes dryer returned almost all laundry to the home.

The Westinghouse pamphlet emphasized that women could control the automatic washer, both by setting the washing time and the water temperature when they first started their machines and by stopping it at any time (the machine would "resume the operation where it was stopped").

Nonetheless, the automatic washing machine, especially the less expensive machines and the heavy-duty models sold to coin laundries for those who could not afford their own, took control of the labor process away from the housewife; costlier models, especially as time went on, had more knobs and dials that allowed the operator to choose wash and rinse times, temperatures, agitating speeds, and water levels. Laundry, once a set of skills requiring considerable judgment, became a job done by machines; expensive machines produced better laundry.

Competition over the clothesline, then, became a matter not of skill and craft satisfaction but of products; many laundry-product ads, inquiring who had the brightest and whitest wash, based their answers on who did the best job of buying. "I BEAT MY MOTHER-IN-LAW," declared Mrs. Claudia Fortson in a 1980 Tide ad. Holding up two pairs of socks, one definitely whiter than the other, Mrs. Fortson explained that her mother-in-law "swore by her liquid for years" until Claudia showed her that Tide

Although the power laundry industry mechanized, it lost the competition with individual home machines. Seattle laundry operation, around 1930.

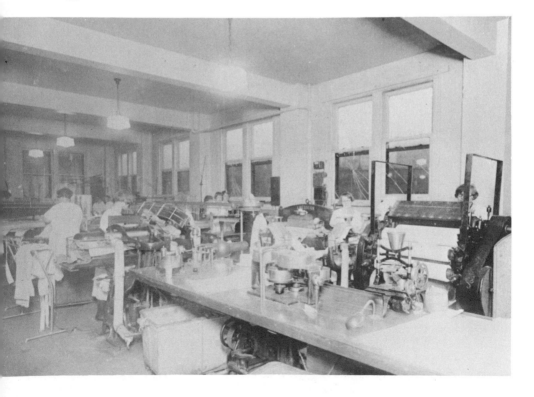

worked better; modern women, in other words, understood not only modern methods (the theme of the thirties Rinso ad that discouraged boiling) but modern products. At one time, the woman with the better wash displayed her skill and her stamina at the washboard—her superiority at work, not at buying; now the control of the outcome, like the control of the process itself, rested on proper purchasing. Proper purchasing, in turn, depended on the full use of the many interdependent products: machine-dried synthetic fabrics, for example, generated static electricity and a "need" for static-reducing products.

Women who had once compared their wash over back fences or the clotheslines they strung up across alleys, in a day of grueling labor that nevertheless provided the company of other women, often put non-automatic machines on porches in the summer where they could call out to friends. Those without basement space hung clothes outside even in the winter. The permanently installed automatic washer and dryer, however, brought the work inside, isolating women in their houses and denying them the companionship that had once enlivened washday, compensating for the woes of the chore they hated most. At the same time, the new machines altered the seasonal nature of the chore: freed from both the unbearable heat of summer laundry work and the frozen fingers of winter washing, women and their work moved away from the natural cycles that had once defined it.

First marketed during the early 1950s, the home freezer further modified the seasons and the structure of the housewife's time. The 1952 Ben-Hur Farm and Home Freezer, its manufacturers claimed, ended seasonal eating forever: now families could enjoy their favorite foods "in Fall and Winter, too, not just a few weeks during the summer." The freezer diminished seasonal inconvenience while it saved shopping time—"no need to go out in snow or rain for your daily menus" because "it's like having a 'supermarket' right at your elbow"; it cut cooking time by permitting women to prepare large quantities of food in advance ("pack a week's sandwiches for childrens' lunches at once") and remove it from the freezer ready to reheat ("a party banquet in 30 minutes!").

Ben-Hur implied that the freezer could even improve family relations: now husbands could bring home unexpected guests without inconveniencing their wives or convince them to take a "vacation hunting or fishing trip" that would "pay for itself by saving on the food bill." Everybody would help out with vegetable and fruit preservation—"fun for the whole family"—now that freezing ended "hours of hard work over boiling kettles and a hot stove." Because home freezing simplified home production, manufacturers initially advertised freezers to a rural market and stressed the money-saving qualities. The Ben-Hur, its flyer emphasized, paid for itself many times over because women could buy food in large quantities —fruits and vegetables in season by the crate or bushel, meat by the half or quarter—"at savings to taste even better, and you eat them with a free conscience, too, if you grew them yourself or bought them in quantity at low in-season prices."

Although freezers never sold as widely as washing machines or refrigerators, the manufacturers' intensive campaign worked: nearly half of electrified households owned freezers by 1977. They did allow women to shop in quantity and to prepare food in advance to use later, offering the technological adjunct to Christine Frederick's idea of the "planned-over," but the freezer's new brand of home production placed an additional burden on housewives, who felt compelled to fill the freezers they bought. One suburban New Jersey woman spent months preparing hors d'oeuvres for a daughter's wedding and storing them in her freezer; eighteen years later, despite the satisfactions of cooking for the wedding instead of hiring a caterer, she remembered those months primarily as an ordeal that she never wanted to repeat. The freezer also created a new problem for those who forgot to defrost their dinners in time, which contributed to the

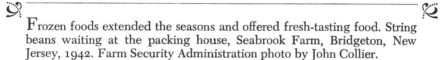

Frozen foods extended the seasons and offered fresh-tasting food. String beans waiting at the packing house, Seabrook Farm, Bridgeton, New Jersey, 1942. Farm Security Administration photo by John Collier.

popularity of restaurant dining. Finally, the new brand of home production fostered a new brand of dependence on purchased energy, evident whenever extended power failures wiped out all those savings in time and money, leaving hundreds of pounds of rotten meat and soggy hors d'oeuvres in thawed freezers.

The Ben-Hur pamphlet never suggested home freezers for storing commercial frozen food because of the prohibitive price of this food in the early 1950s (the source of that unfree conscience), but freezer sales eventually boosted factory frozen-food production, and vice versa. Birds Eye first introduced its "frosted foods" in Springfield, Massachusetts, in 1930, choosing the word "frosted" because "frozen" commonly referred to food ruined by cold weather. Announcing itself in a local paper, the company told residents to watch for "the most revolutionary idea in the history of food": eighteen frozen meats, two vegetables (peas and spinach), three fruits (cherries, loganberries, and raspberries), and three seafoods (oysters and fillets of haddock and sole), to be displayed at six Thrift Store chain locations and four other Springfield groceries. Like other frozen-food manufacturers during the early years, Birds Eye supplied the freezer cabinets and controlled its own prices; stores usually stocked only one brand of frozen food, essentially buying a service from a manufacturer who set the price, rented the freezer, and stocked the food. Birds Eye dropped both price control and its cabinet rental policy in 1940.

Birds Eye's first Springfield ad lauded all the essential qualities of frozen foods. It praised the meats for their uniformity: housewives need worry no longer whether the steak was as good or as bad "as the one you bought a week ago," because Birds Eye "takes the guess out of meat buying" by freezing only good meat. In their identical packages, pieces of meat became "as uniform in quality as packages of breakfast food, or cans of coffee. . . . Every Birds Eye steak is as tender and juicy as the last one!" Freshness distinguished the seafoods: landlocked Springfielders could enjoy haddock "as fresh-flavored as the day the fish was drawn from the cold blue waters of the North Atlantic." The copywriter reserved the best rhetoric for the fruits and vegetables, "the most wondrous magic of all!" On March 7, Birds Eye told Springfield consumers, they would be able to buy "June peas, as gloriously green as any you will see next Summer," as well as berries and cherries, all "ready to cook or eat! The peas are shelled; the spinach is washed clean of sand and grit. The cherries are pitted, ready to make a luscious *fresh* cherry pie—in *March*! And the vegetables take only a fraction of the time to cook that ordinary fresh vegetables do." The sales pitch, like Westinghouse's praise of its automatic washer, rang true to contemporary consumers. Winter-weary families, their menus confined to stored root vegetables and canned goods, might well rejoice at the prospect of fresh-tasting raspberries in March;

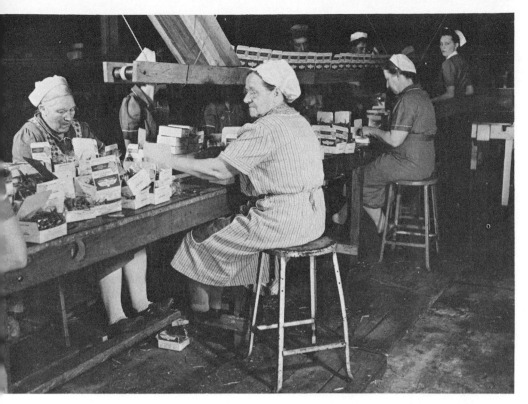

String beans being packed for Birds Eye quick freezing, Seabrook Farm, Bridgeton, New Jersey, 1942. Farm Security Administration photo by John Collier.

advertising had not yet thoroughly devalued words like "revolution" and "magic" as it had by 1980, when a new furniture polish was a "revolutionary new product" and an ad for brownie mix called the product "magic" because the brownies were so moist that they adhered to each other.

The magic of frozen fruits and vegetables kept them dominant among frozen foods for about thirty years. Fruit constituted well over half the total frozen-food output in 1939; vegetables surpassed them in 1948, growing steadily thereafter; fruits, vegetables, and frozen juice concentrates together made up over half of commercial frozen-food production until the 1960s, when frozen poultry, meats, seafoods, and prepared foods finally overtook them. The first frozen prepared foods appeared in the early 1940s, when Birds Eye froze baked beans, a New York firm froze hors-d'oeuvre rolls with ten different fillings, and a Boston establishment offered frozen chicken à la king, roast turkey, and lobster à la Newburg. In 1945, the W. L. Maxson Corporation developed the first complete frozen dinner, freezing meals consisting of meat, vegetables, and potatoes in three-compartmented Pyrex and bakeware trays; the army bought Maxson's entire output to use on airplanes. Bamberger's of Newark, New Jersey's largest department store, first retailed frozen dinners in 1946; called "Strato Meals," their prices ranged from $.98 for beef goulash with gravy, peas with butter sauce, and a potato patty to $1.98 for chicken paprika with French beans and a potato patty. Strato Meals came on trays of heat-resistant paper with a foil-lined cover; a month later, another company introduced the Frigidinner brand with a foil tray and cover. Swanson entered the field with its TV Dinners in 1953, the first year that frozen prepared foods constituted more than 5 percent of frozen-food output. They passed the 10 percent mark during the sixties and the 25 percent mark in the mid-seventies, with more than twice the output that the entire frozen food industry had produced during the early fifties.

Frozen dinners took the guesswork out of eating, not just out of buying food: now the dinner you ate tonight could look, taste, and smell precisely like the one you ate last week. They put the "work-free" box of spinach to shame and applied the "uniformity" of Birds Eye's original frozen meats to whole meals. Housewives who followed the package directions saved labor and time but lost all control of the work process: the manufacturer shelled the peas, put the butter on them, made the menu decisions, determined serving sizes, and arranged the food on the disposable "plate." Many Americans apparently preferred the manufacturers' control to the work of making dinner and washing dishes; by 1977, prepared platters outsold every other category of retail prepared frozen food in dollar value, and only frozen baked goods surpassed them in poundage.

Others, still seeking creativity in their cooking and craft satisfaction in the central ritual of their day, used frozen foods and the other convenience foods that came in boxes and cans as ingredients for more elaborate recipes. Manufacturers encouraged this "creative" use of their products by including recipes in their ads: Stouffer's, for example, suggested turning its frozen spinach soufflé into an appetizer (baked in chili peppers), lunch (baked in tomatoes), or dinner as a pseudo-quiche (baked in a pie shell, mixed with eggs, mushrooms, sausage, and cheese). Pillsbury, making more profit on its highly processed cake and frosting mixes than on its flour, suggested combining Pillsbury Plus Chocolate Mint (or Devil's Food) Cake Mix with part of a package of Pillsbury Ready-To-Spread Chocolate Fudge Frosting Supreme to make a crust for a Frosty Mint Ice Cream Pie—a "refreshing idea" that sold two products at once. By the late 1970s, nearly every recipe in the women's magazine food articles listed at least one canned, packaged, or frozen product as an ingredient, and frequently those articles depended on convenience foods for their themes. "Everyone knows you can make a cake with a cake mix—but did you know you can also make pie with a frosting mix and flavor chicken with pie filling?" asked *Better Homes and Gardens* in 1978. "All sorts of delicious possibilities open up when you start thinking of convenience products in an unconventional way. By saving you time and work, these handy packages, boxes, envelopes, and cans make it easier for you to cook creatively." Many of the recipes that followed required little measuring but elaborate preparation: the woman who prepared Spiced Doughnut Balls from buttermilk pancake mix, for example, had plenty of work and spent plenty of time frying the easily prepared batter.

The manufacturers designed their convenience foods for profit, not for the housewife's convenience; she could follow the package directions or concoct elaborate treats with them, so long as she bought them. Their stress on convenience, however, encouraged both the attitude that cooking—always the most important arena for most women's creativity— should be fast and easy and the use of other devices (and purchased energy) that made the new foods even more convenient. By 1980, most cake-mix packages gave hand-mixing directions parenthetically or as a second choice; some, like Betty Crocker's Traditional Angel Food Cake, offered no alternative to the electric mixer. Some major appliance manu- facturers offered the products that went with them: Whirlpool packed a Tide coupon in every 1980 washer, following the lead of Philco, which gave twenty-one packages of Birds Eye foods to anyone who bought its new refrigerator-freezer combination in 1940.

Food manufacturers and appliance makers encouraged this product interdependence during the late 1970s as they worked together to develop frozen foods compatible with the microwave oven: traditional frozen foods, packed in foil that blocked the microwaves and even damaged the ovens, often used formulas with too much moisture for microwave cook- ing. One microwave oven manufacturer's representative, who "had to beg food companies to come in to talk about microwave cooking" in the mid- seventies, reported that he could not "keep them away" by 1978; another, pleased by Swanson's 1979 announcement of a line of fourteen frozen- food products formulated and packaged for microwave cooking, said that "it can only help our business, but it will help theirs as well." A Swanson vice-president expressed equal optimism: "Color TV plodded along in an unexciting way in the 1950's," he said. "Then as color programming grew —and, in particular, with NBC's decision to go to all-color programming in 1964—it exploded. We think the same takeoff will occur with the introduction of microwave-compatible foods."

Microwave oven manufacturers encouraged the food processors, hoping to boost microwave sales as their growth rate decreased consistently every year after 1974; in 1978, fewer than 10 percent of America's homes owned microwave ovens. *Business Week*, reporting the slow demand without a

Frozen-food section of a supermarket, late 1940s.

definitive explanation, cited the expense, "a proliferation of brands and models that confuses consumers and appliance salesmen alike," "complicated controls that make the ovens look too much like computers," and consumer fears about hazardous radiation. With microwave-compatible foods, the manufacturers maintained, the microwave oven could "redefine what we mean by convenience foods" and counteract this consumer resistance, making possible the one-minute pancake and three-minute popcorn. "Twenty minutes in a regular oven is too long" for a frozen breakfast, the Swanson vice-president maintained. "Most people would rather skip the meal altogether. As for snacks, you should be able to make them during station breaks between television programs."

Although manufacturers touted microwaves for the instant breakfast and the TV commercial snack, they aimed also to convince working wives and mothers to buy the ovens for their time-saving qualities, essentially reinforcing the notion that cooking remained a woman's responsibility even if she worked full-time outside the home. Whirlpool, for example, advertised in 1980 that its "new dishwashers, ranges and microwave ovens are life-style oriented. Designed to go to work exactly when you want, whether you're at home or not." The smaller and cheaper electric crock pot, marketed extensively in the mid-seventies, presented the same possibility: now Mom could prepare dinner before she went to work, leaving it to cook slowly until everybody came home to eat it.

The dishwasher, a major appliance that almost half of American households owned by 1980, saved time and labor in a task that many women had traditionally delegated to or shared with husbands, children, and other family members. Once the machine reduced the work to loading and unloading, many women took the task back in order to reduce breakage, or because it became a simple part of postmeal cleaning. One California woman suggested that the dishwasher completely altered family relations: "We never get together to chat in the kitchen, because why should we be in the kitchen with the dishwasher? A lot of elderly women curse the dishwasher. It takes away the one thing that they were useful for. . . . If we didn't want our mothers around at least we would put up with them because they would do what we didn't want to do. They would do the dishes and they would change the curtains. But with the advent of the automatic dishwasher we got rid of our mothers." Another woman remembered the intimacy of sharing the after-dinner work with her daughter; if the girl "wanted to ask me some questions that were on the sexy side, she didn't have to look at me, because I was at the sink, or she was some other place. . . . It was a nice feeling that we had when we were in the kitchen together." Children who did the dishes together learned their responsibilities to the others they lived with, developing routines that combined work, play, and sibling rivalry.

The extra controls that make the Whirlpool dishwasher "life-style oriented" allow Mother to do the dishes while she works at an office, but they add little to the design of the product itself. Like many of the features manufacturers added to major appliances during the sixties and seventies, they represented an attempt to convince women that an old appliance should be replaced by a new one that promised to do the work no differently. Once a family had replaced its small, old-fashioned refrigerator with one that could store an adequate amount of commercially frozen food, the corporations had little to offer—automatic ice makers, side-by-side refrigerator-freezer combinations, drinks and ice through the door, and the self-defrosting freezer, which eliminated an odious but infrequent chore by using massive amounts of electricity. The fundamental features of the electric stove changed little after its first introduction in the 1920s. Eventually the appliance manufacturers could no longer rely on features or even styling to sell new devices to families whose old ones still worked, and they turned to color: the all-white kitchen disappeared during the sixties. The manufacturers created fashions in kitchen colors; a year after General Electric introduced a whole line of avocado-colored appliances, so much of the new color appeared at the national housewares industry trade exposition that many called it "the avocado show."

The battle of the blender buttons probably best demonstrates the absurdity of the manufacturers' competitive gadgetry. First patented in 1922, blenders had one switch—on and off—until the fifties, when Waring introduced high and low. In the mid-sixties, the buttons began to mount: Waring, Oster, and Sunbeam all offered six to eight buttons, doubling the speeds in the next few years with dual-control circuitry and introducing "flash blend" buttons during the early seventies. Some industry spokesmen defended the new gadgetry, admitting "that such an advanced piece of equipment does not belong in the hands of a beginner" but maintaining that "the present sophistication of blender cookery not only invites but practically necessitates the kind of operational versatility the multi-speed models provide." A few made more candid remarks. "It was crazy," remembered one executive of a company that had stopped producing blenders. "The more buttons, the better they sold. We got as high as 16, and the things still couldn't do much more than whip cream. At most, there was a 100 rpm difference between one speed and another— virtually indistinguishable." Another recalled that "when we came out with our 16-speed blender, eight of us sat up two nights straight, trying to get words with five letters, each one sounding a bit higher than the other. It was like trying to fit 14 words between 'dull' and 'bright.' "

Nobody needed sixteen-speed blenders, by any reasonable definition of need, but the multispeed gadgets served the manufacturers' prime consideration: they sold well, and they suited the concept of "convenience" that appliance manufacturers and food processors developed in order to make things sell well. Disregarding the massive waste of natural resources required to produce replacements for appliances that still worked and new goods that offered only marginal advantages, manufacturers hawked "convenience" to promote the continuation of the economic expansion that had been bringing increasing numbers of products to American households over the previous century: by 1870, most people could buy soap and candles; by 1920, they could afford to purchase most of their clothes; by 1970, they could stop cooking. As it ended home production, economic expansion also eased the tasks of home maintenance, offering cast-iron heating stoves during the second half of the nineteenth century, plumbing and the new fuels during the first decades of the twentieth, and automatic laundry machines and dishwashers after World War II.

Although advertising created an artificial demand for some products, economic expansion itself generated needs as it brought more women into the organized economy as workers. When Christine Frederick taught "household engineering" and recommended manufactured products to early-twentieth-century readers, she had to explain why they should want to save time and to suggest ways for them to spend their newfound leisure. The manufacturers of the 1960s and 1970s did not need to tell their consumers what their products were convenient *for*; they knew that more and more women were coming home from full-time jobs to do another at home, and they suggested "creative" and time-consuming uses for their products to women who had not yet joined the trend. In the healthy economy of the sixties and early seventies, they sold their convenience products despite the ascendancy of another industry: fast-food restaurants, which offered Mom a chance to dispense with the cooking and the dishwashing entirely.

FIFTEEN

You Deserve a Break

When Charlotte Perkins Gilman described the food of her ideal future, she envisioned kitchenless houses; individuals and families would patronize establishments that served hot cooked food ready to eat, produced according to the industrial principles of the division of labor and economies of scale. Eighty years later, her dream has come true at McDonald's, Kentucky Fried Chicken, Taco Bell, Arby's, Pizza Hut, and the innumerable smaller restaurant chains that compete with these industry leaders; as Gilman hoped, many men and women stop by these establishments to pick up dinner on the way home from work, or bring their families to eat there. Her accurate prophecy stopped there: she expected that the system that ended women's kitchen fatigue would serve better food than the private home, in better surroundings, thus contributing to general human progress and liberation. Instead, industrial food preparation has controlled and distorted the central ritual of daily life by subordinating all of its values to profit, and decisions about intimate matters get made in the central offices of large corporations.

Restaurant eating predated the twentieth century: travelers patronized inns and taverns in colonial America, and Lorenzo Delmonico established the first modern restaurant in New York around 1834, but at the turn of the century, most people ate nothing but meals prepared at home. Only the very wealthy went out for dinner. Workers and schoolchildren brought lunches from home: in Homestead, Pennsylvania, steelworkers' wives took pains to make good cold lunches after the mill owners refused to let them bring hot ones to the plant, while in Manchester, New Hampshire, boardinghouses hired young boys to bring hot lunches to the textile factories. Progressive reformers organized lunches as a major feature of their charitable work, establishing school lunch programs for children from impoverished immigrant households and opening cafeterias to provide cheap lunches for workers, especially single women who boarded in other people's houses and could not bring lunch from home. For the first half of the century, commercial establishments serving prepared lunches proliferated: drug and variety store lunch counters gave downtown shoppers a place to rest and pick up a bite to eat; company and school cafeterias became daily gathering places, their food the butt of many jokes; soda fountains and drive-ins served hungry teen-agers their between-meal snacks. By the end of the 1950s, Americans ate out frequently, although dinner at a restaurant still usually marked a special occasion.

All that accelerated during the 1960s and 1970s, as married women with children joined the labor force in unprecedented numbers and as chain restaurants, especially fast-food chains, restructured the restaurant industry. The number of fast-food restaurants nearly tripled during the sixties, while the number of other restaurants declined 9 percent; burger and fried chicken and taco and pizza places crowded the "strips" in every developed suburb, moving into large cities during the seventies, as traditional "Mom and Pop" restaurants closed their doors forever. Rich people consumed more restaurant meals than poor ones, employed people ate out more often than the unemployed, young people more than older ones, men more than women, but by the end of the 1970s everybody ate out sometimes, about a third of the population on any given day spending

about a third of the nation's food dollars on restaurant meals. By 1978, dinner made up about 40 percent of those meals; although most people preferred medium-priced table-service restaurants for their evening meal, they increasingly patronized both takeout and sit-down fast-food restaurants for dinner.

By the mid-seventies, the supermarket business—with a historically low profit margin that left little room for competition—had begun to suffer; the only segment of the industry showing significant growth, the late-night convenience stores, did 30 percent of their business in beer and cigarettes, while the stores that depended on food sales began to look for new solutions to increasingly serious competition from restaurants. Their concern received public attention after December 1976 when Grant Gentry, chairman of the A&P, warned a San Francisco convention of wholesale food brokers that fast food constituted their challenge for the next decade. Their suppliers, the big food processors, noticed the same challenge: a month after Gentry's speech, Banquet frozen chicken took on Kentucky Fried with a new advertising campaign: "The Outs eat out, the Ins eat in." In April 1977, the *New York Times* saw fit to print on the front page of its Sunday edition, "Rising Popularity of Eating Out Puts a Pinch on Supermarkets." "Because more people live alone, more women work and more leisure money is available," the *Times* correspondent wrote, "one of the great American merchandising institutions, the supermarket, is in economic trouble." The article quoted Gentry calling the challenge an "opportunity"; a former Kroger executive, Robert O. Aders of the Food Marketing Institute, had scheduled a special seminar for industry leaders to consider the problem.

In the fall, *Dun's Review* subjected the issue to serious economic analysis: supermarkets' real growth "had virtually come to a halt by 1972," a fact obscured by inflation, the shift of consumers' dollars from individual supermarkets to chain stores, and growing sales of nonfood items. The supermarkets, misreading the signs, continued to enlarge their stores during the early seventies, despite rising energy and labor costs; most seriously, they had failed "to appreciate the social changes that came over the country in the late 1960's and early 1970's." More women worked, family size had decreased, and per capita income had risen, producing a demand for convenience that beset the large food stores with 7-Elevens and Kentucky Fried Chicken outlets. "Like the radio industry after the development of television, supermarkets will have to adapt," declared *Dun's* writer.

Some industry leaders expressed confidence that they could adapt. "Supermarkets won't disappear," claimed the vice-president of Supermarkets General. "They'll just find a niche in the marketplace." Aders, the Food Marketing Institute man, worried more: "Nobody is actually going under yet," he said, "but when you're not growing, you've got big trou-

The Noonday Lunch Army

Do You Belong to it?

If you are a worker in the shop, in the office, or in the home you should eat a food that contains the phosphates and nitrates—the brain and muscle makers—prepared in a digestible form.

Many of the foods that are advertised as "builders of brawn and brain" are merely makers of fat. The ideal food for the desk man and for all indoor workers is

Shredded Whole Wheat

It contains in well balanced proportion the elements that build bone, brain and muscle and these are made digestible by steam-cooking, shredding and baking.

Two Shredded Wheat Biscuits (heated in oven) for lunch with "half and half" will supply all the energy needed for a half day's work and leaves a feeling of stomach comfort and satisfaction.

Shredded wheat with strawberries, raspberries or other fresh fruits and cream forms a lunch that is deliciously wholesome and nourishing. Try it tomorrow.

TRISCUIT, the shredded wheat TOAST, is crisp, snappy and nourishing—just the thing for light luncheons, picnics or excursions.

Shredded Wheat contains no baking powder, yeast, fats or chemicals of any kind. It is not "flavored" or "compounded" with anything. It is just a pure whole wheat cleaned, steam-cooked, shredded and baked. Made in the cleanest, finest, most hygienic food factory in the world, a plant that is visited every year by nearly 100,000 persons from all parts of the habitable globe.

The Shredded Wheat Company, Niagara Falls, N. Y.
(Formerly the Natural Food Company)

An early idea for fast food for working people. From *Collier's*, 1908.

bles." One grocery industry trade magazine tried ironic humor, interviewing Colonel Harland Sanders "in the hope of decoding the nation's attraction to fast foods. . . . If the Colonel could so adroitly draw the populace away from supers over the past two decades, what advice might he offer supermarket operators on reversing the flow?" Quality and service, the Colonel answered, were the keys to business success, hardly the kind of advice likely to rescue a major industry keeling in the seas of social change.

The supermarkets embarked on several new strategies. A few attacked directly through advertising, like the North Carolina stores that offered eight raw hamburgers for the price of three at a fast-food restaurant; more expanded their nonfood operations, opening extra-large "superstores" that provided "one-stop shopping" for clothing and auto supplies along with the spinach and the Cheerios. Nonfood items had always offered supermarket operators larger profit margins than food, and the number of stores dealing in stationery, tobacco, health and beauty aids,

The Star Lunch, just outside the shipyard in Bath, Maine, 1940. About two hundred men came in for lunch every day; the owner had to build an addition to the restaurant to make room for all the men during the lunch-hour rush. Farm Security Administration photo by Jack Delano.

drugs, cleaning products, and small housewares rose consistently after World War II, but few stores before the seventies allocated enough floor or shelf space to establish complete houseware or clothing departments. By 1977, the jumbo stores accounted for one-third of all supermarket sales, and a supermarket trade journal reported that the superstore "is where the industry is going," spurred on by the combination of the high profits from nonfood items and the fast-food competition.

Other supermarkets met the restaurant challenge head-on. Kings Soopers in Denver offered to "fry your chicken while you shop"; many stores opened delicatessen counters and installed warming cabinets full of barbecued ribs and fried chicken. Publix markets in Florida and Supermarkets General of New Jersey established in-store cafeterias; the Schnucks chain in Saint Louis and California's Alpha Beta stores opened sit-down restaurants in their stores, the latter open around the clock. Some chains tried to achieve the same financial effect by purchasing fast-food restaurants: Lucky Stores created a new corporate branch, the 189-restaurant Sirloin Stockade steak chain; Jewel Tea, the Midwestern grocery chain, owned Brigham's, the Eastern ice-cream parlor chain. Skipper's fish-and-chips restaurants invited smaller supermarket chains and individual grocers to purchase individual fast-food franchises instead of whole chains. "Supermarkets have the real estate and the resources," Skipper's president stated, "and fast foods fit very nicely into their business."

While the supermarket industry fretted, restaurant industry leaders told each other that they had gained from "a new American life style" and discounted their competition. "Supermarkets sell food; restaurants sell eating experiences," wrote Arnold Deutsch, research director of *Restaurant Business*, the fast-food and chain restaurant magazine. "The consumer knows eating out may cost more and may not be as nutritious as a home cooked meal but will still eat out. Supermarkets cannot compete with the fact that eating out is seen as an experience that is more pleasurable than eating at home." Restaurant operators should concentrate on their real competition, "the operation that is trying to provide the patron with a better eating experience."

The typical restaurant eating experience changed during the sixties and seventies as the Mom and Pop restaurants died out and the chains took over, dominated by the fast-food burger and chicken operations. Mom's daily special, which she served on thick china plates to customers sitting at tables or on stools, gave way to paper-wrapped sandwiches garnished with precise amounts of ketchup, served by a teen-ager over the counter. The Bureau of Labor Statistics reported that between 1958 and 1972, the number of chain restaurants and drinking establishments almost doubled, while owner-operated restaurants and bars without paid help declined by one-third. The top hundred chains accounted for 25 percent of commer-

cial food-service sales in 1970, 40 percent in 1978, and would go to 50 percent by 1982, according to a food market research firm; one-third of the $23 billion those hundred firms took in during 1977 went to only five companies: McDonald's, Kentucky Fried Chicken, Pillsbury (which owned Burger King and Steak and Ale), International Dairy Queen, and Big Boy. Real growth in commercial food-service sales during the seventies, reported the publisher of a restaurant trade magazine, "can be entirely attributed to the top 100 chain restaurant companies."

The fast-food explosion created new problems for the industry. Financial experts, theorizing that Americans could eat only so many hamburgers, worried about "market saturation" and kept fast-food stock prices low. The same spring that supermarket executives attended their seminar on the fast-food challenge, *Business Week*'s "Inside Wall Street" column reported that bad winter weather had cut into fast-food sales, the chains had not bounced back, "and the perennial question about this classic growth industry is arising again: Have the chains at last saturated most of their markets?" Although the burger and chicken markets showed little likelihood of expansion, the *Business Week* analysis maintained, coffee-shop chains, ethnic and seafood restaurants, and chains catering to an older and wealthier dinner crowd promised continuing growth; the market was nowhere near saturated. In the next year, two successful new chains, Wendy's International and Church's Fried Chicken, challenged the saturation theory even for hamburgers and chicken, but stock market analysts continued to raise the question. "Maturation, or saturation, or overbuilding, is not yet on the horizon. How far beyond the horizon is an open question," remarked one in *Financial World* in 1978; even a restaurant trade magazine projected market saturation and predicted that corporate marketing strategy would shift from increasing the number of restaurants to increasing sales at existing ones.

While the analysts debated, the stock prices stayed low, leaving fast-food companies with their hands tied. Frank Carney, president of Pizza Hut, had hoped to promote his company's growth by expanding into different kinds of restaurants, but "lacked the financial resources" to do so because of undervalued stock. "It might take twenty years before Wall Street came to understand our business," Carney complained. "At first they saw us as a bunch of shady, get-rich-quick artists. Then, when they realized that we were here to stay, they began to preach that there were too many of us in the marketplace and . . . that market saturation would force many of us out of business and erode the growth of those who remained." Carney did not allow his company to go out of business, despite hampered growth; instead, he sold out to Pepsico, one of the many major food companies to buy out fast-food chains. In 1978, larger food companies owned eleven of the top twenty-five fast-food chains, ten through purchase and only one as the result of a food company deciding to open its own chain. Pillsbury owned Burger King and Steak and Ale; General Foods owned Burger Chef and two Canadian chains; Ralston Purina owned Jack-in-the-Box; Herfy's belonged to Campbell's, A&W to United Brands, and Kentucky Fried Chicken to Heublein.

By attaching themselves to the food giants, which had more money to

People's Drug Store on G Street NW, Washington, D.C., at noon, 1942. Farm Security Administration photo by Marjory Collins.

invest in new ventures, the fast-food chains acquired capital for expansion, while the larger companies made money buying up their competition. "What do you do with all that money you earn from your lock on the chilled cookie dough market or the corn flakes market?" asked an analyst at a major institutional stock brokerage. "You either pay it out in greater dividends to your stockholders or you channel it into new businesses that will give you a high rate of return." The food giants achieved only limited success by marketing "takeout-style" frozen chicken, as Swanson did, or by advertising "chunky soups" as the perfect answer for the beleaguered working wife, as Campbell's did; if they bought the fast-food chains, they could even manufacture products to be distributed at their outlets, as Ralston did with Jack-in-the-Box. The eateries provided healthy earnings to the big food companies: 35 percent of Pillsbury's sales and 41 percent of its earnings in 1978 came from its fast-food subsidiaries, and General Mill's new Red Lobster Inns and York Steak Houses grew faster than any other part of the company during the late seventies.

Fast-food investors gained from the sales as well. Restaurant stocks

White Tower hamburger stand, Amsterdam, New York, 1941. Farm Security Administration photo by John Collier.

paid low dividends to investors because the fast-food companies put so much of their profits into expansion, and the fast-food stockholder whose company sold out stood to gain in higher dividends. Low dividends as much as the saturation scare had kept fast-food stock prices low; particularly in a depressed market like that of the late 1970s, investors who could not expect to earn money by selling their stocks found those with high dividends especially attractive. In 1978, McDonald's (obviously the industry leader in many other respects) paid out 6 percent of its earnings in dividends; most other fast-food companies paid almost as little. Even Sambo's 31 percent payback rate paled beside those of the big food companies: Pillsbury, General Mills, Heinz, Carnation, Beatrice Foods, Kraft, Pet, and General Foods all paid out between 34 and 52 percent of earnings, and Kellogg a whopping 67 percent. Investors who received stock in the larger food companies in trade for restaurant stock they held before a sale gained even more than the companies they owned.

Although the fast-food chains lost control by attaching themselves to big companies as subsidiaries, they gained liquid assets; in a rapidly

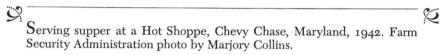

Serving supper at a Hot Shoppe, Chevy Chase, Maryland, 1942. Farm Security Administration photo by Marjory Collins.

expanding industry, liquidity—money to *use*, to build new outlets and expand to new territories—took on particular significance. No fast-food company could make enough money from sales; even McDonald's "billions and billions" of burgers failed to match its investments in real estate. Short of selling out, they had limited options for financing expansion; with stock prices already low, they could hardly expect to gain by issuing new stock, which would flood the market and further depress the price, and they had begun to abandon their traditional source of expansion capital, franchising.

Franchising, while neither a new phenomenon nor one limited to the restaurant business, financed the initial rapid expansion of the fast-foods industry; an extraordinary economic instrument for growing corporations, it allowed them to expand their operations using the capital of the smaller franchise holders, who maintained more autonomy than managers of company-owned outlets. Fast foods contributed to the general growth of franchising; by 1979, franchise operations sold about $200 billion worth of goods and services, about 12 percent of the gross national product, while the possibilities for independent small business contracted. United States Congressman Abner Mikva of Illinois, sponsoring the 1979 Franchise Reform Bill, called franchises "the primary method of entry into the commercial world for small businessmen and women." They did not necessarily provide easy entry for previously disadvantaged groups. In 1976, according to *Black Enterprise* magazine, starting a fast-food restaurant required a minimum of about $165,000, which paid for land (except in the case of McDonald's, which leased property to its franchisees), the initial franchise fee, equipment, and the first monthly royalty payment (a percentage of sales paid to the company for advertising, training, and consultation). Some franchises cost even more—nobody could start a McDonald's without at least $200,000.

Anybody new in business and not in contact with established local commercial circles would have difficulty scraping up $200,000. It was easier for the more typical franchisee of fast food's early days—the proprietor of a thriving independent restaurant who wanted to stop working eighteen hours a day, had contacts among local businessmen and bankers through the Rotary or Kiwanis, and perceived that McDonald's or Kentucky Fried Chicken just might have a better idea. The company would advertise, train personnel, and most important, design systems intended to put out a higher volume of food at a lower cost; cheap and inexperienced teen-age helpers acted more reliably as specialized component parts of those systems than as general helpers in a more traditional restaurant, and the fast-food systems nearly guaranteed profits. Franchising helped the chains, too, in the early days when business success depended on quick expansion: the corporations expanded using other people's money, growing by incorporating small business rather than risking the hazards of overrunning it. With local franchisees active in local business communities, the corporations could more easily obtain zoning variances or their own versions of new urban plans, essential when they intended to erect fast-food outlets over the frequent opposition of community residents.

Franchising provided the capital to finance rapid expansion. Church's Fried Chicken, one of the most profitable companies in the industry, initially depended on tight control (the company owned 702 of its 830 outlets in 1978), but abandoned that policy when it expanded quickly into two new regions, the Northeast and Northwest. Wendy's International—the company that succeeded in the supposedly saturated hamburger market by offering an even more limited menu than most, featuring larger burgers that cost more but used the same amount of labor, and advertising them to a "new" market segment (wealthier, single people)—had a formula attractive to large investors. They issued franchises, but only 150 of them; franchising not individual restaurants but large geographical territories, Wendy's managed to sell the franchises to wealthy operators with long experience in the business, including the former chairman of Kentucky Fried Chicken and the founder of Long John Silver's. Wendy's new kind of franchise provided the parent company with greater control than the old one-restaurant-at-a-time style; the company could work in closer collaboration with its fewer franchisees.

Companies with great enough financial resources, however, moved away from franchising altogether; McDonald's could do so earlier than most because of its phenomenal success in both burgers and real estate. Verne H. Winchell, who worked his way to the top of Denny's, Inc., after that coffee-shop company bought his chain of doughnut shops in 1968, declared as his primary strategy as president the end of new franchising for financial reasons; although franchisees provided large lump sums initially, they took larger shares of operating profits over the long run. But most of all, companies gained control by ending franchising and owning their own restaurants: control over locations, expenses, all aspects of operations, and profits. Just before Winchell took over, for example, some of Denny's franchisees sued the company for forcing them to buy high-priced supplies from the company. Sambo's salaried managers (who owned and reaped the profits on up to 50 percent of their restaurants without holding franchises) rebelled when the company restructured to bolster its stock prices, raising managers' salaries but demanding more of the future earnings; 130 of them quit, half refused to sell shares back to the company, and Sambo's worried whether discontented managers living primarily on their salaries would work as hard to turn out high profits. Like the managers who owned large shares of their restaurants, franchisees who owned the whole operation and saw themselves as independent businessmen in collaboration with large companies could come to

North 83rd Street, Hazel Dell, Oregon, 1981. Photo by Margaret Stratton.

value their independence over the collaboration. Companies therefore used their power to terminate the franchise; in 1971, one fast-food corporation terminated 682 franchises in a single day, a case Congressman Mikva emphasized in promoting legislation designed to confront the issue. The corporations could enhance their powers over operations and their control over profits by exercising this final power, terminating franchises and assuming total control over a chain of company-owned restaurants.

Only the largest companies could afford to do this; as fast-food companies tightened their control over operations and sold out to food conglomerates that could provide them with expansion money, fast food assumed the structure of other American industries, dominated by a few large corporations. As fast foods grew, those few large corporations increasingly dominated not only their industry and their franchisees but Americans' daily lives: McDonald's and Burger Chef and the innumerable smaller chains revamped American eating habits. The average person consumed almost five times as many frozen potatoes in 1976 as in 1960; the fast-food industry used three-quarters of the frozen french fries. Soft-drink consumption more than doubled during the same period. Americans averaged 1.2 pounds of ice milk apiece in 1950, 7.4 pounds in 1976. The consumption of salad and cooking oils tripled between 1947–1949 and 1976. Canned tomatoes, tomato products, and pickles all showed similar increases, testifying to the carloads of ketchup and piles of pickles that garnished all the hamburgers sold with all those fries and shakes.

Nor, if the women's magazine writers had their way, would the new foods keep to their place on the street corner. "Everyone's busy these days," declared the *Ladies' Home Journal* in a 1977 article entitled "Fast Food at Home." "But even in the busiest of families, there's no need to go out: food at home can be just as fast, with the added personal touch of grace and style." The *Journal* recommended stocking up on processed foods in cans, jars, and packages and depending on them for the main course. "For instance, frozen fish fillets get topped with a cheese slice, slipped in a bun and served with a side of deli-coleslaw and chips. Round out with a tall glass of tomato juice and melon balls for dessert. It's the closest thing to non-cooking—without stepping a foot off the premises." Dependent on the food processors for advertising revenue, the *Journal* turned their products into the true competition for fast foods, supplementing the processors' own advertising efforts: Mrs. Paul assured people that they didn't "have to eat out" if they bought her frozen fish sticks, Swanson marketed "take-out style" chicken, Banquet tried their "Outs eat out" campaign, and Contadina and Carnation offered a four-dollar refund on their products to demonstrate that "Eating At Home Pays Off."

Seventeen and *Mademoiselle*, more allied to the makeup industry than to the food processors and appealing to different audiences, encouraged the new eating habits even more directly. *Seventeen*, apparently suspecting that its readers suffered fast-food withdrawal during the winter, told them in January 1978 that they need not "give up [their] favorite fast foods when it's cold outside" and provided recipes for frozen yogurt, fishburgers, fried pies, frosted shakes, pizza, fried chicken, and coleslaw. While some of these dishes, such as the chicken and the pizza, depended heavily on convenience foods, others such as the fried pies and the frozen yogurt took work and time—"fast foods" only in the sense that they imitated the fare of fast-food restaurants. *Mademoiselle* appealed not to hungry teens but to younger career girls seeking to "whip up company dinner in minutes, from stuff you pick up on the way home. . . . Hide that carton, can or bucket, ritz up the goods, add some candles and wine and they'll never guess the help you had with dinner. (And if they do, they've got to admire your wit . . . and nerve.) Presentation is all—and a twist on the traditional helps. Like melting cheese on the takeout chicken's mashed potatoes. Or toning up Chinese with a tea pot." No recipes followed; readers needed none, since the article recommended simply taking food out of cartons, putting it onto elegant plates, and serving it with tasteful utensils. The Shop section, listing stores where readers could purchase goods pictured throughout the magazine, itemized the plates and utensils; nobody had to be told where to buy fried chicken and mashed potatoes in red-striped cartons.

Fast foods have changed eating habits far beyond the food itself; they have invaded the mealtime ritual even at home. The chief executive officer of Kraft, Inc., maintained that eating out accustomed people to "portion control" and therefore to accepting a processor's statement that a package of macaroni and cheese serves four. "Generally speaking," one writer claimed in *Advertising Age*, "the homemaker no longer sets the table with dishes of food from which the family fills their plates—the individual plates are filled and placed before the family, no second helpings." Eating out even accustoms diners at the same table to eating different foods, putting home meals of different prepared foods within the realm of possibility and altering the nature of parental discipline; freed from the "shut up—you'll eat what we're eating" rule, children experience the pleasures and also the isolation of individual free choice at earlier ages. The common bowl that all diners shared until all the food was eaten both represented and fostered important attitudes toward families, toward sharing, and toward food.

Children learned those attitudes at the daily family dinner, once the central ritual of the day and now a dying institution, following the lead of the family lunch (which largely disappeared long before the beginning of the century) and the family breakfast (now defunct in three-quarters of American households). A survey taken during the summer and fall of 1977 showed that families got together for only half their meals on the weekends, when they presumably had the most time to do so; many who had not entirely abandoned family dinners no longer ate together daily. Individual family members eat whenever, wherever, and with whomever they like; one drug company advertised bottled vitamins to mothers in 1980 on the claim that they could not be sure their teen-agers were eating properly. "In one generation," according to *Advertising Age*, "we have gone from a traditional food producing society to a food grazing society—one where we eat wherever we happen to be."

When Americans graze their way to the fast-food outlets, they encounter and participate in a series of new rituals. As a University of Michigan anthropologist points out, writing specifically about McDonald's, behavior there shares important features with other rituals in all cultures: stylized, repetitive, stereotyped events occur in special places, include costumes and set sequences of words and actions, "translate enduring messages, values, and sentiments into observable action," and "signal" people's "acceptance of an order that transcends their status as individuals." People arrive at McDonald's—and to a lesser extent at the other chains—knowing what they will eat, what they will pay, what to say to the counter person and how she or he will respond, what the restaurant will look like—in short, knowing exactly what to expect and how to behave; children learn these expectations and behaviors early in life. For some, the ritual constitutes an attraction of these restaurants; they neither wish to cook nor to chat with a waitress as she intones and delivers the daily specials. The fast-food ritual requires no responsibility other than ordering (with as few words as possible) and paying; nobody has to set or clear the table, wash the dishes, or compliment the cook on her cuisine, the traditional responsibilities of husbands and children at the family dinner.

If, like other rituals, fast-food restaurant behavior signals acceptance of an order that transcends people's status as individuals, there can be no mistaking the order: corporate intrusion into daily life, the ultimate domination of the public sphere over the formerly private. Advertising, as Leo J. Shapiro and Dwight Bohmbach told Madison Avenue in *Advertising Age*, "has replaced 'pinching the tomatoes' and hand selecting in our choice of foods. A wood-cut illustration of an old-fashioned kitchen on a meat analog package; 'grandfather' smacking his lips over a synthetic lemonade . . . these symbols now tell us what to expect from food someone else picked, prepared and packaged for us." The corporations attempt to compensate for stripping food of its emotional content by using symbols like these and the healthy nuclear families in the McDonald's ads. They try to convince consumers that they can regain what they have lost if they substitute one set of products for another: "Eating at home always pays off . . . in good eating, homey surroundings, and economy," Contadina and Carnation claim, offering a refund to consumers who buy their

Dairy Queen, Canyon Road and U.S. Route 26, Beaverton, Oregon, 1981. Photo by Margaret Stratton.

products instead of Pizza Hut's. Or they develop new "product concepts," like the takeout and frozen ethnic foods that Shapiro and Bohmbach maintain "help to satisfy the desire for really traditional dishes" and the "new" kinds of fast-food restaurants that have inside tables. The advertisers do not care whether anybody actually believes that Taco Bell sells "really traditional" Mexican food or whether families achieve intimacy sitting around a table at Kentucky Fried Chicken. They intend merely to "help to satisfy" a desire sufficiently to sell a product especially attractive to working mothers, whose children prefer fast foods—and the safe ritual, individual choice, and freedom from responsibility that go with them—to anything mothers might cook when they get home from work.

The big companies and their advertising wizards have met resistance from the consumer groups that have lobbied successfully for regulation over advertising, product names, and packaging information, from the health-foods movement, and from leisure-time gourmet cooking, but none of these challenge the fundamental problem. The consumer movement generally takes corporate control as given and attempts to limit its powers; although some regulation is better than none, nutritional packaging information helps concerned consumers make intelligent choices between two processed foods, without challenging the corporations' power to determine what appears in the stores on the sole basis of profit. The health-foods movement has brought nutritional awareness beyond packaging, but the large corporations easily co-opted consumers' nutritional concerns by producing "health foods" like the granola-type breakfast cereals, many of them loaded with sugar and salt, and most more expensive than other products. Gourmet cooking will always be the province of people with money; past the initial investment in cookbooks and equipment, this hobby requires continual spending on expensive ingredients, including the unprocessed foods that may some day be available only to the wealthy, and to those with backyards and green thumbs, because they produce lower profits than highly processed foods.

None of this resistance attacks either the most profound causes or the most profound effects of an increasing dilemma; nutritional labeling and gourmet cookbooks cannot save American culture, insofar as it is reflected in and formed by daily eating habits and rituals, from the control of the corporate boardroom. Under that control, most people will increasingly lose their power to decide about their food, their choices limited to the products of one corporation or another, all uniform, geared to the average palate and produced on the basis of decisions made, not about flavor or quality or freshness, but about profit. They will eat even more of their meals in surroundings that distort fundamental rituals, where corporate managers have decided everything—the color of the floor, the clothing of the teen-ager at the counter, the words employees use, and the amount of ketchup on a hamburger—on the basis of market research, or they will buy food from those restaurants and from factories by way of supermarkets and bring it home, where the public ritual has overtaken the private. Their food at home will be processed; like cotton and wool, now luxury fabrics, fresh broccoli and raw chicken will be supplanted by more profitable synthetics.

Although the corporate executive and the advertising copywriter will remain able longer to afford unprocessed foods and expensive restaurants, they too graze for food, grabbing a bite in transit, and they too have lost the family dinner. Undoubtedly many of them recognize the long-run and society-wide implications of their work; a few may even quit their jobs when the emotional costs run high, to be replaced by others who do the same work. But those who form American eating habits do so in their roles as corporate executives and advertising copywriters, not as individual human beings. A few making decisions for the many, chosen without any semblance of democracy, they make those decisions according to corporate balance sheets, which never reflect emotional costs.

SIXTEEN

Life on the Market

Just as the production of energy and clothing had become work done publicly for profit during the first decades of the twentieth century, so eventually did the functions of housework that long had remained private: by the end of the 1970s, manufactured commodities and commercial services fulfilled many Americans' needs for food, child care, and affection. Substantial numbers of women were entering the paid labor force, the divorce rate had mounted, and changing expectations about long-term affectional relationships left both women and men stranded in the marketplace as individuals, increasingly dependent not on other people but on products. The women's liberation movement, which addressed questions of household work and emotional support in its early years, had abandoned those issues for explicit economic and political goals, leaving the backward-looking activists of the New Right to ponder the substantial questions about how modern society had failed the values women had traditionally been charged to protect. Both movements operated on the legacy of the ideology of separate spheres, which encouraged individuals to construe their private lives as individual problems and to seek solutions that failed to attack the roots of those problems in social and economic development. At the same time, the trends that so often made life difficult for individuals had finally provided American women and men with the prerequisites for equal relationships and the first possibilities for seeking real solutions on a social level.

By the early 1970s, the women's movement had begun to transform social attitudes about women working outside the home, and pressure from women activists had resulted in slightly better employment opportunities for women, with higher wages. Nonetheless, the main reason most married women with children joined the labor force during the 1960s and 1970s continued to be economic pressure, and the jobs they found continued to pay poorly, provide little self-fulfillment, and offer few opportunities for advancement. They worked not for pin money but for subsistence: the cost of such basics as food, personal taxes, and automobiles rose sharply during the decade between 1966 and 1976, while the average worker's income remained stagnant, pay raises barely keeping abreast of inflation. Housing costs soared beyond most people's means: by 1977, *Business Week* reported that the prices of new homes had mounted "out of reach of blue collar and nonprofessional, nonmanagerial heads of household whose spouses do not work," yet the price of shelter continued to spiral upward in the next few years, worsened by higher energy costs and by a tight money market that raised finance charges. Only "the numbers game of more workers per dependent," the magazine explained, could account for the fact that consumers had any money to spend on nonessential items. In other words, the women who solved their families' financial woes by going out to work kept the economy going. Fewer than a third of the married women with husbands at home and children under eighteen worked for pay in 1960; by 1977, their labor-force participation had risen to 48 percent, and analysts projected that two-thirds of these women would be in the labor force by 1990.

As a nationwide survey showed, those women retained their primary responsibility for housework as they took on other jobs; husbands of employed women studied in the mid-1960s gave no more help with

housework than husbands of women who stayed home. Individual solutions varied: some women fought with their spouses, some cut their own household work to a minimum with no compunction, some cut the work but felt guilty about neglecting their families, and most struggled endlessly to balance responsibilities. As a group, encouraged by advertisements that promised convenience, these women came to depend on purchased goods and services to do the work of the household, stopping at the Colonel's on the way home from work to buy their kids some chicken, or sticking Swanson's "takeout-style" into the oven.

Employed mothers used part of their paychecks to pay others to care for their children. Some found other women who took small numbers of children into their homes, a new twist on the traditional ways of making money at home, but one regulated by state agencies that licensed child care, limited the number of children, set ratios for staffing and space, and prescribed physical conditions in day-care facilities. Churches and charitable institutions established child-care centers, and others ran under the guidance of parent cooperatives, but as the demand for day care mounted, entrepreneurs set up more centers to make money. Businessmen "who would never have sat still for an argument on day care from the liberated-women's standpoint" began to understand the profitable opportunities in day care and applied the business methods that had served so well in other industries. "Infants is good business," remarked Perry Mendel, the corporate head of Kinder-Care, a child-care chain that operated 170 centers in eighteen states in 1977, when it anticipated expanding to 500 centers and 50,000 children by 1980. Kinder-Care paid its teachers slightly above the minimum wage; the more expensive psychologists and educators that other centers hired, Mendel claimed, "don't know the value of a dollar." Joseph Lelyveld, who reported on Kinder-Care in the *New York Times*, maintained that although individual teachers made their mark on the care their Kinder-Care outlets provided, the corporation aimed "to be safe and predictable—a common denominator that's appreciably higher than the lowest but not so high as to interfere with its own expansion"—at a 30 percent annual growth rate. The most dedicated individual teachers need materials and decent compensation for their work, which (as many nonprofit child-care operations have discovered) may conflict with breaking even, much less making money; industrialized child care, designed by and for profit-making corporations, operates on the basis of priorities unlikely to result in the superior care that every child deserves and that the American future depends upon. The current trends can only serve to reinforce class distinctions: wealthy children, whose mothers can afford to stay at home to care for them or to send them to nonprofit child-care centers, will benefit from early care based on their needs, while most others will have those needs subordinated to the profit requirements of the corporations that provide their care.

Charlotte Perkins Gilman, who at the turn of the century predicted industrialized child care and cooking with better results, maintained that when industry assumed those functions and women worked outside the home for pay, the home would better fulfill its highest and most important functions—as the resting place for family and friends, "the recognized base and background" of lives lived in the world, the place "to return to the dear old ties, to the great primal basis, that we may rise refreshed and strengthened." The absence of productive work, she envisioned, would strengthen the long-term affectional bonds of the family and provide a better basis for its crucial emotional work. Recent trends, however, suggest the opposite: long-term intimate bonds dissolve as the divorce rate rises, and Americans buy both intimacy and leisure as market commodities, becoming dependent on products instead of people to do their emotional work, or on paid surrogates who provide the emotional support that used to be free.

Few Americans now marry without understanding that divorce offers them an option increasingly common and acceptable socially, although most still take their vows seriously and suffer from a profound sense of failure if they find themselves in court seeking the dissolution of their marriages. As the divorce rate increased, doubling between 1965 and 1976, individual states relaxed requirements and procedures, bringing divorcing couples into court without their having to degrade or shame themselves or each other. Children, who understand the new trends better than their parents, experience both the failure and a sense of the prevalence of divorce; now a child of divorcing parents tells an older friend (whose own childhood acquaintances included only one set of divorced parents) that he had considered his parents "the perfect Mom and Dad" because he knew so few other children with parents still married. The disappearing taboo, both cause and effect of the new laws and the new demand for divorce, had political implications by 1980: right-wing Republicans, who had taunted divorced Nelson Rockefeller as a "dirty lover" at the 1964 GOP convention, nominated Ronald Reagan without mentioning his divorce, despite their own profamily platform.

Most of the people who divorce now remarry later; the Census Bureau, acknowledging the increase in divorce in 1979, maintained that "Americans spend most of their adult lives married," establishing patterns of legal serial monogamy. Many others live with members of the opposite sex out of wedlock—the number who acknowledged doing so doubled between 1970 and 1976—and have begun to demand legal and societal recognition for those arrangements, asking companies for such benefits as maternity leaves for unmarried women, company trips, and medical insurance, and asking courts for the financial equivalent to alimony made famous by the Lee Marvin case. In between marriages and cohabitations, more and more adults live alone or in households where unrelated adults

share little other than space; for the first time in human history, large numbers of women and men live by themselves without social stigma, a boon to the economic system that depends on selling as many household goods as possible.

These patterns and the profound transition they represent have thrown Americans' expectations of their families and their living arrangements into confusion. The Census Bureau decided in 1977 to discard the "head of household" label in the 1980 census, a step that required significant revisions in statistical methods; as one analyst at the Bureau of Labor Statistics pointed out, the old label encouraged policy makers to regard the "average" family as one with a husband who supports his wife and two children, "a profile matched by only 6 percent of all American families." The people who live the trends that the government statisticians count have had to discard traditional expectations without yet establishing new ones. Couples no longer marry until death them do part; children no longer expect to see their fathers daily throughout their childhood; wives no longer count on their husbands' continuing financial or emotional support for themselves or their children; in-laws no longer assume that marriage has permanently extended the group they can call family. Without a clear sense of appropriate expectations, and without dependable intimate relationships that afford daily interactions over many years, individuals seek substitutes to provide them with the security that the expectations used to allow and the emotional life that the relationships used to furnish.

Old-fashioned emotional life often failed its participants; probably few couples achieved the "perfect union" even in their own terms, much less in partnerships that blended love, responsibility, interesting companionship, and mutually satisfying sex as most people now expect their marriages to do. Nineteenth-century manuals warned economically dependent women not to expect too much; like Catharine Beecher, Lydia Maria Child, who stressed "the importance of a perfect union between husband and wife" for good child rearing, advised women with "unfortunate" marriages and untrustworthy husbands, "If patience, humility and love cannot win him to a sense of duty . . . redouble your vigilance for the good of your children, and as far as possible withdraw them from his influence." Rachel Haskell, who spent her evenings in the intimate circle of her family and guests, sewing, reading, playing games, making music, and talking around the lamp, complained often in her diary that her husband had spent *his* evening on the town. Living in close quarters, especially during the winter, individuals complained that they lacked privacy. Nonetheless, dependent on each other's services and bolstered by the certainty that they could expect those services to continue as long as both partners lived, most couples established routines and made at least minimally satisfactory accommodation to their marriages. Now, without that security or those expectations, women and men seek intimacy on the market.

They buy emotional support from psychological therapists of all stripes and all schools, from self-help groups and movements, and from the bookstores and magazine racks where written versions of popular psychological theories abound. The advice from those sources during the seventies gave the period its name of "the 'Me' Decade"; individuals learned from them not only to look out for themselves but how to live without expectations of others. In the modern world, they must depend only on themselves; others (who did the same) could never be trusted. Self-reliance costs money—to pay for the books and magazines, the services of the shrink, the group fees, the vacations and clothes and good food that supposedly demonstrate good self-treatment, and the many other products through which people more directly purchase their intimacy.

Some buy it from the telephone company, which sells a way to maintain and extend intimate ties with people to whom the caller has no daily responsibilities. The Bell System encourages long-distance calling with its pricing policies, setting low rates on Mother's Day and other traditional family holidays, and lowering them after business hours, bringing the company extra revenue on already existing equipment. Its advertisements sell long-distance calling less subtly; although the company at one time admitted that long distance was merely "the next best thing to being there," in 1980 it announced that callers could "reach out and touch someone" with a phone call: "Though family and friends move far apart, you can continue to grow together. Just reach out and walk back into each other's lives." For a fee, grandparents could "touch" their grand-children, aunts their sisters' kids, former college roommates their distant friends. In fact, nobody touches anybody on the telephone: telephone conversation, while it may indeed be the "next best thing," constitutes a wholly different kind of communication from face-to-face conversation, in which participants read each other's faces, watch each other's hand gestures, and have an opportunity to really touch. Nineteenth-century American society, at least as mobile as that of today, had no such technology; many people moved thousands of miles, never expecting to see or converse with friends and relations again. When they arrived in their new homes, they established new day-to-day intimacies, free of charge: women who hung their laundry outside knew their neighbors, who genuinely filled some of the needs the telephone meets inadequately.

Those who prefer to pay for a real touch can find that commodity, too, not only in the sexual massage parlors and other modern variants of the "oldest profession" but in the popular nonsexual massage services and classes, touted for their relaxing therapeutic value. The person who massages for pay demands nothing but money, asking for no reciprocal care; the money frees the massage buyer, like the prostitute's customer, of any

responsibility in a relationship with another human being who provides intimate care. The massage that relieves the tensions of modern society capitalizes on them at the same time.

Sexual massage parlors and public pornography appeal primarily to men; despite *Playgirl* and bars with male go-go dancers, most women prefer to keep sex private, and many have bought themselves machines for sex partners. The vibrator—a one-time purchase that demands even less conversation than a prostitute—has left the sex shops and now appears in department and variety stores, manufactured by the same respectable corporations that market electric razors and hair dryers, with names like Feelin' Good and Body Language, and instruction booklets that refer to "a soft touch body massager for . . . tender areas." Sex researchers and therapists agree that the vibrator's intense stimulation produces orgasms fast and consistently; many recommend them to patients, sometimes with warnings about the possibility of dependence on the gadget. The housewares industry's entry into the market takes the device beyond therapy; as one writer points out, it "poses new questions: Has achieving orgasm become just another way of releasing the tensions of day-to-day living? Has the vibrator, once considered a therapeutic device, become a sort of microwave oven of the bedroom—a fast, efficient means of getting sexual pleasure? Is the most efficient orgasm the best orgasm? Is the bedroom really the place for a time-saving device? If so, what are we saving all this time for?"

The question applies equally well to microwave ovens. Americans save time and value convenience in order to meet the demands of unsatisfying jobs that give them money to pay for a plethora of products. Those commodities, in turn, promise to fulfill the functions of the old private sphere—now including those of food, child care, and emotional life, which remained there at the turn of the century—without making demands on the individual or infringing on individual privacy. Accustomed to privacy and to meeting intimate needs free of responsibilities, many modern Americans find intimacy in the old style difficult. When volcanic ash kept everyone indoors in Yakima, Washington, after Mount Saint Helens erupted in May 1980, police reported that they had their hands full with family disputes. "Everyone is cooped up, it's pretty warm here, people can't open their doors and windows and aren't using their air conditioners, so tempers are frayed," a police captain said. People learned to control their tempers in the stuffy Victorian house—to their detriment, modern psychological theory suggests, recommending anger as an emotion to be expressed, not repressed. Modern Americans, free to marry the partner of their own choice rather than their parents', to plan their children's births or decide to have no children, and to leave unsatisfactory marriages, are also free to express their anger and to ponder the entwined nature of intimacy, sexuality, and emotional dependency. Many decide, at least temporarily, that intimacy has become too great a problem, and choose to buy it in the form of commodities that make no demands.

Most people combine the solutions offered by the market with their own individual attempts to achieve intimacy with others because real people offer greater satisfactions than products; the intimacy of the therapist, the vibrator, and the long-distance phone call cannot compensate for touching and talking with loved ones in the same room. The products fulfill their promises so inadequately that people even pay for the opportunity to *search* for the real thing at singles bars and through newspapers' personal advertisement columns. When they think they have found it, they commit themselves and their romantic hopes to another marriage or another relationship, attempting an individual accommodation to a system that places them in impossible binds, making commodities out of affection and love.

Two recent political movements have looked beyond individual solutions. In the early days of women's liberation, the movement examined all aspects of women's lives; movement writers and activists stressed the concept that "the personal is political." Organizing their movement in small consciousness-raising groups, essentially reinstating the sewing circle and the other support groups that women lost when their work isolated them within their homes, these women aimed to demonstrate the common nature of personal problems that often appeared to be wholly individual: these small groups discussed their members' relationships with men at home and at their jobs, finding and analyzing similar experiences. Eventually, wanting to take political action beyond simply organizing the movement, they turned to issues that had tangible political goals. Abandoning private problems of home life, movement activists concentrated on public issues like the Equal Rights Amendment, fair hiring, abortion laws, and equal pay for equal work in the paid labor market. Like the early twentieth-century feminists who narrowed their movement to women's suffrage, the feminists of the seventies narrowed theirs to money and public forms of power, challenging women's economic inequality in the labor market and the systematic discrimination that denied them entry into satisfying jobs. But few challenged a system that depends on unsatisfying jobs and unsatisfying products, and therefore most never addressed the basic issue for most women who remain at home: Why should a woman whose husband can afford to support her go to work at the oppressive jobs that most women can get, exchanging the freedom of private work in the household and the pleasures of home production for supervised labor that makes profits for somebody else and products that fail to deliver the satisfactions they promise?

The women's movement, coinciding with economic changes that made it impossible for many husbands to support their wives with one paycheck, eventually reached every woman in the United States, whether she liked it or not, and affected her life, her relationships with men, and her sense of her own career and life choices. For many, "women's liberation"

became synonymous with the double burden of working full time and caring for a household, as if the movement's goal had been to make women's lives more difficult. Because so many women shouldered that double burden, the issues of the consciousness-raising group moved to the women's magazines, stripped of the "women's liberation" label and of their political content. Ellen Goodman's "The Grateful Wife," published in the July 1980 *McCall's Working Mother*, for example, spoke to the same issue as Pat Mainardi's "The Politics of Housework," an early women's liberation tract: Who does the housework when both partners work outside the home? A decade after Mainardi argued that men who live with working women should do part of the housework, Goodman went much further, suggesting that even helpful husbands who made dinner or picked up children at soccer practice still refused to take their full share of responsibility for household administration. Wives still had to keep all the household details in their own heads and to interpret gratefully the men's activities as "help" with the "women's jobs." But Goodman's article had none of the essential political content suggested by Mainardi's title and by the arguments she offered for women to use on their recalcitrant mates, all rooted in the position that personal matters had fundamental political implications.

By narrowing its position to the tangible economic and political issues, the women's liberation movement left the field of personal issues to the women of the New Right, who made a political campaign against the ERA and reproductive rights, supposedly in the interests of "saving the family." Without articulating the "personal is political" line, this "constellation of traditionalist, individualist, and fundamentalist movements" acted on it, mobilizing women's support around personal issues and lending that support to established right-wing politicians; their activism contributed to the defeat of the ERA in many states and to the 1980 Republican platform planks that upheld "traditional family values." Their defense of an institution "in a form that hardly exists any more," *Time* magazine pointed out after the Republican convention, quoting a Denver Republican leader, appeals to people who "sense that events are out of an individual's control." Many of those people also seek and find community in fundamentalist religion, which offers intensely emotional group experiences to people otherwise isolated in their homes in front of their television sets or communicating with others through radio talk shows.

With their campaign to re-establish lost values, the women activists of the New Right place themselves in the same dilemma Catharine Beecher faced in the mid-nineteenth century: they celebrate the separation of the public and private spheres, actively working in the public sphere to communicate the message that women belong at home and to establish public policy that will keep them there. "I'd rather be home cooking and caring for my family, doing embroidery, than what I'm doing," one right-wing activist told a reporter. "But a force greater than myself is magnetically drawing me to pursue it. I guess I feel a responsibility to inform other women what's going on. We've just got to protect the family." In a society where money determines value and jobs provide social contact and self-definition, women who depend on their husbands for economic support, most of their adult conversation, and their definition in society have difficulty maintaining their self-respect and establishing relationships with their husbands that grant them and their work equal status. The New Right women demand that status as Beecher did: they want to "redeem woman's profession from dishonor," to establish women's supremacy in a separate but equal sphere. They seek a return not merely to past values but to a picture of reality already inadequate when Beecher published *The American Woman's Home* in 1869; by then the home was already changing from an arena for internal production to a handmaiden of the labor and consumer markets. Preindustrial reality will not return.

These backward-looking activists share a predicament with the activist feminists whom they blame for the family's woes. The rhetoric of both movements presupposes separate spheres, the right celebrating the private, the recent feminists the public, but the concept now makes little sense. Women who believe they belong at home, therefore, go out to lobby legislators and learn political tactics that permit them to dominate statewide conferences, while feminists come home from work to confront privately the dilemmas they no longer define as political. Although the major differences between women's independent work at home and their husbands' supervised jobs have kept the ideology of separate spheres alive in various forms for a century and a half, the spheres have never actually been separate: from the beginnings of American industrialization businesses manufactured goods for household use, and households served business by consuming those products and reproducing the labor force. By the end of the Civil War, household theorists like Beecher and Peirce understood that the ideology of separate spheres failed to account for obvious social and economic trends; by the turn of the century, their successors in the home economics movement, along with such extremists as Charlotte Perkins Gilman and Christine Frederick, abandoned the concept because industrial expansion had brought so many households within the domain of the money economy. Since that time, the increasing control of private life by large corporations in the interest of their own profits has presented a grim picture, especially when set against an easily over-romanticized past. Nonetheless, the latest trends constitute the minimum prerequisites for equal relationships between women and men, and for asserting the values of intimacy, love, and community that women were called upon to protect as soon as people came to see the spheres as separate in the first place.

Although few women have left the home for the office or factory by choice, work for pay provides the potential for economic independence; no longer constrained to marry or to remain married for their livelihood,

women may at last be able to approach relationships with men free of the calculation, the intense fear, and the weakness and self-abasement that, as Simone de Beauvoir wrote, has made love "a source of mortal danger" for women. Although many women learn from sad experience that most jobs stultify as much of the self as they fulfill, even when they have returned to school in search of a guarantee of satisfying work, they do find support in their jobs; the women's community that once met over clotheslines and at quilting parties now gathers during coffee breaks and around lunch tables. As the demands of the women's movement and the individual actions of the many women who do not think of themselves as "women's libbers" but fight for equal pay and equal work create expanded opportunities, more women interact with men as equals on the job—as doctors and executives, as fire fighters and skilled carpenters. Nurses, secretaries, and others in traditional women's occupations are demanding respect and decent pay for the work they do. Women who earn and spend their own money, who have the support of other women, and who define themselves for at least part of the day in terms of their paid work do not have to subordinate themselves to their husbands as economically dependent women must. Like Ellen Goodman's "Grateful Wife," they will demand far more than the first activists of the women's liberation movement dared: equal relationships with men who share the tasks, the responsibilities, and the pleasures of sustaining life for both adults and children.

Men who relate to women as equals on the job will more easily accept such expectations from the women they live with; men who live alone for periods of time learn skills to bring to equal living relationships with women. Of course, many men depend even more than working women on purchased goods and services. A California woman who started an expensive "Rent-A-Wife" service in 1979 reported that her phones "haven't stopped ringing" since her first small ad; wealthy bachelors and divorced men paid $25 an hour, $150 a day, or $600 a week for women who organized their household affairs, ran their errands, planned and supervised the redecoration of their homes, entertained their clients and their grandchildren, and did the cooking and cleaning that others sold for much less. But most men living alone have to fend for themselves; even those who buy services carry their own dirty wash to the laundry, trek to the supermarket to fill their own carts with convenience foods, and supervise their own entertaining at restaurants. Finding the burdens of their own care too great, some divorced men soon remarry, perhaps hoping to find a woman who, like the Rent-A-Wife, demands nothing but money in return for her services; increasingly, however, family life requires two paychecks, and they marry working women with their own potential for economic independence, who make demands on them. Other men take as much pride in their everyday self-reliance as women do in their economic independence, and discover the pleasures and compensations that cooking and entertaining and home decoration still offer; many of them assert that self-reliance and demand their share of those pleasures when they live with women again. Single men do their own buying, and when they remarry many continue to do so; consumption, the major economic function of the modern household, is no longer strictly a woman's job. *Time* magazine, offering its advertising space to food companies in 1978, called this "the growth of dual purchase influence," stemming from "a continuing dissolution of male-female stereotypes. Women simply have less time for home interests, and men are accepting a greater share of the purchasing responsibilities."

Few achieve equal relationships in a society still dominated by those dissolving stereotypes, and women's equality at home and on the job represents a necessary but not sufficient solution to the dissatisfactions of American daily life. The married women who now enter the labor market join the men and the single women whose growing participation as workers has expanded the money economy for the past 150 years, giving up the freedom of self-sufficiency and the pleasures of home production to work at stultifying jobs to make money to buy products that provide them with industrialized subsistence. For most of that time, industrialization clearly improved the quality of life at home, eliminating backbreaking labor, raising standards of health and nutrition, and freeing people from virtual slavery to natural cycles. More recently, that quality has begun to decline as the corporations manufacture food, child care, and emotional life in the form of purchased commodities, and the market distorts daily ritual and the values of love and community. No better quality may be expected from an economic system that delegates decision-making power over daily life to private corporations that base those decisions on profit, wasting resources and blatantly ignoring human needs both in their product designs and in the organization of their labor.

The strong legacy of the ideology of separate spheres fuels individual attempts to accommodate to a society that distorts human values: women and men attempt to establish private havens from an ugly world. Although most have dropped the idea that women will work full time at guarding that haven, they depend on the romantic notion that they can nourish a private partnership sufficiently to remain immune to social and economic trends. To the extent that their havens fail to provide well-being, they buy it on the market. Most people find temporary sanity and private pleasures in both their relationships and their purchases, yet also suffer from the emotional ravages of failed romance and unsatisfactory attempts to meet their needs with the things they buy.

Extricating American society and individual women and men from the personal dilemmas that corporate control of daily life imposes takes, first, an understanding that daily life is neither free nor private but bound inextricably with economic and social change; individuals, couples, and families have only limited control over decisions they often construe as their own. With that understanding, they may learn to live in the consolidated sphere, envisioning new kinds of products and services, and new kinds of work patterns that account for the values that women guarded for so long in the so-called private sphere. Women who can now gain their economic independence, their worldly self-definition, and the support of their fellow workers must enter the public world with those old-fashioned values. They must begin to question many of the requirements of male-style jobs and careers; the notion that paid work must take precedence at all times over other concerns; the separation of parenthood from the rest of adult life; the workplace hazards and the minute division of labor and intense supervision that make working for pay so different from women's traditional work at home. They must challenge the failure of industry to provide services that would make housework into socially provided work; its sacrifice of other such services (like the commercial laundry) to the profit motive; and its insistence on providing still others in ways that disregard human nutritional and emotional needs and ever scarcer natural resources in favor of profit and efficiency. Men who now experience the work and the pleasures of the home directly instead of leaving them to women must likewise bring those values to the rest of their lives. Both sexes must seek public solutions to problems they have formerly construed as private, bringing pressure to bear on those who conceive and direct American production, employment, and consumption in the upper echelons of the corporations that give people jobs and produce the goods they buy.

Making those challenges will take the vision and imagination that can extend the optimistic romantic viewpoint beyond the individual, the couple, and the family to the society as a whole. Despite the divorce rate, people marry with a vision of a partnership that can serve their needs, achieving that magic blending of emotional interdependence, daily help and support, and individual autonomy. Although many now suspect that vision to be a legacy of the past, inconsistent with the realities of modern life, the vision is both what keeps people going back to the altar and what keeps good partnerships together. Neither the past nor the present offers any such vision of the social future: the choices often appear to be limited to nuclear holocaust, economic collapse, the computerized supermarket, and Thanksgiving dinner at Burger King. The public actions that will result in anything else demand a vision of a better future, based on the real achievements of industrial society, on a recognition that private life and public decision-making are and always have been linked, and on a celebration of the human values of love and community that lost their status, connected for so long to women's arduous and unstinting unpaid labor in a sphere only apparently separate and private.

Bibliographic Note

Readers who intend to pursue the theoretical questions about the economic function of household labor discussed in the Prologue would do well to begin with one of two excellent summaries of the literature: Nona Glazer-Malbin, "Housework: A Review Essay," *Signs* 1 (Summer 1976): 905–22, and Heidi Hartmann, "Capitalism and Women's Work in the Home, 1900–1930" (Ph.D. dissertation, Yale University, 1974), pp. 8–31. Ann Oakley presents an historical overview of the connections between housework and the economy in Great Britain, in *Woman's Work: The Housewife, Past and Present* (New York: Pantheon Books, 1974). For a more technical treatment of my own stance on the theoretical questions—and on other matters in this book—see my "Never Done: The Ideology and Technology of Household Work, 1850–1930" (Ph.D. dissertation, State University of New York, Stony Brook, 1977).

On household technology, discussed in chapters 1 through 7, Hartmanns' and my dissertations should be supplemented with Susan J. Kleinberg, "Technology and Women's Work: The Lives of Working Class Women in Pittsburgh, 1870–1900," *Labor History* 17 (Winter 1976): 58–72, and with the work of Ruth Schwartz Cowan, especially "The 'Industrial Revolution' in the Home: Household Technology and Social Change in the 20th Century," *Technology and Culture* 17 (January 1976): 1–23. Cowan is currently working on a book; when it is published, the labor of half the population will finally have a historiography as well as a history. Siegfried Giedion's idiosyncratic *Mechanization Takes Command: A Contribution to Anonymous History* (New York: W. W. Norton & Co., 1948) is essential reading, although Giedion relies heavily on patent records, thereby disregarding the question of the diffusion of technology. I returned continually to three older compendia of information: Elizabeth Mickle Bacon, "The Growth of Household Conveniences in the United States from 1865 to 1900" (Ph.D. dissertation, Radcliffe College, 1942); Edgar W. Martin, *The Standard of Living in 1860: American Consumption Levels on the Eve of the Civil War* (Chicago: University of Chicago Press, 1942); and Victor S. Clark, *History of Manufactures in the United States*, 3 vols. (New York: McGraw-Hill Book Co. for Carnegie Institution of Washington, 1929). David Handlin, in *The American Home: Architecture and Society, 1815–1915* (Boston: Little, Brown & Co., 1979), provides an architectural overview and a discussion of utilities.

My discussion of housework as work and of married women's options for earning money at home, in chapters 7 through 9, is framed by categories described by E. P. Thompson, "Time, Work Discipline, and Industrial Capitalism," *Past and Present* 38 (1967): 56–97; see also Keith Thomas, "Work and Leisure in Pre-Industrial Society," *Past and Present* 29 (1964): 50–66. On boarding, see John Modell and Tamara K. Hareven, "Urbanization and the Malleable Household: An Examination of Boarding and Lodging in American Families," *Journal of Marriage and the Family* 35 (August 1973): 467–79. David Katzman has provided the first thorough modern discussion of the major form of paid housework for unmarried women, domestic service, in *Seven Days a Week: Women and Domestic Service in Industrializing America* (New York: Oxford University Press, 1978); see his excellent annotated bibliography for additional references.

Probably no aspect of my subject matter has received as much recent scholarly attention as the nineteenth-century ideology of separate spheres. My thinking, like that of others, was formed in the context of Barbara Welter's seminal description, "The Cult of True Womanhood: 1820–1860," *American Quarterly* 18 (Summer 1966): 151–74, and of Eli Zaretsky's work, published in book form as *Capitalism, the Family and Personal Life* (New York: Harper & Row, Colophon Books, 1976); although I developed fundamental criticisms of Zaretsky's theory, evidence, and political stance, he provided a clear and provocative model. Nancy Cott altered scholarship on separate spheres in *The Bonds of Womanhood: "Woman's Sphere" in New England, 1780–1835* (New Haven, Conn.: Yale University Press, 1977); like myself, she searched for the reality behind the ideological construct, and using very different kinds of evidence, we came to some similar conclusions, especially about the relationship between sex and class in the early nineteenth century. Two important recent interpretations link the ideology of separate spheres to broader issues: Ann Douglas, in *The Femini-*

zation of American Culture (New York: Alfred A. Knopf, 1977), puts insights about women's place outside the economic system in a cultural, religious, and literary context, while William Leach, in *True Love and Perfect Union: The Feminist Reform of Sex and Society* (New York: Basic Books, 1980), puts feminist responses to the ideology in the context of the possessive individualism that developed with capitalism. And for those whose enthusiasm for the connection between the development of separate spheres and the development of American industrialism leads them to overstatement about a "golden age" of sexual equality in the colonial period, two recent books provide an important corrective: Linda Kerber's *Women of the Republic: Intellect and Ideology in Revolutionary America* (Chapel Hill: University of North Carolina Press, 1980), and Mary Beth Norton's *Liberty's Daughters: The Revolutionary Experience of American Women, 1750–1800* (Boston: Little, Brown & Co., 1980).

No student of separate spheres can afford to ignore Kathryn Kish Sklar, *Catharine Beecher: A Study in American Domesticity* (New Haven, Conn.: Yale University Press, 1973), a model of biography as social history. On Melusina Fay Peirce, see Sylvia Wright Mitarachi, "Melusina Fay Peirce: The Making of a Feminist" (Radcliffe Institute Working Paper, Radcliffe College, 1978), and Dolores Hayden, *The Grand Domestic Revolution: A History of Feminist Designs for American Homes, Neighborhoods and Cities* (Cambridge, Mass.: MIT Press, 1981). Hayden's careful and imaginative book places Peirce, Beecher, and Charlotte Perkins Gilman in a comprehensible tradition of domestic reform, and explores the architectural implications of what she calls "material feminism"; readers of my book will find in Hayden's work a very different but complementary scholarly treatment of many of the same issues, as well as some superb illustrations that will supplement the ones here. Another architectural viewpoint on similar issues may be found in Gwendolyn Wright, *Moralism and the Model Home: Domestic Architecture and Cultural Conflict in Chicago, 1873–1913* (Chicago: University of Chicago Press, 1980); Wright establishes connections between domestic reform and the architectural ideal of the single-family dwelling that supplement Hayden's discussion of collective dwellings.

With the exception of the work of Barbara Ehrenreich and Deirdre English, and of Emma Seifrit Weigley's generally uncritical "It Might Have Been Euthenics: The Lake Placid Conferences and the Home Economics Movement," *American Quarterly* 26 (March 1974): 79–96, modern discussion of the home economics movement is notably lacking. Ehrenreich and English, many of whose conclusions in "The Manufacture of Housework," *Socialist Revolution* 5 (October–December 1975): 5–40, and in *For Her Own Good: 150 Years of the Experts' Advice to Women* (New York: Doubleday & Co., Anchor Press, 1978), differ from my own, nonetheless provide an insightful critique essential to students who wish to understand early-twentieth-century domestic reform. See also my "The Business of Housekeeping," *Insurgent Sociologist* 8 (Fall 1978). Another perspective, particularly on child-rearing advice during this period, appears in Sheila M. Rothman, *Woman's Proper Place: A History of Changing Ideals and Practices, 1870 to the Present* (New York: Basic Books, 1978), which offers insight on the relationship between the experts' ideas and policy formation.

I owe much of my understanding of business and labor during the transition to monopoly capitalism to two very different books, Harry Braverman's *Labor and Monopoly Capital: The Degradation of Work in the Twentieth Century* (New York: Monthly Review Press, 1974) and Alfred Chandler's *The Visible Hand: The Managerial Revolution in American Business* (Cambridge, Mass.: Harvard University Press, 1977). Students of the issues Braverman discusses should supplement his work with Raymond Callahan, *Education and the Cult of Efficiency* (Chicago: University of Chicago Press, 1962); David Noble, *America by Design: Science, Technology, and the Rise of Corporate Capitalism* (New York: Oxford University Press, 1977); and Dan Clawson, *Bureaucracy and the Labor Process: The Transformation of U.S. Industry, 1860–1920* (New York: Monthly Review Press, 1980).

On the connections between twentieth-century household technology, advertising, and housework as a job, see again the work of Ruth Schwartz Cowan, especially "Two Washes in the Morning and a Bridge Party at Night: The American Housewife Between the Wars," *Women's Studies* 3 (1976): 147–71. Stuart Ewen's *Captains of Consciousness: Advertising and the Social Roots of the Consumer Culture* (New York: McGraw-Hill Book Co., 1976) contains indispensable information and unforgettable insights. Joann Vanek discusses time studies of housework in "Keeping Busy: Time Spent in Housework, United States, 1920–1970" (Ph.D. dissertation, University of Michigan, 1973) and in "Time Spent in Housework," *Scientific American*, November 1974, pp. 116–20. A broader sociological analysis may be found in Christine Bose, "Technology and Changes in the Division of Labor in the American Home," *Women's Studies International Quarterly* 2 (1979): 000–00.

Although our analyses and evidence differ profoundly, many of the concerns I express in the final chapters parallel those of Christopher Lasch, in *Haven in a Heartless World: The Family Besieged* (New York: Basic Books, 1977), *The Culture of Narcissism: American Life in an Age of Diminishing Expectations* (New York: Warner Books, 1979), and his many articles in the *New York Review of Books*. A different and intriguing twist from a global perspective may be found in Ivan Illich, *Shadow Work* (Boston: Marion Boyers, 1981), which links housework to other kinds of unpaid work in capitalist societies.

Source Notes

PREFACE

PAGE xiii "Handle unambiguous terms": E. P. Thompson, *The Poverty of Theory and Other Essays* (New York: Monthly Review Press, 1979), p. 38.

PROLOGUE. NEVER DONE

PAGE 4 Colonial household "the little commonwealth": John Demos, *A Little Commonwealth: Family Life in Plymouth Colony* (London: Oxford University Press, 1970).

CHAPTER 1. DAILY BREAD

PAGE 12 Colonial self-sufficiency: James T. Lemon, "Household Consumption in Eighteenth-Century America and Its Relationship to Production and Trade: The Situation Among Farmers in Southeastern Pennsylvania," *Agricultural History* 41 (1967): 59–70; Rodney Loehr, "Self-Sufficiency on the Farm (1759–1819)," *Agricultural History* 26 (1952): 37–42.

Rebecca Burlend: Rebecca Burlend, "A Yorkshire Family Settles in Illinois," in David B. Greenberg, ed., *Land That Our Fathers Plowed* (Norman: University of Oklahoma Press, 1969), pp. 67–84.

PAGE 14   "A form of condensed corn": Richard Osborn Cummings, *The American and His Food: A History of Food Habits in the United States* (Chicago: University of Chicago Press, 1940), p. 15.

Aversion to fresh meat: Cummings, *American and His Food*, pp. 16–17.

Hucksters: Karen J. Friedmann, "Victualling Colonial Boston," *Agricultural History* 47 (July 1973): 189–205; Carl Bridenbaugh, *Cities in the Wilderness: The First Century of Urban Life in America, 1625–1742* (New York: Capricorn Books, 1964), pp. 192–95, 349–53.

PAGE 15   "At the end of the Streets": Bridenbaugh, *Cities in the Wilderness*, p. 350.

PAGE 16   Housewives battle cart drivers: Cummings, *American and His Food*, p. 28.

Dickens on pigs in New York: Charles Dickens, *American Notes and Pictures from Italy* (London: Macmillan & Co., 1923), pp. 74–75.

Trollope on cows: Frances Trollope, *Domestic Manners of the Americans*, ed. Donald Smalley (New York: Vintage Books, 1960), pp. 61–62.

City diets: Cummings, *American and His Food*, pp. 25–36.

Rancid cream at Washington's: Cummings, *American and His Food*, p. 26.

Milk consumption: Cummings, *American and His Food*, pp. 53–57.

PAGE 17   Truck farms: Cummings, *American and His Food*, pp. 57–59; Edgar W. Martin, *The Standard of Living in 1860: American Consumption Levels on the Eve of the Civil War* (Chicago: University of Chicago Press, 1942), p. 29.

Wild game: Thomas F. Devoe, *The Market Assistant: Containing a Brief Description of Every Article of Human Food Sold in the Public Markets of the Cities of New York, Boston, Philadelphia, and Brooklyn* (New York: privately printed at the Riverside Press, 1867), pp. 110ff.

PAGE 18   Boston, Saint Louis, San Francisco markets: Martin, *Standard of Living in 1860*, pp. 20–21.

Small Midwest towns: Lewis Atherton, *Main Street on the Middle Border* (Chicago: Quadrangle Books, 1954), p. 62.

Household products at farmers' stalls: Devoe, *Market Assistant*, pp. 114ff., 400–16.

Hucksters: Martin, *Standard of Living in 1860*, p. 34.

Manuals: Devoe, *Market Assistant*, p. 25; F. B. Goddard, *Marketing: A Reliable Guide to the Purchase of Meats, Poultry, Game, Fish, Vegetables, Fruits, & All Other Articles of Food to be Found in the Markets of any City in the United States* (New York: Tradesman's Publishing Co., 1887), pp. 27–28.

Jo March: Louisa May Alcott, *Little Women* (New York: Penguin Books, 1953), p. 158.

Deteriorated and adulterated food: Martin, *Standard of Living in 1860*, p. 20n.

PAGE 19   "A singular agglomeration": quoted in Martin, *Standard of Living in 1860*, p. 19.

Ice harvesting: Cummings, *American and His Food*, pp. 36–39; see also Cummings's definitive work on the subject, *The American Ice Harvests: A Historical Study in Technology, 1800–1918* (Berkeley: University of California Press, 1949).

Walden ice harvest: Henry David Thoreau, *Walden, or, Life in the Woods* (New York: New American Library, Signet Classics, 1960), pp. 196–98.

City ice deliveries: Martin, *Standard of Living in 1860*, pp. 46–67.

Amy and Beth March: Alcott, *Little Women*, p. 43.

PAGE 20   Hale on snow packing: Sarah Josepha Hale, *The Good Housekeeper, or The Way to Live Well, and to Be Well While We Live*, 7th ed. (Boston: Otis, Broaders & Co., 1844), p. 37. See also (Mary Randolph), *The Virginia Housewife* (Washington, D.C.: Davis & Force, 1824), p. 23.

Refrigerator out of barrel: Catharine E. Beecher, *Miss Beecher's Domestic Receipt Book; Designed as a Supplement to Her Treatise on Domestic Economy*, 3rd ed. (New York: Harper & Brothers, 1848), p. 276.

Refrigerator description: Catharine E. Beecher and Harriet Beecher Stowe, *The American Woman's Home, or, Principles of Domestic Science* (New York: J. B. Ford & Co., 1869), p. 376.

PAGE 21   Artificial ice: Oscar Edward Anderson, Jr., *Refrigeration in America: A History of a New Technology and Its Impact* (Princeton, N.J.: Princeton University Press, 1953), pp. 86–96.

Ice statistics: Anderson, *Refrigeration in America*, pp. 114–15.

PAGE 22   New York workingmen: Robert Coit Chapin, *The Standard of Living Among Workingmen's Families in New York City* (New York: Russell Sage Foundation, Charities Publication Committee, 1909), p. 153.

Ice industry estimate: Anderson, *Refrigeration in America*, pp. 27, 115.

Portland, Oregon: "Cost of Living Survey—Portland, Oregon," *Reed College Bulletin* 4 (January 1925): 12.

"Housekeeper's Guide": Smith and Swinney, Chemists, etc., *The House-Keeper's Guide & Everybody's Handbook*, 10th ed. (Cincinnati, Ohio: privately published, 1871), pp. 81–83, 39–45.

Sugar preserving: Helen Campbell, *The Easiest Way in Housekeeping and Cooking* (New York: Fords, Howard & Hulbert, 1881), pp. 244–47.

Canning invention: Cummings, *American and His Food*, p. 68.

Canning supplies in country stores: Cummings, *American and His Food*, p. 85.

Pressure cooker: Earl Lifshey, *The Housewares Story: A History of the American Housewares Industry* (Chicago: National Housewares Manufacturers Association, 1973), pp. 176–80.

"The only method recommended": Irma S. Rombauer and Marion Rombauer Becker, *The Joy of Cooking*, rev. ed. (Indianapolis: Bobbs-Merrill Co., 1964), p. 746.

Campbell on vegetables: Campbell, *Easiest Way*, pp. 244–47.

Another 1880s cookbook: Mrs. F. L. Gillette and Hugo Ziemann, *The White House Cook Book* (New York: J. A. Hill & Co., 1889), pp. 389–93.

PAGE 23   Glass blowing: Robert S. Lynd and Helen Merrell Lynd, *Middletown: A Study in Modern American Culture* (New York: Harcourt, Brace & World, 1929), p. 41.

"We Can Can Vegetables": Cummings, *American and His Food*, p. 139.

Gold rush and Civil War: Cummings, *American and His Food*, pp. 67–69; James Collins, *The Story of Canned Foods* (New York: E. P. Dutton & Co., 1924), pp. 95–104.

Can openers recommended: Campbell, *Easiest Way*, p. 268; Gillette and Ziemann, *White House Cook Book*, p. 539.

Franco-American advertising: O. Blardot, "Advertising of Soups," *Printer's Ink*, March 29, 1893, p. 420.

Bakers in colonial towns: Bridenbaugh, *Cities in the Wilderness*, p. 36; see also Friedmann, "Victualling Colonial Boston," p. 138.

Hale on bread baking: Hale, *Good Housekeeper*, pp. 30–31.

Midwestern baker: Lynd and Lynd, *Middletown*, p. 155.

PAGE 24   Cracker bakeries: Martin, *Standard of Living in 1860*, p. 54.

"Business was carried on in much the same manner": Alfred D. Chandler, Jr., *The Visible Hand: The Managerial Revolution in American Business* (Cambridge, Mass.: Harvard University Press, 1977), p. 37. The following discussion relies heavily on Chandler's interpretation.

PAGE 26   "New process" mills: Chandler, *Visible Hand*, p. 253.

Can factories: Earl C. May, *The Canning Clan* (New York: Macmillan Co., 1937), pp. 350–51.

PAGE 28   Homestead chickens: Margaret F. Byington, *Homestead: The Households of a Mill Town* (New York: Russell Sage Foundation, 1910), p. 48.

Manchester livestock: Tamara K. Hareven and Randolph Langenbach, *Amoskeag: Life and Work in an American Factory-City* (New York: Pantheon Books, 1978), p. 165.

Muncie seed-store proprietor: Lynd and Lynd, *Middletown*, p. 95.

Homestead gardens: Byington, *Homestead*, p. 48.

Frontier sharing: Burlend, "A Yorkshire Family Settles in Illinois," p. 69.

PAGE 29   Month-by-month market list: Gillette and Ziemann, *White House Cook Book*, pp. 421–27.

Muncie winter diet: Lynd and Lynd, *Middletown*, p. 156.

CHAPTER 2. OUT OF THE FRYING PAN

PAGE 33   "Hall" in colonial New England: John Demos, *A Little Commonwealth: Family Life in Plymouth Colony* (London: Oxford University Press, 1970), pp. 30ff.

Plantation eating ritual more elaborate: Julia Cherry Spruill, *Women's Life and Work in the Southern Colonies* (New York: W. W. Norton & Co., 1972), pp. 68–72.

Fireplace utensils: Demos, *A Little Commonwealth*, pp. 39–41; Alice Morse

Earle, *Home Life in Colonial Days* (New York: Macmillan Co., 1898), pp. 52–68; Allison Ravetz, "The Victorian Coal Kitchen and Its Reformers," *Victorian Studies* 11 (June 1968): 435–60.

PAGE 35   "So hot as to allow it to be closed": Catharine E. Beecher, *Miss Beecher's Domestic Receipt Book; Designed as a Supplement to Her Treatise on Domestic Economy*, 3rd ed. (New York: Harper & Brothers, 1848), p. 83.

PAGE 36   Foundries: Victor S. Clark, *History of Manufactures in the United States*, vol. 1, *1607–1860* (New York: McGraw-Hill Book Co. for Carnegie Institution of Washington, 1929), p. 503.

Cooking adjustments for stoves: Beecher, *Domestic Receipt Book*, pp. 260ff, 83. See also Sarah Josepha Hale, *The Ladies' New Book of Cookery*, 5th ed. (New York: H. Long & Brother, 1852): for pictures, pp. 5, 28, 75, 221; roasting, p. 71; adjustments, p. 262.

"Put it on the fire," etc.: Mary Randolph, *The Virginia Housewife: or Methodical Cook* (Philadelphia: E. H. Butler & Co., 1860), *passim*. This is a late edition of an extremely popular early cookbook which was published many times, by many publishers.

"Set the pot in the chimney corner": Hale, *Ladies' New Book of Cookery*, p. 236.

"Baked Beef": Mrs. Washington [pseud.], *The Unrivalled Cook-Book & Housekeeper's Guide* (New York: Harper & Brothers, 1885), pp. 85, 87.

"The most convenient mode": Catharine E. Beecher and Harriet Beecher Stowe, *The American Woman's Home, or, Principles of Domestic Science* (New York: J. B. Ford & Co., 1869), p. 69.

PAGE 37   "We cannot but regret": Beecher and Stowe, *American Woman's Home*, p. 175.

"A common tin oven": Beecher and Stowe, *American Woman's Home*, p. 73.

"A vigorously plastic type": Siegfried Giedion, *Mechanization Takes Command: A Contribution to Anonymous History* (New York: W. W. Norton & Co., 1948), p. 536.

PAGE 38   Sears's 1897 stoves: Sears, Roebuck & Co., *1897 Sears Catalogue*, ed. Fred L. Israel (New York: Chelsea House, 1968), pp. 119–24.

New metal processes: Clark, *History of Manufactures*, vol. 3, *1893–1928*, pp. 84–85.

Sears's 1908 stoves: Sears, Roebuck & Co., *1908 Catalogue No. 117*, ed. Joseph J. Schroeder, Jr. (Chicago: Follett Publishing Co., 1969), pp. 626–41.

Nellie Kedzie Jones: Jeanne Hunnicutt Delgado, "Nellie Kedzie Jones's Advise to Farm Women: Letters from Wisconsin, 1912–1916," *Wisconsin Magazine of History* 57 (Autumn 1973): 7.

PAGE 40   "The most common modes of cooking": Beecher and Stowe, *American Woman's Home*, p. 69.

Dampers: Sears, *1897 Catalogue*, p. 119.

"Here's a sweet prospect": Louisa May Alcott, *Little Women* (New York: Penguin Books, 1953), p. 158.

PAGE 41   Stove directions: Helen Campbell, *The Easiest Way in Housekeeping and Cooking* (New York: Fords, Howard & Hulbert, 1881), pp. 46–47.

Boston experiment: Massachusetts Bureau of Statistics of Labor, *Comparison of the Cost of Home-Made and Prepared Food*, reprint from *Massachusetts Labor Bulletin* no. 19, August 1901 (Boston: Wright & Potter Printing Co., State Printers, 1901), pp. 11–12.

Amounts of coal and wood: Beecher and Stowe, *American Woman's Home*, p. 361.

Scavenged fuel or paid dearly: See Oscar Handlin, *Boston's Immigrants: A Study in Acculturation*, rev. ed. (New York: Atheneum Publishers, 1968), p. 112.

Campbell on coal: *Easiest Way*, p. 47.

PAGE 42   "Be sure and buy the same size": Sears, *1897 Catalogue*, p. 128.

"Convenient little device": Sears, *1908 Catalogue*, p. 63.

Enamelware: Earl Lifshey, *The Housewares Story: A History of the American Housewares Industry* (Chicago: National Housewares Manufacturers Association, 1973), pp. 153–54.

PAGE 43   Sears enamel: Sears, *1897 Catalogue*, pp. 130–31.

Aluminum ware: Lifshey, *Housewares Story*, pp. 164–68.

PAGE 44   "First quality and guaranteed perfect": Sears, *1897 Catalogue*, p. 128.

"Aluminum being now nearly as cheap": Sears, *1897 Catalogue*, pp. 128, 130, 135–36.

Crockery, basketry, wood, tin: Beecher and Stowe, *American Woman's Home*, p. 373; Catharine E. Beecher, *A Treatise on Domestic Economy for the Use of Young Ladies at Home and at School* (New York: Marsh, Capen, Lyon & Webb, 1841), p. 373. See also Count Rumford [Benjamin Thompson], *Collected Works*, vol. 3, *Devices and Techniques*, ed. Sanborn C. Brown (Cambridge, Mass.: Harvard University Press, Belknap Press, 1969), pp. 231–42.

"A mill, for spice": Beecher and Stowe, *American Woman's Home*, p. 374.

"Every article required": Campbell, *Easiest Way*, p. 51.

PAGE 45   Campbell's list: *Easist Way*, pp. 267–69.

"Celebrated as the best beater made": Sears, *1897 Catalogue*, p. 134.

"Many complicated patent arrangements": Campbell, *Easiest Way*, p. 51.

Sears's prices: *1897 Catalogue*, pp. 102, 128, 133–34.

PAGE 46   Hannah Lambertson: Dorothy Gallagher, *Hannah's Daughters: Six Generations of an American Family, 1876–1976* (New York: Thomas Y. Crowell Co., 1976), p. 55.

Gadget prices: Montgomery Ward & Co., *1894–95 Catalogue and Buyers Guide No. 56.*, ed. Joseph J. Schroeder, Jr. (Northfield, Ill.: DBI Books, 1977), p. 548. For nearly identical prices, see Sears, *1897 Catalogue*, pp. 143–44.

Government estimate: U.S. Department of Labor, Bureau of Labor Statistics, *Tentative Quantity and Cost Budget Necessary to Maintain a Family of Five in Washington, D.C. at a Level of Health and Decency* (Washington, D.C.: Government Printing Office, 1919), p. 63.

PAGE 47   Rachel Haskell: "A Literate Woman in the Mines: The Diary of Rachel Haskell," in Christiane Fischer, ed., *Let Them Speak for Themselves: Women in the American West, 1849–1900* (New York: E. P. Dutton & Co., 1977), pp. 62–66.

Emily Dickinson: Millicent Todd Bingham, *Emily Dickinson's Home: The Early Years as Revealed in Family Correspondence and Reminiscences* (New York: Dover Publications, 1967), pp. 114–15.

CHAPTER 3. THE HOME FIRES

PAGE 51   Early colonists confined to "hall": John Demos, *A Little Commonwealth: Family Life in Plymouth Colony* (London: Oxford University Press, 1970), p. 46.

Colonial diaries: Alice Morse Earle, *Home Life in Colonial Days* (New York: Macmillan Co., 1898), pp. 70–71.

Dutch and German stoves: Earle, *Home Life in Colonial Days*, pp. 70–71; Siegfried Giedion, *Mechanization Takes Command: A Contribution to Anonymous History* (New York: W. W. Norton & Co., 1948), pp. 528–30.

PAGE 53   "There is no sight of the fire": quoted in Giedion, *Mechanization Takes Command*, p. 530.

Translucent mica doors: Sears, Roebuck & Co., *1897 Sears Catalogue*, ed. Fred L. Israel (New York: Chelsea House, 1968), p. 125.

Harriet Beecher Stowe on hearth fires: Quoted in David Handlin, *The American Home: Architecture and Society, 1815–1915* (Boston: Little, Brown & Co., 1979), pp. 478–79.

Furnaces: Reyner Banham, *The Architecture of the Well-Tempered Environment* (Chicago: University of Chicago Press, 1969), p. 49; Edgar W. Martin, *The Standard of Living in 1860: American Consumption Levels on the Eve of the Civil War* (Chicago: University of Chicago Press, 1942), p. 93.

Beecher's 1869 heating plans: Catharine E. Beecher and Harriet Beecher Stowe, *The American Woman's Home, or, Principles of Domestic Science* (New York: J. B. Ford & Co., 1869), pp. 79–83, 419–27.

PAGE 54   Beecher's 1841 heating plans: Catharine E. Beecher, *A Treatise on Domestic Economy for the Use of Young Ladies at Home and at School* (New York: Marsh, Capen, Lyon & Webb, 1841), pp. 274–88. For a comparison of Beecher's 1841 and 1869 plans, see James Marston Fitch, *Architecture and the Esthetics of Plenty* (New York: Columbia University Press, 1961), pp. 73, 77.

Sears's 1908 furnaces: Sears, Roebuck & Co., *1908 Catalogue No. 117*, ed. Joseph J. Schroeder, Jr. (Chicago: Follett Publishing Co., 1969), pp. 159, 613.

"Although most of the working class . . .": Robert S. Lynd and Helen Merrell Lynd, *Middletown: A Study in Modern American Culture* (New York: Harcourt, Brace & World, 1929), p. 96.

Wood and coal in colonial towns: Carl Bridenbaugh, *Cities in the Wilderness: The First Century of Urban Life in America, 1625–1742* (New York: Capricorn Books, 1964), pp. 12, 151–52, 311–13.

Domestic versus imported coal: Victor S. Clark, *History of Manufactures in the United States*, vol. 1, *1607–1860* (New York: McGraw-Hill Book Co. for Carnegie Institution of Washington, 1929), p. 331.

Coal statistics: U.S. Department of Commerce, Bureau of the Census, *Historical Statistics of the United States, Colonial Times to 1970* (Washington, D.C.: Government Printing Office, 1975), p. 580.

Grates: Beecher and Stowe, *American Woman's Home*, p. 361.

PAGE 55   "Start your fire in the fall": Sears, *1908 Catalogue*, p. 650.

Central steam heat: Handlin, *American Home*, p. 479; Lynd and Lynd, *Middletown*, p. 96.

PAGE 56   "Communism in Hot-Air": from *American Architect and Building News*, quoted in Handlin, *American Home*, p. 479.

PAGE 57   "It saves, too, more than that": Harriet Beecher Stowe, *House and Home Papers*, quoted in Beecher and Stowe, *American Woman's Home*, p. 50.

Carbon monoxide and carbon dioxide: Beecher and Stowe, *American Woman's Home*, pp. 47ff, 82.

Stove defects: Beecher and Stowe, *American Woman's Home*, pp. 76–78.

"Sucks up, like a sponge": Beecher and Stowe, *American Woman's Home*, p. 80.

Alice LaCasse: Tamara K. Hareven and Randolph Langenbach, *Amoskeag: Life and Work in an American Factory-City* (New York: Pantheon Books, 1978), p. 258.

Jo March: Louisa May Alcott, *Little Women* (New York: Penguin Books, 1953), pp. 47, 50, 55.

Beecher on fire danger: *Treatise on Domestic Economy*, p. 372.

PAGE 58   Christie Devon: Louisa May Alcott, *Work, A Story of Experience* (New York: Schocken Books, 1977), p. 32.

Candlemaking: Earle, *Home Life in Colonial Days*, pp. 35–38.

Cooperative candlemaking: Julia Cherry Spruill, *Women's Life and Work in the Southern Colonies* (New York: W. W. Norton & Co., 1972), p. 110.

Pine knots: Earle, *Home Life in Colonial Days*, pp. 31ff.

Rebecca Burlend: Rebecca Burlend, "A Yorkshire Family Settles in Illinois," in David B. Greenberg, *Land That Our Fathers Plowed* (Norman: University of Oklahoma Press, 1969), p. 71.

Floating tapers: Beecher, *Treatise on Domestic Economy*, p. 306.

PAGE 60   "Used only on rare occasions": Beecher and Stowe, *American Woman's Home*, p. 362.

Candle industry: Clark, *History of Manufactures*, vol. 1, pp. 86, 97, 184, 271, 492.

Argand burner: Beecher and Stowe, *American Woman's Home*, p. 362.

"Afford a clearer and steadier light": Beecher, *Treatise on Domestic Economy*, p. 303.

Illuminants: Clark, *History of Manufactures*, vol. 1, pp. 493–94.

"To such an extent . . .": Beecher and Stowe, *American Woman's Home*, p. 363.

PAGE 61   "Always attended by great peril": Beecher and Stowe, *American Woman's Home*, p. 364.

"We do not solicit kerosene oil trade": Sears, *1897 Catalogue*, p. 20.

Candlepower of lamps: Martin, *Standard of Living in 1860*, p. 96.

Beecher warnings: reading in bed, *Treatise on Domestic Economy*, p. 372; *American Woman's Home*, p. 352; heat of lamp, *American Woman's Home*, p. 363.

Other lamp advice: Helen Campbell, *The Easiest Way in Housekeeping and Cooking* (New York: Fords, Howard & Hulbert, 1881), p. 66.

Haskell on lamp cleaning: "A Literate Woman in the Mines: The Diary of Rachel Haskell," in Christiane Fischer, ed., *Let Them Speak for Themselves: Women in the American West, 1849–1900* (New York: E. P. Dutton & Co., 1977), p. 66.

Domestic writers' advice: Beecher and Stowe, *American Woman's Home*, p. 364; Campbell, *Easiest Way*, p. 50.

PAGE 62   Emily Dickinson: Millicent Todd Bingham, *Emily Dickinson's Home: The Early Years as Revealed in Family Correspondence and Reminiscences* (New York: Dover Publications, 1967), p. 117.

Campbell on housecleaning: *Easiest Way*, pp. 60–62.

"A general housewrecking process": Jeanne Hunnicutt Delgado, "Nellie Kedzie Jones's Advice to Farm Women: Letters from Wisconsin, 1912–1916," *Wisconsin Magazine of History* 57 (Autumn 1973): 17.

Muncie merchant on housecleaning: Lynd and Lynd, *Middletown*, p. 171n.

PAGE 63   Stowe on spring: *House and Home Papers*, quoted in Beecher and Stowe, *American Woman's Home*, pp. 50–51.

"Where it escaped the espionage": Sarah A. Emery, "Reminiscences of a Nonagenarian" (1879), quoted in David H. Flaherty, *Privacy in Colonial New England* (Charlottesville: University Press of Virginia, 1972), p. 73n.

"Aunt Nellie": Delgado, "Nellie Kedzie Jones's Advice," pp. 11–12.

PAGE 64   Focussed versus framed space: Banham, *Architecture of the Well-Tempered Environment*, p. 55.

Homestead, Pennsylvania: Margaret F. Byington, *Homestead: The Households of a Mill Town* (1910; reprint ed., Pittsburgh: University Center for International Studies, 1974), p. 55.

PAGE 65   Rachel Haskell: "A Literate Woman," in Fischer, ed., *Let Them Speak*, pp. 58–72.

CHAPTER 4. AT THE FLICK OF A SWITCH

PAGE 68   Baltimore gas company: Louis Stotz and Alexander Jamison, *History of the Gas Industry* (New York: Press of Stettiner Bros., 1938), pp. 13–16.

New York City gas company: Stotz and Jamison, *History of the Gas Industry*, pp. 20–40.

PAGE 69   Three hundred gas companies: see chronological list in Denys Peter Myers, *Gaslighting in America: A Guide for Historic Preservation* (Washington, D.C.: U.S. Department of the Interior, Heritage Conservation and Recreation Service, 1978), pp. 249–52. See also Edgar W. Martin, *The Standard of Living in 1860: American Consumption Levels on the Eve of the Civil War* (Chicago: University of Chicago Press, 1942), pp. 96–97.

PAGE 70   Coke and gas manufacturing: Victor S. Clark, *History of Manufactures in the United States*, vol. 2, *1860–1893* (New York: McGraw-Hill Book Co. for Carnegie Institution of Washington, 1929), pp. 515–16.

Coal gas and water gas methods of manufacture: Clark, *History of Manufactures*, vol. 2, p. 516; Stotz and Jamison, *History of the Gas Industry*, pp. 4–5; Elizabeth Mickle Bacon, "The Growth of Household Conveniences in the United States from 1865 to 1900" (unpublished Ph.D. dissertation, Radcliffe,

1942); "Gas, an Ideal Fuel," (New York: Dominick and Dominick, 1930), pp. 6–7.

Natural gas: "Gas, an Ideal Fuel," p. 5; Stotz and Jamison, *History of the Gas Industry*, pp. 67–91; Clark, *History of Manufactures*, vol. 2, p. 517; Alfred M. Leeston, John A. Crichton, and John C. Jacobs, *The Dynamic Natural Gas Industry* (Norman: University of Oklahoma Press, 1963), pp. 4–9.

PAGE 71 Public-building fixtures: Myers, *Gaslighting in America*, pp. 3, 35, 43, 115–27.

Stewart and Vanderbilt fixtures: Myers, *Gaslighting in America*, pp. 141–43, 147.

"An increasingly futile rearguard action": Myers, *Gaslighting in America*, p. 207.

Living Among Workingmen's Families in New York City (New York: Russell Sage Foundation, Charities Publication Committee, 1909), p. 117; New York City Bureau of Standards, *Report on the Cost of Living for an Unskilled Laborer's Family in New York City* (n.p., n.d.—1915 stamped in Library of Congress copy), p. 36.

PAGE 72 Columbian Exposition: William E. Cameron, *The World's Fair, Being a Pictorial History of the Columbian Exposition* (Chicago: Chicago Publication & Lithograph Co., 1893), pp. 327, 467, 718.

PAGE 73 A total system "for generating," etc.: Reyner Banham, *The Architecture of the Well-Tempered Environment* (Chicago: University of Chicago Press, 1969), pp. 60–61.

"A minor invention every ten days": Edison, quoted in David F. Noble, *America by Design: Science, Technology, and the Rise of Corporate Capitalism* (New York: Oxford University Press, 1977), p. 8.

Edison's financial backing: Noble, *America by Design*, pp. 8–9; Alfred D. Chandler, Jr., *The Visible Hand: The Managerial Revolution in American Business* (Cambridge, Mass.: Harvard University Press, 1977), pp. 426–28.

PAGE 74 Financiers and electrical manufacturers: Chandler, *Visible Hand*, p. 426.

"The basic organizational form": Chandler, *Visible Hand*, p. 417.

"Pricing, competitors' activities": Chandler, *Visible Hand*, p. 430.

Electrical salesmen: Chandler, *Visible Hand*, pp. 309–10.

Toaster and Cousin Mary's waffle iron: "When You Buy Electrical Equipment," *American Cookery* 29 (February 1925): 606.

"It is unwise to attempt repairs": R. C. Tarr, "Electrical Measurements in the Household," *American Cookery* 29 (March 1925): 606.

PAGE 76 Mrs. Cornelius Vanderbilt: David P. Handlin, *The American Home: Architecture and Society, 1815–1915* (Boston: Little, Brown & Co., 1979), p. 474.

Columbian Exposition model house: Cameron, *The World's Fair*, p. 327.

GE ad in *McClure's*: "The Lamp That Lights the Way to Lighter Housework," *McClure's*, September 1917, p. 55.

PAGE 78 Ads after World War I, and "tell-tale gray" quotation: Ruth Schwartz Cowan, "Two Washes in the Morning and a Bridge Party at Night: The American Housewife Between the Wars," *Women's Studies* 3 (1976): pp. 149–51.

Muncie electric company ad: quoted in Robert S. Lynd and Helen Merrell

Lynd, *Middletown: A Study in Modern American Culture* (New York: Harcourt, Brace & World, 1929), p. 173.

Electric irons: Earl Lifshey, *The Housewares Story: A History of the American Housewares Industry* (Chicago: National Housewares Manufacturers Association, 1973), pp. 229–31.

Zanesville and thirty-six other cities: R. O. Eastman, Inc., *Zanesville and Thirty-Six Other American Communities: A Study of Markets and of the Telephone as a Market Index* (New York: Literary Digest, 1927), pp. 68–69.

Carpet sweepers and vacuum cleaners: Lifshey, *Housewares Story*, pp. 290–300.

PAGE 79   "Almost every woman": Marion Harland, *The New Common Sense in the Household" by Marion Harland Revised for Gas and Electricity by her Daughter Christine Terhune Herrick* (New York: Frederick A. Stokes Co., 1926), p. 323.

The New Common Sense on vacuum cleaners: Harland, *New Common Sense*, pp. 322–25.

PAGE 80   Toasters: Lifshey, *Housewares Story*, pp. 254–57; in Zanesville: Eastman, Inc., *Zanesville*, p. 71.

Toastmaster ad: *Saturday Evening Post*, March 5, 1927, reproduced in Lifshey, *Housewares Story*, p. 256.

Highly specialized appliances: E. S. Lincoln, *The Electric Home, A Standard Ready Reference Book* (New York: Electric Home Publishing Co., 1934), pp. 344–47.

PAGE 81   Economy in ads: reproduced in Lifshey, *Housewares Story*: GE toaster, p. 255; Hoover sweeper, p. 297; GE iron, p. 233.

"Replace the old-style lamps": 1912 GE ad reproduced in Lifshey, *Housewares Story*, p. 226.

"What Every Woman Wants": reproduced in Lifshey, *Housewares Story*, p. 226.

Electricity statistics: U.S. Department of Commerce, Bureau of the Census, *Historical Statistics of the United States, Colonial Times to 1970* (Washington, D.C.: Government Printing Office, 1975), p. 827.

Bureau of Labor Statistics study: U.S. Department of Labor, Bureau of Labor Statistics, *Cost of Living in the United States*, Bulletin no. 357 (Washington, D.C.: Government Printing Office, 1924), p. 391.

PAGE 82   Bryn Mawr graduate seminar: Quoted in Belle Boone Beard, *Electricity in the Home* (New York: Workers Education Bureau Press, 1927), p. 11.

"Relatively recent factors": Beard, *Electricity in the Home*, p. 9.

CHAPTER 5. FETCH A PAIL OF WATER

PAGE 86   George Vanderbilt's bathroom: Siegfried Giedion, *Mechanization Takes Command: A Contribution to Anonymous History* (New York: W. W. Norton & Co., 1948), pp. 686–87, 699.

Farmer's Alliance organizer: *The Progressive Farmer* (Winston, N.C.), December 3, 1886, p. 4.

PAGE 87   "Aunt Nellie": Jeanne Hunnicutt Delgado, "Nellie Kedzie Jones's

Advice to Farm Women: Letters from Wisconsin, 1912–1916," *Wisconsin Magazine of History* 57 (Autumn 1973): 8.

PAGE 88   "If the washerwoman . . .": Catharine E. Beecher, *A Treatise on Domestic Economy for the Use of Young Ladies at Home and at School* (New York: Marsh, Capen, Lyon & Webb, 1841), p. 308.

Laundry directions: Beecher, *Treatise on Domestic Economy*, pp. 310–11.

PAGE 89   "Wire dish cloth": Helen Campbell, *The Easiest Way in Housekeeping and Cooking* (New York: Fords, Howard & Hulbert, 1881), p. 89.

Soap: Edgar W. Martin, *The Standard of Living in 1860: American Consumption Levels on the Eve of the Civil War* (Chicago: University of Chicago Press, 1942), p. 216.

Other cleaning agents: Elizabeth Mickle Bacon, "The Growth of Household Conveniences in the United States from 1865 to 1900" (unpublished Ph.D. dissertation, Radcliffe College, 1942), pp. 48, 58.

Dishwashing instructions: Beecher, *Treatise on Domestic Economy*, p. 368; Campbell, *Easiest Way*, p. 40; Catharine Beecher and Harriet Beecher Stowe, *The American Woman's Home, or, Principles of Domestic Science* (New York: J. B. Ford & Co., 1869), pp. 372–73.

Philadelphia water: Sam Bass Warner, Jr., *The Private City: Philadelphia in Three Periods of Its Growth* (Philadelphia: University of Pennsylvania Press, 1968), pp. 107–8.

PAGE 90   Lydia Maria Child on bathing: Lydia Maria Child, *Letters from New York*, 11th ed. (New York: C. S. Francis & Co., 1850), p. 169.

PAGE 92   James Marston Fitch: *American Building: The Historical Forces That Shaped It*, 2nd ed. (Boston: Houghton Mifflin Co., 1966), p. 69.

Philadelphia waterworks: Warner, *Private City*, pp. 102–7.

Dickens on Philadelphia waterworks: Charles Dickens, *American Notes and Pictures from Italy* (London: Macmillan & Co., 1923), p. 85.

Child on Croton Aqueduct: *Letters from New York*, pp. 167–69.

PAGE 93   Cities with waterworks: Everett Dick, *The Sod House Frontier, 1854–1890* (New York: D. Appleton-Century Co., 1937), p. 398; F. E. Turneaure and H. L. Russell, *Public Water-Supplies*, 3rd ed. (New York: John Wiley & Sons, 1924), p. 9.

PAGE 94   Chicago sewers: Bacon, "Growth of Household Conveniences," p. 118; Martin, *Standard of Living in 1860*, pp. 242–43.

Boston sewers: Sam Bass Warner, Jr., *Streetcar Suburbs: The Process of Growth in Boston, 1870–1900* (Cambridge: Harvard University Press and M.I.T. Press, 1962), p. 30.

Boston reformer Atkinson: Edward Atkinson, "Invention in Its Effects Upon Household Economy," *Proceedings and Addresses, Celebration of the Beginning of the Second Century of the American Patent System at Washington City, D.C., April 8, 9, 10, 1891* (Washington: Press of Gedney & Roberts Co., 1892), pp. 221–22.

Sewage and porous brickwork: George E. Waring, Jr., *Draining for Profit and Draining for Health*, rev. ed. (New York: Orange Judd Co., 1911), p. 228.

Sewer gas: James C. Bayles, *House Drainage and Water Service: In Cities, Villages, and Rural Neighborhoods, with Incidental Consideration of Causes*

Affecting the Healthfulness of Dwellings (New York: David Williams, 1878), pp. 23–43.

One architectural historian: David Handlin, *The American Home: Architecture and Society, 1815–1915* (Boston: Little, Brown & Co., 1979), pp. 455–71.

PAGE 95   Earth closet: Centennial: U.S. Centennial Commission, *International Exhibition 1876, Reports and Awards* (Philadelphia: J. B. Lippincott Co., 1877), group 14, pp. 37–38. Beecher: *American Woman's Home*, pp. 403–18. Waring: Handlin, *American Home*, pp. 460–63.

"The chance to get rid of human wastes": Handlin, *American Home*, p. 463.

"The most disagreeable item": Beecher and Stowe, *American Woman's Home*, p. 403.

PAGE 96   "Their visits to the privy": Bayles, *House Drainage and Water Service*, p. 268. For similar comments from Waring, see Handlin, *American Home*, pp. 459–60.

Extra fee for bathtubs: Martin, *Standard of Living in 1860*, p. 112.

Beecher 1841 house plan: *Treatise on Domestic Economy*, pp. 293–94.

Beecher 1869 house plan: *American Woman's Home*, pp. 32–41.

"The water closets must have the latest improvements": Beecher and Stowe, *American Woman's Home*, p. 38.

Sears's sanitary supplies: Sears, Roebuck & Co., *1897 Sears Catalogue*, ed. Fred L. Israel (New York: Chelsea House, 1968), pp. 55–56, 134, 682–83.

PAGE 97   Muncie plumbing: Robert S. Lynd and Helen Merrell Lynd, *Middletown: A Study in Modern American Culture* (New York: Harcourt, Brace & World, 1929), p. 27.

Harriet Beecher Stowe's sink: Annie Fields, ed., *Life and Letters of Harriet Beecher Stowe* (Boston: Houghton Mifflin Co., 1898), pp. 125–28.

Sanitary facilities in Homestead: Margaret F. Byington, *Homestead: The Households of a Mill Town* (1910; reprint ed., Pittsburgh: University Center for International Studies, 1974), pp. 53–55.

PAGE 100   Chapin on New York workers: Robert Coit Chapin, *The Standard of Living Among Workingmen's Families in New York City* (New York: Russell Sage Foundation, Charities Publication Committee, 1909), p. 79.

Florence Nesbitt: Florence Nesbitt, *The Chicago Standard Budget for Dependent Families* (Chicago: Committee on Relief of Chicago Council of Social Agencies, 1919), p. 4.

Ernest Anderson: Tamara K. Hareven and Randolph Langenbach, *Amoskeag: Life and Work in an American Factory-City* (New York: Pantheon Books, 1978), p. 145.

Sears's plumbing outfits: Sears, Roebuck & Co., *1908 Catalogue No. 117*, ed. Joseph J. Schroeder, Jr. (Chicago: Follett Publishing Co., 1969), pp. 604ff.

Mass production of tubs: Giedion, *Mechanization Takes Command*, p. 703.

Production of sanitary fixtures: Giedion, *Mechanization Takes Command*, p. 685.

PAGE 102   Zanesville, Ohio: R. O. Eastman, Inc., *Zanesville and Thirty-Six Other American Communities: A Study of Markets and of the Telephone as a Market Index* (New York: Literary Digest, 1927), p. 63.

Chicago public welfare: Elizabeth A. Hughes, *Living Conditions for Small-*

Wage Earners in Chicago (Chicago: Department of Public Welfare, 1925), p. 30.

PAGE 103   President's Conference: quoted in Ruth Schwartz Cowan, "The 'Industrial Revolution' in the Home: Household Technology and Social Change in the 20th Century," *Technology and Culture* 17 (January 1976): 4.

CHAPTER 6. BLUE MONDAY

PAGE 104   Haskell on laundry: "A Literate Woman in the Mines: The Diary of Rachel Haskell," in Christiane Fischer, ed., *Let Them Speak for Themselves: Women in the American West, 1849–1900* (New York: E. P. Dutton & Co., 1977), pp. 65, 68.

PAGE 105   "The American housekeeper's hardest problem": Catharine E. Beecher and Harriet Beecher Stowe, *The American Woman's Home, or, Principles of Domestic Science* (New York: J. B. Ford & Co., 1869), p. 334.

Washing instructions: Catharine E. Beecher, *A Treatise on Domestic Economy for the Use of Young Ladies at Home and at School* (New York: Marsh, Capen, Lyon & Webb, 1841), pp. 310–12; Helen Campbell, *The Easiest Way in Housekeeping and Cooking* (New York: Fords, Howard & Hulbert, 1881), pp. 55–58.

PAGE 106   "Before dirt has had time to harden": Campbell, *Easiest Way*, p. 54.

PAGE 107   "Said she'd wash on the day she wanted to": Karen V. Hansen, "Taking Back the Day: The Historical Recovery of Women's Household Work Experience," unpublished manuscript, August 1979, p. 91.

PAGE 108   "Awaiting their turn at the pump": Margaret F. Byington, *Homestead: The Households of a Mill Town* (1910; reprint ed., Pittsburgh: University Center for International Studies, 1974), p. 131; see also p. 136.

Washday meals: Hansen, "Taking Back the Day," p. 70.

"Eat a cold dinner on washday": Susan J. Kleinberg, "Technology and Women's Work: The Lives of Working Class Women in Pittsburgh, 1870–1900," *Labor History* 17 (Winter 1976): 70.

Ironing advice: Beecher, *Treatise on Domestic Economy*, pp. 323–25; Campbell, *Easiest Way*, pp. 58–59.

Montgomery Ward's ironing boards: Montgomery Ward & Co., *1894–95 Catalogue & Buyers Guide No. 56*, ed. Joseph J. Schroeder, Jr. (Northfield, Ill.: DBI Books, 1977), p. 552.

"Would really get the pressing done": Hansen, "Taking Back the Day," p. 71.

PAGE 109   Colonial newspapers: Julia Cherry Spruill, *Women's Life and Work in the Southern Colonies* (New York: W. W. Norton & Co., 1972), pp. 286–87.

Letter from California: Abby Mansur, "MS Letters Written to Her Sister, 1852–1854," in Fischer, ed., *Let Them Speak for Themselves*, pp. 55–56.

"The washing was too much for me": Mary Mathews, "Ten Years in Nevada, or, Life on the Pacific Coast," in Fischer, *Let Them Speak for Themselves*, p. 180.

PAGE 111   Mary Mathews: "Ten Years in Nevada," in Fischer, *Let Them Speak for Themselves*, pp. 183–89.

PAGE 112   Neighborhood laundries: Beecher and Stowe, *American Woman's Home*, p. 334.

Melusina Fay Peirce: Mrs. C. F. Peirce, "Cooperative Housekeeping," *Atlantic Monthly*, November 1868, pp. 513–24; December 1868, pp. 682–97; January 1869, pp. 29–39; February 1869, pp. 161–71; March 1869, pp. 282–94.

Cambridge Cooperative Housekeeping Society: Dolores Hayden, "Melusina Fay Peirce and Cooperative Housekeeping," *International Journal of Urban and Regional Research* 2 (1978): 409–10.

PAGE 113   *Wisconsin Agriculturalist*: quoted in Jeanne Hunnicutt Delgado, "Nellie Kedzie Jones's Advice to Farm Women: Letters from Wisconsin, 1912–1916," *Wisconsin Magazine of History* 57 (Autumn 1973): 14.

Power-laundry industry statistics: Heidi Irmgard Hartmann, "Capitalism and Women's Work in the Home, 1900–1930" (Ph.D. dissertation, Yale University, 1974), p. 287.

Russell Sage Foundation report: Robert Coit Chapin, *The Standard of Living Among Workingmen's Families in New York City* (New York: Russell Sage Foundation, Charities Publication Committee, 1909), pp. 165, 179.

PAGE 116   Curved-surface washing machine: Siegfried Giedion, *Mechanization Takes Command: A Contribution to Anonymous History* (New York: W. W. Norton & Co., 1948), p. 561; Sears, Roebuck & Co., *1927 Edition of the Sears, Roebuck Catalogue*, ed. Alan Mirken (New York: Crown Publishers, 1970), p. 913.

Union Washing Machine: Elizabeth Mickle Bacon, "The Growth of Household Conveniences in the United States from 1865 to 1900" (Ph.D. dissertation, Radcliffe College, 1942), p. 22.

Washing machines in catalogues: Sears, Roebuck & Co., *1897 Sears Catalogue*, ed. Fred L. Israel (New York: Chelsea House, 1968), p. 139; Montgomery Ward, *1894–95 Catalogue*, pp. 552–53. Quoted copy for Cline's Improved Steam Washer appeared in both catalogues.

PAGE 117   Sears's wringers: *1897 Sears Catalogue*, pp. 100–1.

General-purpose soaps: Bacon, "Growth of Household Conveniences," p. 167.

Laundry soaps: Ruth Schwartz Cowan, "The 'Industrial Revolution' in the Home: Household Technology and Social Change in the 20th Century," *Technology and Culture* 17 (January 1976): 5–6.

PAGE 118   Washing-machine statistics: Hartmann, "Capitalism and Women's Work," pp. 295, 311.

PAGE 119   More than a quarter of nonfarm households: calculated from Hartmann, "Capitalism and Women's Work," p. 297, and U.S. Department of Commerce, Bureau of the Census, *Historical Statistics of the United States from Colonial Times to 1970* (Washington, D.C.: Government Printing Office, 1975), p. 827.

Laundry service descriptions: letter from Ethel Erickson, Industrial Assistant, U.S. Department of Labor Women's Bureau, to Harry Hoerr, Sr., President, Ohio Laundrymen's Association, July 20, 1928, in folder 51–101, box 2, Women's Bureau papers, U.S. National Archives.

Luncheon talk: "Suggested Laundry Talk for Luncheon Clubs—Complete," typescript sent to Ethel Best, Industrial Supervisor, U.S. Department of Labor

Women's Bureau, by L. C. Ball, Department of Sales Promotion, Laundry-owners National Association of the United States and Canada, March 12, 1929, in folder 51-A-101, box 2, Women's Bureau papers, National Archives.

PAGE 120   Trade association negotiations: Hartmann, "Capitalism and Women's Work," p. 299.

"Remained highly decentralized": Hartmann, "Capitalism and Women's Work," p. 301.

"To extract direct financial benefits": Hartmann, "Capitalism and Women's Work," p. 309.

Average firm sizes: Hartmann, "Capitalism and Women's Work," p. 303.

PAGE 121   "It would seem unreasonable": U.S. Department of Labor, Bureau of Labor Statistics, *Tentative Quantity and Cost Budget Necessary to Maintain a Family of Five in Washington, D.C. at a Level of Health and Decency* (Washington, D.C.: Government Printing Office, 1919), p. 40.

"Expenditure in assistance": U.S. Department of Labor, Bureau of Labor Statistics, *Minimum Quantity Budget Necessary to Maintain a Worker's Family of Five at a Level of Health and Decency* (Washington, D.C.: Government Printing Office, 1920), p. 18.

"Almost universal" practice: Bureau of Labor Statistics, *Tentative Quantity and Cost Budget*, pp. 73–74.

CHAPTER 7. A STITCH IN TIME

PAGE 125   Classic history of textile industry: Caroline F. Ware, *The Early New England Cotton Manufacture: A Study in Industrial Beginnings* (New York: Russell & Russell, 1966), p. 3.

PAGE 126   Flax processing: For a good description, see Alice Morse Earle, *Home Life in Colonial Days* (New York: Macmillan Co., 1898), pp. 167–74.

Gallatin homespun estimate: Alfred D. Chandler, Jr., *The Visible Hand: The Managerial Revolution in American Business* (Cambridge, Mass.: Harvard University Press, 1977), p. 51.

Colonial craftspeople: Earle, *Home Life in Colonial Days*, pp. 212–13; Julia Cherry Spruill, *Women's Life and Work in the Southern Colonies* (New York: W. W. Norton & Co., 1972), pp. 285–86.

Mantua-makers: R. Turner Wilcox, *The Mode in Costume* (New York: Charles Scribner's Sons, 1948), p. 179.

PAGE 128   Imported cloth: Spruill, *Women's Life and Work*, pp. 74–76.

PAGE 130   "All of us thrown upon our own resources": Lucy Larcom, *A New England Girlhood*, in Rosalyn Baxandall, Linda Gordon and Susan Reverby, eds., *America's Working Women: A Documentary History—1600 to the Present* (New York: Vintage Books, 1976), p. 44.

"Who left their homes in order to maintain them": Victor S. Clark, *History of Manufactures in the United States*, vol. 1, *1607–1860* (New York: McGraw-Hill Book Co. for Carnegie Institution of Washington, 1929), p. 529.

"The half-live creature": Lucy Larcom, quoted in Steve Dunwell, *The Run of the Mill: A Pictorial Narrative of the Expansion, Dominion, Decline and Enduring Impact of the New England Textile Industry* (Boston: David R. Godine Publisher, 1978), p. 100.

Cloth at frontier stores: Lewis E. Atherton, *The Frontier Merchant in Mid-America* (Columbia: University of Missouri Press, 1971), p. 52.

Household manufacture dead by 1860: Rolla Milton Tryon, *Household Manufactures in the United States, 1640–1860* (Chicago: University of Chicago Press, 1917), pp. 310–76; Edgar W. Martin, *The Standard of Living in 1860: American Consumption Levels on the Eve of the Civil War* (Chicago: University of Chicago Press, 1942), pp. 190, 201.

PAGE 131   Haskell on sewing: "A Literate Woman in the Mines: the Diary of Rachel Haskell," in Christiane Fischer, ed., *Let Them Speak for Themselves: Women in the American West, 1849–1900* (New York: E. P. Dutton & Co., 1977), pp. 58–72.

"Ripping out the sleeves": Catharine E. Beecher and Harriet Beecher Stowe, *The American Woman's Home, or, Principles of Domestic Science* (New York: J. B. Ford & Co., 1869), p. 358.

Farrar on darning: Eliza Farrar, *The Young Lady's Friend*, rev. ed. (New York: Samuel S. & William Wood, 1849), pp. 117–19.

"Get a dress fitted": Beecher and Stowe, *American Woman's Home*, p. 355.

Dickinson seamstresses: Millicent Todd Bingham, *Emily Dickinson's Home: The Early Years as Revealed in Family Correspondence and Reminiscences* (New York: Dover Publications, 1967), pp. 116, 139, 175, 299, 311, 318, 328, 345, 351, 358.

Emily's sister Vinnie: Bingham, *Emily Dickinson's Home*, p. 318.

PAGE 132   "A woman who does not know how to sew": Farrar, *Young Lady's Friend*, p. 116.

PAGE 133   Philadelphia sewing circle: Frances Trollope, *Domestic Manners of the Americans*, ed. Donald Smalley (New York: Vintage Books, 1960), pp. 281–82.

"Quilting frolics": Trollope, *Domestic Manners*, p. 416n.

Colonial quilting parties: Earle, *Home Life in Colonial Days*, p. 274; Spruill, *Women's Life and Work*, p. 110.

PAGE 134   Rachel Haskell and Mrs. Mack: Quoted in Fischer, *Let Them Speak for Themselves*, p. 66.

"Little Women" sewing together: Louisa May Alcott, *Little Women* (New York: Penguin Books, 1953), pp. 31–32.

Sewing in family circle: Farrar, *Young Lady's Friend*, p. 116.

Value of women's wear: Clark, *History of Manufactures*, vol. 2, *1860–1893*, p. 446.

"Made it possible to sell the *design*": Caroline Bird, *Enterprising Women* (New York: W. W. Norton & Co., 1976), p. 75. On paper patterns, see Margaret Walsh, "The Democratization of Fashion: The Emergence of the Women's Dress Pattern Industry," *Journal of American History* 66 (September 1979): 299–313.

PAGE 135   Army tailor shop: Claudia B. Kidwell and Margaret C. Christman, *Suiting Everyone: The Democratization of Clothing in America* (Washington, D.C.: Smithsonian Institution Press, 1974), pp. 47–49.

PAGE 136   "Outside shops": Egal Feldman, *Fit for Men: A Study of New York's Clothing Trade* (Washington, D.C.: Public Affairs Press, 1960), pp. 102–4.

"Inside shops": Feldman, *Fit for Men*, pp. 95–101; Jesse Eliphalet Pope, *The Clothing Industry in New York*, University of Missouri Studies, Social Science Series, vol. 1 (Columbia: University of Missouri, 1905), pp. 12–13.

Sewing girls in fashionable establishments: Farrar, *Young Lady's Friend*, pp. 126–27.

Laborers' clothes: Pope, *Clothing Industry in New York*, pp. 6–7, 9–10.

PAGE 137   Union Army measures conscripts: Kidwell and Christman, *Suiting Everyone*, p. 105.

PAGE 138   Measured sleeves: Kidwell and Christman, *Suiting Everyone*, p. 101.

Howe and sewing machine: Ruth Brandon, *A Capitalist Romance: Singer and the Sewing Machine* (Philadelphia: J. P. Lippincott Co., 1977), pp. 53–99.

Machines in inside shops: Brandon, *Capitalist Romance*, p. 135.

Expansion of ready-made in 1850s: Martin, *Standard of Living in 1860*, pp. 190–91; Feldman, *Fit for Men*, pp. 98, 105–11.

PAGE 139   *Godey's* plan for collective ownership: quoted in Brandon, *Capitalist Romance*, p. 117.

Installment plan and trade-in allowance: Brandon, *Capitalist Romance*, pp. 117–19; Penrose Scull, with Prescott C. Fuller, *From Peddlers to Merchant Princes* (Chicago: Follett Publishing Co., 1967), pp. 184–87.

PAGE 141   "The principal sale of sewing machines": quoted in Brandon, *Capitalist Romance*, p. 99.

Mary Mathews: Mary Mathews, "Ten Years in Nevada, or, Life on the Pacific Coast," in Fischer, *Let Them Speak*, pp. 177–92.

Putting-out system remains: See Edith Abbott, *Women in Industry: A Study in American Economic History* (New York: D. Appleton & Co., 1910), chap. 6.

"I considered it very kind of her": Mathews, in Fischer, *Let Them Speak*, p. 185.

PAGE 142   Contract system and task system: Moses Rischin, *The Promised City: New York's Jews, 1870–1914* (Cambridge: Harvard University Press, 1962), pp. 64–65.

PAGE 143   Women's wear and men's wear figures: Clark, *History of Manufactures*, vol. 2, p. 446.

Government report: U.S. Department of Labor, Bureau of Labor Statistics, *Minimum Quantity Budget Necessary to Maintain a Worker's Family of Five at a Level of Health and Decency* (Washington, D.C.: Government Printing Office, 1920), pp. 9–10.

Midwestern industrial city: Robert S. Lynd and Helen Merrell Lynd, *Middletown: A Study in Modern American Culture* (New York: Harcourt, Brace & World, 1929), p. 165.

"The needle will soon be consigned to oblivion": Quoted in Kidwell and Christman, *Suiting Everyone*, p. 79.

CHAPTER 8. THE BOARDER

PAGE 146   Colonial family structure: See Philip J. Greven, Jr., *Four Generations: Land and Family in Colonial Andover, Massachusetts* (Ithaca, N.Y.: Cornell University Press, 1970), especially chaps. 7–9; and Kenneth Lockridge, *A New England Town: The First Hundred Years* (New York: W. W. Norton & Co., 1970), especially chap. 8.

PAGE 148 Boarders in different societies: See Lutz K. Berkner, "The Stem Family and the Developmental Cycle of the Peasant Household: An 18th-Century Austrian Example," in Michael Gordon, ed., *The American Family in Social-Historical Perspective* (New York: St. Martin's Press, 1973), pp. 45–47; Michael B. Katz, *The People of Hamilton, Canada West: Family and Class in a Mid-Nineteenth Century City* (Cambridge, Mass.: Harvard University Press, 1975); Michael Anderson, "Family, Household, and the Industrial Revolution," in Gordon, *American Family*, pp. 59–75.

"The idea that nearly all Americans lived in hotels": Edgar W. Martin, *The Standard of Living in 1860: American Consumption Levels on the Eve of the Civil War* (Chicago: University of Chicago Press, 1942), pp. 148–49.

Hotels and boarding houses: Martin, *Standard of Living in 1860*, p. 167.

One North American city and "a close check": Katz, *People of Hamilton*, p. 36.

"Money Making for Ladies": *Harper's New Monthly Magazine*, June 1882, pp. 112–13.

PAGE 149 Mrs. Trollope on women boarders: Frances Trollope, *Domestic Manners of the Americans*, ed. Donald Smalley (New York: Vintage Books, 1960), pp. 282–84.

Ten Dollars Enough: Catharine Owen [Helen Alice Matthews Nitsch], *Ten Dollars Enough*, 13th ed. (Boston: Houghton, Mifflin & Co., 1897), pp. 1–6, 269–76.

PAGE 150 "It would seem that a far larger number of people are boarding": Catharine Owen, in "Is Housekeeping a Failure?" *North American Review*, February 1889, p. 254.

"The family is an institution of God": Rose Terry Cook, in "Is Housekeeping a Failure?" p. 249.

"People who eat by contract": Marion Harland, in "Is Housekeeping a Failure?" p. 252.

PAGE 151 "A natural institution": Quoted in Irving Howe, *World of Our Fathers* (New York: Harcourt Brace Jovanovich, 1976), p. 88.

For statistics on immigration, see U.S. Department of Commerce, Bureau of the Census, *Historical Statistics of the United States, Colonial Times to 1970* (Washington, D.C.: Government Printing Office, 1975), pp. 8, 23, 116–17; Alba M. Edwards, *Comparative Occupation Statistics for the United States, 1870 to 1940*, Sixteenth Census of the United States: 1940. Population (Washington, D.C.: Government Printing Office, 1943), pp. 158, 185–88.

Immigrant networks: Edward C. Kirkland, *Industry Comes of Age: Business, Labor and Public Policy, 1860–1897* (Chicago: Quadrangle Books, 1961), pp. 328–29; David Brody, *Steelworkers in America: The Nonunion Era* (New York: Harper Torchbooks, 1960), p. 109.

Pennsylvania steel towns: Brody, *Steelworkers in America*, p. 98. See also Sophonisba P. Breckinridge, *New Homes for Old* (New York: Harper & Brothers, 1921), pp. 20–23.

25 to 50 percent: See Laurence A. Glasco, "The Life Cycles and Household

Structures of American Ethnic Groups," *Journal of Urban History* 1 (May 1975): 339–64; Katz, *People of Hamilton*; John Modell and Tamara K. Hareven, "Urbanization and the Malleable Household: An Examination of Boarding and Lodging in American Families," *Journal of Marriage and the Family* 35 (1973): 470; Robert Coit Chapin, *The Standard of Living Among Workingmen's Families in New York City* (New York: Charities Publication Committee, 1909), p. 57; Louise Bolard More, *Wage-Earners' Budgets* (New York: Henry Holt & Co., 1907), p. 84; J. C. Kennedy et al., *Wages and Family Budgets in the Chicago Stockyards District* (Chicago: University of Chicago Press, 1914), p. 63.

Boarding and the life cycle: See Modell and Hareven, "Urbanization and the Malleable Household," p. 476.

PAGE 152   "A star boarder": Quoted in Howe, *World of Our Fathers*, p. 88.

Food accounts: Margaret F. Byington, *Homestead: The Households of a Mill Town* (New York: Russell Sage Foundation, 1910), p. 139; Howe, *World of Our Fathers*, p. 178; Breckinridge, *New Homes for Old*, pp. 24–25.

1921 Chicago study: Breckinridge, *New Homes for Old*, p. 23.

"Mother aged 35 years": Quoted in John Bodnar, "Immigration and Modernization: The Case of Slavic Peasants in Industrial America," *Journal of Social History* 10 (Fall 1976): 59.

"Taking lodgers": Byington, *Homestead*, p. 144.

Social workers' studies: Chapin, *Standard of Living Among Workingmen's Families*, pp. 55–57; Roy Lubove, *The Progressives and the Slums* (Pittsburgh: University of Pittsburgh Press, 1962), pp. 197–98.

New York State Conference of Charities and Corrections: Quoted in Lubove, *Progressives and the Slums*, p. 197.

PAGE 154   Yvonne Dionne and Alice LaCasse: Quoted in Tamara K. Hareven and Randolph Langenbach, *Amoskeag: Life and Work in an American Factory-City* (New York: Pantheon Books, 1978), pp. 197, 255.

Homestead steelworkers and boarders: Byington, *Homestead*, pp. 42, 87.

PAGE 155   "Each with a tag of some sort": Byington, *Homestead*, p. 139; see also Breckinridge, *New Homes for Old*, p. 64.

Cora Pellerin: In Hareven and Langenbach, *Amoskeag*, pp. 202–3.

The boarder and the faithless wife: See Howe, *World of Our Fathers*, p. 89; for a fictional account, see Abraham Cahan, *Yekl: A Tale of the New York Ghetto* (New York: D. Appleton & Co., 1896), which served as inspiration for Joan Micklin Silver's 1975 film *Hester Street*.

Manhattan had world's densest population: Lubove, *Progressives and the Slums*, p. 94.

"A two-room apartment on Allen Street": Howe, *World of Our Fathers*, p. 88.

One Yiddish novel: Anzia Yezierska, *Bread Givers: A Struggle Between a Father of the Old World and a Daughter of the New World* (1925; reprint ed., New York: Persea Books, 1975), p. 28.

PAGE 156   "Only millionaires can be alone": Yezierska, *Bread Givers*, pp. 13–14.

"The best interests of the immigrant": Lubove, *Progressives and the Slums*, pp. 96–97.

U.S. Bureau of Labor report: U.S. Bureau of Labor, *Report on the Condition of Woman and Child Wage Earners in the United States* (Washington, D.C.: Government Printing Office, 1910–1913), vol. 5, p. 62.

"Fraught with great danger": Lawrence T. Veiller, *Housing Reform* (New York: Charities Publication Committee, 1911), p. 33.

PAGE 157 Workers at Amoskeag mill: Tamara K. Hareven, "Family Time and Industrial Time: Family and Work in a Planned Corporation Town, 1900–1924," *Journal of Urban History* 1 (May 1975): 375.

"One room for everything": Breckinridge, *New Homes for Old*, p. 63.

"Men of executive ability": Jane Addams, "The Subjective Necessity for Social Settlements," in Anselm L. Strauss, ed., *The American City* (Chicago: Aldine Publishing Co., 1968), pp. 209–10.

"An army of inspectors": Veiller, *Housing Reform*, pp. 34–35.

"Why they should always have been 'widows' ": Lawrence T. Veiller, "Room Overcrowding and the Lodger Evil," in *Housing in America*, Proceedings of the Second National Conference on Housing (Philadelphia, 1912), p. 66.

PAGE 158 Jordan's response to Veiller: Thomas Jordan, "Discussion," in *Housing in America*, pp. 171–75.

PAGE 159 California commission: University of California, Heller Commission, *Cost of Living Studies II. How Workers Spend a Living Wage*, prepared by Jessica B. Peixotto, University of California Publications in Economics, vol. 5, no. 3 (Berkeley, 1929), p. 179; University of California, Heller Commission, *Cost of Living Studies IV. Spending Ways of a Semi-Skilled Group*, University of California Publications in Economics, vol. 5, no. 5 (Berkeley, 1931), p. 309.

Chicago small wage earners: Elizabeth A. Hughes, *Living Conditions for Small-Wage Earners in Chicago* (Chicago: Department of Public Welfare, 1925), p. 13.

Boardinghouse and lodging-house keepers in census: Edwards, *Comparative Occupation Statistics*, pp. 122, 129.

PAGE 160 Population statistics: Bureau of the Census, *Historical Statistics*, pp. 8, 41.

CHAPTER 9. MISTRESS AND MAID

PAGE 163 Hannah and March family: Louisa May Alcott, *Little Women* (New York: Penguin Books, 1953), p. 34.

One domestic service worker for every 8.4 families: Janet M. Hooks, *Women's Occupations Through Seven Decades*, U.S. Department of Labor Women's Bureau Bulletin no. 218 (Washington, D.C.: Government Printing Office, 1947), pp. 139–40. These figures include women working in boardinghouses, hotels, and restaurants, but that overcount is probably counterbalanced by underreporting of domestic servants.

PAGE 165 Irish women 59 percent of applicants: Society for the Encouragement of Faithful Domestic Servants in New York, *First Annual Report* (New York: Printed by D. Fanshaw, at the American Tract Society's House, 1826), p. 3.

End-of-the-century study: Gail Laughlin, "Domestic Service, A Report Prepared Under the Direction of the Industrial Commission," *Report of the In-*

dustrial Commission on the Relations and Conditions of Capital and Labor Employed in Manufacture and General Business, vol. 14 of the Commission's Reports (Washington, D.C.: Government Printing Office, 1901), p. 745; see also Lucy Salmon, *Domestic Service* (New York: Macmillan Co., 1897), pp. 74–80.

Irish immigrants as servants: Oscar Handlin, *Boston's Immigrants: A Study in Acculturation* (New York: Atheneum Publishers, 1968), pp. 60–63.

PAGE 166   "Friendly advice to servants": Society for the Encouragement, *First Annual Report*, pp. 4, 11–12, 31–32.

Christian Inquirer and *Mechanics' Free Press*: Quoted in Helen L. Sumner, *History of Women in Industry in the United States*, vol. 9 of U.S. Bureau of Labor, *Report on Condition of Woman and Child Wage Earners in the United States* (Washington, D.C.: Government Printing Office, 1910), pp. 181–82.

"Miseries of Mistresses": *Harper's New Monthly Magazine*, October 1856, pp. 717–18; January 1857, pp. 285–86.

Hale on American servants: Sarah Josepha Hale, *The Good Housekeeper, or The Way to Live Well, and to Be Well While We Live*, 7th ed. (Boston: Otis, Broaders, & Co., 1844), p. 122.

"Acknowledge their ignorance": Hale, *Good Housekeeper*, pp. 125–26.

"Every mistress of a family": Catharine E. Beecher, *Miss Beecher's Housekeeper and Healthkeeper* (New York: Harper & Brothers, 1876), p. 342; for the Golden Rule, see Catharine E. Beecher and Harriet Beecher Stowe, *The American Woman's Home, or, Principles of Domestic Science* (New York: J. B. Ford & Co., 1869), p. 328.

PAGE 167   "It is a tax which the rich must pay": "Hints About Help," *American Ladies' Magazine*, September 1832, p. 423.

"Who mean to make domestic service a profession": Beecher and Stowe, *American Woman's Home*, p. 321.

"An unsuspected spirit of superiority": Beecher and Stowe, *American Woman's Home*, pp. 322–23.

"The most delicate lady": Hale, *Good Housekeeper*, pp. 127–28.

"Large houses, many servants, poor health": Beecher, *Housekeeper and Healthkeeper*, p. 17.

The fifty largest cities: Salmon, *Domestic Service*, p. 83.

Half of all working women: Hooks, *Women's Occupations*, pp. 139–41.

PAGE 169   "Perplexities real and puzzling": Lillian Pettengill, *Toilers of the Home* (New York: Doubleday, Page & Co., 1903), pp. 362–66. For strikingly similar lists of the problems associated with domestic service from the standpoint of the employee, see also Salmon, *Domestic Service*, pp. 140–65; Laughlin, "Domestic Service," pp. 757–59; YWCA Commission on Household Employment, *First Report, to the Fifth National Convention* (Los Angeles, 1915), pp. 8–34; Henrietta Roelofs, "The Road to Trained Service in the Household," YWCA Commission on Household Employment *Bulletin*, no. 2 (1915–1916), pp. 5–10.

Salmon on social stigma: *Domestic Service*, p. 158.

Laughlin on social stigma: "Domestic Service," p. 759.

PAGE 170   "A teacher or cashier": Quoted in David M. Katzman, *Seven Days a Week: Women and Domestic Service in Industrializing America* (New York: Oxford University Press, 1978), p. 10.

PAGE 171   Salmon on working hours: *Domestic Service*, p. 146.
   Laughlin on working hours: "Domestic Service," p. 758.
   "My first employer": Quoted in Katzman, *Seven Days a Week*, p. 10.

PAGE 172   Salmon on domestic employees' social life: *Domestic Service*, pp. 152–53.
   "Do they not desire something else": Quoted in Roelofs, "Road to Trained Service," p. 12.
   "It is the person who is hired": Laughlin, "Domestic Service," p. 759.
   YWCA bulletin of 1915–1916: Quoted in Roelofs, "Road to Trained Service," pp. 12–13.
   "The survival of mediaeval terms of contract": I. M. Rubinow, "The Problem of Domestic Service," *Journal of Political Economy* 2 (1905): 514.
   "Back in the eighteenth century": Ida Tarbell, "What a Factory Can Teach a Housewife," YWCA Commission on Household Employment *Bulletin*, no. 4 (1915–1916), p. 2.

PAGE 173   "A dinner ordered at half past six": Pettengill, *Toilers of the Home*, p. 370.
   Household employment must move "into the current": Salmon, *Domestic Service*, pp. 194–98.
   Laughlin on written contract: "Domestic Service," p. 760.
   Domestic Reform League contract: "History of the Domestic Reform League," reprint from the *Federation Bulletin*, November 1903, in Women's Educational and Industrial Union Papers, box 1, folder 5, Arthur and Elizabeth Schlesinger Library on the History of Women in America.
   Legal Aid Society contract: Legal Aid Society of New York, *Domestic Employment* (New York, 1908), p. 10.
   Employment agencies and white-slaving: See also Frances Kellor, *Out of Work: A Study of Employment Agencies, Their Treatment of the Unemployed, and Their Influence on Home and Business* (New York: Macmillan Co., 1904).
   Domestic Reform League employment bureau: Domestic Reform League, *Bulletin*, vol. 2, no. 1 (November 1907), in WEIU papers, Schlesinger Library.

PAGE 175   "Whether present domestic difficulties could be alleviated": Massachusetts Bureau of Statistics of Labor, *Trained and Supplemental Employees for Domestic Service*, Part 2 of the Annual Report for 1906 (Boston: State Printers, 1906), pp. 91, 100.
   Salmon on day labor: *Domestic Service*, pp. 224–25.
   "Would be in line with the industrial organization": Jane Addams, *Democracy and Social Ethics* (New York: Macmillan Co., 1916), p. 110.
   "The privilege of unlimited smoking": Rubinow, "Problem of Domestic Service," pp. 515–16.

PAGE 176   "The new way is coming": Pettengill, *Toilers of the Home*, p. 371.
   Statistics on black women servants: Joseph A. Hill, *Women in Gainful Occupations, 1870 to 1920*, U.S. Bureau of the Census Monographs, no. 9 (Washington, D.C.: Government Printing Office, 1943), pp. 114–17.

Employment agents recruit domestic workers: Robert Hamburger, "A Stranger in the House," *Southern Exposure* 5 (Spring 1977): 22–23.

Black women in servant population: George J. Stigler, *Domestic Servants in the United States, 1900–1940*, Occasional Paper no. 24 (New York: National Bureau of Economic Research, 1946), p. 7.

Black women as servant class: Katzman, *Seven Days a Week*, pp. 78–79.

PAGE 178 Roena Bethune: Quoted in Hamburger, "A Stranger in the House," p. 24.

"Our well-trained employees work": Honor Maid Cleaning Company advertisement, 1980–81 Seattle *Yellow Pages*.

Coralee Kern of Maid-To-Order: Quoted in "Maid Firm Makes Life More Livable," *Nation's Business* 67 (January 1979): 53–54.

CHAPTER 10. REDEEMING WOMAN'S PROFESSION

PAGE 181 Times versus task-oriented labor: See E. P. Thompson, "Time, Work Discipline, and Industrial Capitalism," *Past and Present* 38 (1967): 56–97, and Keith Thomas, "Work and Leisure in Pre-Industrial Society," *Past and Present* 29 (1964): 61–62.

Ladies' Magazine article: "Home," *Ladies' Magazine*, May 1830, p. 217, quoted in Kirk Jeffrey, "The Family as Utopian Retreat from the City," in Sallie Teselle, ed., *The Family, Communes, and Utopian Societies* (New York: Harper Torchbooks, 1971), p. 28.

PAGE 182 "What a lesson is taught a girl": Lydia Maria Child, *The American Frugal Housewife*, 30th ed. (New York: Samuel S. & William Wood, 1844), p. 95.

"Purity, piety, submissiveness, and domesticity": Barbara Welter, "The Cult of True Womanhood, 1820–1860," *American Quarterly* 18 (Summer 1966): 151–74.

John Todd: Quoted in Ben Barker-Benfield, "The Spermatic Economy: A Nineteenth-Century View of Sexuality," in Michael Gordon, ed., *The American Family in Social-Historical Perspective* (New York: St. Martin's Press, 1973), pp. 336, 338.

"How then could men dare to leave home": Jeffrey, "The Family as Utopian Retreat," p. 30.

Avoiding physical contact: Eliza Farrar, *The Young Lady's Friend* rev. ed. (New York: Samuel S. & William Wood, 1849), p. 263.

"Wholesome dread": Farrar, *Young Lady's Friend*, pp. 280–81.

"So many temptations beset young men": Farrar, *Young Lady's Friend*, p. 201.

PAGE 183 Avoid loveless marriage: Farrar, *Young Lady's Friend*, p. 187.

"Such words imply a separate existence": The Authoress of "Olive," etc., "Fragments from a Young Wife's Diary," *Harper's New Monthy Magazine*, October 1852, p. 627.

Chaste but controlled: See Carroll Smith-Rosenberg, "Puberty to Menopause: The Cycle of Femininity in Nineteenth-Century America," in Mary Hartman and Lois W. Banner, eds., *Clio's Consciousness Raised* (New York: Harper Colophon Books, 1974), p. 24.

Paradoxes in separate-spheres ideology: See Carroll Smith-Rosenberg, "The Hysterical Woman: Sex Roles and Role Conflict in 19th-Century America," *Social Research* 39 (Winter 1972): 656; Donald Meyer, *The Positive Thinkers* (Garden City, N.Y.: Doubleday & Co., 1965), pp. 54–56; Nancy F. Cott, *The Bonds of Womanhood: "Woman's Sphere" in New England, 1780–1835* (New Haven, Conn.: Yale University Press, 1977), p. 69.

PAGE 185   Christian family state: Catharine Beecher and Harriet Beecher Stowe, *The American Woman's Home, or, Principles of Domestic Science* (New York: J. B. Ford & Co., 1869), pp. 17–22, 453–61.

PAGE 186   "There is no housekeeper so expert": This advertisement for Beecher and Stowe, *American Woman's Home*, appeared on the flyleaves of the book.

List of sciences: Catharine E. Beecher, *Miss Beecher's Housekeeper and Healthkeeper* (New York: Harper & Brothers, 1876), pp. 127–32.

Ten years of teaching and study: Beecher, *Housekeeper and Healthkeeper*, p. 16.

Women would "constantly be interested and cheered": Beecher, *Housekeeper and Healthkeeper*, p. 212.

God "made woman to do the work": Beecher, *Housekeeper and Healthkeeper*, p. 16.

Democratic custom: Beecher, *Housekeeper and Healthkeeper*, p. 254.

"You are training young minds": Beecher, *Housekeeper and Healthkeeper*, p. 462.

Beecher on early rising: Beecher and Stowe, *American Woman's Home*, pp. 195–96.

PAGE 188   "There is no one thing more necessary": Beecher and Stowe, *American Woman's Home*, p. 222.

Weekly schedule: Beecher and Stowe, *American Woman's Home*, pp. 226–27.

Ordered closets and house plans: Beecher and Stowe, *American Woman's Home*, p. 227.

"In many large kitchens": Catharine E. Beecher, "How to Redeem Woman's Profession from Dishonor," *Harper's New Monthly Magazine*, November 1865, p. 713.

"A true machine for living": James Marston Fitch, *Architecture and the Esthetics of Plenty* (New York: Columbia University Press, 1961), pp. 77–81.

PAGE 189   "We must give account to God": Beecher and Stowe, *American Woman's Home*, p. 247.

Child on domestic apprenticeship: *American Frugal Housewife*, p. 92.

PAGE 191   "Institutions should be established": Beecher, "How to Redeem Woman's Profession," p. 711.

"Young women are taught": Beecher, *Housekeeper and Healthkeeper*, p. 170.

"The first problems of Geometry": Beecher, *Housekeeper and Healthkeeper*, p. 183.

Training for professions: Beecher, "How to Redeem Woman's Profession," p. 716.

Adopting orphans: Beecher, "How to Redeem Woman's Profession," p. 716.

The remedy "is not in leading women . . .": Beecher, "How to Redeem Woman's Profession," p. 710.

PAGE 192   Declaration of Sentiments and Resolutions: Aileen S. Kraditor, ed., *Up from the Pedestal: Selected Writings in the History of American Feminism* (Chicago: Quadrangle Books, 1968).

"Head and chief magistrate": Beecher, *Housekeeper and Healthkeeper*, p. 265.

PAGE 193   Rules for preservation of temper: Beecher, *Housekeeper and Healthkeeper*, pp. 274–79, and Beecher and Stowe, *American Woman's Home*, pp. 212–19.

Rules One and Two: Beecher, *Housekeeper and Healthkeeper*, p. 276.

"You really *have* great trials to meet": Beecher, *Housekeeper and Healthkeeper*, p. 460.

"Take charge of a *man-of-war*": Beecher, *Housekeeper and Healthkeeper*, p. 461.

"The next word of comfort": Beecher, *Housekeeper and Healthkeeper*, p. 461.

PAGE 194   Beecher on industrialized laundry service: Beecher and Stowe, *American Woman's Home*, p. 334.

Beecher denounces communal housekeeping: "How to Redeem Woman's Profession," p. 716.

PAGE 195   Peirce articles: Mrs. C. F. Peirce, "Cooperative Housekeeping," *Atlantic Monthly*, November 1868, pp. 513–24; December 1868, pp. 682–97; January 1869, pp. 29–39; February 1869, pp. 161–71; March 1869, pp. 282–94.

PAGE 196   Blaming men and machines: Peirce, "Cooperative Housekeeping," November 1868, pp. 517–18.

Male degeneration: Peirce, "Cooperative Housekeeping," November 1868, pp. 522–23.

PAGE 197   "Back, sirs, back!": Peirce, "Cooperative Housekeeping," January 1869, pp. 29–30.

PAGE 198   "Willful independence": Peirce, "Cooperative Housekeeping," February 1869, p. 168.

Peirce's following: See Dolores Hayden, "Melusina Fay Peirce and Cooperative Housekeeping," *International Journal of Urban and Regional Research* 2 (1978): 408–15.

PAGE 199   Council of husbands: Peirce, "Cooperative Housekeeping," December 1868, p. 687.

"I regret to believe": Melusina Fay Peirce, *Co-operative Housekeeping* (Boston: James R. Osgood & Co., 1884), pp. 106–7.

"It is just as necessary": Peirce, "Cooperative Housekeeping," December 1868, p. 684.

PAGE 200   Women as a class: See Cott, *Bonds of Womanhood*, pp. 98–100; Kathryn Kish Sklar, *Catharine Beecher: A Study in American Domesticity* (New Haven, Conn.: Yale University Press, 1973), pp. 158–60, 173–74.

CHAPTER 11. THE BUSINESS OF HOUSEKEEPING

PAGE 203   Mary Lyon: *Notable American Women* (Cambridge, Mass.: Harvard University Press, 1971), vol. 2, p. 446.

Mary Welsh: Quoted in Isabel Bevier and Susannah Usher, *The Home Economics Movement* (Boston: Whitcomb & Barrows, 1906), p. 27.

Lou Allen Gregory: Quoted in Bevier and Usher, *Home Economics Movement*, p. 31.

"Not enough elements of intellectual growth": Quoted in Bevier and Usher, *Home Economics Movement*, p. 15.

PAGE 204   College home-economics courses: Hazel T. Craig, *History of Home Economics*, ed. Blanche M. Stover (New York: Practical Home Economics, 1945), p. 15.

Juliet Corson's "Ladies' Class": F. E. Fryatt, "The New York Cooking School," *Harper's New Monthly Magazine*, December 1879, p. 23.

Boston Domestic Reform League School of Housekeeping: Announcements for the school may be found in Women's Educational and Industrial Union papers, Schlesinger Library on the History of Women in America, box I, folder 9.

"Encouraging habits of carefulness and industry": Quoted in Marvin Lazerson, *Origins of the Urban School* (Cambridge, Mass.: Harvard University Press, 1971), p. 105.

PAGE 206   Worcester school superintendent: Lazerson, *Origins of the Urban School*, p. 106.

Jane Addams: Quoted in Barbara Ehrenreich and Deirdre English, "The Manufacture of Housework," *Socialist Revolution*, no. 26 (October–December 1975), p. 31.

" 'Good for the children' ": Irving Howe, *World of Our Fathers* (New York: Harcourt Brace Jovanovich, 1976), p. 175.

Emily Huntington: Quoted in Huntington biography, *Notable American Women* (Cambridge, Mass.: Harvard University Press, 1971), vol. 2, p. 239. See also Isabel F. Hyams, "The Louisa May Alcott Club," *Proceedings of the Second Lake Placid Conference on Home Economics* (1900), pp. 18–23.

PAGE 207   Goodrich's plan: Henrietta Goodrich, "Suggestions for a Professional School of Home and Social Economics," in WEIU papers, Schlesinger Library, folder 9; also in *Second Lake Placid Conference Proceedings*, pp. 26–40.

Goodrich on Ph.D.: Goodrich, "Suggestions," p. 6.

PAGE 208   Course for Home-Makers: Goodrich, "Suggestions," p. 6.

Lucy Salmon on professional education: Lucy Salmon, *Domestic Service* (New York: Macmillan Co., 1897), pp. 259–60.

PAGE 209   Julia Lathrop: Julia Lathrop, "The Family," lecture no. 15, February 8, 1916, in Bureau of Vocational Information mss., Schlesinger Library.

PAGE 210   Ellen Richards: Quoted in Bevier and Usher, *Home Economics Movement*, p. 21.

"Something more than the idea of personal relationships": *Proceedings of the Lake Placid Conference on Home Economics* (1902), p. 36.

"In line with the great social and industrial forces": Goodrich, "Suggestions."

"HOME ECONOMICS STANDS FOR": Quoted in Bevier and Usher, *Home Economics Movement*, p. 21.

Secretary of Agriculture James Wilson: Quoted in Bevier and Usher, *Home Economics Movement*, p. 38.

"Scientific investigation of social phenomena": Goodrich, "Suggestions," p. 7.
Juliet Corson: See Fryatt, "The New York Cooking School," pp. 23–24.

PAGE 212   Teaching people how to use money: See John Bodnar, "Immigration and Modernization: The Case of Slavic Peasants in Industrial America," *Journal of Social History* 10 (Fall 1976): 49; Margaret F. Byington, *Homestead: The Households of a Mill Town* (New York: Russell Sage Foundation, 1910), pp. 152–57; Barbara Laslett, "The Family as a Public and Private Institution," *Journal of Marriage and the Family* 35 (August 1973): 483.

Florence Nesbitt: Florence Nesbitt, *Household Management* (New York: Russell Sage Foundation, 1918), pp. 20–21, 59–60; Florence Nesbitt, *Low Cost Cooking* (Chicago: American School of Home Economics, 1915), pp. 5–6, 11–12.

"We are all consumers": *Proceedings of the Eighth Lake Placid Conference on Home Economics* (1906), p. 42; for Hunt, see p. 39.

"A broader term": Craig, *History of Home Economics*, p. 13.

Expanding business opportunities: See the following documents in Bureau of Vocational Information mss., Schlesinger Library, folder 115: "List of Home Economics Women in Business," n.d.; "Home Economics in Banks," 1922; Rosalyn Bloch Frank, "A Survey of Household Experiment Stations in the City of New York," 1921; "Women Trained in Home Economics," 1921.

"In many ways the business of housemaking": Nesbitt, *Low Cost Cooking*, p. 5.

PAGE 213   A $100 prize: Documents in WEIU papers, folder 11, Schlesinger Library.

Tracts on the relationship between household and society: See Martha Bensley Bruere and Robert W. Bruere, *Increasing Home Efficiency* (New York: Macmillan Co., 1912), especially the chapter called "The Basis of Efficiency."

"Pin or string plan": Lillian Gilbreth, *The Homemaker and Her Job* (New York: D. Appleton-Century Co., 1927), pp. 92–93.

PAGE 214   Scheduling: Christine Frederick, *Household Engineering: Scientific Management in the Home* (Chicago: American School of Home Economics, 1920), p. 69.

Housewife as executive: Frederick, *Household Engineering*, p. 92.

PAGE 215   "Standard practice": Frederick, *Household Engineering*, p. 152.

PAGE 216   "If a woman were doing nothing": Frederick, *Household Engineering*, p. 66.

"*Arbitrary standards*": Frederick, *Household Engineering*, p. 381.

PAGE 218   "*What is the best order*": Frederick, *Household Engineering*, p. 67.
"*The real object in saving time*": Frederick, *Household Engineering*, p. 504.
"*To subordinate housekeeping routine*": Frederick, *Household Engineering*, p. 509.

"Ten Things to Do in Leisure Time": Frederick, *Household Engineering*, pp. 503–10.

"Our greatest enemy": Christine Frederick, "Points in Efficiency," *Journal of Home Economics* 6 (June 1914): 280.

PAGE 220   "We are the only animal species": Charlotte Perkins Gilman,

Women and Economics, ed. Carl Degler (New York: Harper Torchbooks, 1966), p. 5.

"Quite the greatest man I have ever known": Charlotte Perkins Gilman, *The Living of Charlotte Perkins Gilman* (New York: Harper & Brothers, 1935), p. 187.

Lester Frank Ward: Quoted in Degler introduction to Gilman, *Woman and Economics,* p. xxxiv.

Monogamous marriage and sex-distinction: Gilman, *Women and Economics,* p. 38.

Belief in progress, shaping the future: Gilman, *Women and Economics,* pp. 122, 340.

Reviews of *The Home*: Collected in folder 299, Gilman papers, Schlesinger Library.

PAGE 221   "All industries were once 'domestic' ": Charlotte Perkins Gilman, *The Home: Its Work and Influence* (1903; reprint ed., Urbana: University of Illinois Press, 1972), pp. 30–31; see also pp. 82–83.

"To give a general impression": Gilman, *The Home,* pp. 28–29.

"The savage works by himself": Gilman, *The Home,* pp. 84–85.

"What would shoes be like": Gilman, *The Home,* pp. 90–91.

"No other ambition": Gilman, *The Home,* p. 91.

PAGE 222   "We have to pay severally": Gilman, *The Home,* p. 18.

"There is nothing private and special": Gilman, *The Home,* p. 115.

"If we are willing to receive our water": Gilman, *The Home,* p. 330.

"Our housewife does not go out": Gilman, *The Home,* p. 331.

"In their true arena, the world": Gilman, *The Home,* p. 347.

CHAPTER 12. WHEN THE BOUGH BREAKS

PAGE 225   "Fast disappearing into professional hands": Charlotte Perkins Gilman, *The Home: Its Work and Influence* (1903; reprint ed., Urbana: University of Illinois Press, 1972), p. 338.

"Built and furnished for several mixed and conflicting industries": Gilman, *The Home,* p. 238.

"With heavy masses of stiff cloth": Gilman, *The Home,* p. 240.

"The infallible power of 'a mother's love' ": Gilman, *The Home,* p. 242.

"Collected from one newspaper": Gilman, *The Home,* p. 244.

PAGE 226   "Grow up with a burning ambition": Gilman, *The Home,* p. 248.

"This deep, new, thrilling mystery of life": Gilman, *The Home,* p. 251.

"A newborn baby" and "What if she does not?": Gilman, *The Home,* p. 340.

PAGE 227   "Calm, wise, experienced professional care": Gilman, *The Home,* p. 339.

"Citizens with rights to be guaranteed": Gilman, *The Home,* pp. 334–35.

"The home-love and care of the Armenians": Gilman, *The Home,* p. 340.

PAGE 228   Statistics on women's occupations: Most of the statistics in this section come from Joseph A. Hill, *Women in Gainful Occupations, 1870 to 1920,* U.S. Bureau of the Census Monographs, no. 9 (Washington, D.C.: Government Printing Office, 1929). For a full statistical discussion of the assertions made here, see my unpublished work "Never Done: The Ideology and Technology of Household Work, 1850–1930" (Ph.D. dissertation, State University of New York, Stony Brook, 1977), pp. 364–75.

PAGE 230   "The line of progress": "Ellen Key, *The Century of the Child* (1909; reprint ed., New York: Arno Press, 1972), p. 95.
"People will regard the maternal function": Key, *Century of the Child*, p. 85.
"The mother is the most precious possession": Key, *Century of the Child*, pp. 84–85.
Theodore Roosevelt on motherhood: Quoted in Barbara Ehrenreich and Deirdre English, *For Her Own Good: 150 Years of the Experts' Advice to Women* (New York: Doubleday & Co., 1978), p. 171.
"The keeper of the gates of to-morrow": Quoted in Ehrenreich and English, *For Her Own Good*, p. 172.

PAGE 232   G. Stanley Hall on child rearing: Quoted in Ehrenreich and English *For Her Own Good*, p. 173.
Dr. Luther Emmett Holt on motherhood: Quoted in Ehrenreich and English, *For Her Own Good*, p. 181.
Holt and Mrs. Max West on infant care: Quoted in Daniel Beekman, *The Mechanical Baby: A Popular History of the Theory and Practice of Child Raising* (Westport, Conn.: Lawrence Hill & Co., 1977), p. 117.
Mrs. West on playing: Mrs. Max West, *Infant Care*, Children's Bureau Publication no. 8 (Washington, D.C.: U.S. Department of Labor, 1914), pp. 59–60.
Mrs. West on toilet training: Quoted in Beekman, *Mechanical Baby*, p. 116; *Infant Care*, p. 51.

PAGE 233   Mrs. West on thumb-sucking: *Infant Care*, p. 61.
Mrs. West on masturbation: *Infant Care*, p. 62.
Other books and mechanical devices: Beekman, *Mechanical Baby*, pp. 121–24.
Justifications for discipline: West, *Infant Care*, p. 59.

PAGE 234   Historians on industrial child rearing: Ehrenreich and English, *For Her Own Good*, pp. 181–82; Beekman, *Mechanical Baby*, pp. 109–33.
"Some person not altogether competent": West, *Infant Care*, p. 26.
"A conscientious young mother": West, *Infant Care*, p. 34.
"The very love of the mother for her child": D. A. Thom, *Child Management*, Children's Bureau Publication no. 143 (Washington, D.C.: U.S. Department of Labor, 1925), p. 3.
Description of cries: Quoted in Beekman, *Mechanical Baby*, p. 116.

PAGE 235   Dutch and French child care: Lydia Maria Child, *The Mother's Book* (1831; reprint ed., New York: Arno Press, 1972), p. 1.
Instinct for fondness: Child, *Mother's Book*, p. 5.

PAGE 236   Midwives: Ehrenreich and English, *For Her Own Good*, pp. 84–88.

PAGE 237   Holt infant formulas: Beekman, *Mechanical Baby*, p. 114.
Weighing breast-fed babies: West, *Infant Care*, p. 37.
"More nearly proper percentage of fat": West, *Infant Care*, p. 40.
Lydia Maria Child's leading principles: *Mother's Book*, pp. v–vi.
Comparison of two mothers: Child, *Mother's Book*, pp. 46–50.

PAGE 238 *How I Kept My Baby Well*: Beekman, *Mechanical Baby*, pp. 126–33.

PAGE 239 "An inexperienced mother": West, *Infant Care*, p. 51.

PAGE 240 Sally, a Boston housewife: Quoted in Ellen Goodman, "The Changing World of the Full-Time Housewife," *McCall's*, February 1979, pp. 131–32.

PAGE 241 "A smile, or a look of fondness": Child, *Mother's Book*, p. 4.
"Even very little children are happy": Child, *Mother's Book*, p. 62.

CHAPTER 13. SELLING MRS. CONSUMER

PAGE 243 "The smartest men" in Cincinnati: Frances Trollope, *Domestic Manners of the Americans*, ed. Donald Smalley (New York: Vintage Books, 1960), p. 85. See also p. 419, and Harriet Martineau, *Society in America*, ed. Seymour Martin Lipset (Gloucester, Mass.: Peter Smith, 1962), p. 302.
"Every young woman": Catharine E. Beecher, *Miss Beecher's Housekeeper and Healthkeeper* (New York: Harper & Brothers, 1873), p. 18.

PAGE 244 "Until I believe I have a right to claim": Advertisement for *Ladies' World*, *Printer's Ink*, August 5, 1891, p. 113, quoting from article by Fowler in *Printer's Ink*, July 22, 1891.
Maher response: William H. Maher, "Advertising for Women," *Printer's Ink*, August 5, 1891, p. 103.

PAGE 245 Fowler response to Maher: Nathaniel C. Fowler, Jr., "Advertising for Women," *Printer's Ink*, August 26, 1891, p. 174.
Juliet Corson: F. E. Fryatt, "The New York Cooking School," *Harper's New Monthly Magazine*, December 1879, pp. 22–29.
"Economizing on food": Florence Nesbitt, *Low Cost Cooking* (Chicago: American School of Home Economics, 1915), pp. 5–6.

PAGE 246 "Uncolored facts": Florence Nesbitt, *Household Management* (New York: Russell Sage Foundation, 1918), pp. 59–60.

PAGE 247 Housewife as purchasing agent: Christine Frederick, *Household Engineering: Scientific Management in the Home* (Chicago: American School of Home Economics, 1920), pp. 315–16.

PAGE 248 Frederick on family budget: *Household Engineering*, p. 275.
"Typical divisions for all incomes": Frederick, *Household Engineering*, p. 273.
"Just as each need seems to arise": Frederick, *Household Engineering*, p. 272.
"How many times has one seen a 'bargain' ": Frederick, *Household Engineering*, p. 302.
Marking bedsheets: Frederick, *Household Engineering*, p. 303.

PAGE 249 Canned-goods storage records: Frederick, *Household Engineering*, p. 304.
"Business corner": Frederick, *Household Engineering*, p. 312.
"Think of the hours you spent": Frederick, *Household Engineering*, p. 310.
"In other words, some of the time saved": Frederick, *Household Engineering*, p. 317.

PAGE 250   "A woman's virtue and excellence": *The Ladies' Home Journal,* March 1928, p. 43, quoted in Ruth Schwartz Cowan, "Two Washes in the Morning and a Bridge Party at Night: The American Housewife Between the Wars," *Women's Studies* 3 (1976): 152.

PAGE 251   Hand-crocheted tablecloth: Anzia Yezierska, *Bread Givers: A Struggle Between a Father of the Old World and a Daughter of the New World* (1925; reprint ed., New York: Persea Books, 1975), pp. 32–33.

Sociologists' time studies: See Joann Vanek, "Time Spent in Housework," *Scientific American,* November 1974, pp. 116–20; Kathryn E. Walker, "Homemaking Still Takes Time," *Journal of Home Economics* 61 (October 1969): 621–24; Heidi Irmgard Hartmann, "Capitalism and Women's Work in the Home, 1900–1930" (Ph.D. dissertation, Yale University, 1974), chap. 5.

PAGE 252   Early advertising: Alfred D. Chandler, Jr., *The Visible Hand: The Managerial Revolution in American Business* (Cambridge, Mass.: Harvard University Press, 1977), pp. 227–28, 298.

PAGE 253   Magazine revenue figures: Stuart Ewen, *Captains of Consciousness: Advertising and the Social Roots of the Consumer Culture* (New York: McGraw-Hill Book Co., 1976), p. 32.

Fear in advertising: Ewen, *Captains of Consciousness,* pp. 97–99, 178–79.

"Sneaker smell," etc.: Ewen, *Captains of Consciousness,* p. 97.

"How This Vacation Romance Was SAVED": *Good Housekeeping,* August 1933, p. 101.

French's mustard ad: *Good Housekeeping,* August 1933, p. 149.

One elderly California woman: Quoted in Karen V. Hansen, "Taking Back the Day: The Historical Recovery of Women's Household Work Experience," unpublished manuscript, August 1979, p. 93.

PAGE 254   Rinso ad: *Good Housekeeping,* August 1933, inside back cover.

Franco-American ad: *Good Housekeeping,* August 1933, p. 93.

Gerber's ad: *Good Housekeeping,* August 1933, p. 130.

Debunking old ways: See Ewen, *Captains of Consciousness,* pp. 161–62.

National Biscuit Company: Chandler, *Visible Hand,* pp. 334–35.

PAGE 256   "Some kind of label" and "All 'bulk' goods": Frederick, *Household Engineering,* p. 353.

Advertising raises quality of articles: Frederick, *Household Engineering,* p. 357.

Selling Mrs. Consumer: Christine Frederick, *Selling Mrs. Consumer* (New York: Business Bourse, 1929).

"If someone else bakes your bread": Nesbitt, *Low Cost Cooking,* pp. 11–12.

Nesbitt on working mothers: "When the Mother Works Outside the Home," *Low Cost Cooking,* pp. 113–16. On fireless cookers, see pp. 107–8.

PAGE 257   *Bread Givers* on manufactured goods: Yezierska, *Bread Givers,* pp. 28–29.

"The new system": Chandler, *Visible Hand,* p. 232.

PAGE 259   A&P statistics: Godfrey M. Lebhar, *Chain Stores in America* (New York: Chain Store Publishing Co., 1952), pp. 21–26.

Number of chains: M. M. Zimmerman, *The Supermarket: A Revolution in Distribution* (New York: McGraw-Hill Book Co., 1955), p. 2.

Lower trade margin: U.S. Department of Commerce, Bureau of the Census, *Historical Statistics of the United States, Colonial Times to 1970* (Washington, D.C.: Government Printing Office, 1975), p. 848.

Poorer people use chains: See Time, Inc., *Markets by Incomes: A Study of the Relationship of Income to Retail Purchases in Appleton, Wisconsin*, vol. 1 (New York: Time, Inc., 1932), p. 45.

Michael Cullen: Zimmerman, *The Supermarket*, pp. 30–39; Rom J. Markin, *The Supermarket: An Analysis of Growth, Development and Change*, rev. ed., Washington State University Bureau of Economic and Business Research Bulletin no. 43 (Pullman, February 1968), p. 11.

Chains versus supermarkets: Markin, *The Supermarket*, pp. 13–17.

PAGE 260 Work in the twentieth century: Harry Braverman, *Labor and Monopoly Capital: The Degradation of Work in the Twentieth Century* (New York: Monthly Review Press, 1974).

CHAPTER 14. QUICK AND EASY

PAGE 264 Cleveland utilities: Calculated from Howard Whipple Green, *Standards of Living in the Cleveland Metropolitan District as Depicted by the Federal Real Property Inventory* (Cleveland: Special Report of the Real Property Inventory of Metropolitan Cleveland, 1935), pp. 48–49.

Smaller cities: See Faith M. Williams and Alice C. Hanson, *Money Disbursements of Wage Earners and Clerical Workers in Eight Cities in the East North Central Region, 1934–36* (Washington, D.C.: U.S. Department of Labor, Bureau of Labor Statistics Bulletin no. 636, 1940), p. 52.

One elderly California woman: Karen V. Hansen, "Taking Back the Day: The Historical Recovery of Women's Household Work Experience" (unpublished manuscript, 1979), p. 102.

PAGE 265 Massive selling campaign: Heidi Irmgard Hartmann, "Capitalism and Women's Work in the Home, 1900–1930" (Ph.D. dissertation, Yale University, 1974), pp. 361–62.

General Electric ad: *House Beautiful*, August 1930, opposite p. 100.

Other refrigerator ads: *Good Housekeeping*, July 1934, pp. 9, 120, 127, 158, 164, 176, 204.

Refrigerator article: Arthur J. Donniez, "About Refrigerators," *Good Housekeeping*, July 1934, pp. 113, 190.

Zanesville refrigerators: R. O. Eastman, Inc., *Zanesville and Thirty-Six Other American Communities: A Study of Markets and of the Telephone as a Market Index* (New York: Literary Digest, 1927), p. 63.

"In the U.S. as a whole": Time, Inc., *Markets by Incomes: A Study of the Relationship of Income to Retail Purchases in Appleton, Wisconsin*, vol. 1 (New York: Time, Inc., 1932), p. 22.

Appleton refrigerators: Time, Inc., *Markets by Incomes*, p. 23.

PAGE 267 According to one writer: Neil Borden, *Economic Effects of Advertising* (Chicago: R. D. Irwin, 1942), cited in Hartmann, "Capitalism and Women's Work," pp. 361–62.

About three times as many washing machines: Hartmann, "Capitalism and Women's Work," p. 295.

"Some day soon . . . you'll be free": Westinghouse Home Economics Institute, "Home Laundering Guide for Clothes and Fabrics" (Mansfield, Ohio, 1944), p. 41.

PAGE 268   Test marketing of Laundromat: Westinghouse, "Home Laundering Guide," p. 45.

"Reduces clothes washing to three simple steps": Westinghouse, "Home Laundering Guide," p. 41.

"Torn off buttons" and "An entire new day": Westinghouse, "Home Laundering Guide," p. 48.

Clothes dryers in model floor plan: Westinghouse, "Home Laundering Guide," pp. 46–47.

California studies: University of California, Heller Commission, *Cost of Living Studies IV. Spending Ways of a Semi-Skilled Group*, University of California Publications in Economics, vol. 5, no. 5 (Berkeley, 1931), p. 327; Jessica B. Peixotto, *Getting and Spending at the Professional Standard of Living* (New York: Macmillan Co., 1927), pp. 182–83.

PAGE 270   Family laundry expenditures: Hartmann, "Capitalism and Women's Work," pp. 289, 293.

PAGE 271   "I BEAT MY MOTHER-IN-LAW": Tide ad, *Ladies' Home Journal*, August 1980, p. 118.

PAGE 272   Ben-Hur freezer: 1952 Ben-Hur Farm and Home Freezer announcement, Ben-Hur Manufacturing Co., Milwaukee, Wisconsin.

PAGE 273   Nearly half owned freezers: Joan A. Rothschild, "Technology, 'Women's Work', and the Social Control of Women" (paper prepared for International Political Science Association, Eleventh World Congress, Moscow, 1979), p. 12.

PAGE 274   Frozen-food history: Unless otherwise cited, all frozen-food history comes from Sam Martin and Saul Beck, "Forty Years of *Quick Frozen Foods*," *Quick Frozen Foods*, August 1978, pp. 16–66. Birds Eye's Springfield ad is reproduced on p. 20 of this article.

PAGE 275   "Revolutionary new product": Complete ad, *Ladies' Home Journal*, August 1980, p. 57.

"Magic" packaged brownies: Duncan Hines ad, *Redbook*, August 1980, p. G-2.

Frozen-food production figures: "A Collection of Facts and Figures," *Quick Frozen Foods*, November 1978, pp. 162–63.

PAGE 276   Ideas for frozen spinach soufflé: Stouffer's ad, *Woman's Day*, August 5, 1980, pp. 130–31.

Frosty Mint Ice Cream Pie: Pillsbury ad, *Good Housekeeping*, August 1980, p. 149.

PAGE 277   "Everyone knows you can make a cake": Diane Nelson, "Do Something Different with Convenience Foods," *Better Homes and Gardens*, September 1978, p. 122.

"Had to beg food companies": Larry Kai Elbert, "Microwave Success Draws Items from Food Makers," *Advertising Age*, October 30, 1978, p. 88.

"It can only help our business" and "Color TV plodded along": Peter J.

Schuyten, "Special Frozen Foods for Microwave Ovens," *Seattle Post-Intelligencer*, December 17, 1979, p. B8.

Sagging microwave sales: "Microwave Oven Sales Lose Some Speed," *Business Week*, July 31, 1978, pp. 99–100.

PAGE 278 "Redefine what we mean by convenience foods": David M. Ehlens, Pillsbury vice-president, quoted in "Microwave Oven Sales," *Business Week*, July 31, 1978, p. 100.

"Twenty minutes in a regular oven": Quoted in Schuyten, "Special Frozen Foods," p. B8.

PAGE 279 New appliances are "life-style oriented": Whirlpool ad, *Redbook*, August 1980, p. 42.

"We never get together to chat": Quoted in Hansen, "Taking Back the Day," p. 104.

"Wanted to ask me some questions": Quoted in Hansen, "Taking Back the Day," p. 64.

PAGE 280 "The avocado show": Earl Lifshey, *The Housewares Story: A History of the American Housewares Industry* (Chicago: National Housewares Manufacturers Association, 1973), p. 147.

Industry spokesmen defend new gadgetry: Lifshey, *Housewares Story*, p. 274.

"It was crazy" and "When we came out with our 16-speed blender": "The Sociology of the Blender," *New Times*, April 29, 1977, p. 25.

CHAPTER 15. YOU DESERVE A BREAK

PAGE 283 Homestead lunches: Margaret Byington, *Homestead: The Households of a Mill Town* (New York: Russell Sage Foundation, 1910), p. 64.

Manchester lunches: Tamara K. Hareven and Randolph Langenbach, *Amoskeag: Life and Work in an American Factory-City* (New York: Pantheon Books, 1978), p. 223.

Number of fast-food restaurants nearly tripled: Richard B. Carnes and Horst Brand, "Productivity and New Technology in Eating and Drinking Places," *Monthly Labor Review*, September 1977, p. 12.

Who eats out and where: See Gallup surveys in the following: "45,728,000 Adults Go Out to Eat Daily," *Food Service Marketing*, April 1978, p. 8; "Where Are Americans Eating Out?" *Food Service Marketing*, April 1978, pp. 71–73; "Working Women Are Boon to Food Service," *Food Service Marketing*, June 1978, p. 12.

General growth of fast foods: John C. Maxwell, Jr., "Fast-feeders Draw a Bead on Continued Growth," *Advertising Age*, September 11, 1978, pp. 117–18.

PAGE 284 Supermarket profit margins: *Standard and Poor's Industry Surveys*, April 1979, vol. 2, p. R166.

Late-night convenience stores: "Convenience Stores: A $7.4 Billion Mushroom," *Business Week*, March 21, 1977, pp. 61–64.

Banquet ad campaign: "The Supermarkets Fight Back," *Dun's Review*, October 1977, p. 108.

New York Times article: B. Drummond Ayres, Jr., "Rising Popularity of Eating Out Puts a Pinch on Supermarkets," *New York Times*, April 10, 1977, p. 1.

Dun's Review analysis: "Supermarkets Fight Back," pp. 108–10.

"Supermarkets won't disappear": "Supermarkets Fight Back," p. 110.

Aders of Food Marketing Institute: Quoted in Ayres, "Rising Popularity," p. 26.

PAGE 286   Colonel Sanders: "Some Finger-Lickin' Good Advice for Supers," *Progressive Grocer*, August 1978, pp. 82–84.

1970s "superstores": Ayres, "Rising Popularity."

Nonfoods before 1970: M. M. Zimmerman, *The Super Market: A Revolution in Distribution* (New York: McGraw-Hill Book Co., 1955), pp. 127, 150–52, 236–55.

PAGE 287   Head-on competition and purchase of restaurants: "Supermarkets Fight Back"; Christy Marshall, "Supermarkets Fight Fast-Food Challenge," *Advertising Age*, October 30, 1978, pp. 30–31.

"Supermarkets have the real estate": "Marketing Observer," *Business Week*, September 26, 1977, p. 158.

"A new American life-style": Patrick O'Malley, president of the National Restaurant Association, quoted in Ayres, "Rising Popularity."

"Supermarkets sell food": Arnold Deutsch, "Ignoring the Supermarkets," *Restaurant Business*, July 1978, p. 176.

Bureau of Labor Statistics: Carnes and Brand, "Productivity and New Technology," p. 11.

Top hundred chains: Phillip L. Rane, "Are 'Mom and Pops' Dead?" *Food Service Marketing*, November 1978, p. 12.

PAGE 288   "Inside Wall Street": Jeffrey Madrick, "Inside Wall Street: A Cautious Approach to Fast-Food Chains," *Business Week*, March 28, 1977, p. 85. See also Robert Z. Chew, "Taking Stock: Fast Food Expert Shoots Down Oversaturation Theory," *Advertising Age*, May 8, 1978, p. 90.

"Maturation, or saturation": Edward Kulkosky, "The Frantic Fast-Food Fracas," *Financial World*, August 1, 1978, p. 36.

A restaurant trade magazine: Rane, "Are 'Mom and Pops' Dead?"

Carney and Pizza Hut: Pete Berlinski, "The Corporate Mating Game," *Restaurant Business*, May 1978, pp. 151–53. See also "The Fast-Food Stars: Three Strategies for Fast Growth," *Business Week*, July 11, 1977, pp. 65–67.

PAGE 289   Buying up competition: Marshall, "Supermarkets Fight," p. 34; Walter Kiechel III, "The Food Giants Struggle to Stay in Step with Consumers," *Fortune*, September 11, 1978, pp. 53–54.

PAGE 290   "What do you do with all that money": Berlinski, "Corporate Mating Game," p. 148.

PAGE 291   Payback to investors: Berlinski, "Corporate Mating Game," p. 154.

PAGE 292   "The primary method of entry": Abner J. Mikva, Letter to Colleagues, February 27, 1979.

Start-up cash for fast foods: Phil W. Petrie, "Fast Food and Quick Bucks," *Black Enterprise*, April 1978, p. 30.

PAGE 293   Church's Fried Chicken: "Church's: A Fast-Food Recipe That Is Light on Marketing," *Business Week*, February 20, 1978, pp. 110–12.

Wendy's International: Kulkosky, "Frantic Fast-Food Fracas," p. 38; "The Fast-Food Stars," pp. 60, 64.

McDonald's phases out franchises: "The Fast-Food Stars," pp. 56–60.

Winchell and Denny's: "Denny's Takes Its Menu East," *Business Week*, September 19, 1977, pp. 110–14.

Sambo's revolt: "Sambo's Restructures to Bolster Its Stock," *Business Week*, February 20, 1978, pp. 93–96.

PAGE 295   One company terminated 682 franchises: Abner J. Mikva, "Franchise Reform Will Protect Small Business," *Food Service Marketing*, August 1978, p. 32.

Frozen-potato consumption: Kiechel, "Food Giants Struggle," p. 52; Louise Page and Berta Friend, "The Changing United States Diet," *Bioscience*, March 1978, p. 194.

Soft drinks and ice milk: Leo J. Shapiro and Dwight Bohmbach, "Eating Habits Force Changes in Marketing," *Advertising Age*, October 30, 1978, p. 65.

Salad and cooking oils: Page and Friend, "Changing United States Diet," p. 193.

"Everyone's busy these days": "Fast Food at Home," *Ladies Home Journal*, October 1977, p. 138.

"Eating At Home Pays Off!": Carnation and Contadina ad, *Parade*, February 11, 1979.

PAGE 296   *Seventeen* article: "Homemade Takeouts," *Seventeen*, January 1978, pp. 76–77.

Mademoiselle article: "Four Fast-Food Makeovers," *Mademoiselle*, February 1979, pp. 160–61.

Kraft executive and "Generally speaking, the homemaker no longer sets the table": Larry Edwards, "Soft Sales Challenge Food Marketers," *Advertising Age*, October 30, 1978, p. 27.

Breakfast defunct: Shapiro and Bohmbach, "Eating Habits Force Changes," p. 65.

PAGE 297   One drug company: Roche ad, *Ladies' Home Journal*, August 1980, p. 6.

"In one generation": Shapiro and Bohmbach, "Eating Habits Force Changes," p. 27.

"Translate enduring messages": Conrad P. Kottak, "Rituals at McDonald's," *Natural History*, January 1978, p. 74.

Advertising "has replaced 'pinching the tomatoes' ": Shapiro and Bohmbach, "Eating Habits Force Changes," p. 66.

CHAPTER 16. LIFE ON THE MARKET

PAGE 301   Cost of subsistence versus income: "The New Two-Tier Market for Consumer Goods," *Business Week*, April 11, 1977, pp. 80–83.

New home prices "out of reach": "The New Two-Tier Market," p. 82.

Married women's labor-force participation: U.S. Bureau of the Census, *Recent Social and Economic Trends* (Washington, D.C.: Government Printing Office, 1978), p. xviii; "'Most 1990 Mothers' to Work Outside Home," *Seattle Post-Intelligencer*, September 24, 1979, p. A2. For a variety of statements of the statistical trends, see U.S. Department of Labor, Bureau of Labor Statistics, *Perspectives on Working Women: A Databook*, Bulletin 2080 (Washington, D.C.: Government Printing Office, October 1980).

Husbands helping, in nationwide survey: John P. Robinson and Philip E. Converse, *United States Time Use Survey*, cited in Joann Vanek, "Time Spent in Housework," *Scientific American*, November 1974, p. 118.

PAGE 302   "Who would never have sat still" and Kinder-Care: Joseph Lelyveld, "Drive-In Day Care," *New York Times Magazine*, June 5, 1977, p. 110.

PAGE 303   "The recognized base and background": Charlotte Perkins Gilman, *The Home: Its Work and Influence* (1903; reprint ed., Urbana: University of Illinois Press, 1972), pp. 346–47.

Divorce rate: Census Bureau, "Recent Trends," p. xiv.

"Dirty lover": "American Notes: Disappearing Taboo," *Time*, September 6, 1976, p. 42.

"Americans spend most of their adult lives married": Susanna McBee, "Americans Remain the Marrying Kind," *Washington Post*, January 14, 1979, p. A2.

Out-of-wedlock living: See *Los Angeles Times*, "Housemates Delicate Business Problem," *Daily Olympian*, July 13, 1977, p. D1.

PAGE 304   "Head of household" label: "'Head of Household' Label Passé," *Daily Olympian*, July 5, 1977, p. A3; U.S. Department of Labor, Bureau of Labor Statistics, *Marital and Family Characteristics of the Labor Force in March 1976* (Washington, D.C.: Government Printing Office, 1977), p. A-2, "Technical Note on the Comparability of Data."

Child on marriage expectations: Lydia Maria Child, *The Mother's Book* (1831; reprint ed., New York: Arno Press, 1972), pp. 50–51.

PAGE 305   Bell System ads: *Ladies' Home Journal*, August 1980, p. 125; *Good Housekeeping*, August 1980, p. 56; *McCall's Working Mother*, July 1980, p. 13.

Nineteenth-century mobility: See Stephan Thernstrom and Peter R. Knights, "Men in Motion: Some Data and Speculations on Urban Population Mobility in Nineteenth Century America," *Journal of Interdisciplinary History* 1 (1970): 7–35.

PAGE 306   Vibrators: Mimi Swartz, "For the Woman Who Has Almost Everything," *Esquire*, July 1980, pp. 56–63.

"Everyone is cooped up": "Crime Falls With the Ash in Yakima," *Seattle Post-Intelligencer*, May 21, 1980. Not everyone argued: nine months later, the same paper reported a baby boom in eastern Washington and Idaho. See "Out of Volcano's Ashes Come BABIES!" *Seattle Post-Intelligencer*, February 19, 1981.

PAGE 308   Goodman: Ellen Goodman, "The Grateful Wife," *McCall's Working Mother*, July 1980, p. 82.

Mainardi: Pat Mainardi, "The Politics of Housework," in Robin Morgan, ed., *Sisterhood Is Powerful* (New York: Vintage Books, 1970), pp. 447–54.

"Constellation of traditionalist . . . movements": Andrew Kopkind, "America's New Right," *New Times*, September 30, 1977, p. 22.

Time on Republican family planks: "On Traditional Family Values," *Time*, July 28, 1980, p. 30.

"I'd rather be home cooking": quoted in Kopkind, "America's New Right," p. 22.

PAGE 309   Maintaining self-respect: See Ellen Goodman, "The Changing World of the Full-Time Housewife," *McCall's*, February 1979, pp. 85, 127–34.

PAGE 310   "A source of mortal danger": Simone de Beauvoir, *The Second Sex* (New York: Bantam Books, 1961), p. 629.

Rent-A-Wife: Phyllis Battelle, "For $25 an Hour, Anyone Can Rent a Wife," *Seattle Post-Intelligencer*, July 20, 1980, p. D1.

PAGE 311   "The growth of dual purchase influence": *Time* advertisement, *Advertising Age*, October 30, 1978, pp. 61–64.

PICTURE CREDITS

Crane Company: pp. 101, 102. Courtesy of Crane Company.
Community Service Society of New York: p. 153. Courtesy of the Community Service Society of New York.
General Electric Company: pp. 77, 266. Courtesy of General Electric Company.
Historical Society of Seattle and King County: pp. 95, 118, 226, 231, 233, 238, 271.
Idaho State Historical Society: pp. 132, 170. Reprinted by permission of the Idaho State Historical Society Collection.
International Museum of Photography: p. 142. Reprinted by permission of the International Museum of Photography at George Eastman House.
Arthur C. Johnson: p. 114. Reprinted by permission.
Ladies' Home Journal: p. 177. Copyright 1918 by LHJ Publishing, Inc. Reprinted by permission of Ladies' Home Journal.
The Library of Congress: pp. 13, 15, 17, 20, 21, 24, 25, 27, 55, 59, 72, 75, 98, 99, 106, 111, 115, 119, 122, 129, 136, 139, 140, 165, 184, 189, 190, 198, 200, 244, 247, 252, 258, 260, 270, 273, 275, 286, 289, 290, 291, 294.
The National Archives: pp. 34, 158.
New York Public Library Picture Collection: pp. 62, 64, 79, 83, 101, 114, 127, 168, 174, 177, 205, 228, 236.
Progressive Grocer: p. 278. Courtesy of Progressive Grocer.
Smithsonian Institution Collection of Business Americana: pp. 91, 285.
State Historical Society of North Dakota: p. 133. Reprinted by permission of the State Historical Society of North Dakota.
State Historical Society of Wisconsin: jacket and cover photograph; pp. 26, 30, 35, 42, 48, 52, 56, 65, 87, 88, 90, 93, 110, 123, 160, 195, 208, 209, 216, 246, 250, 261.
Westinghouse Electric Corporation: p. 269.

Index

ABOUT THE AUTHOR

Susan Strasser received her doctorate in American history from the State University of New York at Stony Brook. She now teaches American history and labor studies at The Evergreen State College in Washington.